D1807492

ARTHURIAN STUDIES LXIV

THE FORTUNES OF KING ARTHUR

ARTHURIAN STUDIES

ISSN 0261–9814

General Editor: Norris J. Lacy

Previously published volumes in the series
are listed at the back of this book

THE FORTUNES OF KING ARTHUR

Edited by Norris J. Lacy

D. S. BREWER

First published 2005
D. S. Brewer, Cambridge

ISBN 1 84384 061 8

D. S. Brewer is an imprint of Boydell & Brewer Ltd
PO Box 9, Woodbridge, Suffolk IP12 3DF, UK
and of Boydell & Brewer Inc.
668 Mt Hope Avenue, Rochester, NY 14620, USA
website: www.boydellandbrewer.com

A catalogue record for this book is available from the British Library

This publication is printed on acid-free paper

Typeset by Pru Harrison, Hacheston, Suffolk
Printed in Great Britain by
Cromwell Press, Trowbridge, Wiltshire

Contents

Illustrations

Illustrations 1–32 appear between pages 165 and 166

Colour plate 33 appears after page 200

Contributors

†W.R.J. BARRON, having studied at St Andrews, Yale and Strasbourg and taught at Aberdeen, Manchester and Shiraz, was, at the time of his death, a Senior Research Fellow of the University of Exeter. He was series editor of 'Arthurian Literature in the Middle Ages', having himself edited vol. II, *The Arthur of the English*. Among his other publications are *English Medieval Romance*, an edition and translation of *Sir Gawain and the Green Knight* and (with S.C. Weinberg) of Laȝamon's *Brut*.

SIAN ECHARD is Professor of English and Distinguished University Scholar at the University of British Columbia, where she publishes on Anglo-Latin literature, John Gower and Arthurian subjects. In the Arthurian field she is the author of *Arthurian Narrative in the Latin Tradition*, and she recently edited *A Companion to Gower*. Her current project is a study of post-medieval printings of medieval texts. She is President of the Medieval Association of the Pacific.

CAROLINE D. ECKHARDT is Director of the School of Languages and Literatures and Department Head of Comparative Literature at the Pennsylvania State University. Her specializations include medieval chronicles, Chaucer, Arthurian tradition, and medieval manuscripts, readers and book production. Among her books and editions are *Essays in the Numerical Criticism of Medieval Literature*, *Castleford's Chronicle, or the Boke of Brut* and *The Prophetia Merlini of Geoffrey of Monmouth: A Fifteenth-Century Commentary*.

DENNIS GREEN is Schröder Professor Emeritus of German at the University of Cambridge and is a Fellow of Trinity College, Cambridge. He has published widely on subjects such as orality and literacy, irony, and fictionality and history in courtly romance. Among his books are *Irony in the Medieval Romance*, *The Art of Recognition in Wolfram's Parzival*, *Medieval Listening and Reading: The Primary Reception of German Literature, 800–1300*, *Language and History in the Early Germanic World* and *The Beginnings of Medieval Romance*.

JOAN TASKER GRIMBERT is Professor and Chair of Modern Languages and Literatures at Catholic University of America, where she teaches French and medieval studies. Her publications, concentrating on Arthurian literature and film, include *'Yvain' dans le miroir: une poétique de la réflexion dans le 'Chevalier au lion' de Chrétien de Troyes*, *Tristan and Isolde: A Casebook*, and *Songs of the Women Trouvères*. She has co-edited *A Companion to Chrétien de Troyes* with Norris Lacy. Past secretary-treasurer of the International Arthurian Society North American Branch, she is currently international treasurer of the IAS.

EDWARD DONALD KENNEDY is Professor of English and Comparative Literature at the University of North Carolina at Chapel Hill. His publications include *Chronicles and Other Historical Writing* (vol. 8 of *A Manual of the Writings in Middle English*), *King Arthur: A Casebook*, and numerous articles and reviews, primarily on Arthurian subjects and medieval chronicles. He is currently collaborating on an edition of short Scottish chronicles. He is editor of *Studies in Philology* and Associate Editor of *The Comparatist*.

NORRIS J. LACY is the Edwin Erle Sparks Professor of French and Medieval Studies at the Pennsylvania State University. His books include *The Craft of Chrétien de Troyes*, *The Arthurian Handbook* (with Geoffrey Ashe) and *Reading Fabliaux*. He is general editor of *The New Arthurian Encyclopedia* and of *Lancelot-Grail: The Old French Arthurian Vulgate and Post-Vulgate Cycles in Translation*. He has co-edited (with Joan Grimbert) *A Companion to Chrétien de Troyes* and is preparing a critical edition of the fourteenth-century *Prose Yvain*. He is past president of The International Arthurian Society.

CERIDWEN LLOYD-MORGAN is Head of the Manuscripts Unit at the National Library of Wales, Aberystwyth, and Honorary Research Fellow in the School of Welsh at the University of Cardiff. She has published widely in the field of Arthurian studies, her special interests being Middle Welsh prose traditions and French influences on the literature of medieval Wales. She also guest-edited the 2004 volume of *Arthurian Literature*, devoted to Celtic Arthurian Literature.

ALAN LUPACK is Adjunct Professor of English and Director of the Rossell Hope Robbins Library at the University of Rochester; creator of *The Camelot Project* (an electronic database of Arthurian texts, images, bibliographies, and information); and Associate Editor of the TEAMS Middle English Texts series. He has edited medieval and modern Arthurian texts and is the co-author of *King Arthur in America* and author of numerous articles on medieval and modern Arthurian literature. He has recently published *The Oxford Guide to Arthurian Literature and Legend* for the Oxford University Press.

CHRISTOPHER A. SNYDER is Associate Professor of European History and Chair of the Department of History and Politics at Marymount University. He is the author of *An Age of Tyrants: Britain and the Britons, AD 400–600* (1998), *The World of King Arthur* (2000), and *The Britons* (2003). He is a member of the editorial board of *Arthuriana*.

ALISON STONES is Professor of History of Art and Architecture at the University of Pittsburgh. She writes about medieval manuscript illumination, mostly French, and is the co-editor and co-author of *Les Manuscrits de Chrétien de Troyes* and *The Pilgrim's Guide to Santiago de Compostela, Critical Edition*, and the author of *Le Livre d'images de Madame Marie (Paris, BNF n.a.fr. 16251*). Her current research is *Illuminated Manuscripts Made in France* and the Lancelot-Grail Project (for which see <http://vrcoll.fa.pitt.edu/stones-www/MASHome page/lancelot-project.html>). Her web site on monuments of medieval art and architecture is <http://www.pitt.edu/~medart>. She is a member of the Société nationale des antiquaires de France and a Fellow of the Society of Antiquaries of London.

JANE H.M. TAYLOR is Professor of Modern Languages at Durham University, and Principal of Collingwood College. She has worked extensively on the literature of the late Middle Ages in France, especially on the late Arthurian romances and on the lyric. She is currently working on the lyric anthologies of the late Middle Ages and the early Renaissance. Her books and editions include *Dies illa: Death in the Middle Ages*, *Le Roman de Perceforest* (Part I), *The Poetry of François Villon: Text and Context* and *Double Vision: Studies in Literary Translation*. She is past president of The International Arthurian Society.

NEIL THOMAS is reader in German in the University of Durham (UK) and has just finished a three-year tenure as president of the British Branch of the International Arthurian Society. He has published a number of monographs on the Arthurian romances, on Gottfried's *Tristan* and on the *Nibelungenlied*. His latest volumes are *Diu Crône and the Medieval Arthurian Cycle* (2002) and *Wirnt von Gravenberg's Wigalois: Intertextuality and Interpretation* (2005).

Introduction

The title of this volume is intentionally ambiguous. The more general intent is to reflect the vicissitudes of the legend itself, as it develops, flowers – more accurately, explodes – during the High Middle Ages, then wanes and nearly dies during the early-modern period before its dramatic revival beginning in the nineteenth century and continuing unabated to the present. This cycle of birth, vigorous life, decline, and rebirth stands also as a metaphor, approximate but appropriate, for the fortunes of King Arthur himself, of Camelot, of the Round Table. Indeed, even the final element of the cycle metaphor, the king's survival and anticipated return, has by now become a standard or canonical part of the Arthurian story, even though it is absent from some earlier versions of the legend.

Despite nearly infinite variations of detail from text to text, this cyclical structure is a standard feature of most works that purport to tell the whole Arthurian story. The most familiar and influential examples include the French Lancelot-Grail Cycle and the account offered by Sir Thomas Malory. As Derek Brewer has observed in regard to Malory, his work 'may be said to follow a roughly threefold movement. Movement I . . . shows Arthur's upward rise; Movement II . . . surveys the varied greatness of the knights of the Round Table and the peak of Arthur's glory; in Movement III the wheel of Fortune, starting at its height, goes on to its downward movement, showing the downfall of the Round Table and of Arthur, Lancelot and Guenevere'.[1] As noted, too, a good many texts offer a fourth movement, implied if not always realized: Arthur's sleep in Avalon, whence he will return in the hour of Britain's greatest need.

In speaking of the fortunes of Arthur himself, however, we are frequently speaking not only metaphorically but also mythologically, for the figure of Fortune – Lady Fortuna herself, most often with her wheel – is ubiquitous in medieval Arthuriana. Fortune brings eventual ruin even, or especially, to those who are most exalted, and Arthur is a prime example. In the early fourteenth century, he would be accorded a place in that pantheon of noble personages known as the Nine Worthies and would often be identified as first among the three Christian Worthies, thus as the most illustrious of all.[2] Yet, well before the

1 *The Morte Darthur, Parts Seven and Eight*, by Sir Thomas Malory, ed. and intro. D.S. Brewer (Evanston, 1974), p. 40. Brewer's precise formulation is quoted in the essay by Caroline D. Eckhardt in the present volume.

2 The initial list was offered by Jacques de Longuyon in his *Voeux du paon*. The 'standard' group of Worthies consists of three pagans (Hector, Caesar and Alexander), three Christians (Arthur, Charlemagne and Godefroy de Bouillon), and three Jews (Joshua, David and Judas Maccabeus).

list of the Worthies was formulated and set, authors of Arthurian fiction were depicting the king's imperfections alongside his noble qualities. Morever, a number of those writers were explicitly dramatizing his fall from power and relating it to the inexorable turning of Fortune's wheel, which lifts up the downtrodden and miserable and casts down those who have enjoyed privilege and power. Thus Fortune, whether working through human frailties or historical forces, brings to an end the glory that was Camelot.

The medieval Fortune topos was inspired in particular by the second book of Boethius's *Consolation of Philosophy*, in the early pages of which we are asked, 'What is fickle Fortune except a promise of future distress?'[3] Furthermore, 'If you try to stop the turning of her wheel, you are the most foolish man alive. If it stopped turning, it would cease to be Fortune's wheel.' (However, occasionally it does stop turning, as we shall later see later in this volume.)

Finally, we are told that when Fortune turns her wheel, 'she exalts the humbled even as she dashes the exalted to earth. Yet, she does not hear or care about the tears of those who suffer; she callously laughs at the pain she causes. This is how she amuses herself and demonstrates her power. She shows her servants the remarkable sight of a man who is in despair and then happy within the same hour.'

Even where Fortune herself is not invoked, Arthur's fall and the end of Camelot are seen as inevitable, whether we think of his reign as 'one brief shining moment' (following T.H. White) or as the explicitly cyclical 'The old order changeth, yielding place to new' (the line used by Tennyson to announce both 'The Coming of Arthur' and 'The Passing of Arthur'). Both phrases accurately emphasize the transitoriness of Camelot. Even so do the essays in the present volume deal both with the changing Arthurian order and with the reception of Arthurian themes through the centuries.

This volume grew out of a conference held at Pennsylvania State University and sponsored by the university's Center for Medieval Studies. The conference title was the same as that of this volume. During the conference, nine papers were presented and discussed; the presenters were then accorded the time to revise their work for publication, and four additional contributions were invited. The resulting essays offer a mix of broad studies and specific illustrations of the volume's theme.

The first section of the book, devoted to 'History, Chronicle and the Invention of Arthur', includes five of the thirteen essays. Christopher Snyder opens the volume with a study of Arthur and notions of kingship in the *Historia Brittonum*, and Siân Echard examines the theme of fortune in Geoffrey of Monmouth's *Historia regum Britanniae*, considering both the Latin and the Welsh manuscripts. The essay by the late W.R.J. Barron continues the emphasis on chronicles, but traces also the evolution from Geoffrey to Laȝamon and on to *Sir Gawain and the*

3 Boethius, *De consolatione philosophiae; Opuscula theologica*, ed. Claudio Moreschini (Munich, 2000). An English translation was prepared by P.G. Walsh, *The Consolation of Philosophy* (Oxford, 1999). The brief passages offered in my discussion are my paraphrases and translations of excerpts drawn from Book II.

Green Knight. The relationship of chronicle to romance (specifically Robert de Boron) provides the subject of Edward D. Kennedy's chapter, which studies both the ways in which Robert's use of Christian elements transformed the Arthurian story and the curious failure of that christianization to exert a substantial influence on most of the English Arthurian chronicles in the later Middle Ages. Dennis Green offers a further transition in his 'King Arthur: From History to Fiction', discussing the interrelations of medieval historiography and fiction, examining the extent to which medieval and specifically Arthurian fiction may have arisen out of history.

In the second group of essays, Ceridwen Lloyd-Morgan, emphasizing the crucial role of the Welsh tradition but concentrating on a later manifestation of that tradition, offers an analysis of a little-known Arthurian text: a biography of the king by Elis Gruffydd. Norris J. Lacy focuses in particular on thirteenth-century French materials but mentions as well Norse, German and other texts in a study of the figure of Fortune in relation to traditionally ambiguous representations of the king. Next, Joan Tasker Grimbert examines the influence of the Tristan legend on attitudes toward the love affair of Lancelot and Guenevere; she deals in particular with the French Prose *Tristan* and the Italian *Tavola Ritonda*. Alison Stones contributes a study of the presentation of Arthur in manuscript illustration, concentrating on major and familiar themes, including Fortune.

The third section of the volume is concerned especially with later medieval and modern works. First, Neil Thomas analyzes the fortunes of the king in the 'post-classical' German romances, with especial emphasis on Heinrich von dem Türlin and Wirnt von Gravenberg. Jane H.M. Taylor examines the figure of Arthur in the strange and fascinating French romance *Le Chevalier du papegau*. Caroline D. Eckhardt turns her attention to Malory, treating him not just as the culmination of the medieval Arthurian tradition, but also as something of a transitional figure, whose selectivity in regard to material inherited from the past is matched by the selectivity exercised *on* his work by later generations of writers. Finally, to illustrate the continuing turn of Fortune's wheel, Alan Lupack focuses on the Arthurian revival that began in the nineteenth century and continues to the present. His essay considers post-medieval treatments of the legend – what they owe to the past and the way they are adapted to more modern tastes and times.

When the conference subject was originally considered, it was of course obvious already that a baker's dozen studies could not begin to treat the theme fully. Such a thorough treatment, though devoutly to be desired, has not been our intent. Rather, we have endeavored to provide authoritative essays, by major Arthurian scholars, that investigate either large stages or smaller steps in the elaboration of the legend, from the chronicle tradition to the major authors of Arthurian fiction to the story's modern revival. Gaps are of course as regrettable as they are inevitable. We might wish for more studies of the most prominent literatures – Latin, Welsh, French, German, English – and many readers may lament, as we do, the impossibility of giving more attention to Norse and Italian works (mentioned or discussed only briefly) and to Dutch and Hispanic texts (omitted entirely). What is not represented here must, by necessity, await another time and another volume.

As volume editor, I wish to express my gratitude to Professor Vickie Ziegler, Director of the Center for Medieval Studies at the Pennsylvania State University. Though I selected speakers and organized the presentations for the original conference, I had her invaluable support at every step, and neither the conference nor this volume could be a reality without her help and encouragement. I am no less grateful to Boydell & Brewer, and in particular to Caroline Palmer, for encouragement and assistance in bringing this book to publication.

January 2005 Norris J. Lacy

Arthur and Kingship in the Historia Brittonum

CHRISTOPHER A. SNYDER

> At that time the English increased their numbers and grew in Britain. On Hengest's death, his son Octha came down from the north of Britain to the kingdom of the Kentishmen, and from him are sprung the kings of the Kentishmen. Then Arthur fought against them in those days, together with the kings of the British; but he was their leader in battle.[1]

This passage from the *Historia Brittonum* ('History of the Britons'), along with two entries in the *Annales Cambriae* ('Welsh Annals'), marks Arthur's first appearance in literature.[2] The passage is followed by a description of Arthur's twelve battles against the Saxons, in which he performs great feats and is always victorious. From this Geoffrey of Monmouth, Thomas Malory and countless writers of medieval romance were able to construct a notable saga of *King* Arthur. Yet, neither in the *Historia* nor in the *Annales* is Arthur specifically identified as a king. This fact, observed by the legion of students pursuing the case for a historical Arthur, has led to the now widely accepted conclusion that the *real* or original Arthur was not king but rather warrior or perhaps general.

In this essay, I will question that assumption by examining what specifically the author of the *Historia Brittonum* is trying to say about Arthur and British kingship in general. This has implications not just for the quest for the historical Arthur, but also for our understanding of early medieval British kingship.

It must be said at the outset that the *Historia Brittonum*, despite its popularity among medieval historians,[3] is a problematic historical source for modern scholars.[4] There are scholarly disputes concerning its date and authorship. Traditionally the work has been ascribed to a Welsh monk named Nennius, pupil of the historically attested Elfoddw (Elvodug), the archbishop of Gwynedd who

1 *Historia Brittonum*, ch. 56, in John Morris, ed. and trans., *Nennius: British History and the Welsh Annals* (London, 1980). Translations of the *Historia* in this article are by Morris unless otherwise stated.

2 The reference to Arthur in the vernacular poem *Y Gododdin*, composed c. 600, may predate these Latin sources, but the manuscript tradition is late and a matter of much dispute. See note 50 below.

3 The *Historia* survives in some forty manuscripts, with nine different Latin recensions and one Middle Irish translation.

4 See, for example, the angst exhibited by some recent historians: David N. Dumville, 'Sub-Roman-Britain: History and Legend', *History*, 62 (1977), 173–92; Michael E. Jones, *The End of Roman Britain* (Ithaca, NY, 1996), app. 4; and Christopher A. Snyder, *An Age of Tyrants: Britain and the Britons, AD 400–600* (University Park, PA, 1998), 48.

finally convinced the Welsh to adopt the Roman Easter in 768. This attribution rests upon a prolog in the so-called 'Nennian recension' of the *Historia*:

> Here begins a very brief eulogy of the island of Britain, which *Ninnius* disciple of *Elvodugus* put together.
>
> I *Ninnius*, disciple of *Elvodugus*, have undertaken to write down some extracts that the stupidity of the British cast out; for the scholars of the island of Britain had no skill, and set down no record in books. I have therefore made a heap of all that I have found, both from the annals of the Romans and from the chronicles of the Holy Fathers (that is, Jerome, Eusebius, Isidore, and Prosper), and from the annals of the Irish and the Saxons, and out of the tradition of our elders, which many learned scholars and copyists have tried to write. But somehow they have left the subject more obscure, whether through repeated pestilence or frequent military disasters. I ask every reader who reads this book to pardon me for daring to write so much here after so many, like a chattering bird or an incompetent judge. I yield to whoever may be better acquainted with this skill than I am.[5]

The 'Nennian recension' was copied into a manuscript between 1164 and 1166 and is not in the oldest recension of the *Historia*, which dates to 831.[6] David Dumville has argued that the prolog was a later addition to the main body of the *Historia*, and thus that the attribution to Nennius is fraudulent (he calls it 'a literary conceit').[7] Dumville's argument has been so persuasive that almost all subsequent scholarly discussion of the *Historia* has either neglected to identify its author or else consigned 'Nennius' to parentheses.

A few years ago Peter Field took up this challenge.[8] He argued that the original author was indeed Nennius, a disciple of Elfoddw (d. 809) who is recorded in 817 as the author of a satirical tract on the Welsh alphabet.[9] Field believes that this Nennius (or *Nemnius*) wrote the *Historia* in the late eighth century, and that his prolog was purposely left out of some recensions because it denigrated both the author and British scholarship in general.[10] We will never know why such decisions over spelling and inclusion or exclusion of the prolog were made by the various copyists. Both the 'Nennian recension' prolog and later tradition, however, argue for Nennius's authorship of the *Historia*. Since we have no claim

5 This translation is a slight emendation of that made by Peter Field based upon David Dumville's transcription of the Corpus Christi manuscript, folio 168v. See notes 6 and 7 below.

6 The 'Nennian recension' is known from five manuscripts, the oldest of which is Corpus Christi College Cambridge MS 139. The Corpus Christi manuscript appears to be the source of the other four. The oldest recension of the *Historia*, however, is that in British Library MS Harleian 3859, which was copied c. 1100 but, based on internal evidence, may have taken shape as early as 831. See P.J.C. Field, 'Nennius and His History', *Studia Celtica*, 30 (1996), 159–65, here citing 159.

7 In three articles reprinted in David N. Dumville, *Histories and Pseudo-Histories of the Insular Middle Ages* (Aldershot, 1990).

8 Field, 'Nennius'.

9 The so-called *Oxoniensis Prior* (Oxford Bodleian Library MS Auct. F.4.32) is a rebuttal of the allegation made by an English scholar that the Britons were illiterate. The text employs a concocted Welsh alphabet to parody English runes. See Morris, *Nennius*, pp. 1–2; and Field, 'Nennius', p. 161.

10 Field, 'Nennius', p. 164.

for any other candidate, it is perfectly legitimate to describe the author as Nennius, with a footnote rather than parentheses.[11] I do, however, favor Dumville's dating of the composition to the early ninth century, consistent with the internal references to the kings Merfyn Frych (r. 825–44) and Egferth, son of Offa (d. 796) and absence of mention of Rhodri Mawr (r. 844–78) and the powerful Wessex dynasty of Egbert (d. 839).

The author of the *Historia*, whatever his name, appears to have been, despite the claim of the prolog, a talented compiler of a great variety of sources. These include the *De Excidio Britanniae* of the British cleric Gildas, the church chronicle of Jerome and Eusebius, Orosius's *Adversum Paganos*, the *Chronicle* of Prosper of Aquitaine, the writings of Isidore of Seville, the *Cursus Paschalis* of Victorius of Aquitaine, an eighth-century *Book of St Germanus*, the early hagiography of St Patrick, lost British chronicles, a Kentish chronicle, a Northumbrian regnal list, Mercian genealogies, Welsh genealogies, English legendary material about Hengist and Horsa and a good deal of local Welsh tradition. Since many of these sources are not of an overtly historical nature, this has left the *Historia* with a chronology that is confusing at best.

Further compromising the integrity of the *Historia* is an appendix attached to it (in the Harleian recension) called 'The Marvels of Britain'. This compilation of local lore includes two items concerning Arthur. The first is a heap of stones at Buelt (Builth Wells in south-central Wales) that bears a dog's paw-print, supposedly belonging to Cabal the hound of 'the warrior Arthur', who set his foot on it during a boar-hunt. This stone cannot, it is said, be removed from the heap, for it will always return to the spot. The second Arthurian marvel, in the Welsh district of Ercing, is the tomb of 'Amr, son of Arthur'. Each time one tries to measure it, says the author (who has tried it himself), it appears to be a different length!

The Arthurian material in the *Historia* proper is believed by many scholars to derive from a Welsh (vernacular) poem on the battles of Arthur.[12] Though we do not possess even a fragment of this poem, some Arthurian scholars believe that the battle list transmits details of real military campaigns around the year 500.[13] More recently, there has been a trend to view such material in the *Historia* as biblically inspired, with Arthur playing the role of an Old Testament hero like Joshua.[14] While the 'battle poem' and 'biblical style' theories are not mutually exclusive, I am working under the assumption that Nennius was neither entirely fictive in writing this section of the *Historia* nor was able to reproduce accurate details of sixth-century campaigns. Rather, what we should expect to find here

11 Even Dumville ('Sub-Roman Britain', p. 176) admits that 'the name of the author is unimportant in itself'. Cf. N.J. Higham, *King Arthur: Myth-Making and History* (London, 2002), p. 121.

12 A theory first proposed in H.M and N.K. Chadwick, *The Growth of Literature*, vol. I (Cambridge, 1932). See also John T. Koch and John Carey, *The Celtic Heroic Age* (Malden, MA, 1995), p. 281.

13 See, for example, Kenneth H. Jackson, 'Once Again Arthur's Battles', *Modern Philology*, 43 (1945), 44–57; Rachel Bromwich, 'Concepts of Arthur', *Studia Celtica*, 10–11 (1975–76), 163–81; and Bernard S. Bachrach, 'The Questions of King Arthur's Existence and of Romano-British Naval Operations', *Haskins Society Journal*, 2 (1991), 13–28.

14 See D.H. Howlett, *Cambro-Latin Compositions: Their Competence and Craftsmanship* (Dublin, 1998); and Higham, *King Arthur*, pp. 144ff.

are perspectives on warfare, kingship and Anglo-British relations shared by early-ninth-century Britons.

Let us now examine the relevant passage in the *Historia* in its entirety:

> At that time the English increased their numbers and grew in Britain. On Hengest's death, his son Octha came down from the north of Britain to the kingdom of the Kentishmen, and from him are sprung the kings of the Kentishmen. Then Arthur fought against them in those days with the kings of the Britons but he himself was the leader of the battles (*dux bellorum*). The first battle was at the mouth of the river which is called Glen (*Glein*). The second and third and fourth and fifth were upon another river which is called Douglas (*Dubglas*) and is in the district of Lindsey (*Linnuis*). The sixth battle was upon the river which is called *Bassas*. The seventh battle was in the Caledonian wood, that is, *Cat Coit Celidon*. The eighth battle was in Fort *Guinnion* in which Arthur carried the image of St Mary, ever virgin, on his shoulders and the pagans were turned to flight on that day and a great slaughter was upon them through the virtue of our Lord Jesus Christ and through the virtue of St Mary the Virgin, his mother. The ninth battle was waged in the City of the Legion. The tenth battle he waged on the shore of the river which is called *Tribruit*. The eleventh battle took place on the mountain which is called *Agned*. The twelfth battle was on mount Badon, in which nine hundred and sixty men fell in one day from one charge by Arthur, and no one overthrew them except himself alone. And in all the battles he stood forth as victor.[15]

Here, for the first time in a written document, Arthur is presented as the preeminent military hero of the Britons in their struggle with the Saxons. He fights 'with the kings of the Britons', as 'the leader of the battles', but is not himself called a king. He is, however, credited with twelve great victories over the Saxons, in which his martial prowess is complemented by his Christian devotion. Though we hear nothing more about Arthur in the *Historia*, this brief passage established a foundation for his career that would be taken up and expanded by such writers as Geoffrey of Monmouth, Wace and Laȝamon.

As was said in the beginning of this essay, many have focused on the point that Nennius did not specifically call Arthur 'king' in this passage. We will examine this *ex silentio* argument in detail a bit later. The positive evidence presented by Nennius is that Arthur was a leader of armies, a great soldier himself and a paragon of Christian devotion. These are surely the qualities of the ideal early medieval monarch. Let us assume then for the sake of argument that Nennius either implies here that Arthur is a king, or that he assumes that his audience would of course know that the famous Arthur was a king. If this was the case, in order to understand Nennius's depiction of British kings we must ask ourselves two questions: What were real British kings of the fifth and sixth centuries like? What were British kings of Nennius's time like?

Dynastic kingship was characteristic of Britain during the Iron Age and throughout the Middle Ages. Only the Roman period witnessed an interruption,

15 *Historia Brittonum*, ch. 56.

but there is good reason to believe that native Britons preserved both tribal and aristocratic identities during the period of Roman occupation.[16] Many archaeologists have linked the reoccupation of hillforts in the late fourth and fifth centuries with the emergence of the British kings and kingdoms described in the written sources. 'The hillforts', writes Richard Hodges, 'reveal a powerfully centralized elite able to mobilize labour to repair hundreds of metres of fortifications . . . an exercise of military command quite unlike that found in [early Anglo-Saxon] England.'[17] Dyke construction around British towns like Verulamium and Chichester also shows the vast human resources that some British communities, or British lords, could still command.

'Britain has kings', writes Gildas in the early sixth century, 'but they are tyrants'.[18] One of the questions that has most puzzled scholars of this period – which I have termed the Brittonic Age[19] – is how we get from Roman officials governing Britain in the early fifth century to a land of kings and kingdoms by the sixth century. I have argued elsewhere that the key to this transition is the *tyrannus*, the British tyrant who appears so frequently in the written sources.[20] In Britain imperial usurpers, city magistrates and dynastic kings were all called 'tyrants' in fifth- and sixth-century writings. The similarly sounding vernacular term *tigernos* (or *tiern*), which appears in Welsh and Breton sources and in inscriptions and meant simply 'lord', provided Latin commentators like Gildas with a convenient rhetorical sting for rulers they disliked: to a man who boasted of being a *tigernos*, they could call him *tyrannus*. Thus a man whose very name meant 'Over lord' – Vortigern – could be described quite acerbically as a *superbus tyrannus* by Gildas.

Britain's reputation for tyrants goes back at least to the time of Magnus Maximus, who usurped the title of the Western Roman emperor in 383. In the year 407 Britain launched no fewer than three imperial usurpers; after those men were disposed of, and Britain no longer was ruled by Rome, whatever men assumed control in Britain were viewed by outsiders like Jerome and Procopius as illegitimate tyrants. When Patrick referred to the 'tyranny' of a British warlord named Coroticus, he had both illegitimacy and despotism in mind.[21] Gildas similarly describes British kings as tyrants because their wicked behavior contrasts with the virtues of the Old Testament monarchs which he extols. 'If [in Gildas's view] all present authority was illegitimate,' writes Dumville, 'it was because of the origins of its power in rebellion against Rome and because of the current unjust exercise of its authority.'[22]

16 See discussion in Christopher A. Snyder, *The Britons* (Oxford, 2002), ch. 4.

17 Richard Hodges, *The Anglo-Saxon Achievement* (Ithaca, NY, 1989), p. 32.

18 Gildas, *De Excidio Britanniae*, p. 27, in Michael Winterbottom, ed. and trans., *Gildas: 'The Ruin of Britain' and Other Works* (London, 1978). All citations herein refer to this edition unless otherwise stated.

19 Snyder, *An Age of Tyrants*, pp. 251ff.

20 Snyder, *An Age of Tyrants*, esp. ch. 9.

21 Patrick, *Epistola*, 6, in A.B.E. Hood, ed. and trans., *St. Patrick: His Writings and Muirchu's 'Life'* (London, 1978).

22 David Dumville, 'The Idea of Government in Sub-Roman Britain', in *After Empire: Towards an Ethnology of Europe's Barbarians*, ed. Giorgio Ausenda (San Marino, 1995), pp. 177–216, here 187.

Ironically, Rome may have contributed to the rise of the British tyrants. Dumville believes that Rome had effectively ceased to govern the upland regions of Britain in the third century, and thus native governance survived or revived in those areas.[23] This could explain the reoccupation of hillforts before 400, as well as the many Iron Age tribal and royal names that survive into the Brittonic Age. Still this period is characterized by a mixture of Roman and native political institutions, such as, for example, the many inscribed stones that commemorate local Welsh magnates with Latin titles. From the epigraphic evidence it is not always clear whether we are seeing titles or names when we encounter a TRIBVNI or a TIGERNI.[24] But by the sixth century we find individuals explicitly identified on their memorials as *rex* and *princeps*.[25]

The picture that emerges, however blurry, is one of local magnates of all sorts who assert control in Britain after 410 and who eventually reestablish dynastic rule. A council still held some authority in the mid fifth century, but it shared power with the *tyrannus superbus*, remembered in later sources as the king Vortigern.[26] The council, if it is a remnant of Roman governance, likely included representatives of the tribal *civitates* of Britain, most of which survive as the basis of early medieval British kingdoms. That Vortigern held something like an overkingship in Britain is strongly indicated by Gildas's biblical metaphor of Pharaoh and the princes of Zoan used to describe the relationship between the *tyrannus superbus* and the British council.[27] Ambrosius Aurelianus, one of the few British leaders specifically named by Gildas, may have had similar authority.

In whatever guise these sub-Roman potentates took, they must have controlled both human and material resources. Many have posited a quasi-feudal model for post-Roman Britain, with a declining money economy that gave way, by the middle of the fifth century, to a barter system. In such a system lords were defined by the amount of land they owned and by the number of warriors they could maintain, supporting these retainers with feasts and prestige gifts. They could also collect taxes (probably in the form of produce and livestock) from the farmers and other laborers whom their walls and warbands protected.

Rewards to warriors and perhaps sub-kings would have come in the form of weapons and imported luxury items. These would come even cheaper if the prince could control the trade and distribution system, which has been posited for the lord of Tintagel, undoubtedly the most important port of the Brittonic Age. Mediterranean ships sailed to Britain in the late fifth and sixth centuries on average of twenty to one hundred voyages per year.[28] Oil, wine, fine table wares and other yet to be discovered goods made their way from Tintagel to other high-status sites like South Cadbury, Glastonbury and Congresbury, where in

23 Dumville, 'The Idea of Government', p. 179.

24 See Elisabeth Okasha, *Corpus of Early Christian Inscribed Stones of Southwestern Britain* (Leicester, 1993), pp. 44, 97, 156, 222.

25 Snyder, *An Age of Tyrants*, p. 87.

26 Gildas, *De Excidio*, 22.3–23.1. See Dumville, 'Sub-Roman Britain'.

27 *De Excidio*, 23.2. See Dumville, 'The Idea of Government', p. 198.

28 According to Michael Fulford, 'Byzantium and Britain', *Medieval Archaeology*, 33 (1989), 1–5.

turn some made their way to lesser landowners at places like Dinas Powys in southeast Wales. On the high end you have kings exchanging goods with their clients, while down the socio-economic scale you have lesser lords exchanging manufactured wares for foodstuffs from their tenants.

Both written and material evidence suggests that tin – referred to in Byzantine sources as 'the Brittanic metal' – was an important commodity that the Britons traded to Gaul and the Mediterranean in exchange for these luxuries. Slaves, hunting dogs and salt may have been other exports. The salt manufacturing center at Droitwich, which shows continuity from the Iron Age to the Anglo-Saxon period, served a wide network of communities while under British control, as well as after passing into Saxon hands.[29]

Gildas describes, in a passage critical of the British kings of his day, what may have been typical royal functions:

> Britain has kings, but they are tyrants; she has judges, but they are wicked. They often plunder and terrorize the innocent; they defend and protect the guilty and thieving; they have many wives – whores and adulteresses; they constantly swear false oaths; they make vows, but almost at once tell lies; they wage wars, civil and unjust; they chase thieves energetically all over the country, but love and even reward the thieves who sit with them at table; they distribute alms profusely, but pile up an immense mountain of crime for all to see; they take their seats as judges, but rarely seek out the rules of right judgment; they despise the harmless and humble, but exalt to the stars, so far as they can, their military companions, bloody, proud and murderous men, adulterers and enemies of God, if chance, as they say, so allows: men who should have been rooted out vigorously, name and all; they keep many prisoners in their jails, who are more often loaded with chafing chains because of intrigue than because they deserve punishment. They hang around the altars swearing oaths, then shortly afterwards scorn them as though they were dirty stones.[30]

Peering through Gildas's venom we see some practical functions of British kingship: kings act as judges, participate in oath-giving ceremonies, lead bands of armed warriors, police and jail criminals, and distribute gifts and alms. From Gildas elsewhere and other contemporary written sources we can add another royal duty to this list: fighting against the barbarians, especially expansionist Anglo-Saxons.

Nennius claims to know the history of these British kings of the fifth and sixth centuries. He has read Gildas and perhaps a lost British chronicle, and he has probably heard a poem describing the battles of Arthur and the British kings against the Anglo-Saxons. We would then expect him to mix this body of information together with what he knows of kings and kingship from direct experience (i.e., how Welsh, and perhaps English, kings of the eighth century behave) and from scripture. Then would he form, in writing the *Historia*, a mixed image of British kingship during the Brittonic Age, just as Homer combined ancient

29 See Della Hooke, *The Landscape of Anglo-Saxon England* (London, 1998), pp. 2–9; and Christopher A. Snyder, *Sub-Roman Britain (AD 400–600): A Gazetteer of Sites* (Oxford, 1996), p. 40.
30 *De Excidio*, p. 27.

Mycenaean memories with Greek Dark Age custom to portray his heroes of the Trojan War.

It may come as a surprise that Welsh kingship of Nennius's day resembled in many respects that of Britons two or three centuries earlier. Many hillforts and other defended settlements like crannogs continued to be occupied by Welsh princes, who continued to import prestige goods and to support warriors, craftsmen, clergy and bards at their courts. This model of the Welsh prince (*teyrn*) and his court (*llys*) is constructed from evidence of the eighth to the eleventh centuries, such as the Welsh laws, Welsh vernacular poetry, the hagiography of the British saints, a few chronicles and a collection known as the Llandaff Charters.[31] While the ecclesiastical authors obviously admire the Christian qualities of Welsh kings, and expect them to be good governors and statesmen, the poets constantly stress their military virtues. A praiseworthy king is bold, powerful, wealthy, generous, a good horseman, able not just to defend his subjects but to extend the boundaries of his kingdom. He often resides in a hall (*neuadd*) with his warband (*teulu*), employs a bard (*bardd*) to sing his praises and craftsmen, witnesses charters and grants land to religious houses, and governs the subjects (*gens*, *clas*, *llwyth*) of his kingdom (*regnum*, *gwlad*).

In the ruling houses of early medieval Wales primogeniture was not strictly established, so all males of the royal line had the right to compete for the throne.[32] Only late did the Welsh adopt the concept of a designated heir, the *gwrthrych* or *edling* (borrowed from the English *aetheling*).[33] Clientship was clearly important at an early date, most likely developing from the *clientela* of the Late Roman aristocracy.[34] Welsh patron/client relationships were more flexible and less permanent than contemporary continental vassalage, but it would not have been a difficult transition to make for Welsh rulers in the twelfth century.

Gwynedd (Latin *Venedotia*) may have been, from the very beginning of post-Roman kingship, the most powerful of the medieval Welsh kingdoms. It is clearly the area most familiar to the author of the *Historia Brittonum*, and some have postulated that Nennius was writing at Bangor. Most likely a local Venedotian dynasty asserted its power in Late Roman Britain and seized control of both local Roman forts and native hillforts after 410. Ken Dark has proposed that this nascent kingdom was overthrown by Maelgwn, perhaps a sub-king controlling Anglesey who Gildas claims killed many kings – including his uncle – along his path to power.[35] Once in power, Maelgwn is described by Gildas as

31 See Leslie Alcock, *Economy, Society and Warfare Among the Britons and Saxons* (Cardiff, 1987); Wendy Davies, *An Early Welsh Microcosm: Studies in the Llandaff Charters* (London, 1978); idem, *Wales in the Early Middle Ages* (Leicester, 1982), pp. 121ff.; and idem, *Patterns of Power in Early Wales* (Oxford, 1990). See, however, the criticisms of this model by some archaeologists: Roberta Gilchrist, 'A Re-appraisal of Dinas Powys: Local Exchange and Specialized Livestock in Fifth-Seventh Century Wales', *Medieval Archaeology*, 32 (1988), 50–62; and Christopher J. Arnold and Jeffrey L. Davies, *Roman and Early Medieval Wales* (Stroud, 2000), pp. 195ff.

32 Kari Maund, *The Welsh Kings* (Stroud, 2000), p. 45.

33 W. Davies, *Wales in the Early Middle Ages*, p. 125.

34 W. Davies, *Patterns of Power*, pp. 22–24.

35 K.R. Dark, *Civitas to Kingdom: British Political Continuity, 300–800* (Leicester, 1994), pp. 77–78.

'higher than almost all the generals in Britain, in your kingdom as in your physique'.[36] Similarly, the *Historia Brittonum* calls Maelgwn *magnus rex*, 'great king'.[37] Clearly the kings of Gwynedd were asserting their superiority among Welsh kings from an early date. Cadfan, the father of Cadwallon (d. 635), is described on his Anglesey memorial stone as 'the wisest and most renowned of all kings'.[38] Bede calls Cadwallon 'the king of the Britons', while Adomnán adds 'the most powerful king of the Britons'.[39] Cadwallon's son Cadwaladr, who died of the plague in 682, is depicted in the poem *Armes Prydein* and by Geoffrey of Monmouth as the most powerful British king of his day. The title *rex Brittonum* is later given to Rhodri of Gwynedd (d. 754) and his son Cynan (c. 815), while Merfyn Frych is called 'glorious king of the Britons' on the ninth-century Bamberg cryptogram.[40] Through conquest and propaganda, the dynasties of Maelgwn and Merfyn made Gwynedd the preeminent kingdom of early medieval Wales.

While the rulers of Gwynedd had little to fear from the southern Welsh kingdoms, their greatest threat was the expansionism of the English states of Northumbria and Mercia. Cadwallon of Gwynedd had to make an alliance with the pagan king of Mercia in order to fight back the Northumbrians in the early seventh century. Mercia itself expanded at the expense of Gwynedd's neighbor Powys, and many Welsh Christians from the south and east appear to have fled to Gwynedd during this period. Gwynedd and Powys attempted to win back the plains to their east in the mid eighth century, prompting Aethelbald of Mercia to construct Wat's Dyke, an earthwork that extends from the Severn valley to the estuary of the Dee and thus marks the boundary of the lowlands. His successor Offa followed with an even more impressive earthwork, Offa's Dyke, and together the two formed an official boundary between Welsh and English lands. Though it did not prevent subsequent raiding from both parties, the Dyke would have made the transportation of stolen livestock more difficult and did serve as a legal boundary in later English laws.

Offa is said to have devastated much Welsh territory. According to the *Anglo-Saxon Chronicle* and the *Welsh Annals*, Saxons strangled Caradog of Gwynedd in 798 and ravaged Snowdon and Rhufoniog in 816. The brothers Cynan and Hywel were engaged in a prolonged struggle for the throne of Gwynedd in the early ninth century. Merfyn Frych, who was not in patrilineal descent in Gwynedd (though his mother may have been of the ruling house), appears to have usurped the throne c. 825 and ruled over a united Gwynedd until his death in 844. It is in this time of uncertainty for Gwynedd, and hostility between the Welsh and the English, that Nennius wrote his *History of the Britons*.[41]

There was a need, then, to portray British kingship as long established and British kings as powerful and worthy Christian monarchs. Also Nennius, like

36 *De Excidio*, 33.2.
37 *Historia Brittonum*, 62.
38 V.E. Nash-Williams, *The Early Christian Monuments of Wales* (Cardiff, 1950), no. 13.
39 Bede, *The Ecclesiastical History of the English People*, 3.1; Adomnán, *The Life of St. Columba*, 1.1.
40 See W. Davies, *Wales in the Early Middle Ages*, p. 104.
41 See Higham, *King Arthur*, pp. 117ff.

other Welsh nationalist writers, felt a need to depict the past unity of Britain in the face of increasing political segmentation. Thus he begins with the famous origin legend for Britain, in which Brutus (or Britto), a descendant of the Trojan Aeneas, sailed to Britain and gave his name to both the island and its inhabitants. It may be significant that Brutus is never specifically called 'king' by Nennius (he is first introduced as 'a Roman consul'), though Nennius does employ the phrase 'when Britto reigned in Britain'.[42]

The next British ruler we encounter in the *Historia* is 'Lucius, the British king', who Nennius says was the first to receive baptism, 'with all the underkings of the British nation'.[43] Nennius continues to refer to these British 'underkings' (*reguli*) as he discusses the various Roman emperors who came to Britain or began usurpations there. Then, in 409, 'the Britons overthrew the rule of the Romans', 'killed their generals', and 'were harassed by the barbarian . . . Irish and Picts'.[44] The Britons 'went in fear for forty years', and this was during the reign of the British king Vortigern, who ruled in fear of a Roman invasion, of barbarian invasions and of a rival named Ambrosius.[45]

It was Vortigern who received the Saxon adventurers, Hengest and Horsa, mercenaries who eventually turned on the Britons. Nennius contrasts the character of Vortigern with that of St Germanus and Vortigern's own son, Vortimer, who is described as fighting vigorously against the Saxon rebels with 'the kings of our nation'.[46] Four battles of Vortimer are described in a manner very similar to the description of Arthur's twelve battles; while Vortimer is not called king here, it is clear that he is representing his beleaguered royal father.

After the deaths of Vortimer and Vortigern, Pascent, another son of Vortigern, ruled in the Welsh lands of Builth and Gwerthrynion, but only by permission of Ambrosius, 'the great king among all the kings of the British nation'.[47] Nennius appears to make Ambrosius contemporary with St Patrick's mission in Ireland. Then in the next generation, of Hengest's son Octha, 'Arthur fought against [the Saxons] . . . together with the kings of the Britons; but he was *dux bellorum*'. 'Taken as a whole', writes Leslie Alcock of this phrase, '[the words] are usually read as implying that Arthur was not himself a king, but rather a soldier acting on behalf of a number of British kings. But this is not actually said'.[48] There are two strains of this *dux bellorum* argument:

A. Arthur was a non-royal native warrior fighting with the British kings;
B. Arthur held a formal military rank akin to the Roman *dux Britanniarum*.

Favoring the first interpretation is the tradition of 'Arthur the warrior' found in much early Welsh legend and poetry. Arthur, for example, appears as *Arthur miles* twice in the 'Marvels of Britain' attached to the Harleian recension of the

42 *Historia Brittonum*, ch. 7 and 11.
43 *Historia Brittonum*, ch. 22.
44 *Historia Brittonum*, ch. 28–30.
45 *Historia Brittonum*, ch. 31.
46 *Historia Brittonum*, ch. 43–44.
47 *Historia Brittonum*, ch. 48.
48 Leslie Alcock, *Arthur's Britain* (London, 1971), p. 60.

Historia.[49] He is also compared to the warrior Gordur in the poem *Y Gododdin*, considered by many to be the earliest appearance of Arthur in literature.[50] But this allusion may not be older than the ninth century. There is, of course, no reason to interpret a 'soldier Arthur' as excluding the possibility that he was also a king, though some have suggested that this phrase was used by Nennius to distinguish two separate Arthurs.

The second interpretation of *dux bellorum* was put forward by the historian R.G. Collingwood more than sixty years ago.[51] Collingwood, believing that Arthur's name derived from the Latin *Artorius*, speculated that he may have held a Roman-derived post similar to the *comes Britanniarum*, with command of a mobile field army consisting of heavily armed cavalry. The archaeologist Leslie Alcock expanded on this theory, depicting Arthur as a *magister militum* (a higher military command than *dux* or *comes*) whose military headquarters was the South Cadbury hillfort.[52]

The exact wording of this key passage is *sed ipse dux erat bellorum*, 'but he himself was leader of the battles'. Although medieval Latin still had flexibility in word ordering, it seems unlikely that Nennius would have separated *dux* and *bellorum* if it was intended to denote a formal title. He never separates *rex* and *Brittonum* when he describes 'British kings' and 'kings of the Britons', for example. In the 'Harleian recension' contents description, moreover, Arthur is called 'King Arthur the warrior' (*Arturo rege belligero*).

As Geoffrey Ashe and others have pointed out, the far-flung geography in Nennius's description of Arthur's twelve battles would seem to make Arthur a national figure rather than a local ruler.[53] Arthur is given no epithet in the earliest recensions of the *Welsh Annals*, which records the accomplishments and deaths of several Britons known to have been kings. But in the *Welsh Annals*, kingship is often implied rather than stated. One of the later recensions of the *Annals* does describe Arthur as *rex Britonum*.[54] In Welsh hagiography, which usually has unfavorable depictions of Arthur's character, Arthur is described as a king. Finally, 'Arthur' (in its various forms) is a royal name from very early on. It was borne by princes in western Scotland and Wales (and even in Ireland) in the sixth and seventh centuries.[55]

Alcock has suggested that *dux erat bellorum* may be translating a Welsh poetic expression, rather than a formal Roman title, and that 'all we are being told [by Nennius] is that Arthur fought in the company of the British kings, but he was pre-eminent in battle'.[56] Unlike the Latin *rex*, there was no single standard for

49 He is also called *Arthur miles* in the Scottish text *Liber Floridus*, written by Lambert of St. Omer c. 1120. See David Dumville, 'The *Liber Floridus* of Lambert of Saint-Omer', *Bulletin of the Board of Celtic Studies*, 26 (1974–76), 103–22.

50 See J.T. Koch, *The 'Gododdin' of Aneirin. Text and Context from Dark-Age North Britain* (Cardiff, 1997).

51 R.G. Collingwood and J.N.L. Myres, *Roman Britain and the English Settlement* (Oxford, 1936).

52 Alcock, *Arthur's Britain*, passim.

53 Ashe in Norris J. Lacy, Geoffrey Ashe and Debra N. Mancoff, *The Arthurian Handbook*, 2nd ed. (New York, 1997), p. 15.

54 See J.B. Coe and S. Young, *The Celtic Sources for the Arthurian Legends* (Lampeter, 1995), p. 13.

55 See Ken Dark, 'A Famous Arthur in the Sixth Century? Reconsidering the Origins of the Arthurian Legend', *Reading Medieval Studies*, 26 (2000), pp. 77–96.

56 Alcock, *Arthur's Britain*, p. 61.

depicting kings in early Welsh poetry, but rather a variety of terms for lord or prince from which the poet could choose, including *teyrn, rwyfadur* and *brenhin.* Nennius need not have had a written text before him as he composed the section on Arthur's battles, nor does this theory require an oral source of any real historical value for events c. 500. In writing the phrase *Arthur . . . dux erat bellorum,* Nennius may be seen as simply the first (known) Latin author to put down in writing a well-known (to early-ninth-century Welsh audiences) vernacular tradition concerning an Arthur who was a prominent British leader of battles against the Saxons in the distant past. To Nennius at least, Arthur was more prominent than the unnamed *reges Brittonum* whom he lead into battle, and it is a reasonable assumption given the evidence presented herein that this Arthur was a king (or held royal status) himself.

It is reasonable now to ask what, if any, implications this understanding of Nennius has on the historicity of Arthur. Unfortunately, problems remain with the *Historia Brittonum* and we cannot upgrade its status as a source for the history of the Brittonic Age. It is not contemporary evidence for a sixth-century Arthur, and we cannot at this stage extract Nennius's source material in uncorrupted form. 'The best we can therefore honestly say', writes Thomas Green, 'is that in the *Historia Brittonum,* a source of very dubious historical value [for the sixth century], we have evidence for the idea that Arthur was a historical figure being current by A.D. 829/30 at the latest'.[57] That is, Arthur was undoubtedly believed to have been a historical figure by British writers of the ninth century, if not earlier.

While we cannot answer what some believe to be the ultimate or most important question about Arthur, I hope that this essay will nevertheless counter two recent assumptions in Arthurian scholarship. Just as there is no real proof that Nennius's authorship of the *Historia Brittonum* is a fabrication, so too must we now abandon the notion that the *Historia* proves that Arthur was no king.

57 Thomas Green, 'The Historicity and Historicisation of King Arthur' (March 1998, rev. Dec. 2001), http://www.arthuriana.co.uk/historicity/arthur.htm (cited March 2002).

'For Mortals are Moved by these Conditions': Fate, Fortune and Providence in Geoffrey of Monmouth

SIÂN ECHARD

Early in Geoffrey of Monmouth's *Historia regum Britannie*, King Leir laments the state to which he has been reduced by the combination of his own foolishness and his elder daughters' unfilial treatment of him. He does not, however, blame himself, but rather berates both the Fates and Fortune:

> 'O irreuocabilia fatorum seria que solito cursu fixum iter tenditis, cur unquam me ad instabilem felicitatem promouere uoluistis cum maior pena sit ipsam amissam recolere quam sequentis infelicitatis presentia urgeri. Magis etenim aggrauat me illius temporis memoria quo tot centenis milibus militum stipatus et menia urbium diruere et prouintias hostium uastare solebam quam calamitas miserie mee que ipsos qui iam sub pedibus meis iacebant debilitatem meam deserere coegit. O irata fortuna! Uenietne unquam dies qua ipsis uicem reddere potero qui sic tempora mea sicuti paupertatem meam diffugierunt?'[1]
>
> ['Oh, you Fates, with your immoveable chain of events, you who hold to your accustomed, ordained course, why did you wish to raise me up to an unstable felicity when it is the greater pain to recall what is lost than for me to consider the present state of unhappiness which follows? For indeed, the memory of that time when, with so many hundreds of thousands of men I used to batter down the walls of cities and lay waste the provinces of my enemies, causes me more pain than the calamity of my current misery, although it has caused those who once lay beneath my feet to abandon me in my weakness. Oh irate Fortune! When, oh when will the day ever come when I will be able to administer vengeance on those who have thus fled me in my poverty?']

In Leir's lament we can see the later medieval fascination with the fall of princes: the king who has been laid low draws an explicit contrast between his power as conqueror and his present distress. This is standard material in the *de casibus* tradition,[2] and the moralistic overtones of that tradition seem at first to be at

1 Geoffrey of Monmouth, *The Historia regum Britannie of Geoffrey of Monmouth I: Bern, Burgerbibliothek, MS. 568*, ed. Neil Wright (Cambridge, 1984), c. 31, p. 21.

2 For a useful summary of the development of the *de casibus* tradition, from Boccaccio's *De casibus virorum illustrium*, see Paul Budra, *A Mirror for Magistrates and the de casibus Tradition* (Toronto, 2000). Budra makes important distinctions between *de casibus* narratives and tragedies: Boccaccio's interest in the fall of the great can be linked to the cumulative didactic potential of these examples, pp. 16–18.

play here, for Geoffrey's Leir, like Shakespeare's, has been a fool, and the reversal in his fortunes is therefore earned. But this Leir does not remain humbled. The finish of his story is not, in the *Historia*, personally tragic (nor is it particularly useful as a moral lesson). Far from ending in madness and misery, Leir succeeds in wreaking vengeance on his sons-in-law, and after their defeat rules Britain for three more years before dying and passing the rule of his kingdom to Cordelia. It is the innocent Cordelia whose end is unhappy: after she has ruled for five years, her nephews rebel against her and imprison her, and she eventually takes her life.

The story of Leir encapsulates many of the contradictions in Geoffrey's treatment of Fortune. The actors in his historical dramas may deserve their ends, or they may not; their fates may be attributed to Fate, or Fortune, or providence; to human error or to human treachery. With its relentless sequence of kings, and its overall structure from the Trojan foundation to the Saxon domination, Geoffrey's *Historia* seems likely to read as an enactment of Fortune's wheel in the lives of men, an early version of British history as what the *Gawain*-poet famously called a cycle of 'blysse and blunder'.[3] But the *Historia* is more complex, or perhaps more incoherent, than that. In the end, a reader is left wondering if Geoffrey has any certitude that any power – whether Fortune or God or anything else – is really in control of human history.[4] Geoffrey's Arthur is thoroughly embedded in these confusions: his fall is one of the most spectacular, and the least deserved, of any king in the whole of the *Historia*.[5] It is *explicable*, in the sense that Mordred's greed and betrayal are nothing new in British history, but the shock of Arthur's end, after the time lavished on his heroic reign, seems to have brought even Geoffrey up short:

> Nec hoc quidem . . . Galfridus Monemutensis tacebit sed, ut in prefato Britannico sermone inuenit et a Gwaltero Oxenefordensi in multis historiis peritissimo uiro audiuit, uili licet stilo breuiter propalabit que prelia inclitus ille rex . . . cum nepote suo commiserit.[6]

3 *Sir Gawain and the Green Knight*, ed. J.R.R. Tolkien and E.V. Gordon, 2nd ed., rev. Norman Davis (Oxford, 1967), vs. 18.

4 Geoffrey's unconventional historiography has been frequently discussed. For Robert W. Hanning, Geoffrey deliberately removes the conventional Christian explanations for historical events, thus producing a radically unprovidential version of history: *The Vision of History in Early Britain: From Gildas to Geoffrey of Monmouth* (New York, 1966), pp. 138–72. Sometimes Geoffrey is read as a parodist; see for example Christopher N.L. Brooke, 'Geoffrey of Monmouth as a Historian', in *Church and Government in the Middle Ages: Essays Presented to C.R. Cheney on his 70th Birthday*, ed. C.N.L. Brooke et al. (Cambridge, 1976), pp. 77–91, and Valerie I.J. Flint, 'The *Historia regum Britanniae* of Geoffrey of Monmouth: Parody and its Purpose. A Suggestion', *Speculum*, 54 (1979), 447–68. I discuss Geoffrey's historiography in *Arthurian Narrative in the Latin Tradition* (Cambridge, 1998).

5 It will be clear that while I share Maureen Fries's view of the importance – and Boethian roots – of the cyclical structure of the *Historia*, I do not agree that Geoffrey intends a reader to see Arthur's fall as the result of 'overreaching appetite for earthly glory' (Maureen Fries, 'Boethian Themes and Tragic Structure in Geoffrey of Monmouth's *Historia regum Britanniae*', in *The Arthurian Tradition: Essays in Convergence*, ed. Mary Flowers Braswell and John Bugge [Tuscaloosa, AL, 1988], p. 37). See below for my discussion of Geoffrey's treatment of Arthurian conquest.

6 *Historia*, c. 177, pp. 129–30.

[But about this . . . Geoffrey of Monmouth will be silent and, as he found it in the aforementioned British writing and as he has heard it from Walter of Oxford, a man most skilled in many histories, he will, in his admittedly humble style, briefly describe the battle which that most famous king fought with his nephew . . .]

While later writers would try to reconcile this end with a providential view of history, sometimes by attributing to Arthur the weaknesses to which kings seem particularly susceptible, Geoffrey simply reports. He returns to his 'British book' instead of turning to God, or to Fortune,[7] and after pages spent on Arthur's reign, dispatches his final battle and apparent death in an almost shockingly bald way:

Set et inclitus ille rex Arturus letaliter uulneratus est; qui illinc ad sananda uulnera sua in insulam Auallonis euectus Constantino cognato suo et filio Cadoris ducis Cornubie diadema Britannie concessit anno ab incarnatione Domini .dxlii.. Anima eius in pace quiescat.[8]

[But that most famous king Arthur was mortally wounded. Arthur having been taken from there to the island of Avalon for the healing of his wounds, he handed over the crown of Britain to his cousin Constantine, son of Cador, duke of Cornwall, in the year 542 after the incarnation of our Lord. May his soul rest in peace.]

Geoffrey then returns to describing British history as a quick-moving cycle of good kings and bad, mimicking the shape of Fortune's wheel, perhaps, but seldom invoking it directly, either as symbol or as explanatory device. Later writers may have found it possible to rework Geoffrey's history along more conventional lines, but to read backwards from these reworkings is to miss what is unique in Geoffrey's vision.[9]

Fortune in fact appears so infrequently in the *Historia* that it is possible to canvas most of those appearances very quickly. These include the invocation

7 Budra argues that, 'Though one of the most prevalent images of the Middle Ages and Renaissance, fortune embodies a concept that has no place in a divinely-ordered, providential universe': but writers are reluctant to give up the rich possibilities of the figure, and thus she may be deployed in various ways; *A Mirror for Magistrates*, p. 50. One such deployment in the medieval histories which concerns me was to see the vagaries of Fortune as functioning under the control of providential history – Fortune as the wheel rolling along the straight line of God's plan, as it were.

8 *Historia*, c. 178, p. 132.

9 I would wish, then, to alter slightly Maureen Fries's argument that subsequent Arthurian authors recognized in this structure Geoffrey's 'implicit debt to Boethian thought' (Fries, 'Boethian Themes', p. 41); I would argue instead that Geoffrey's deliberate detaching of both his overall structure and his occasional explicit references to Fortune from their traditionally medieval association with providence is something which made later vernacular writers uncomfortable, so that they redirected his vision into more conventional paths. Hanning concludes his discussion of Geoffrey's radical historiography by arguing that Geoffrey's facts were absorbed into later history, while his attitudes were not. The 'antipolitical' and 'almost antihistorical' aspects of the *Historia*, for their part, were more congenial to romance, a form which 'presented and examined personal destiny in a deliberately ahistorical context – not at the Christian exegetical level of national and personal providence, nor as a factor in political evolution, but as an index of the human condition considered as a unique, continuous, ethical phenomenon'; *The Vision of History*, pp. 174–75.

(like Leir's) of the Fates – seemingly metonymic for Geoffrey of Fortune – and the occasional use of *forte* to introduce an incident. Chance, or *casus*, is occasionally given credit for events. But these are usually passing references: Leir's outburst is in fact the most developed reference to Fortune or Fate in the whole text. More typical is Goffar, king of the Poitevins, gazing at the encamped Trojans and crying out 'Proh fatum triste!' ['How sad a fate'].[10] Battle sometimes includes the language of chance: for example, we are told that chance arranges matters so that Nennius brother of Cassivelaunus encounters Caesar in battle – the word *casus* in fact occurs twice in the chapter describing that battle.[11] The chance that brings Nennius and Caesar together is at least partially beneficent: the Britons are victorious, though Nennius ultimately dies of his wounds. Chance can also be portrayed in a negative light. A series of unlikely events sets up Vortigern's bid for kingship: Constans the ex-monk is a weak shadow-king, his brothers are infants, and 'Preterea infortuniam illud acciderat quod proceres regni qui maiores erant natu defuncti fuerant solusque Uortegirnus astutus et sapiens magnique consilii uidebatur' [And a further misfortune had befallen in that the older nobles of the kingdom had died and thus Vortigern alone seemed to be wise and astute, the only man of any useful counsel].[12] But to say that a situation is unfortunate is not necessarily to attribute causality to Fortune (as Leir apparently does). The only other place in the *Historia*, besides Leir's outburst, where we are invited to imagine Fortune controlling the destinies of men is in the peculiar, proto-romantic story of Cadwallo and his nephew Brian, near the end of the *Historia*. Cadwallo, sailing to Britanny in search of help to regain his kingdom, is blown off course by a storm, and the rudderless ship travels 'dispositioni fortune' [at the will of fortune]. Cadwallo and Brian eventually land on Guernsey and Brian sets off to seek whatever game 'casus' [chance][13] might send his way (when chance disobliges him, he slices a chunk out of his own thigh, roasts it, and feeds it to his uncle). And chance continues to be a motif in Brian's adventures, as he later encounters his kidnapped sister and then, 'forte',[14] the very magician he wishes to kill. This is the last reference to chance in the *Historia*; what follows are the final events leading up to the Saxon domination, signalled at last when an angelic voice tells Cadwallader that God no longer wishes the Britons to rule, at least not at this time. Divine providence (confirmed by the oracular sayings of Merlin) has the final word, although providence, like Fortune, is only sparingly mentioned throughout the *Historia*.

The *Historia* is in general, by this account, not particularly concerned with the language of Fortune; and there is even less of such language in the Arthuriad than in other sections of the text. All the moments which later versions of Arthur's rise and fall imbue with the iconography or the language of Fortune are in Geoffrey far more straightforward. The dream of the dragon and the bear, which in the *Alliterative Morte Arthure* is elaborated in such a way as to emphasize the up-and-down movement of the two combatants (thus perhaps foreshad-

10 *Historia*, c. 20, p. 12.
11 *Historia*, c. 56, p. 36.
12 *Historia*, c. 95, p. 63.
13 *Historia*, c. 193, p. 138.
14 *Historia*, c. 196, p. 141.

owing the explicit references to Fortune and her wheel in the later prophetic dream), is over quickly:

> Sopitus etiam per somnum uidit ursum quendam in aere uolantem cuius murmure tota litora intremebant; terribilem quoque draconem ab occidenti aduolare, qui splendore oculorum suorum patriam illuminabat. Alterum uero alteri occurrentem miram pugnam committere. Sed prefatum draconem ursum sepius irruentem ignito anhelitu comburere combustumque in terram prosternere.[15]
>
> [As he drowsed, in a dream he saw a certain bear, flying through the air, at whose growling the shores shook; and also a terrible dragon came flying from the west, illuminating the countryside with the splendour of its eyes. When the one encountered the other, a marvellous battle began. But the aforementioned dragon kept attacking the bear, burning it with its fiery breath, and finally cast it down, entirely burned up, to the earth.]

The battle between Arthur and the giant which follows is imbued, in the *Alliterative Morte*'s version, with the language and action of Fortune: Arthur and the giant roll over and over in their struggles, eventually rolling down a hillside. Geoffrey's Arthur, on the other hand, does not roll down the hill in the giant's embrace – he is briefly cast to his knees, but quickly rises and dispatches the giant by driving his sword into the latter's brain. There is a direct reference to Fortune in this section of the text, but it is in the words the old nurse addresses to Bedevere: 'O infelix homo, quod infortunium te in hunc locum subuectat?' ['Oh unfortunate man, what misfortune has brought you to this place?'][16] And Bedevere has no part to play in this drama; in other words, the language seems purely conventional. The case is similar elsewhere in the Arthuriad. Boso encourages his men to follow him through the Roman ranks in order to capture Petreius, 'si fortuna fauerit' [if Fortune favours us],[17] and we are told that the Britons might have suffered a defeat, 'nisi fortuna optatum auxilium eis accelerasset' [had not fortune hastened the aid they needed to them].[18] There is nothing in these passing references to match Leir's accusation of the Fates; nothing either to match Brian's romantic adventures with their characteristic happenstance events. The final battle is not, as it will later be in the vernacular tradition, provoked by a knight's drawing his sword to kill an asp. Geoffrey's Arthur, an apparently perfect king and conqueror, will be destroyed by betrayal within his own family – something which a reader of the whole of the *Historia* has come to expect, as time and again good kings are brought down by treachery.

The contrast Leir contemplates between his past as conqueror and his miserable present underpins many post-Galfridian versions of Arthur's fall, in both Latin and the vernacular. William of Rennes's thirteenth-century adaptation of the *Historia*, the *Gesta regum Britannie*, figures Arthur as a second Alexander, and mingles the admiration and disapproval which such figures traditionally

15 *Historia*, c. 164, pp. 116–17.
16 *Historia*, c. 165, p. 117.
17 *Historia*, c. 166, p. 121.
18 *Historia*, c. 167, p. 122.

evoke.[19] While Geoffrey is careful to provide justifications for all of Arthur's battles, William is more critical. Arthur's bloodthirsty speech to his troops before the battle at Siesia provokes this outburst:

> Quis furor, o fortes, pro regno deperituro
> Perdere perpetuum regnum? Perdetis utrumque
> Excedendo modum: contenta Britannia fine
> Debuit esse suo; potuit quoque Roma tributum
> Quod petit iniuste non exegisse.[20]
>
> [What madness, oh brave men! Is that perpetual kingdom to be lost for an earthly one? You will lose in both ways through your excess. Britain should be content with its own borders. Rome, too, should not seek to exact tribute unjustly.]

In William of Rennes's version, Arthur learns of Mordred's treachery as he prepares to march on Rome, and we are told that 'Deus opposuit tantis sua numina uotis' [God opposed these vows with his powers].[21] Fate is set in motion, it seems, by the behaviour of men: as the final battle approaches: 'quia fatorum contra decreta uenire / Nulli permissum est, ad bellum tendit uterque / Ante datum fatis'[22] [since it is not permitted for anyone to go against the laws of the fates, both set out for the battle fate had decreed]. In an apostrophe at the end of the *Gesta*, William makes explicit the link between Fortune's wheel and British history, and it is a link which is unequivocal in its moral judgements:

> O Bruti regio, miserande condicionis
> Insula, plena doli, ueneris domus, hospita martis,
> Sanguinis urna, capax uiciorum sportula: testis
> Fortune stabilis, mendaces esse poetas
> Conuincis, qui stare deam, quam uoluit in orbe
> Orbita, posse negant. Fortunam stare tenaci
> Proposito te teste probas nusquamque moueri:
> Nam qualis tecum cepit persistere, talis
> Perstat adhuc. Regni cepisti nomen habere
> Ui gladii; tua cepta tenes, tua cepta tenebis,
> Dum poterunt Britones et Saxones arma tenere.
> Progenies Priami, fera gens, quam blanda molestat
> Pax, quam bella iuuant, que semper uiuis in armis,
> Cui semper discors concordia, scismaque concors,
> Ecce uenit uindicta Dei dignaque reatus
> Punit clade tuos.[23]

19 In his edition of the *Gesta*, Neil Wright points out that William adds a passage on Fortune and her wheel to the Leir story, too, in addition to using Geoffrey's 'fully Classical imagery'; see *The Historia Regum Britannie of Geoffrey of Monmouth V: Gesta regum Britannie*, ed. Neil Wright (Cambridge, 1991), p. xxiii. Rosemary Morris discusses William's Arthuriad at length in 'The *Gesta Regum Britanniae* of William of Rennes: An Arthurian Epic?', *Arthurian Literature* VI (1986), 60–123. She argues that, as in some later vernacular versions of Arthur's story, the king moves from just to unjust conquest – as the quotations discussed below illustrate.

20 William of Rennes, *Gesta regum Britannie*, VIII.474–78.

21 *Gesta regum Britannie* IX.145.

22 *Gesta regum Britannie* IX.241–43.

23 *Gesta regum Britannie* X.429–44.

[O realm of Brutus, island of miserable events, full of deceit, home of lust, host to war, vessel of blood, capacious basket of vices: you are a witness to the stability of Fortune, and you show poets to be liars when they say that the goddess, whose wheel whirls her round, cannot stand still. You offer testimony that Fortune can stand in a fixed purpose; you show her to be moving nowhere: for just as she took up with you in the first place, so she remains even now. You seized the name of kingdom by the power of the sword; you continue as you have begun, and as you have begun you will continue, while the Britons and the Saxons are still able to bear arms. Progeny of Priam, savage people, whom gentle Peace troubles, whom war delights, who live always in arms, to whom harmony is always discord, and schism, peace – lo, the vengeance of God comes to punish you with deserved ruin.]

This is the conventional medieval view of Fortune: functioning under God's providential purpose, she governs the destinies of those who are most susceptible – and kings and conquerors are particularly prone to fall under her rule. The reversals they suffer are earned, no matter how splendid a picture they present on their way up the wheel.

While we do not anywhere in the *Historia* encounter anything like Arthur's dream of Fortune and her wheel in such texts as *La mort le roi Artu* or the *Alliterative Morte Arthure*, it is nevertheless the case that Geoffrey does return, more than once, to the idea that there is *something* intervening in the destinies of men. The *Historia* may not focus on the machinations of Fortune, but it is a book structured around prophecy. Prophecy can be understood as the revelation of an underlying plan for humanity – and these prophecies mark the overarching movement of the *Historia*, from the British beginnings with Brutus, to the apex of British power in Arthur and, finally, to the moment when the Britons lose control of their island. Yet even these prophetic moments are varying and ambiguous when it comes to revealing just who or what is behind the destiny of Britain and her kings. The first prophetic voice is that of the goddess Diana:

Tunc uisum est illi deam astare ante ipsum et sese in hunc modum affari:
'Brute, sub occasu solis trans Gallica regna
Insula in occeano est <undique clausa mari.
Insula in occeano est>, habitata gigantibus olim,
Nunc deserta quidem, gentibus apta tuis.
Hanc pete: namque tibi sedes erit illa perennis;
Hic fiet natis altera Troia tuis.
Hic de prole tua reges nascentur, et ipsis
Totius terre subditus orbis erit'.[24]

[Then a vision came to him of the goddess standing before him and addressing him in this manner: 'Brutus, below the setting sun, beyond the realms of Gaul, there is an island in the ocean, surrounded by the sea. There is an island in the ocean, formerly the

24 *Historia*, c. 16, p. 9.

> habitation of giants, but now deserted, and ready for your people. Seek it: for it will be your seat through the years; here another Troy will be made for your descendants, here kings will be born from your people, and the whole globe of the world will be subject to them.']

Diana's prophecy is fulfilled by Brutus and his descendants, and its imperial aspects are echoed in the next direct prophecy, when Merlin (with whose other prophecies I will deal later) explicates the appearance of a comet for Utherpendragon:

> 'Te etenim sydus istud significat et igneus draco sub sydere. Radius autem qui uersus Gallicanam plagam porrigitur portendit tibi futurum filium et potentissimum cuius potestas omnia regna que proteget habebit. Alter uero radius significat filiam, cuius filii et nepotes regnum Britannie succedenter habebunt.'[25]

> ['For that star signifies you, as does the fiery dragon beneath the star. The ray which stretches towards the shores of Gaul portends your future son, who will be most powerful, and whose power will extend over all the kingdoms which he will protect. And the other ray signifies your daughter, whose sons and grandsons will hold the kingship of Britain in turn.']

This time it is not a goddess who speaks, but the message is the same – another prophecy concerned with rule. The final prophecy is assigned to an angelic voice, and signals the end of the imperial state forecast by the first two, for as Cadwallader prepares to return to reclaim his kingdom with the help of Alan, King of Britanny, '. . . intonuit ei uox angelica dum classem pararet ut ceptis suis desisteret. Nolebat enim Deus Britones in <insula> Britannie diutius regnare antequam tempus illud uenisset quod Merlinus Arturo prophetauerat'[26] [an angelic voice spoke to him while he was preparing his ship, and told him to cease his preparations. For God did not wish the Britons to reign any longer in the island of Britain, until the time should come which Merlin had prophesied to Arthur].

Once Alan, by consulting the Sybelline oracles and Merlin's prophecies, has satisfied himself that Cadwallader has heard a true prophecy, he encourages Cadwallader to go to Rome as the voice had instructed. Cadwallader's sons Yvor and Yni return to the island and battle the Saxons, but finally to no avail, and Geoffrey's *Historia* draws to a close. It is significant that the final words of the *Historia* stress, not prophecy or providence, but rather human behaviour: the Britons fail, we are told, because of their habit of internal strife [consuetudinarium discidium]. The Saxons, on the other hand, 'sapientius agentes, pacem et concordiam inter se habentes' [acted more wisely, keeping peace and harmony among themselves].[27] It seems, then, that the power behind the prophecies has correctly recognized the weaknesses of the Britons: human beings have the ability to control their own fates, and the unseen powers simply have a longer view as to the consequences of those actions.

25 *Historia*, c. 133, p. 94.
26 *Historia*, c. 205, p. 146.
27 *Historia*, c. 207, pp. 146–47.

However, that final prophecy bears closer examination, for it refers to Merlin prophesying to Arthur. This is something Merlin never does, or at least, something that Geoffrey never shows Merlin doing: Merlin's last appearance in the *Historia* occurs when he arranges the deception by which Uther engenders Arthur. The reference seems to be to the most concentrated prophetic section of the *Historia*, the *Prophetia Merlini*. These prophecies circulated separately from the *Historia* proper,[28] and although they have a place in the narrative arc of the *Historia* – Merlin delivers them before Vortigern, in order to demonstrate that Vortigern's magicians are charlatans – they reach beyond and outside the narrative of Britain's kings up to Cadwallader. The moment which the angelic voice anticipates is perhaps this one:

> Tunc erumpent Armorici montes et diademate Bruti coronabitur. Replebitur Kambria letitia et robora Cornubie uirescent. Nomine Bruti uocabitur insula et nuncupatio extraneorum peribit.[29]
>
> [Then the mountains of Armorica shall erupt and it will be crowned with the diadem of Brutus. Cambria shall be filled with joy and the oaks of Cornwall shall flourish. The island shall be called by the name of Brutus, and the naming given it by the foreigners shall perish.]

This is the stuff of Welsh nationalist prophecy, and although it predicts a reversal for the hated occupiers, it is not a conventional Fortune narrative. It is also not the final prophetic word in this section, and it is in the degeneration of Merlin's prophecies that we can begin to see what lies behind Geoffrey's portrayal of human history. The prophecies concern themselves obliquely with the rise and fall of rulers, but the animal imagery used to figure those rulers – imagery which becomes denser as the prophecies progress – inevitably aligns the human with the bestial. A final movement shifts to celestial display, and this display – unlike the comet interpreted for Uther by Merlin – seems designed to show that the heavenly powers are inimical to mankind:

> 'Splendor solis electro Mercurii languebit et erit horror inspicientibus. Mutabit clipeum Stilbon Archadie, uocabit Uenerem galea Martis. Galea Martis umbram conficiet, transsibit terminos furor Mercurii. Nudabit ensem Orion ferreus, uexabit nubes <Phebus> equoreus. Exibit Iupiter licitas semitas et Uenus deseret statutas lineas. Saturni syderis liuido corruet et falce recurua mortales perimet. ... In ictu radii exurgent equora et puluis ueterum renouabitur. Confligent uenti diro sufflamine et sonitum inter sydera conficient.'[30]
>
> ['The splendour of the sun will languish in the amber of Mercury, and there will be horror among those who see this. Mercury of Arcady will change its shield,

28 See Julia Crick, *The Historia regum Britannie of Geoffrey of Monmouth III: A Summary Catalogue of the Manuscripts* (Cambridge, 1989) and *The Historia regum Britannie of Geoffrey of Monmouth IV: Dissemination and Reception in the Later Middle Ages* (Cambridge, 1991); and Caroline D. Eckhardt, *The Prophetia Merlini of Geoffrey of Monmouth: A Fifteenth-century Commentary* (Cambridge, MA, 1982) and 'The *Prophetia Merlini* of Geoffrey of Monmouth: Latin Manuscript Copies', *Manuscripta*, 26 (1982), 167–76.

29 *Historia*, c. 115.20, p. 77.

30 *Historia*, c. 117.73–74, p. 84.

and the Helmet of Mars will call to Venus. The helmet of Mars will cast a shadow, and the rage of Mercury will cross over its orbit. Iron Orion will bare its sword, and watery Phoebus will torment the clouds. Jupiter will leave its ordained paths and Venus will desert its appointed lines. The anger of the star Saturn will fall and kill mortals with a curved sickle. . . . The oceans shall surge up and the dust of the ancients shall be made new in the blink of an eye. The winds will do battle with a dire blast, and they shall make noise among the stars.']

This final apocalyptic vision is not accompanied by references to God or to providence: Robert Hanning argues that the *Prophecies* show that 'the impersonal universe which has presided over the rise and fall of kingdoms will lose control of itself and history will dissolve into nothingness'.[31] It is worth remembering that the only *angelic* prophecy in the *Historia* is the one which ends both the work and the reign of the Britons, the latter until some indistinct future – a future predicted by Merlin. The *Historia* has no Fortuna (nor Philosophia) explicitly governing its movement; Merlin is in some ways as close as we come, and before making a final assessment of the powers that control Geoffrey's *Historia*, we should look at Merlin's other appearance, in the *Vita Merlini*.

Like Leir in the *Historia*, the Merlin of the *Vita* complains about fate. The poem opens with the maddened prophet lamenting the loss of his men in battle:

'Ergo ne sic potuit sors importuna nocere
ut michi surriperet tantos talesque sodales
quos modo tot reges tot regna remota timebant?
O dubios hominum casus mortemque propinquam
que penes est illos semper stimuloque latenti
percutit et miseram pellit de corpore vitam!'[32]

['Surely, malignant chance has not been so vicious as to take away all my companions, such men as until now kings and distant kingdoms were accustomed to fear? O, the doubtful fates of men, with death ever near, always able to strike them with a hidden goad, and drive out the miserable life from the body!']

Like Leir's lament, there is specific reference to the fate of rulers here, as Merlin remembers the former power of his warband. And as in the *Historia*, Merlin's prophecies also concern themselves with the fate of kings and kingdoms, vacillating between an emphasis on human weakness on the one hand, and a sense of inimical celestial powers on the other. Here, for example, the Merlin of the *Vita* chastises the Britons:

'O rabiem Britonum, quos copia diviciarum
usque superveniens ultra quam debeat effert!
Nolunt pace frui, stimulis agitantur Herinis.
Civiles acies cognataque prelia miscent.
Ecclesias Domini paciuntur habere ruinam
pontificesque sacros ad regna remota repellunt.'[33]

31 Hanning, *The Vision of History*, pp. 171–72.
32 Geoffrey of Monmouth, *Life of Merlin: Vita Merlini*, ed. Basil Clarke (Cardiff, 1973), lines 40–45.
33 *Vita Merlini*, lines 580–85.

['Oh, the madness of the Britons, whose overflowing riches lead them to seek even more than they ought! They do not wish to enjoy peace, but are goaded by a Fury. They mix civil strife and domestic battles. They allow the churches of the Lord to fall to ruin, and they drive its holy bishops to remote lands.']

As this prophetic outburst continues, Merlin foretells the coming of the Normans, and it seems that the fate of the Britons is also the fate of the island of Britain; that is, each successive king or conqueror brings more misery. After the Normans, Merlin prophesies a complete social breakdown:

'Tum pax atque fides et virtus omnis abibit,
undique per patrias committent prelia cives
virque virum prodet, non invenietur amicus.
Conjuge despecta meretrices sponsus adibit
sponsaque cui cupiet despecto conjuge nubet.
Non honor ecclesiis servabitur, ordo peribit.
Pontifices tunc arma ferent, tunc castra sequentur,
in tellure sacra turres et menia ponent
militibusque dabunt quod deberetur egenis.'[34]

['Then peace and faith and virtue will all depart, and there will be civil war throughout the lands, and man will betray his fellow, and no friend will be found. The husband, despising his wife, will mate with whores, and the wife will join with whomever she desires, despising her husband. Honour for the churches will not remain, and the order will perish. Then bishops will bear arms, then they will follow the camps, they will place towers and walls on sacred ground and give to soldiers what they ought to give to the poor.']

Like William of Rennes, the Merlin of the *Prophetia Merlini* has a grim view of the tendencies of the British people. But while William's final apostrophe linked sin, Fortune and God's punishment, is there a similarly strong change of causation/ explanation in the *Vita*? Can we find in Geoffrey's later poem a tendency that offsets what sometimes seems like nihilism in his earlier history?

Merlin's is not the only voice of lament and prophecy in the *Vita*. His sister Ganieda, wife of Rodarch, also prophesies. While Penelope Doob has argued that the *Vita* is a 'profoundly religious poem' in which Merlin is 'a Christian first and a king second',[35] it is worth noting that it is Ganieda and not Merlin who produces the more conventionally Christian prophecies in the poem. First, she laments her husband's death in terms which stress the frailty of the human condition, referring this mystery to the Creator:

'Sic equidem, nam sors hominum miseranda per evum
ducitur ut nequeant ad pristina jura reduci.
Ergo nichil prodest pereuntis gloria mundi
que fugit atque redit fallit leditque potentes.

34 *Vita Merlini*, lines 661–69.
35 Penelope Doob, *Nebuchadnezzar's Children: Conventions of Madness in Middle English Literature* (New Haven, 1974), p. 153.

Melle suo delinit apes quod postmodo pungit.
Sic quos demulsit divertens gloria mundi
fallit et ingrate collidit verbere caude.
Fit breve quod prestat, quod habet durabile non est,
more fluentis aque transit quodcumque ministrat.
Quid rosa si rutilet, si candida lilia vernent,
si sit pulcher homo vel equus vel cetera plura?
Ista Creatori non mundo sunt referenda.
Felices igitur qui perstant corde piato
obsequiumque Deo faciunt mundumque relinquunt.
Illis perpetuo fungi concedet honore
qui sine fine regit Christus qui cuncta creavit.'[36]

['But so it is, for the pitiable lot of men through the ages is such that they may never be returned to their former state. Therefore there is no profit in the passing glory of the world, which flees and fails and wounds the great. The bee seduces with its honey what afterwards it stings. Thus the glory of the world deceives those whom it caressed, turning and harming with the unwelcome scourge in its tail. That which is glorious, is brief; it does not endure, and whatever it brings passes away like flowing water. What if the rose blooms, if the white lilies flourish, if a man or a horse or anything else be fair? These are things to be asked of the Creator, not for the world. Happy are they, then, who are firm in their piety and obedience to God, and who give up the world. Christ, who created all things, who rules without end, will give them everlasting glory.']

While this evocation of the human condition ends with a retreat to Christ – for the *Vita* is certainly more explicitly Christian than is the *Historia* – the nightmarish quality of Merlin's prophecies in the *Historia* is also to be found everywhere in the *Vita*, in both Merlin's rehearsing of material also found in the *Historia*, and even in Ganieda's passages. For after her lament for Rodarch, Ganieda returns at the end of the poem with a prophecy whose animal and celestial imagery are familiar from the *Prophetia Merlini*:

'Armoricanus aper, quercu protectus avita,
abducit lunam gladiis post terga rotatis.
Sidera bina feris video committere pugnam
colle sub Urgenio quo convenere Deyri
Gewissique simul magno regnante Cohelo.
O quanto sudore viri tellusque cruore
manat, in externas dum dantur vulnera gentes!
Concidit in latebras collisum sydere sidus
absconditque suum renovato lumine lumen.'[37]

['The Armorican boar, protected by an ancient oak, takes away the moon, waving swords behind backs. I see two stars at war with wild beast under the hill of Urien, where the men of Deira and the men of

[36] *Vita Merlini*, lines 708–23.
[37] *Vita Merlini*, lines 1496–504.

> Gwent convened when the great Coel was ruling. O, how the men flow with sweat and the ground with gore, as wounds are given to foreign people! A star, having collided with another, falls into the shadows, hiding her own light when the light is restored.']

Unlike the last section of Merlin's prophecies, Ganieda's may be identified with particular historical events,[38] and while Merlin's prophecy concentrates on the bad behaviour of the Britons, Ganieda's evocation of the same celestial display which ended Merlin's prophecies in the *Historia* is here aligned with the nationalist dream of expelling the hated invaders:

> 'Iteque Neustrenses, cessate diutius arma
> ferre per ingenuum violento milite regnum!
> [. . .]
> Christe, tuo populo fer opem, compesce leones,
> da regno placidam bello cessante quietem!'[39]

> ['Go, Normans, and end your violent soldiers' passage of arms through our native kingdom! . . . Christ, bring help to your people, suppress the lions, and, having brought an end to war, give the kingdom a time of peace!']

Furthermore, Ganieda explicitly calls upon Christ, something that the prophesying Merlin of the *Historia* does not do. Is this, then, an indication that behind Geoffrey's graphic evocation of the ruin which comes when the British cooperate in their own destruction, is a sense of divine purpose or providence? To return once again to the question of Geoffrey's treatment of Fortune and Fate, does he in the end show these things to be under the ultimate direction of God?

To answer this question we must return to the *Historia*, and note that, while references to God are rather more frequent than references to Fortune, they, too, are fewer than one might expect. To be sure, many of Britain's early kings are pagan – Leir is one – but one does find the occasional good king acknowledging the help of God. Thus Cassivellaunus thanks God for his victory over Julius Caesar and the worthy King Lucius seeks of his own accord to be converted to Christianity.[40] God cares for the Britons during the Diocletian persecutions by encouraging the holy martyrs.[41] Perhaps not surprisingly, given his reliance on Gildas and Bede for the period preceding Arthur, Geoffrey figures the struggles of the Britons against the Saxons as a crusade, and there are many references to God-given leaders, or to God's favour in battle. Even here, however, the references to divine power move quickly into the berating of human folly, as for example when the Romans abandon the Britons:

> O diuinam ob preterita scelera ultionem! O tot bellicosorum militum per uesaniam Maximiani absentiam! Qui si in tanta calamitate adessent, non superuenisset populus quem non in fuga propellerent. Quod manifestum fuit

38 As may the earlier prophecies in the *Historia*, of course.
39 *Vita Merlini*, lines 1511–12, 1516–17.
40 See *Historia*, c. 57, p. 37; c. 72, p. 46.
41 *Historia*, 77, p. 50.

dum manebant: nam et longe posita regna adiciebant postestati sue et Britanniam cum tran<q>uillitate possidebant. Sic est cum regnum tutamini rusticorum deseritur.[42]

[Oh, divine reparations for former sins! Oh, the absence of so many soldiers, through the madness of Maximianus! If they had been present in this great disaster, no people could have come whom they would not have driven to flight. This was manifest while they remained: for they possessed Britain in tranquillity and added distant realms to their power. Thus it is when a kingdom is abandoned to the protection of peasants.]

Like Gildas, Geoffrey is assigning blame to the Britons – their foolishness and ineptitude has left them prey to the Saxons. But Geoffrey is not Gildas, and certain disquieting notes begin to creep into this picture of divine (if stern) providence. The arrival of Hengist and Horsa seems to Vortigern as if 'siue Deus siue alius' [either God or someone else] has sent them.[43] Aurelius successfully combats the Saxons 'nutu Dei' [with God's help],[44] and his victory induces Octa to acknowledge that Aurelius's God is supreme.[45] But Aurelius is slain by treachery. His brother Uther is in his turn aided by Christ to victory in battle, but soon gives way to his unseemly lust for Ygerna, conceiving Arthur and later himself falling prey to poison, as had his brother. In other words, even when God is with the Britons, either the treachery of others, or their own folly (or sometimes both) becomes the final determinant of their fate.

What is striking in the case of Arthur, however, is that he is a most explicitly Christian hero. Geoffrey's good kings often do thank God, and they often set their realms in order by, among other things, rebuilding churches. But Arthur is the figure who is presented most consistently as a Christian crusader.[46] His first battle-speech invokes Christ:

'Quoniam impiissimi atque inuisi nominis Saxones fidem mihi dedignati sunt tenere, ego fidem Deo meo conseruans sanguinem conciuium meorum hodie in ipsos uindicare conabor. Armate uos, uiri, armate et proditores istos uiriliter inuadite quos proculdubio auxiliante Deo triumphabimus.'[47]

['Although the Saxons, of impious and hateful name, disdain to keep faith with me, I will keep my faith with my God and I will strive to defeat them today, avenging the blood of my countrymen. Arm yourselves, men, and armed, attack these traitors manfully – for without a doubt, we shall triumph, with Christ's help.']

His next act is to take up his shield, with its image of the Blessed Virgin. Michelle Warren has recently and convincingly read the *Historia* as a 'border narrative', one which demonstrates that colonization and conquest also invites

42 *Historia*, 91, p. 60.
43 *Historia*, c. 98, p. 66.
44 *Historia*, c. 123, p. 87.
45 *Historia*, c. 126, p. 89.
46 Aurelius could also be seen in this light, of course, but because Arthur is treated at more length, this aspect of his portrayal is more fully developed.
47 *Historia*, c. 146, p. 103.

counterconquest. She rightly points out that Geoffrey's Arthur deftly shifts his rhetorical ground in arguing for a violent response to the Romans,[48] and certainly the grounds for some of the later readings of Arthur I have discussed are implicit in these passages. But Arthur's defeat of the Romans is unequivocally attributed to God – an attribution which is all the more noteworthy for being relatively unusual in Geoffrey's *Historia*:

> Quod diuine potentie stabat loco cum et ueteres eorum priscis temporibus auos istorum inuisis inquietationibus infestassent; et isti tunc libertatem quam illi eisdem demere affectabant tueri instarent, abnegantes tributum quod ab ipsis iniuste exigebatur.[49]
>
> [This was arranged by divine providence, for just as in earlier times their ancestors had harrassed the ancestors of the Britons with their oppressions, so now did these Britons try to protect the liberty which they sought to take from them, by denying the tribute which those Romans unjustly required of them.]

Thus even if Arthur's reasoning is specious or self-serving, his victory is clearly part of God's plan. But does this sense of providential design hold?

Ganieda's final appeal to Christ suggests that the divine power is the ultimate one, and the way to escape the vagaries of the human world – yet Geoffrey's Arthur no sooner wins his divinely-ordained victory, than he learns of Mordred's treachery. And at this point, Geoffrey falls silent on the subject of providence (or, indeed, of Fortune), returning instead to the ancient British book to which he initially attributed the whole of his *Historia*. The final battle is all the more shockingly brief, when we consider the length of time we have spent on Arthur's reign. Arthur's death is famously ambiguous – he goes off to Avalon after handing the crown over to Constantine son of Cador – and the *Historia* begins to wind down towards the inevitable overthrow of the Britons. Where, then, does this leave us?

One answer would be to say that Geoffrey's views about Fortune, Fate, free will, and providence are as eclectic as are his sources. One moment we have the pagan Leir's lament for his past glories in a purely classical evocation of the role of the Fates in the lives of men.[50] The next, Geoffrey seems to be channelling Gildas, and the whole of British history is a record of God's just wrath against a lazy and corrupt people – there *is* a plan, even if its outcome is not immediately beneficial to the Britons. Yet the angelic voice which ends the *Historia* suggests a return to rule in a future time as prophesied by Merlin – the same Merlin whose prophecies in fact end in destructive chaos.[51] Does a coherent vision emerge? And does it tell us anything about the Fortunes of Arthur in Geoffrey's writings?

48 Michelle R. Warren, *History on the Edge: Excalibur and the Borders of Britain, 1100–1300* (Minneapolis, 2000), pp. 52–59.

49 *Historia*, c. 175, p. 129.

50 J.S.P. Tatlock, who saw the story of Arthur as the climax of the whole of the *Historia*, seems to find classical tragedy in the Arthuriad too, remarking 'it is hard to think of a single medieval work of any extent with such foresighted, indeed classical symmetry; it recalls the structure of good tragedy'; *The Legendary History of Britain: Geoffrey of Monmouth's Historia regum Britanniae and its Early Vernacular Versions* (Berkeley, 1950), p. 393. He seems here to be speaking as much about form as about a possible classical-Christian distinction.

51 Jan Ziolkowski makes a similar argument when he suggests that the Merlin of the *Vita* is

When Julius Caesar invades Britain, he is aided by Androgeus, Cassivelaunus's nephew. The two Britons are locked in a feud, and Androgeus writes to Julius with his offer of help, concluding his letter in this way: 'Ea enim conditione mouentur mortales ut post inimicicias amici fiant et post fugam ad triumphum accedant' ['Mortals are moved by this state of affairs, that after strife they may become friends, and after flight they may achieve victory'].[52] This self-serving reference to the conditions that govern human life is on one level simply another instance of the 'self-betrayal of Britain',[53] but it also tells us something about Geoffrey's view of history. The whole of the *Historia* – and the Arthurian section is no exception – is structured around the relentless cycle of good and bad, as good kings and bad kings both fall, sometimes through their own guilt, and sometimes through the malign interventions of others. All of this, the angelic voice at the end would have us believe, is part of the providential plan so clear to historians like Gildas. But Geoffrey seems more at home with Leir's pagan Fates, applying as they do to all men, good or bad. While the Britons often seem to cooperate in their own destruction, the nightmare imagery of Merlin's prophecies also makes space for the more devastating notion that this apparent cooperation is mere coincidence: the heavenly powers do what they do, and mortals are moved, to use Androgeus's phrase, by powers over which they have no control. Lady Philosophy tells Boethius that Fortune is fickle – in her vision, one does not necessarily deserve either Fortune's blessings or her curses. One must simply live in such a way that these are alike neutral. Medieval historians, and medieval Arthurian writers, seem generally to be more comfortable with a closer tie between Fortune's actions and God's ultimate design, and Geoffrey's foolish kings suggest he feels the pull of that link too. But the refusal in the Arthuriad to blame Arthur for what happens to his kingdom is, given the later history of the treatment of Arthur's Fortunes, particularly remarkable. In the *Vita Merlini*, after Ganieda calls upon Christ, Merlin allows his prophetic voice to fall silent. It is tempting to hear this silence as Geoffrey's own – the silence of one who would like to believe that the cycles of history are ultimately wrapped in a beneficent plan, but whose own pursuit of history has instead led, more often than is ultimately comfortable, to another conclusion.

eclectic: 'one part a wild man engaged in shamanlike practices that were widespread in the pre-Christian era, one part a political prophect of a type still found in Wales when Geoffrey wrote, and one part a Christian prophet combining traits of Old Testament prophets and Christian saints'; 'The Nature of Prophecy in Geoffrey of Monmouth's *Vita Merlini*', in *Poetry and Prophecy: The Beginnings of a Literary Tradition*, ed. James L. Kugel (Ithaca, NY, 1990), p. 154.

52 *Historia*, 61, p. 40.

53 The phrase is Susan M. Shwartz's; see 'The Founding and Self-Betrayal of Britain: An Augustinian Approach to Geoffrey of Monmouth's *Historia regum Britanniae*', *Medievalia et Humanistica*, 10 (1981), 33–53. I think Shwartz is absolutely right to argue that the *Historia* is about 'the struggle of people in a mutable, fallen world against evil' (p. 47); it will have become clear from my argument about Geoffrey's treatment of providence that I am not at all certain this is harmonized, for Geoffrey, with an Augustinian view of history.

Visions of History: Robert de Boron and English Arthurian Chroniclers

EDWARD DONALD KENNEDY

Robert de Boron, as Norris Lacy has observed, is, with the exception of Chrétien de Troyes, perhaps 'the most influential writer within the French romance tradition',[1] and there are several reasons for his influence:

(1) He introduced in the late twelfth century the concept of cyclic romance, a series of romances intended to follow one another, instead of the usually independent romances that Chrétien wrote. Robert wrote at least two verse romances: one, known as the *Joseph d'Arimathie*, concerns the origins of the Grail; the other, the *Merlin*, is a continuation of the *Joseph* that survives in only a 502-line fragment. There also survive in two manuscripts – E.39 of the Bibioteca Estense in Modena and nouv. acq. 4166 of the Bibliothèque Nationale (often called the 'Didot' manuscript after the name of a former owner) – prose adaptations of Robert's *Joseph* and a complete *Merlin*, followed by two short prose romances, a *Perceval*, concerning the quest for the Grail, and a brief concluding prose account concerning the death of Arthur. Although scholars have debated whether these last two romances were based upon verse romances by Robert, the surviving four prose romances form a series that tell the Arthurian story from the origin of the Grail to the death of Arthur. This concept of a series of related romances would be important to the development of Arthurian romance from the French prose romances of the thirteenth century to Sir Thomas Malory's *Morte Darthur* in the fifteenth.

(2) Robert was also influential because he transformed the Grail from Chrétien's mysterious platter containing a wafer that may or may not have been a Christian symbol to a definite Christian object, a vessel from the Last Supper that Joseph of Arimathea used to collect the blood of Christ after his body had been removed from the cross. Despite the importance of Chrétien de Troyes to Arthurian tradition, Robert's conception of the Grail is probably the one that is most familiar today.

1 Norris J. Lacy, 'The Evolution and Legacy of French Prose Romance', *The Cambridge Companion to Medieval Romance*, ed. Roberta L. Krueger (Cambridge, 2000), pp. 167–82, here quoting 169.

(3) In addition to giving new significance to the Grail, Robert incorporated Christian elements into the story of Arthur that became important to later versions of the legend. He added to the account of the birth of Merlin, for example, the motif of the anti-Christ and to the story of Arthur's becoming king, the account of the miraculous appearance of the sword in the stone. Moreover, he described Arthur's Round Table as a figure of Christ's table at the Last Supper, and if the *Perceval* romance in this series is based upon a verse original by Robert, he made the greatest event in the history of Arthur's kingdom not the conquest of Europe, as it had been in earlier chronicles, but the miraculous appearance of the Grail at Arthur's court.

In this essay I shall emphasize some ways in which the addition of these latter Christian elements radically transformed the story of Arthur that Robert inherited from earlier chroniclers, and I shall suggest why, with the exception of the widely circulated fifteenth-century chronicle of John Hardyng, these modifications had little influence upon the later Arthurian chronicles that were important in England throughout the Middle Ages.

Although Robert had several sources, he appears to have based his *Merlin* primarily upon a version of the Arthurian story, the Anglo-Norman verse chronicle known as the *Roman de Brut* written in 1155 by Wace. Some details indicate that he had at one time also read Wace's Latin prose source, the *Historia Regum Britanniae* of Geoffrey of Monmouth that had been written about twenty years before Wace's version.[2] Although Wace had made significant additions to Geoffrey's account, the basic story and view of history are essentially the same in both works. Geoffrey of Monmouth presents a history of the British from their founding by Brutus, the great grandson of Aeneas, until their conquest by the Anglo-Saxons, and his chronicle includes the first substantial account of the reign of Arthur. In it Arthur becomes king at the age of fifteen after the death of his father Uther Pendragon; he defeats his enemies in Britain, marries a woman named Guenevere and goes on to conquer France and much of the rest of Europe. After he returns to Britain, emissaries from the Roman procurator Lucius arrive at his court and unjustly demand tribute. Arthur conseqently declares war on Rome and defeats the Romans, but just before he is to march into Rome to be proclaimed emperor, he receives word that his nephew Mordred, whom he had appointed regent of Britain, has usurped the throne and is living adulterously with Guenevere. Arthur returns to Britain, and in the ensuing battle, Mordred is killed, and Arthur is mortally wounded and taken to Avalon for the healing of his wounds in the year 542. The final parts of the book describe the further decline of the British and their eventual replacement by the Anglo-Saxons.

Robert Hanning describes Geoffrey's *Historia* as a humanist vision of history largely devoid of Christian assumptions. He contrasts it with earlier histories like those of the sixth-century British writer Gildas and the eighth-century English historian Bede, both of whom had the assumption, drawn from Christian and Jewish historical and biblical traditions, that God had an interest in the

2 Alexandre Micha, *Étude sur le 'Merlin' de Robert de Boron* (Geneva, 1980), pp. 36–37.

fate of particular nations. Gildas, drawing an analogy to Old Testament accounts of God's punishment of the Isrealites, had seen God punishing the British for their sins. Bede presented in the *Ecclesiastical History of the English People* a vision of history in which God had replaced the sinful British with a new chosen people, the English. Geoffrey's assumptions about history, however, were for the most part different.[3] Admittedly, the story is not as secular as Hanning describes it: there are statements in which a bishop says that Christ will help Arthur's men defeat the pagan Saxons; and at the end an angelic voice tells the last British king Cadwallader that God did not want the Britons to rule any longer in Britain, but the voice promises that they will someday occupy the island again.[4] Nevertheless, Geoffrey's history is primarily the story of the rise and fall of various kings with little indication that God has any part in the process. Hanning notes particularly the part of Geoffrey's book concerning the prophecies of Merlin, prophecies that end, Hanning writes, with 'a terrifying apocalypse in which all the elements of heaven and earth are set free from their order and go whirling into chaos. Here is no triumph of divine providence, no judgment which will reward the good, punish the bad, and reveal the forces moving all history; instead, the impersonal universe which has presided over the rise and fall of kingdoms will lose control of itself and history will dissolve into nothingness.' Hanning believes that Geoffrey's vision of the past has little to do with Christian theology but instead is similar to the cyclic view of the repetitious rise and fall of people found among the Greeks. 'The fatal and conflicting forces ruling man and society', he writes, 'partake less of the Christian historical imagination of the early medieval centuries than of the classical historiography which it supplanted. With Geoffrey, the wheel has indeed come full circle.'[5]

The part of Geoffrey's *Historia* concerning Arthur marks the beginning of the Arthurian tragedy. Although Fortune is not specifically mentioned, the story of Arthur follows the pattern of a protagonist rising on Fortune's wheel, reaching the height of his power, in this case the conquest of Rome, and then falling, not necessarily as in Aristotelian tragedy because of some flaw or error, but because Fortune is capricious, things of the world are transient, and uncertainty and insecurity are part of life. Such a world view is compatible with Christian views, but it is not particularly Christian and goes back at least to the concept of the goddess Fortuna in pagan Rome.[6] Arthur is one of a series of rulers who rise and fall; and his story, Hanning believes, is similar to the cyclic view of history that can be found in ancient Greece.[7] Although Wace, in adapting Geoffrey's Latin prose into French verse, added courtly elements and allusions to other stories of Arthur that were orally circulating and introduced the Round Table into the

3 See Robert W. Hanning, *The Vision of History in Early Britain* (New York, 1966).

4 Geoffrey of Monmouth, *Historia Regum Britanniae*, ed. Acton Griscom (London, 1929), ix.4 and xii.17, pp. 437–38, 532–33; *The History of the Kings of Britain*, trans. Lewis Thorpe (Harmondsworth, 1966), pp. 216, 282–83.

5 Hanning, *Vision of History*, p. 172.

6 For the classical background of this concept, see Howard R. Patch, *The Goddess Fortuna in Medieval Literature* (1927; repr. New York, 1967), pp. 8–34.

7 Hanning, *Vision of History*, pp. 171–72.

Arthurian legend,[8] the historical perspective remains essentially what it is in Geoffrey's account. The story of Arthur is primarily a humanist one, a history devoid of the assumptions found in Gildas or Bede.

Although Geoffrey claimed he was translating from a previously unknown book written in Celtic, most today would describe the *Historia* as creative writing. Medieval historical writing was, to be sure, different from historical writing today, and most medieval historians, following the tradition of classical historians, had a role similar to that of poets: they hoped to delight and instruct and were free to invent speeches that a person might have said in given circumstances and invent details that would make the historian's portrait of the past convincing.[9] Bernard Guenée writes:

> [L']historien, au Moyen Age, n'eut pas simplement le pouvoir de réinterpréter le passé; il eut celui de le réinventer. S'adressant à un public dont la culture historique était des plus limitées, et à des confrères qui n'avaient que de faibles moyens pour vérifier et critiquer ses dires, il était maître d'un passé singulièrement flexible. . . . Le passé, au Moyen Age, était aussi complaisant qu'il était respecté, aussi malléable qu'il était prestigieux.[10]
>
> [The historian in the Middle Ages had not simply the power to reinterpret the past; he had the power to reinvent it. Addressing himself to a public whose historical knowledge was most limited and to colleagues who had only inadequate ways to verify and criticize what he said, he was master of a past that was singularly flexible. . . . The past in the Middle Ages was as accommodating as it was respected, as malleable as it was prestigious.]

There were, however, limits to this malleability, limits to the extent to which the truth might be manipulated. Geoffrey's contemporary William of Newburgh condemned the *Historia* because Geoffrey had disguised under the honorable name of history the fables of Arthur. As Ruth Morse and before her E.K. Chambers observed, William's anger was not that Geoffrey had ' "embroidered" or "filled in" the British past, but that he had done it to such an extreme degree – and in Latin'.[11] Similarly Giraldus Cambrensis in his *Itinerarium Kambriae*, written in 1191, had scoffed at Geoffrey's work by telling the story of a man named Meilerius, who was an associate of evil spirits that could help him determine true and false passages of a book. When the gospel of St. John was placed on Meilerius's chest, the evil spirits could not come near him, but when

8 See Judith Weiss, ed. and trans., *Wace's Roman de Brut: A History of the British* (Exeter, 1999), pp. xviii–xxiv; Charles Foulon, 'Wace', in *Arthurian Literature in the Middle Ages*, ed. Roger Sherman Loomis (Oxford, 1959), pp. 94–103; C.S. Lewis, 'The Genesis of a Medieval Book: 1. Laȝamon's "Brut" ', in C.S. Lewis, *Studies in Medieval and Renaissance Literature*, collected by Walter Hooper (Cambridge, 1966), pp. 18–33.

9 See Ruth Morse, *Truth and Convention in the Middle Ages: Rhetoric, Representation, and Reality* (Cambridge, 1991), p. 92. Also see her ' "This Vague Relation": Historical Fiction and Historical Veracity in the Later Middle Ages', *Leeds Studies in English*, n.s. 13 (1982), pp. 85–103, here 89.

10 Bernard Guenée, *Histoire et culture historique dans l'Occident médiéval* (Paris, 1980), pp. 351–52.

11 Morse, ' "This Vague Relation," ' p. 96; E.K. Chambers, *Arthur of Britain* (1927; repr. Cambridge, 1964), p. 107.

Geoffrey's book was substituted for it, the devils clustered around in greater number and more loathsomely than ever.[12]

A few others expressed concerns about Geoffrey's account. A near contemporary, the twelfth-century chronicler Alfred of Beverley, who believed in the basic truth of Geoffrey's story of Arthur, nevertheless asked why there was no external confirmation of Geoffrey's account. The fourteenth-century chronicler Ranulf Higden had more serious reservations. Having written a history of the world and having examined some of the chronicles written on the Continent, he asked why if Arthur had conquered most of Europe none of the chroniclers on the Continent had been aware of it.[13] Geoffrey, writing in the scholarly Latin prose of history, had gone beyond the limits of what was permitted. Such criticism of Geoffrey, however, was not widespread. Most of the later English chroniclers who told the story of the British seem to have accepted his work as valid, although some questioned certain passages in the book.[14]

If Geoffrey's book had remained simply a history of Britain up to the Anglo-Saxon conquest, it might later have been dismissed as a work of fiction or a fable. In England, however, it was incorporated into other chronicles that told of the periods following the downfall of the British, histories of the Anglo-Saxons and of the years following the Norman conquest. It consequently became difficult to dismiss as fable, for if one believed the later parts of the chronicles, if one believed, for example, that there was a Henry V and before that an Edward II and before that a William the Conqueror and before that a King Alfred, one could also believe that there had been a King Arthur. The context in which Geoffrey's book was placed gave it legitimacy.[15]

With the notable acceptions of the twelfth-century historians Alfred of Beverley and Geoffrey Gaimar,[16] the absorption of Geoffrey's Arthurian tragedy into this greater scheme occurred primarily in the thirteenth century and later. In the twelfth century when Robert de Boron was writing, Geoffrey's *Historia* and Wace's verse adaptation of it were still isolated, largely secular histories of the British, and it is uncertain that a writer like Robert de Boron would have considered them any more true than the romances of Chrétien. Wace was Robert's primary source, and commentators have noted Wace's expressed skepticism about the validity of some of the Arthurian stories and the question of Arthur's return.[17] Moreover, Wace wrote in verse, the language of entertainment, and his account might not have been taken seriously as history. It would not be long before French chroniclers would be abandoning verse in order to

12 Chambers, *Arthur of Britain*, pp. 107–08.

13 T.D. Kendrick, *British Antiquity* (London, 1950), pp. 12–14.

14 See Laura Keeler, *Geoffrey of Monmouth and the Late Latin Chroniclers* (Berkeley, 1946).

15 On the popularity of these chronicles, see Felicity Riddy, 'Reading for England: Arthurian Literature and National Consciousness', *Bibliographical Bulletin of the International Arthurian Society*, 43 (1991), 314–32.

16 On Alfred of Beverley, see besides Kendrick, *British Antiquity*, cited n. 13 above, Antonia Gransden, *Historical Writing in England c. 550 to c. 1307* (Ithaca, NY, 1974), p. 212; on Geoffrey Gaimar, see Gransden, *Historical Writing in England*, pp. 209–12 and M. Dominica Legge, *Anglo-Norman Literature and Its Background* (Oxford, 1963), pp. 28–36.

17 See, for example, Foulon, 'Wace', p. 98.

authenticate their vernacular narratives by writing them in prose, the language of 'truth'.[18]

In any event, Robert approached the story of the early history of Arthur's kingdom with assumptions different from those of Geoffrey or Wace, and his adaptation changed the story of Arthur every bit as radically as did his adaptation of Chrétien's conception of the Grail. While the sacred elements in Chrétien's vision of the Grail – a platter containing a wafer – were implicit and Robert made them explicit by changing the Grail into the vessel used at the Last Supper, the story of Arthur as presented in Geoffrey and Wace had relatively little religious significance. In Geoffrey, Merlin's father is an incubus, a creature made of air that in pagan classical tradition inhabits the region between the earth and the moon; in Robert, by contrast, the story of Merlin's birth is associated with the legend of the anti-Christ, the attempt to send a son of a devil into the world made familiar through films like *Rosemary's Baby* (1968) and *The Omen* (1976). Robert's story begins in Hell where a council of devils recruit an incubus to find and impregnate a virtuous maiden worthy of bearing the son of a devil. However, through the prayers of the maiden's confessor, when Merlin is born, he inherits his father's supernatural powers but his mother's goodness, and his story becomes an exemplum of the ultimate triumph of good over evil. Merlin becomes an agent of God, who says, 'Diex m'a esleu a un suen servise faire que nus ne porroit faire se je non, quar nus ne set les choses si com je sai' ['Our Lord has chosen me to serve Him in a way that I alone could do, for no-one shares my knowledge'.][19]

In Geoffrey and Wace Arthur simply becomes king after the death of his father Uther Pendragon. In Robert, Arthur is proclaimed king only after the miraculous appearance on Christmas Eve of a sword in an anvil on a stone, and the sword bears the inscription that whoever can draw it from the stone will become king 'par l'election Jhesu Crist' ['by the choice of Jesus Christ'].[20] Arthur's Round Table, which Wace says Arthur established so that no knight could be exalted above any other, becomes in Robert's account a table that corresponds to the Grail table established by Joseph of Arimathea which in turn corresponds to the table that Christ used at the Last Supper.[21] Thus Arthur and his knights become figures of both the Grail society and of Christ and his disciples.

18 Gabrielle M. Spiegel, *Romancing the Past: The Rise of Vernacular Prose Historiography in Thirteenth-Century France* (Berkeley, 1993), p. 2.

19 *Merlin: Roman du XIIIe siècle*, ed. Alexandre Micha (Paris, 1980), p. 99; translation from *Merlin and the Grail: 'Joseph of Arimathea', 'Merlin', 'Perceval': The Trilogy of Prose Romances Attributed to Robert de Boron*, trans. Nigel Bryant (Cambridge, 2001), p. 70. Although Micha bases his text upon the prose version of Robert's *Merlin* in Bibliothèque Nationale f. fr. 747 and Bryant bases his translation upon E.39 of the Bibioteca Estense in Modena, the passages quoted are identical in both. There is a modern edition, without scholarly apparatus or extensive introduction, of the Modena manuscript, which I have also consulted: *Le Roman du Graal: Manuscrit de Modène*, ed. Bernard Cerquiglini (Paris, 1981). The older scholarly edition of the two concluding parts of the cycle is that of William Roach, ed., *The Didot Perceval, According to the Manuscripts of Modena and Paris* (Philadelphia, 1941). For the verse romances attributed to Robert, see *Le Roman de l'Estoire dou Graal*, ed. William A. Nitze (Paris, 1971).

20 *Merlin*, p. 269; *Merlin and the Grail*, trans. Bryant, p. 107.

21 *Merlin*, pp. 184–85; *Merlin and the Grail*, trans. Bryant, p. 92.

As mentioned above, two manuscripts of the prose versions of Robert's romances conclude with a version of the story of Perceval's quest for the Grail and a story of the fall of Arthur's kingdom. Because of inconsistencies between the *Perceval* romance and the earlier romances of *Joseph d'Arimathie* and *Merlin*, scholars have debated whether the *Perceval* and the *Mort Artu* parts of the cycle are derived from original verse romances by Robert. William Roach, who in his 1941 edition of the last two parts of the cycle, summarizes scholarship up to that time, agrees with the earlier scholar Ernst Brugger that Robert had originally written a verse cycle of four parts which were adapted into prose shortly after they were written and then 'reworked by a none-too-intelligent redactor'.[22] More recently, Nigel Bryant has suggested that the *Perceval*, including the account of the death of Arthur, was 'the work of a talented redactor and in no way from Robert's pen'.[23] Alexandre Micha, on the other hand, believes that the *Perceval* could be based upon a lost verse romance by Robert, but suspects that the final account of the death of Arthur adapted from the chronicles may not be, in part because of inconsistencies between it and earlier parts of the cycle and doubts about whether a reference to the *Mort Artu* at the conclusion of the prose *Merlin* was originally a part of Robert's work.[24] It is certainly possible that even if Robert intended a concluding *Mort Artu* section that he nevertheless wished to emphasize Perceval's triumph in the Grail quest and his return to Arthur's court. The concluding *Mort Artu* makes up only about ten per cent of the whole cycle; and Pierre le Gentil, who doubts that Robert had anything to do with either the *Perceval* or *Mort Artu* sections, notes that the latter 'seems a post-script'.[25] As Micha points out, Perceval, who is descended from the family of Joseph of Arimathea, unites the chivalry of the Round Table with the spirituality of the Grail Table and that of Christ and his disciples.[26] At the end of the *Perceval* romance, Merlin tells Arthur,

> 'Artu, saces que a ton tans est acomplie li plus haute prophetie qui onques avenist; car li Rois Pesciere est garis, et sont cheü li encantement de la terre de Bretagne. Et Percevaus est sire del Graal par l'avenement de nostre Segnor.'
> ['Arthur, . . . you should know that your reign has seen the fulfilling of the greatest prophecy of all time. For the Fisher King is healed and the enchantments of the land of Britain are cast out. And Perceval is lord of the Grail by Our Lord's decree'.][27]

This is the major point of Robert's story: the emphasis is not upon the tragedy of Arthur but upon the triumph of Perceval and of Arthurian chivalry in the fulfillment of a quest ordained by God. Robert could have intended to recreate the Arthurian story as a providential vision of history that, like Bede's *Ecclesias-*

22 Roach, ed., *Didot*, p. 118.
23 Bryant also summarizes the debate in *Merlin and the Grail*, pp. 2–8. See especially p. 7, n. 15.
24 Micha, *Étude sur le 'Merlin'*, pp. 5–29, esp. p. 22.
25 Pierre le Gentil, 'The Work of Robert de Boron and the Didot *Perceval*', in Loomis, ed., *Arthurian Literature in the Middle Ages*, pp. 251–62, here 260.
26 Micha, *Étude sur le 'Merlin'*, p. 28.
27 *Didot 'Perceval'*, ed. Roach, p. 243; *Roman du Graal*, ed. Cerquiglini, p. 272; *Merlin and the Grail*, trans. Bryant, p. 156.

tical History, showed God's interest in a people, a vision of Arthurian history in which Arthur's knights become worthy successors to the disciples of Christ.

A major difference in the type of work Robert was writing compared to that of Geoffrey of Monmouth is that Robert, unlike Geoffrey, may never have expected his work to be taken seriously as history any more than Chrétien expected his verse romances to be. Robert's work might be compared to saints' lives, or to the apocryphal Gospels, works that, as Ruth Morse points out, manipulate the past in order to teach moral lessons.[28] Hipolyte Delehaye long ago described the saints' lives as hagiographical romances, works that were intended to be works of inspiration rather than works of historical truth.[29] Like authors of the saints' lives, Robert may never have intended his verse adaptation of the Arthurian chronicle to be understood as historically true. It could have been intended primarily as a moral lesson concerning the virtuous potential of chivalric life.[30]

How widely the verse or prose versions of Robert's work were read in England is unknown. Either of these appear to have been a source for the early thirteenth-century French prose romance *Perlesvaus*, a work associated with Glastonbury Abbey, and Micha suggests that Robert de Boron's *Merlin* influenced several details in the chronicle of Laȝamon, who adapted Wace's *Brut* into alliterative English verse probably in the early thirteenth century.[31] This is possible particularly if Robert's work was known at Glastonbury, since Laȝamon lived in western England and says he traveled far to obtain information for his chronicle. Glastonbury would not have been too distant from his home in King's Arley, Worcestershire. In fact, the discovery of what was supposedly Arthur's body at Glastonbury in 1191 could have inspired Laȝamon to write his English adaptation of Wace's *Brut*. After the mid-thirteenth century, however, it is difficult to determine if there was direct influence of the original versions of Robert's work, because the prose version of Robert's *Merlin* was incorporated into both the Vulgate (or *Lancelot-Grail*) Cycle and the Post-Vulgate *Roman du Graal*. The latter cycles were known in England, and it is probably through these that Robert's revisions of the Arthurian legend became best known.

Robert's series of romances, either in its verse or prose form, is often seen as an inspiration for the long Arthurian prose romances of the Vulgate Cycle, the first of which were written between approximately 1215 and 1230 or 1235, apparently according to a plan developed by – to use Jean Frappier's term – an

28 Morse, ' "This Vague Relation" ', p. 90.

29 Hipolyte Delehaye, *The Legends of the Saints*, trans. Donald Attwater (Dublin, 1998), pp. xxxii, 3–9, translation of *Les Légendes hagiographiques* (1905), 4th ed. (Brussels, 1955).

30 On the moral purpose of Robert's work and the later Vulgate romances, see Robert W. Hanning, 'Arthurian Evangelists: The Language of Truth in Thirteenth-Century French Prose Romances', *Philological Quarterly*, 64 (1985), 347–65. Hanning observes that the use of prose was for the purpose of 'redeeming vernacular narrative from its perverse (and dangerous) fictiveness' (p. 356).

31 Micha, *Étude sur le 'Merlin'*, pp. 34–35. Laȝamon's *Brut* appears to have been written between 1189 and 1216. See Françoise H.M. Le Saux, *Laȝamon's 'Brut': the Poem and Its Sources* (Cambridge, 1989), pp. 9–10. (On p. 10 there is a typographical error: '1185' appears instead of '1189', the intended date judging from comments Le Saux makes on p. 9.)

architect who outlined a series of romances written by a group of different authors.[32] However, while Robert's series begins with the early history of the Grail and the early history of Arthur's kingdom, the original authors of the Vulgate Cycle planned their series as the story of Lancelot from his birth to his death. The immediate source for the Vulgate Cycle appears to have been an early thirteenth-century non-cyclic independent prose romance of *Lancelot* that begins with Lancelot's birth and ends happily with the consummation of the love of Lancelot and Guenevere.[33] Some later author must have felt that there was something inherently wrong with a romance that presented lovers committing adultery and happily getting away with it and consequently planned to incorporate this non-cyclic romance into a series of three romances. The three romances that originally made up the Vulgate Cycle, the *Lancelot*, *La Queste del Saint Graal* and *La Mort le Roi Artu*, told not of the triumph of this love but of its disastrous consequences. In the *Queste*, Lancelot, once Arthur's greatest knight, is unable to achieve the Grail because of his sin, and most of Arthur's other knights are also too sinful to be worthy of the quest. Thus, in contrast to Robert de Boron's *Perceval*, where the achievement of the Grail becomes a major success in the history of Arthur's court, in the Vulgate *Queste*, the ideals of the Grail have become incompatible with those of Arthur's court. In the *Mort Artu* the love of Lancelot and Guenevere becomes a major cause for the destruction of Arthur's kingdom. These romances, although written by several authors, form a biographical series, and the earlier *Lancelot* foreshadows events in the later romances, and the later ones allude to events in the earlier.

Shortly after the original romances of the Vulgate Cycle were written, other writers added to them romances based on the prose versions of Robert de Boron's *Joseph of Arimathea* and the *Merlin*. These tell the early history of the Grail and the early history of Arthur's kingdom before the birth of Lancelot; the Vulgate stories of Joseph (*Estoire del Saint Graal*) and of Merlin (*Estoire de Merlin*) thus provide 'prequels' to the original stories. The French romances of the Vulgate Cycle were widely read in England by whose who could read French, and a few English versions of the *Estoire* and the *Merlin* were produced in England between the thirteenth and fifteenth centuries before Malory based his *Morte Darthur* upon the Vulgate Cycle and other French and English romances.

Although these French prose romances were known in England, they did not have much influence on most of the English chronicles that were derived from Geoffrey's *Historia*. In light of what Bernard Guenée refers to as the malleability of the past when in the hands of medieval chroniclers,[34] it is surprising how closely the English chroniclers followed Geoffrey of Monmouth and avoided incorporating much material from the romances. It was as if the story that Geoffrey had invented had been a canonical text that few wished to tamper with. For one thing, it provided the English with a story that must have been

32 Jean Frappier, *Étude sur 'La Mort le Roi Artu'*, 3rd ed. (Geneva, 1972), p. 144; also Frappier, 'The Vulgate Cycle', in Loomis, ed., *Arthurian Literature in the Middle Ages*, p. 316.

33 On the non-cyclic version, see Elspeth Kennedy, ed., *Lancelot do Lac: The Non-Cyclic Old French Prose Romance*, 2 vols (Oxford, 1980), and her *Lancelot and the Grail: A Study of the Prose Lancelot* (Oxford, 1986).

34 Guenée, *Histoire et culture*, p. 352.

satisfying to them. Although Arthur had been a British hero fighting the invading Saxons, the English accepted him as one of their own, a great hero who, in conquering most of Europe, had brought the island to its greatest period of glory. In the later Middle Ages, Arthur's Celtic origins were often forgotten; later writers like Malory refer to him as an English king; and English kings used his alleged conquests in Geoffrey's *Historia* to help justify their claims on Scotland, Wales and France.[35]

The French attitude toward the truth of Geoffrey's *Historia* appears to have been considerably different. In France there were a few chroniclers, particularly in Brittany, who seem to have believed the Arthurian story, and there was even one early sixteenth-century Breton chronicler, Alain Bouchart, who credited Arthur with building a chapel to the Virgin Mary in Paris where Notre Dame now stands.[36] However, most French chroniclers do not appear to have taken the Arthurian story seriously. Having been conquered by the British was generally not a part of their historical tradition; their views were probably similar to those of Boccaccio, who, apparently unable to believe that the British had defeated the Romans, dismissed the Arthurian story as a fable.[37] In any event, the French took more liberties with the Arthurian story than the English chroniclers, who seemed bound to the narrative that Geoffrey of Monmouth had established.

There were a few attempts in chronicles to acknowledge the romances. The early fourteenth-century chronicler Robert Mannyng of Brunne, for example, although unwilling to incorporate romance adventures into his work, nevertheless acknowledged the possible existence of these adventures. As Lesley Johnson and Ad Putter have pointed out, Mannyng indicates that during twelve years of peace mentioned by Geoffrey, the stories told of Arthur 'in ryme' took place, and during the nine years in which, according to Geoffrey, Arthur had ruled in France after his European conquests, the adventures narrated in the French prose romances occurred.[38] Mannyng ignores the fact that the adventures in the Vulgate Cycle from the *Merlin* through the *Death of Arthur* would have occurred over a period of some ninety years, rather than nine, since Arthur is born in the *Merlin* and when he dies fighting Mordred in the *Death of Arthur* he is a rather vigorous 92-year-old. What was important to Mannyng was to find time within Geoffrey of Monmouth's chronology to acknowledge that the adventures in the romances might have taken place. Mannyng probably felt obliged to do this since romance writers, like Chrétien de Troyes, Robert de

[35] On the importance of the legends and their growth during Henry II's reign, see Antonia Gransden, 'The Growth of the Glastonbury Traditions and Legends in the Twelfth Century', *Journal of Ecclesiastical History*, 27 (1976), 337–58.

[36] Robert Huntington Fletcher, *The Arthurian Material in the Chronicles Especially Those of Great Britain and France* (1906; repr. New York, 1966), pp. 230–35.

[37] See my 'Generic Intertextuality in the English *Alliterative Morte Arthure*: The Italian Connection', in *Text and Intertext in Medieval Arthurian Literature*, ed. Norris J. Lacy (New York, 1996), pp. 41–56, here 46.

[38] Lesley Johnson, 'Robert Mannyng's History of Arthurian Literature', in *Church and Chronicle in the Middle Ages*, ed. Ian Wood and G.A. Loud (London, 1991), pp. 129–47; Ad Putter, 'Finding Time for Romance: Medieval Arthurian Literary History', *Medium Aevum*, 63 (1994), 1–16.

Boron and the authors of the Vulgate romances, had included allusions to events in the chronicles to their works; but although acknowledging the existence of these adventures, he did not try to incorporate them into his account.

In other chronicles, there are occasional allusions to romances, such as the brief reference in the Auchinleck manuscript of the fourteenth-century English *Short Metrical Chronicle* to Lancelot's building a castle at Nottingham for Guenevere and defending her honor at Glastonbury.[39] Most tempting to chroniclers must have been the Vulgate account of Joseph of Arimathea's followers bringing the Grail to Britain, since this would have given Britain the prestige of having had a Christian church that dated from apostolic times. Allusions to this occasionally occur. In the thirteenth-century an anonymous monk interpolated a reference to Joseph of Arimathea and a band of disciples founding a church at Glastonbury in A.D. 63 into William of Malmesbury's twelfth-century history of Glastonbury Abbey,[40] and the chronicler John of Glastonbury (fl. c. 1400), who, apparently trying to raise funds for this abbey by promoting it as a tourist attraction, writes that, following instructions of the angel Gabriel, Joseph of Arimathea and 150 followers established a church at Glastonbury in honor of the Virgin Mary; John cites as his source a book called the 'Holy Grail', which could have been the Vulgate *Estoire* or Robert's *Joseph*, although nothing in either of these works corresponds exactly to John of Glastonbury's account. But instead of mentioning the Grail, however, he associates Joseph with vessels containing the blood and sweat of Christ.[41] Although people would have identified this vessel containing Christ's blood with the Grail, John of Glastonbury does not describe it as such. The Grail was associated with the fictions of romance, but relics containing the holy blood were considered authentic and could be found throughout Europe. As James Carley points out, 'the Grail itself might be heterodox and not an actual relic, but the events describing it . . . could all be interpreted as historical fact'.[42] John of Glastonbury's version of the story later influenced a few other manuscripts of chronicles such as a late fifteenth-century version of the English Prose *Brut* found in Lambeth Palace Library MS 84, a fifteenth-century manuscript of the early fourteenth-century chronicle attributed to Robert of Gloucester (College of Arms Arundel 58), a genealogy of Arthur in Robert of Avesbury's fourteenth-century *Historiae Edwardi III*, one Latin prose *Brut* and its English translation, known as *The New Croniclys . . . of the Gestys of the Kynges of England*, and the two versions of the fifteenth-century chronicle by John Hardyng.[43]

39 *An Anonymous Short English Metrical Chronicle*, ed. Ewald Zettl (London, 1935), pp. 70–71.

40 Gransden, 'Growth of the Glastonbury Traditions', p. 358.

41 *The Chronicle of Glastonbury Abbey: An Edition, Translation and Study of John of Glastonbury's Cronica, 'Glastoniensis Ecclesie'*, ed. James P. Carley, trans. David Townsend (Woodbridge, 1985), pp. 47–55.

42 Carley, ed., *The Chronicle of Glastonbury Abbey*, pp. li–lii.

43 For the English Prose *Brut* in Lambeth MS 84, see Lister M. Matheson, 'The Arthurian Stories of Lambeth Palace Library MS 84', *Arthurian Literature* V (1985), 70–91; for the references in *The New Croniclys*, College of Arms Arundel 58, and Hardyng, see my *Chronicles and Other Historical Writing*, vol. 8 of *A Manual of the Writings in Middle English*, ed. Albert E. Hartung (New Haven, 1989), pp. 2638–40, 2642 and 2644–47, and my 'John Hardyng and the Holy Grail', *Arthurian Literature* VIII (1989), 185–206, here 186–87, repr. in *Glastonbury Abbey and the*

Robert's account of Arthur's being selected by Christ through the miracle of the sword in the stone and of the Round Table being a figure of the table used at the Last Supper might, one would think, have appealed to chroniclers interested in enhancing the prestige of Britain; but this was not the case, and it was probably due to the fact that when Robert's account of Arthur was incorporated into the Vulgate Cycle, it was tainted in a rather peculiar way. Some authors of the original three romances of the Vulgate Cycle added a new element to the story. In the chronicles the traitor Mordred had simply been Arthur's nephew, the son of King Lot of Orkney and Arthur's sister Anna. Robert de Boron had adopted a similar genealogy, except that she was his half-sister. The Vulgate authors changed this. In the concluding romance of the cycle, the *Mort Artu*, Arthur tells his men the surprising news that Mordred is his son. He does not identify the mother, and those who had read only the *Mort Artu* might have thought, as Boccaccio apparently did, that she was simply a concubine of Arthur.[44] The mother's identity, however, is revealed in a brief episode in the earlier Vulgate *Lancelot*: there Lancelot finds in the hand of a man whom Mordred has killed a letter intended for Mordred that says, 'Os tu, Mordrez, . . . saches vraiement que li rois Artus . . . t'engendra en la fame le roi Loth d'Orcanie' ['Rash Mordred, . . . know truly that King Arthur . . . sired you in the wife of King Lot of Orkney'].[45] Thus, Mordred's mother is King Arthur's half-sister. It is not certain whether the reference to Mordred's being Arthur's son in the *Lancelot* was composed before the reference to this in the *Mort Artu*: the author of the *Mort Artu* in having Arthur mention that Mordred was his son may have been expecting his readers to remember an earlier reference to the incest in the *Lancelot*; but it is also possible that the reference to the incest in the *Lancelot* was a later interpolation to explain Arthur's allusion to Mordred's being his son in *Mort Artu*.[46] In any event, the Vulgate Cycle introduced a new element into the Arthurian story: King Arthur had committed the sin of incest.

Moreover, while in Geoffrey of Monmouth's *Historia* we are simply told that Mordred and Arthur are killed in the final battle of Camlann, in the Vulgate *Mort Artu* Arthur and Mordred kill each other. Thus the Vulgate cycle added to Arthur's final days the elements of filicide and patricide.[47] Elizabeth Archibald observes that, although in traditional incest stories there is some penance at the end, 'some moral sensibility, some consciousness of sin', in the Vulgate story of Arthur and Mordred, 'there is no demonstration of contrition, no place for penance, no possibility of . . . absolution'. She continues, '[T]he story of Arthur ends with unredeemed and unredeemable personal and political catastrophe.'[48]

As I mentioned above, the Vulgate *Merlin* was written as a 'prequel' to the

Arthurian Tradition, ed. James P. Carley (Cambridge, 2001), pp. 249–68. For Robert of Avesbury, see Fletcher, *Arthurian Material*, pp. 176, 189. Also see Valerie M. Lagorio, 'The Evolving Legend of St Joseph of Glastonbury', *Speculum*, 46 (1971), 209–31, esp. 224–25.

44 See my 'Generic Intertextuality', p. 48.

45 *Lancelot*, ed. Alexandre Micha, 9 vols (Geneva, 1978–83), V, p. 223; trans. Carleton W. Carroll in *Lancelot-Grail*, genl ed. Norris J. Lacy, 5 vols (New York, 1995), III, p. 261.

46 Elizabeth Archibald, *Incest and the Medieval Imagination* (Oxford, 2001), p. 204; Frappier, *Étude*, 32–37, 429 and Frappier, ed., *La Mort le Roi Artu*, 3rd ed. (Geneva, 1964), p. xvi.

47 Archibald, *Incest*, p. 215.

48 Archibald, *Incest*, pp. 215–16.

original three Vulgate romances. It begins with the prose version of Robert de Boron's *Merlin*, which is followed by a long continuation. Toward the end of the prose version of Robert de Boron's *Merlin* King Lot of Orkney marries one of Arthur's half-sisters, one of the daughters of Igerne and her first husband, the duke of Tintagel, and she gives birth to four sons, Mordred, Gawain, Gareés (Guerrehet or Garys) and Gaheriez (Gaheriet or Gareth): 'de ceste fille . . . eissi Mordrez et mes sires Gauvains et Gareés et Gaheriez'.[49] Thus Mordred in Robert de Boron's account is, as he is in the chronicles, simply Arthur's nephew. The author of the Vulgate version of Robert's account incorporated this information except that he added a fifth son Agravaine, who is an important character in later parts of the Vulgate Cycle.[50] However, the author must have soon realized that there was an inconsistency here with the information about incest in the Vulgate *Lancelot*. Shortly after the Robert de Boron section ends, the author of the Vulgate continuation has Merlin tell Arthur that he has fathered one of Lot's sons, but he does not tell him which one.[51] The author later repeats the information that Lot's wife was one of Arthur's half-sisters and then adds: 'de cele dame issi gauaines & agrauains & guerehes & gaheries icil furent fil au roy loth . & dautre part en issi mordret qui fu li maines que li rois artu engendra' [This lady gave birth to Gawainet, Agravain, Guerrehet and Gaheriet, who were all King Lot's sons. Furthermore, she also bore Mordred, who was the offspring whom King Arthur fathered].[52] Apparently to keep readers from thinking too badly of Arthur, however, the author of the Vulgate *Merlin* explains that Arthur did not realize he was committing incest: before he became king, he was attracted to Lot's wife, and not realizing she was his sister, crept into her bed one night when Lot was away, and the lady, thinking Arthur was her husband, received him gladly and conceived Mordred.[53] Thus incest was introduced into the Vulgate *Merlin* as well as into the *Lancelot*, but Arthur had not realized he had committed the sin.

A later shorter cycle, the Post-Vulgate *Roman du Graal* that was adapted from the Vulgate Cycle and written sometime between 1230 and 1240, developed the incest motif still further; for in this work, although Arthur still unknowingly commits incest with his sister, Merlin rebukes him for his sin and calls him 'dyables et anemis Jhesucrist' ['devil and enemy of Jesus Christ'].[54] This work, as Fanni Bogdanow points out, presents Arthur as a great king, but he has nevertheless become a flawed hero whose sin, even though unwitting, will help bring about the destruction of his kingdom.[55] Thus both the Vulgate Cycle and the

49 *Merlin*, ed. Micha, p. 244; *Merlin and the Grail*, trans. Bryant, p. 103.
50 *Lestoire de Merlin*, in *The Vulgate Version of the Arthurian Romances*, ed. H. Oskar Sommer, 8 vols (Washington, 1908–16), II, p. 73; *The Story of Merlin*, trans. Rupert T. Pickens, in *Lancelot-Grail*, ed. Lacy, I, p. 207.
51 *Lestoire de Merlin*, p. 96; *The Story of Merlin*, trans. Pickens, p. 220.
52 *Lestoire de Merlin*, p. 128; *The Story of Merlin*, trans. Pickens, p. 237.
53 *Lestoire de Merlin*, pp. 128–29; *The Story of Merlin*, trans. Pickens, p. 237.
54 *La Suite du Roman de Merlin*, ed. Gilles Roussineau, 2 vols (Geneva, 1996), I, p. 8; *The Post-Vulgate, part I: The Merlin Continuation*, trans. Martha Asher in vol. IV of *Lancelot-Grail*, ed. Lacy, p. 169.
55 Fanni Bogdanow, 'The Evolution of the Theme of the Fall of Arthur's Kingdom', trans. Edward Donald Kennedy in *King Arthur: A Casebook*, ed. Edward Donald Kennedy (New

Post-Vulgate *Roman du Graal* give the story of Arthur a strange new element. While they retain Robert de Boron's conception of the Round Table as a figure of the Grail Table and of the Table used at the Last Supper and the episode of the sword in the stone, which describes Arthur as the king chosen by Christ,[56] this Christian hero also commits incest and filicide.

Thus, thanks to the French authors, the story of Arthur had changed from that of the great British hero whose fall in Geoffrey of Monmouth must be attributed to the capricious workings of Fortune and from Robert de Boron's story of a person destined to be king by the choice of Christ to the story of a man who, although still chosen by Christ, commits two of the worst sins. Incest, in particular, is described by Elizabeth Archibald as 'the most extreme manifestation of lust and bodily appetite', the 'monstrous sin'.[57] An illustration of how seriously it might be viewed can be found in Chaucer's *Canterbury Tales*. There Chaucer criticizes his friend John Gower for having written two stories concerning incest, the stories of Canacee and of Appolonius of Tyre: Chaucer has his Man of Law say 'Of swiche cursed stories I sey fy!' ['Fie on such cursed stories!']. Chaucer's Man of Law points out that that great writer Chaucer would never have written 'of swiche unkynde abhomynacions' ['of such unnatural abominations].[58] The presence of incest in the French Arthurian romances may, in fact, explain something about Chaucer's attitude toward the Arthurian stories. Although details in some of Chaucer's works indicate he knew at least the Vulgate *Lancelot*,[59] Chaucer generally avoided Arthurian material. He has his Nun's Priest briefly dismiss the Vulgate *Lancelot* by saying that his beast fable about two chickens is as true 'as is the book of Launcelot de Lake, / That wommen holde in ful greet reverence' ['that women think of with very great reverence'],[60] a remark that relegates the prose *Lancelot* to the medieval equivalent of the Silhouette romances sold in supermarkets today. His only story loosely associated with Arthurian material in that it is set 'in th'olde dayes of the King Arthour' is appropriately enough assigned to a woman, the Wife of Bath, who is not among the more refined of the Canterbury pilgrims.[61] Chaucer's general lack of interest in and perhaps even contempt for Arthurian material could be associated with his aversion to stories concerned with what his Man of Law called 'unkynde abhomynacions'.

The Vulgate *Merlin* was translated or adapted into English three times. The first of these was a fairly popular early English metrical romance, *Of Arthur and of Merlin*. Surviving in five manuscripts, it was written c. 1250, not long after the

York, 1996, repr. 2002), pp. 91–103, here 94–99. This article was originally published as 'La chute du royaume d'Arthur: Évolution du thème', *Romania*, 107 (1986), 504–19.

56 Both the Vulgate and the Post-Vulgate *Merlin* incorporate these passages from the prose version of Robert de Boron, found in *Merlin*, ed. Micha, pp. 184–85, 269; *Merlin and the Grail*, trans. Bryant, pp. 92, 107.

57 Archibald, *Incest*, p. 6.

58 'Introduction to *The Man of Law's Tale*', lines 80, 88 in *The Riverside Chaucer*, 3rd ed., gen. ed. Larry D. Benson (Boston, 1987), p. 88.

59 See my 'Gower, Chaucer, and French Prose Arthurian Romance', *Mediaevalia*, 16 (1993), 55–90.

60 *The Nun's Priest's Tale*, lines 3212–13, *The Riverside Chaucer*, p. 258.

61 *The Wife of Bath's Tale*, line 857, *The Riverside Chaucer*, p. 116.

French version. It retains the story of the sword in the stone and the announcement that Arthur was chosen by Christ, but it omits references to Mordred as Arthur's son. The story of Arthur's incest does not appear in English until 200 years later in two other translations, an anonymous close prose translation and a bad verse translation by Harry Lovelich, a skinner of London, both written in the mid-fifteenth century when many people were doubting the truth of the Arthurian stories.[62] Not long after that, an adaptation of the version of the incest story found in the Post-Vulgate *Roman du Graal* appeared in Malory's *Morte Darthur*, which was completed between March 1469 and March 1470. Thus it took quite a while for an account of Arthur's incest to appear in English.

The association of Arthur with incest and filicide in the romances could account for the chroniclers' avoiding allusions to a story about Arthur that Robert de Boron had originally written to enhance Arthur's prestige by making him a king chosen by Christ. It may also help explain why most chroniclers did not make radical changes in the material that Geoffrey of Monmouth had written other than by granting, in Robert Mannyng's case, that the adventures in romances occurred during a period of peace or when Arthur ruled in France. I know of only three allusions to the incest in the chronicles, and two of these deny it ever happened: One is in the Scottish Latin chronicle of John of Fordun who indicates that the Scot Mordred was Arthur's nephew and adds that sources that say he had another origin are without foundation.[63] An oblique denial of the incestuous origins of Morded occurs in versions of the Prose *Brut*, which, with about 225 surviving manuscripts in Anglo-Norman and English, were the most widely read vernacular chronicles in England. In the *Brut* account of Arthur's death, we are told that Arthur turned the realm over to his kinsman Constantine 'for-asmiche as he hade none heire of his body bigeten'. The author adds for emphasis: 'and grete harme was hit þat soche a noble Kyng, and so doughty, had none childe of his body bigeten; but al þing þat God wil haue done, moste bene done'.[64] The fifteenth-century chronicler John Hardyng alludes to rumors of the incest in the first version of his chronicle: 'Bot som bokes sayne Arthur was so vnwyse / That he hym [Mordred] gatte on his syster dame Anne',[65] but Hardyng deleted this when he revised his chronicle.

Hardyng's chronicle, however, is the only English chronicle that incorporated much of the material that originated with Robert de Boron. It reached Hardyng through the Vulgate Cycle and, for the Joseph of Arimathea material, apparently

62 For the type of reader for which the English prose translation of the Vulgate *Merlin* might have been intended, see Carol M. Meale, 'The Manuscripts and Early Audience of the Middle English *Prose Merlin*', and Karen Stern, 'The Middle English *Prose Merlin*', both in *The Changing Face of Arthurian Romance*, ed. Alison Adams, Armel H. Diverres, Karen Stern and Kenneth Varty (Woodbridge, 1986), pp. 92–111, 112–22.

63 John of Fordun, *Chronica Gentis Scotorum*, ed. W.F. Skene (Edinburgh, 1871), pp. 109–10, and the translation in *John of Fordun's Chronicle of the Scottish Nation*, trans. F.J.H. Skene (Edinburgh, 1872), pp. 101–02. Fordun's story of Arthur is incorporated into Walter Bower's *Scotichronicon*, genl ed. D.E.R. Watt, vol. II, ed. [and trans.] John and Winifred MacQueen (Aberdeen, 1989), pp. 64–65. Also see my 'John Hardyng and the Holy Grail', p. 200.

64 *The Brut or the Chronicles of England*, ed. Friedrich W.D. Brie, Pt 1 (1906; repr. London, 1960), p. 91.

65 British Library Lansdowne 204, fol. 71v.

through John of Glastonbury's chronicle. Another unusual feature for a chronicle written in English after the mid-fifteenth century is that it is written in verse after prose had become the norm for chronicle writing. The type of verse Hardyng used, rhyme royal, was taken from some of the moral and didactic works written by Chaucer and Lydgate. That Hardyng would have written verse is somewhat surprising, for he was not even a remotely competent poet. Thomas Warton described him as 'the most impotent of our metrical chroniclers', and his verse has been described by Warton as being 'almost beneath criticism' and by Eleanor Hammond as 'doggerel stupidity' with 'no literary merit whatever'.[66] Hardyng has contributed considerably to the reputation of the fifteenth century as a century of really bad English poetry. He may have used verse so that he could more freely adapt the usual chronicle story. Ruth Morse writes that works explicitly intended for a non-scholarly audience seem to have had more latitude than those meant for scholars,[67] and, just as Robert de Boron chose to write the original versions of his Arthurian accounts in verse, Hardyng may have believed that he could manipulate the well-known events of the chronicles more easily if he wrote in verse instead of prose. In any event, it is through Hardyng that some material originally invented by Robert de Boron finally was incorporated into an English chronicle.

Hardyng wrote two versions of his chronicle that covered the period from the founding of Britain until the mid-fifteenth century. The first, the Lansdowne version (cited in n. 65), survives in a single presentation copy intended for the Lancastrian King Henry VI; the second was intended first for Richard, duke of York and after the duke's death in 1460 it was further revised for Edward IV in 1464. The second version, surviving in fifteen manuscripts from the fifteenth, sixteenth and seventeenth centuries and in two sixteenth-century editions, is not well known today but was widely read in its time and was a source for Malory, Spenser and Milton.[68]

The chronicle was possibly used by Edward IV as a part of his propaganda campaign to justify his claim to the throne.[69] Bernard Guenée writes that throughout the Middle Ages whoever wanted firm power needed active propaganda,[70] and indeed Hardyng's chronicle represents history written and was

66 Thomas Warton, *History of English Poetry*, 4 vols (London, 1774–90), ed. W.C. Hazlitt (London, 1871), III, p. 124; Eleanor Hammond, *English Verse between Chaucer and Surrey* (Durham, NC, 1927; repr. New York, 1965), p. 233.

67 Morse, ' "This Vague Relation" ', p. 96.

68 See my 'John Hardyng and the Holy Grail', pp. 186, 191 n. 16; also Felicity Riddy, 'Glastonbury, Joseph of Arimathea and the Grail in John Hardyng's Chronicle', *The Archaeology and History of Glastonbury Abbey*, ed. Lesley Abrams and James P. Carley (Woodbridge, 1991), pp. 317–31, repr. in *Glastonbury Abbey*, ed. Carley, pp. 269–84; and her 'Chivalric Nationalism and the Holy Grail in Hardyng's *Chronicle*', in *The Grail: A Casebook*, ed. Dhira B. Mahoney (New York, 2000), pp. 397–414.

69 See Felicity Riddy, 'John Hardyng's Chronicle and the Wars of the Roses', *Arthurian Literature* XII (1993), 91–108, and A.S.G. Edwards, 'The Manuscripts and Texts of the Second Version of John Hardyng's *Chronicle*', in *England in the Fifteenth Century*, ed. Daniel Williams (Woodbridge, 1987), pp. 75–84. Hardyng probably died before completing the second version of the chronicle, and various scribes completed the rhymes of some of his concluding verses in different ways. Such activity suggests that there may have been efforts to put the manuscripts of the chronicle into circulation, probably as propaganda in support of Edward IV.

70 Guenée, *Histoire et culture historique*, p. 332.

used for that purpose. Even though Hardyng wrote different versions of his chronicle for two opposing groups, the Lancastrians and the Yorkists, his overriding message was that England had a right to rule Scotland, and he used the Arthurian material to stress the superiority of the part of the island that became England. As I mentioned above, he was one of the few English chroniclers to tell of Joseph of Arimathea's establishing a church at Glastonbury, and he did this to give Britain prestige: in order to surpass Scotland's claim that it had been miraculously converted when the bones of St. Andrew were brought to Scotland in the fourth century, he claimed that there had been a British church established by Joseph of Arimathea, who, in some medieval legends, was a kinsman of Christ. Hardyng also includes Robert's association between the Grail Table and Arthur's Round Table: in the first version of Hardyng's chronicle the Round Table is a figure of Joseph's Grail Table, and in the second it is identified as the Grail Table itself.[71]

If, however, the story of Joseph of Arimathea was somewhat unusual in an English chronicle, Hardyng's next addition was unprecedented, for he lifted the story of Galahad's Grail quest from the Vulgate Cycle and added it to the chronicle story of Arthur. In Robert de Boron's account, Perceval's achievement of the Grail represents the height of Arthurian chivalry. In the Vulgate Cycle, the quest for the Grail became a story that showed the weaknesses and decline of Arthurian society, since few of Arthur's knights were worthy of the quest. Hardyng, probably without knowledge of Robert de Boron's version, used the story, much as Robert did, to increase the prestige of Arthur's knights and kingdom; but while in Robert's account it represents the ultimate achievement of Arthurian chivalry, in Hardyng it represents but one high point, for, after the quest, Hardyng tells us, Arthur's 'great honoure encreased more and more'.[72] And indeed it does; for while all of the other English chronicles have Arthur hear of Mordred's treason just before he is to be crowned Roman emperor, Hardyng goes a step further and has Arthur crowned emperor before he hears of Mordred's treason. Hardyng eliminates the religious significance that was so central to the versions of Robert and the Vulgate *Queste*. As Felicity Riddy observes, 'Hardyng's emphasis is public and social, not internal and private.' He ignores the 'inwardness of the religious experience' that the Grail represents and 'the spiritual meanings it might be made to bear'.[73]

Hardyng's emphasis throughout is upon the world rather than the spirit. Although during Arthur's reign, Hardyng tells us that each day seemed 'more like . . . / An heuenly life, then erthely', he emphasizes the 'erthely' rather than the 'heuenly'. His enthusiastic praise of the king as 'peerlesse, / Throughout ye world', the most highly 'gloryfied' prince of all time, the 'Moste redoubted in erth & moste famous', the 'worthiest and wyest without pere', the 'hardyest', 'moste coragious,' 'moste victorious', and 'moste bounteous' is distinctly secular,[74] and his vision contrasts with what was presumably Robert's vision of

71 See my 'John Hardyng and the Holy Grail', p. 203.
72 John Hardyng, *The Chronicle*, ed. Henry Ellis (London, 1812), p. 136.
73 Riddy, 'Chivalric Nationalism', p. 407.
74 Hardyng, *The Chronicle*, pp. 121, 126, 128, 148.

Arthurian society at its height. To Robert, or to the author of the prose *Perceval* associated with Robert's work, the high point was bringing the Grail to Arthur's court and thus the fulfillment of the conception of the Round Table as a figure of the table from which Christ ate at the Last Supper. For Hardyng, the high point was Arthur's conquest of Rome and his coronation as emperor, the achievement of the greatest earthly power.

Robert and Hardyng represent two contrasting visions of Arthurian history, the one emphasizing a spiritual triumph, the other, an earthly. Both were transitory because the tragic conclusion followed, at least in Hardyng for it is not certain that Robert intended the tragic conclusion found in the surviving prose versions of his work. Given the nationalist interests of the later chroniclers, it is not surprising that Hardyng's emphasis would have been upon secular triumphs. Although he incorporated much of the material invented by Robert, he employed it not to show the victory of the spiritual over the earthly, but for nationalist propaganda; and his vision of history was, like the one Geoffrey of Monmouth introduced three hundred years earlier, basically the secular one that Robert had moved away from shortly after the first Arthurian chronicles were written. As Hanning (and before him Shakespeare) observed, Fortune's wheel is indeed come full circle.[75]

75 Hanning, *Vision of History*, p. 172; *King Lear*, 5.3.174. Hanning was referring to Geoffrey of Monmouth's return to classical, rather than Christian historiography.

Bruttene Deorling: *an Arthur for Every Age*

†W.R.J. BARRON

Over the fifteen centuries of his literary life there have been many Arthurs: each age, each culture found in him an iconic figure embodying something significant for its society. For those who wrote of him in English the image was primarily that of a great military leader, champion of his people, embodiment of the nation. What relation that image bore to the putative Arthur of history, a Celtic warlord who for a period around A.D. 500 resisted the southwestern expansion of the invading Anglo-Saxons, cannot be determined. The dynastic role is essentially the creation of Geoffrey of Monmouth in his pseudo-chronicle of 1138, the *Historia Regum Britannie*.* The existence of his proclaimed source, 'a certain very ancient book written in the British language' (§2),[1] and the full extent of his apparent sources, partial, imprecisely identified and no doubt incomplete, are equally irrelevant. It is the role and *persona* of Arthur as established by Geoffrey, so influential for centuries to come, which concern us here.[2]

His role is the apogee of a major thematic pattern in which a native dynasty struggles for possession of Britain against Saxon invaders, introduced by an earlier usurper, who have treacherously poisoned both his immediate predecessors. Coming to the throne, aged fifteen, he continues the struggle with the help of his Breton kinsmen, defeats the Saxons, then other ancient enemies of his people, Scots, Picts and Irish, before conquering Iceland, Norway and the Orkneys. Having married Guinevere, descendent of a noble Roman family, his court becomes renowned for its chivalry and fame inspires him to conquer all Europe. He captures Paris, kills the Roman tribune of Gaul and defies a summons to submit to the emperor. At the height of his power, as he marches on Rome, news reaches him that his nephew Modred has seized the kingdom and taken the queen adulterously. Returning home, he drives the traitor westward, kills him in Cornwall and, himself mortally wounded, is borne away to Avalon.

* Although several of the authors of essays in this volume spell Geoffrey's title the traditional way (*Britanniae*), others including Professor Barron preferred to follow the form given in the Neil Wright edition; see following footnote. [Editor's note]

1 References are to the chapter numbers of the edition of the *Historia* by Neil Wright, *The* Historia Regum Britannie *of Geoffrey of Monmouth*, I: *Bern Burgerbibliothek MS 568* (Cambridge, 1985).

2 For succinct characterisations of the *Historia* see Brynley F. Roberts in Rachel Bromwich, A.O.H. Jarman and B.F. Roberts, eds, *The Arthur of the Welsh* (Cardiff, 1991), pp. 97–116, A.O.H. Jarman, in *The Arthur of the Welsh*, pp. 130–37, and W.R.J. Barron in *The Arthur of the English*, ed. W.R.J. Barron (Cardiff, 1999, rev. ed. 2001), pp. 11–18.

The year is A.D. 542, and Britain is left vulnerable to the Saxons, reintroduced as allies by Modred, domestic treachery achieving what Arthur's ancestors had so long successfully resisted.[3]

Such a role is archetypal, familiar in Homer and Virgil, in the myriad versions of the Alexander legend, in *Beowulf*, the *Nibelungenlied*, the *chansons de geste*, the *romans d'antiquité*, much of it no doubt known to Geoffrey in one form or another. He drew upon the tropes and conventions of heroic literature in creating an appropriate *persona* for his dynastic hero, just as stylistically he allowed the Old Testament, Livy and other Roman historians to lend appropriate gravity to his epic narrative. Mystery, reminiscent of the birth of Alexander, surrounds that of Arthur, sired by Uther upon Ygerne in the likeness of her husband Gorlois, whose timely death allows the boy to be born in wedlock (§§137–38). Merlin, the agent of that transformation, seer and guide to the dynasty, is credited with the incorporated Prophecies (§§111–17), in which the Boar of Cornwall prefigures Arthur's greatness (§112.2). Arthur's imperial obsession which carries him from domestic defence to European conquest, to the gates of Rome, to national and personal disaster, echoes that of Alexander and Caesar. His charismatic leadership and tactical skill are reminiscent of the imperial Charlemagne, a secular leader in a patriotic cause against pagan forces who unites his followers by good government and personal generosity. But these external literary influences may have done no more than strengthen the concept of Arthur inherited from Welsh tradition, perhaps available to Geoffrey in his Monmouth youth: good Christian devoted to the Virgin Mary, valiant war-leader inspiring his followers by his personal prowess (§155, §165), his valour expressed in his ancestral arms with their ancient names and reputations (§147). Unrestrained by historical record, Geoffrey created the figure of an ideal king in whom, nonetheless, many contemporary aspirations to national unity, wise government and just rule are expressed – his chronicle is, after all, in the romance mode.

The strength of this characterisation, the universal appeal of the Arthurian legend so largely created by Geoffrey, was to be demonstrated again and again across the ages until Milton, in an age of historical rationalisation, reluctantly abandoned it as the basis of a national epic. In the intervening years those who made Arthur the subject of dynastic chronicle, dynastic romance and chivalric romance recognised the strength and clarity of the universal hero created by Geoffrey and, to a greater or lesser degree, made his *persona* the core of their presentation. While the Latin original swept through Europe, serving as a model for national chronicles as far afield as Poland, each of the island vernaculars produced versions for native audiences. At least five different translations, of which some sixty texts survive, were produced in Wales where the *Brut y Brenhinedd* remained current until the eighteenth century.[4] The version of Wace,

3 I use standard forms of Arthurian personal and place names throughout to avoid confusion between those proper to the individual texts discussed here.

4 On the remarkable diffusion of the *Historia* see J.C. Crick, *The* Historia Regum Britannie *of Geoffrey of Monmouth*, IV: *Dissemination and Reception in the Later Middle Ages* (Cambridge, 1991). On the versions of the Welsh *Brut y Brenhinedd* see Brynley F. Roberts in Bromwich et al., eds, *Arthur of the Welsh*, pp. 97–116.

a cleric from Jersey educated in France, made in 1155 under the patronage of Henry II and presented to his queen Eleanor, was an instant success on both sides of the Channel. Arthur's dominance is increased by extending his reign from one-sixth of the *Historia* to some 4000 out of the 15,000 lines of the *Roman de Brut*, favouring his imperial conquests rather than victories over the Saxons, introducing new fictional elements such as the founding of the Round Table and expanding Geoffrey's somewhat cryptic account of the Hope of the Britons in Arthur's return. Some of these elaborations have been seen as heralding a new age of courtliness, notably the description of Arthur's Whitsun feast at Camelot where knights in distinctive livery contend for the admiration of ladies similarly dressed whose love inspires their chivalry, but they are, in fact, closely based on Geoffrey. It is Wace's development of detail, invention of lively dialogue inserted among the formal speeches of the *Historia*, his gift for aphoristic summation, above all his use of the octosyllabic couplet and the vocabulary of contemporary French literature which gives the *Roman de Brut* its courtly gloss, a first fleeting glimpse of England as a land of romance.[5]

The earliest English version of Geoffrey's dynastic Arthur, though basically derived from Wace's *Roman*, is so idiosyncratic as to defy cultural expectations, turning a Celtic folk-hero into an iconic personification of his bitterest enemies, the English he was to exemplify for centuries to come. The work of Laȝamon, son of Leovenath, parish priest of Areley Kings in Worcestershire, it came at a moment in the early thirteenth century when the native culture was just beginning to struggle free from the parochialism imposed upon it by the Conquest. Our piecemeal knowledge of the minority tradition makes it difficult to assess the context of Laȝamon's *Brut*, the more so since it constitutes such a massive part of the surviving corpus, at over 16,000 lines the second longest poem in English. Most significantly, its medium is basically the long line of Old English verse whose two halves are linked across the medial caesura by the use of alliteration, but here with many irregularities, variations of stress and syllabic content, notably the use of rhyme or near-rhyme to link almost fifty percent of the half lines. The archaic effect of the medium is compounded by the associated idiom: a distinctive poetic vocabulary including many compound words providing the variants which alliteration requires for terms of frequent occurrence; formulaic phrases applied to repeated narrative situations, some mere tags, others extending to a half or even a whole line; a marked lack of French borrowings. The combination of medium and idiom evokes the native tradition, both Anglo-Saxon poetry and the rhythmical alliterative prose of late homiletic texts, to which Laȝamon might have had access in the monastic libraries of Worcester – an easy ten-mile walk away from his parish – preserved by the enduring influence of the long-lived Bishop Wulfstan (*ob.* 1095). But there can be no question of mere antiquarian imitation: most of Laȝamon's compounds are original with him; so are his poetic formulas, though often modelled on idiomatic expressions or alliterating phrases found in the older prose as well as verse;

5 For a modern text see Judith Weiss, ed. and trans., *Wace's* Roman de Brut: *A History of the British* (Exeter, 1999). For a recent summation of Wace scholarship see Françoise Le Saux in Barron, ed., *Arthur of the English*, pp. 18–22.

his metre, though vulnerable to instability, often achieves the rhythmic variety of blank verse as a narrative medium. The overall effect is not of antiquarian pastiche but of a medium rooted in tradition, individually and experimentally extrapolated, consciously archaistic rather than merely archaic.

But no literary medium can be viable unless at least its basic components are familiar to the audience; and the *Brut* evidently commanded an extensive audience. The two surviving texts, both independently derived from a common version which cannot have been the author's original, show that at least four copies of this massive work must once have existed. Earlier assumptions that its idiom cannot have remained comprehensible long after the presumed early-thirteenth-century date of composition have been undermined by palaeographical evidence dating one text to the second half of the thirteenth century, the other some way into the fourteenth. This extended viability suggests that there was, for some century or more, a south-west Midlands audience for whom Laȝamon's idiom was meaningful, though its composition can only be guessed at. Initially, perhaps, his Areley neighbours who could appreciate a lively narrative read aloud; or the household of a local landowner such as 'the good knight' with whom he is said, in a textual variant, to have lived, perhaps as domestic chaplain; later, perhaps, some antiquarians among the Worcester clerics who, despite doubts as to its historicity, may have helped the *Brut* to find a wider audience.[6]

The relation of idiom to audience is relevant here since Laȝamon's presentation of Arthur suggests a similar archaising tendency whose evocative power must depend to some degree on recognition of its terms of reference. Its function in the dynastic theme is Geoffrey's, its material largely Wace's but supplemented and imaginatively elaborated, the *Brut* as a whole doubling the bulk of the *Roman*. Many of the additions and elaborations heighten the idealisation of Arthur. Echoes from Geoffrey's *Prophecies of Merlin*, omitted by Wace but available to Laȝamon in versions, Latin and French, circulating independently, establish his undying fame even before he has been born:

> 'Longe beoð æuere, dæd ne bið he næuere;
> þe wile þe þis world stænt, ilæsten scal is worðmunt;
> and scal inne Rome walden þa þæines.' (9406–8)

> ['As long as time lasts, he shall never die; while this world lasts, his fame shall endure; and he shall rule the princes in Rome.'][7]

Another of his creative initiatives, invoking the tradition of gift-giving deities at the birth of a prince, defines the sources of Arthur's greatness as warrior, long-living king, and generous patron:

6 Much that is summarised here remains hypothetical; I have outlined some of the emergent evidence in 'The Idiom and the Audience of Laȝamon's *Brut*' in *Layamon: Contexts, Language, and Interpretation*, ed. Rosamund Allen, Lucy Perry and Jane Roberts (London, 2002), pp. 157–84.

7 Text and translation from *Laȝamon's* Brut, ed. and trans. W.R.J. Barron and S.C. Weinberg (Harlow, 1995), whose line-numbering is that of the EETS edition by Brook and Leslie.

heo ȝeuen him mihte to beon bezst alre cnihten;
heo ȝeuen him anoðer þing, þat he scolde beon riche king;
heo ȝiuen him þat þridde, þat he scolde longe libben;
heo ȝifen him, þat kinebern, custen swiðe gode
þat he wes mete-custi of alle quike monnen; (9610–14)

[. . . they gave him strength to be the best of all knights; they gave him another gift, that he should be a mighty king; they gave him a third, that he should live long; they gave him, that royal child, such good qualities that he was the most liberal of all living men.]

Neither prophecy nor gift-giving is evocative of a particular cultural tradition or even a specific literary genre. Description of the hero's armour as emblematic of his warrior status is a commonplace of both epic and romance, though Laȝamon gives it more explicit magical associations than either of his predecessors:

Þa dude he on his burne ibroide of stele
þe makede on aluisc smið mid aðelen his crafte;
he wes ihaten Wygar þe witeȝe wurhte.
His sconken he helede mid hosen of stele.
Calibeorne his sweord he sweinde bi his side;
hit wes iworht in Aualun mid wiȝelefulle craften. (10,543–48)

[. . . then he put on his corslet of woven steel which an elvish smith had made by his noble skill; he, the skilful artificer, was called Wygar. He protected his legs with hose of steel. At his side he hung his sword Caliburn; it was made in Avalon by magic arts.]

So also he recognises the importance of prophetic dreams in guiding a national hero. Having reproduced the passage in which Arthur, sailing to France for his assault on Rome, dreams of a conflict between a dragon and a bear whose ominous meaning his courtiers are too much in dread of him to interpret (12,764–93), Laȝamon invents a second vision whose meaning is brutally clear. On the eve of the final assault on Rome, while his followers hesitate to tell him the news of Modred's treachery, Arthur dreams (13,981–14,021) that he is bestriding a great wooden hall with Gawain seated before him as champion, royal sword in hand; Modred hews through the supporting pillars while Guinevere pulls down the roof, and, as the hall collapses, king and nephew fall, Arthur breaking his right arm and Gawain both of his; but, taking his sword in his left hand, Arthur cuts down the traitors. Structurally and thematically the episode echoes Geoffrey's use of the first dream; but its imagery, evoking the Anglo-Saxon hall as the seat of royal power and the associated concept of the *comitatus* as royal bodyguard and defender of the nation, is characteristic of Laȝamon's tendency to reduplicate a striking effect and to exploit his inventive freedom by using English images to vivify a universal trope. But though greatly increased in the *Brut*, the element of the occult is not thematically engaged; Arthur is not supernaturally guided in his mission as national messiah, as his predecessors were by Merlin whom Arthur never meets. It merely adds a gloss of myth to his more realistic roles as war-leader, world-conqueror, lawgiver and Christian king.

In the medieval manner, Arthur is characterised in relation to those roles rather than in terms of individuality; others are characterised only in relation to him as beautiful, passive consort, loyal or traitorous nephews, obedient followers, rebellious underlings, imperious or humbled opponents. Nor is there any development in his presentation; at his accession aged fifteen, he is already wholly himself – 'and the years had all been well employed, for he was fully mature' (9931). Immediately afterwards, at his coronation, his regal personality is sketched in terms which are to remain constant throughout his reign: the best of warriors, generous to all, a father to the young, a comfort to the old, but stern with wrongdoers – 'and by such means he surpassed all kings, by fierce strength and by generosity; such were his virtues that all nations knew of it' (9957–59). The ambivalence, benevolence and sternness, ferocity and generosity, is Laȝamon's addition to the blander portrait in Wace and Geoffrey. He occasionally restates it aphoristically as the key to Arthur's personality (11,235–36), and as such it manifests itself in each aspect of his multiple role.

His function as lawgiver, foretold by Merlin before his birth, sworn to by the young king at the moment of his accession, is periodically renewed at national hustings, exercised in foreign territories whose conquest is confirmed by the establishment of British law, and finally forms the basis of his charge to his successor, Constantin: ' "Defend my Britons as long as you live, and maintain for them all the laws that have been in force in my day, and all the good laws which existed in Uther's time" ' (14,274–76). But though the king is presented as the fountain of justice, justice is as often equated with punishment as with mercy. The punishments decreed by Arthur for those who started the riot which led to the making of the Round Table seem very rough justice indeed:

'Nimeð me þene ilke mon   þa þis feht ærst bigon,
and doð wiððe an his sweore   and draȝeð hine to ane more,
and doð hine in an ley uen   þer he scal liggen;
and nimeð al his nexte cun   þa ȝe maȝen iuinden
and swengeð of þa hafden   mid breoden eouwer sweorden.
Þa wifmen þa ȝe maȝen ifinden   of his nexten cunden,
kerueð of hire neose   and heore wlite ga to lose;
and swa ich wulle al fordon   þat cun þat he of com.' (11,393–400)

['Seize that man who first began this fight, put a cord about his neck and drag him to a marsh, and thrust him into the bog where he shall lie; and seize all his close kin whom you can find and strike off their heads with your broad swords. The women of his immediate family whom you can find, cut off their noses and let their looks be ruined; and so I will utterly destroy the race from which he came.']

But violence within the court, threatening the king's peace and the stability of the nation, is treason – for which Arthur imposes the traditional sentence: ' "being drawn asunder by horses which is the penalty for all traitors" ' (11,406).

Such passages have been cited as evidence of Laȝamon's sadistic temperament and the unsophisticated nature of his English audience. But an audience, many of whose members may have been born in an age of civil war, remembering the anarchy under Stephen when, according to the *Anglo-Saxon Chronicle*, 'men said openly that Christ and all his saints were asleep', might well have found Laȝamon's picture of a strong and ruthless ruler both realistic and attractive. Though the antique native roots of his idiom may have darkened that picture with epic colouring suggesting a return to more primitive values, the spectacle of Arthur wooing and coercing his followers to rally to the defence of the nation ('And whoever stayed away should suffer mutilation; and whoever came willingly, he should become rich'), restraining them when they assault the Roman ambassadors in his court (a detail not in Wace), and calming violent disputes between his closest kinsmen in council no doubt seemed admirable exercise of authority in the interests of the nation. Laȝamon wrote in an age when fear and favour were equally instruments of government and admits their parity in Arthur's methods of control: 'All the people of Britain loved Arthur. All who dwelt in the land stood in awe of him' (13,526–27). If he acknowledges the darker side of feudal polity to a greater degree than Wace, it is perhaps because the vividness with which his imagination pictures the reign of Arthur instinctively clothes it in the circumstances of his own age. Ultimately he undermines the heroic image he has been at such pains to create by distancing the king from those who should advise and support him: no one dares to offer an interpretation of his first portentous dream, 'lest he should lose limbs which he valued' (12,792–93), and the messenger who brings news of Modred's treachery critically delays its delivery (14,022–34).

The dangers of internal dissension are never entirely forgotten: a sudden passion for a loyal subject's wife may precipitate civil war, rivalry for preeminence at court leads to riot, quarrels erupt between trusted lieutenants in council. Arthur imposes his authority by using the political means of a feudal age: personal example, public ceremonial, royal largess, state religion. His military prowess is demonstrated both as tactician marshalling forces from all over his empire against the might of Rome, and as national champion fighting the Roman tribune Frolle in single combat. Both roles originate with Geoffrey, but Laȝamon has developed them with vigour and imaginative realism. The single combat, four times longer than in Wace (11,755–991), results from a challenge issued by Frolle in the confidence that Arthur will refuse; their meeting on an island in the Seine is treated with all the formality of a trial by combat, and victory over an opponent of equal valour is won by Arthur's personal prowess (11,951–69). As in the other battle passages, Laȝamon relishes the violence: the bodies cut in half, the sword lodging in the teeth of a cloven skull, the showers of arrows 'thick as falling snow', the streams of blood flowing along the forest paths, the wounded soldiers wandering over the wooded countryside. The contrast with Wace's comparatively bland and generalised battle pieces owes more, perhaps, to Laȝamon's preference for concrete detail and the vividness of his vocabulary than to any coarsening of concept. When the king defends his people against the ravages of the giant of Mont St Michel (12,960–13,040), though his beastliness is vividly evoked, there is a significant contrast with Wace's account where Arthur hopes to take the giant unawares; 'Arthur', says Laȝamon, 'would never attack him while asleep lest he should later suffer reproach.' Laȝamon has been said to lack appreciation of chivalry, yet he elaborates descriptively the few lines in the *Roman de Brut* telling how the body of the emperor Lucius was returned to Rome, recognising the honour due to a worthy opponent who 'had been a very brave man while he lived' and underscoring the irony of Arthur's message that the golden coffin was the only tribute he would send the Romans.

Laȝamon's appreciation of the place of ceremonial in medieval governance seems no less acute than Wace's: Arthur's arming is as splendid, his councils as formal if often more impassioned, his crown-wearing at Caerleon no less detailed, ceremonious or courtly, even if his followers show more interest in field sports and ball games than in the gambling and board games of Wace. The English poet is no less aware of the refinements of court life than the French, except in the matter of courtly wooing where he does no more than lip-service to Wace's rare passages of *amour courtois*. He deals quite competently with love where it is necessary to his dynastic theme – witness the Ygerne episode; it is the abstract doctrine which he seems to find irrelevant. Where he omits such references, as when Gawain praises peace as conducive to amorous dalliance (Wace: 10,767–72), it is in favour of a different idealism based on social good rather than personal happiness: 'for peace allows a good man to do good deeds whereby all men are the better and the land the happier' (12,457–58). Ceremonial occasions display the unity and magnificence of the Round Table and the royal munificence which underpins both. Arthur rewards loyal service with kingdoms and castles, dismisses aged knights with rich gifts, restores forfeited lands to pardoned rebels (though not to traitors or perjurers), and feasts his followers to the sound of trumpets.

Religious observance plays an important part in Arthur's public life: clerics bless his enterprises, keep vigil before he fights Frolle, celebrate his victories; he, in turn, nominates archbishops, rebuilds ruined churches, takes oaths upon the relics of saints. Repeatedly, earnestly and with every appearance of sincerity he invokes divine aid: at the moment of his accession when he prays for help in upholding God's laws all his life, addressing before every battle the Virgin whose image he bears on his shield and, on waking in terror from an ominous dream, calling on Christ by formulaic titles as old as the oldest English verse:

> 'Lauerd Drihten, Crist,   domes Waldende,
> midelarde Mund,   monnen Froure,
> þurh þine aðmode wil,   Walden ænglen,
> let þu mi sweuen   to selþen iturnen!' (12,760–63)
>
> ['Christ, our Lord and Master, Lord of destinies, Guardian of the world, Comforter of men, Ruler of angels, let my dream, through your gracious will, lead to a good outcome!']

But here too prayer is a public act in the hearing of his men, just as elsewhere God is invoked in a political act as Arthur is about to execute youthful German hostages in a moment of anger against their leader: ' "If life endures within me, and He who created sun and moon grants it, never again shall Childric deceive me!" ' (10,522–24). Since Arthur, the public figure, has no inner life, there is no indication of his personal faith, even in moments of greatest anguish: when he learns of the treachery of Modred and Guinevere (it is Gawain who invokes

God's law in vowing their destruction); when he laments Gawain's death; or in the slaughter at Camelford. Christian and magical elements having coexisted in his public life as easily as the roles of feudal sovereign and fairy prince in his persona, it comes as no surprise that he invokes the fairy Argante for his bodily healing and that it is Merlin who, like some Old Testament prophet, predicts his messianic return (14,293–97).

Laȝamon's presentation of Arthur and his society is rooted in familiar tropes of heroic literature given an archaic Old English colouring by his idiom and verse medium. The tendency to reduplication and extrapolation evident in his treatment of the inherited narrative leads ultimately to expressive originality whose most striking feature is his introduction of extended similes which have no counterpart in Old English tradition and only brief conventional models in Wace.[8] Where Wace likens a charging warrior to a hunting lion, Laȝamon adapts the image to the experience of his English audience by substituting a wild boar falling upon tame swine browsing on beech mast (10,609–10). There are such single-line similes throughout the *Brut*, but with the entry of Arthur they increase in frequency, length and vividness: Arthur himself leading a charge 'like the frost-grey wolf when he comes from the snow-hung wood, bent on devouring whatever prey he pleases' (10,040–43); his forces falling upon the enemy as a fierce wind presses upon a lofty wood (10,047–48); enemy leaders fleeing like a hunted wolf (10,114) or a wild crane separated from the flock, harried by hawks in the air and by hounds on land (10,061–67). At the climax of Arthur's revenge upon the Saxons for their killing of Uther come eight similes within six hundred lines, each extending over many verses: the defeated Childric as a sportive fox surprised by the hunt, driven over the hills and dug out of his den (10,398–417); Colgrim as a goat held at bay by the wolf Arthur in the hills above Bath (10,628–36); Baldolf looking down on his companions slaughtered in crossing the Avon – 'then the river Avon was all bridged with steel!' (10,616). Arthur comments:

'Ȝurstendæi wes Baldulf cnihten alre baldest;
nu he stant on hulle and Auene bihaldeð,
hu ligeð i þan stræme stelene fisces;
mid sweorde bigeorede heore sund is awemmed;
heore scalen wleoteð swulc gold-faȝe sceldes;
þer fleoteð heore spiten swulc hit spæren weoren.
þis beoð seolcuðe þing isiȝen to þissen londe,
swulche deor an hulle, swulche fisces in wælle!' (10,638–45)

['Yesterday Baldolf was the boldest of warriors; now he stands on the hill and looks upon the Avon, sees how steel fish lie in the river trammelled with swords, their swimming impaired; their scales gleam as if they were gilded shields; their fins drift in the water like spears floating there. This is a marvellous thing come to pass in this land, such beasts on the hill, such fish in the water!']

8 See W.R.J. Barron and Françoise Le Saux, 'Two Aspects of Laȝamon's Narrative Art', *Arthurian Literature* IX (1989), 25–56.

Excited to creative independence by his vision of Arthur triumphant, Laȝamon has elaborated the basic image on which his simile rests to a visionary level matched elsewhere by his conflation of separate fragments from the Prophecies of Merlin into a declaration of his hero's undying fame:

> 'Of him scullen gleomen godliche singen;
> of his breosten scullen æten aðele scopes;
> scullen of his blode beornes beon drunke.
> Of his eȝene scullen fleon furene gleden;
> ælc finger an his hond scarp stelene brond.
> Scullen stan walles biuoren him tofallen;
> beornes scullen rusien, reosen heore mærken.' (9410–16)
>
> ['Of him shall minstrels splendidly sing; of his breast noble bards shall eat; heroes shall be drunk upon his blood. From his eyes shall fly sparks of fire; each finger on his hand shall be a sharp steel blade. Stone walls shall fall down before him; men shall tremble, their banners fall.']

The extrapolation from the concept of a hero's reputation serving as meat and drink to the bards who sing of him to the Eucharistic imagery of a Saviour on whose body and blood his people are spiritually nourished is typical of the verbal exaltation which overcomes Laȝamon in moments of heightened thematic interest.

This emotional climax to his initial presentation of Arthur suggests some patriotic feeling on the poet's part – but for what nation? For him Arthur was 'Bruttene deorling', but the cognomen seems to have been modelled on the medieval title for Alfred the Great, 'England's darling' and elsewhere Laȝamon appears to use the racial terms interchangeably. At Arthur's departure to Avalon, he replaces Wace's version of Merlin's prophecy 'that his death would remain in doubt' with an emphatic promise 'that an Arthur should again come to aid the people of England' (14,297) – 'corrected' in the later manuscript to 'Britain', but perhaps erroneously. In his proem to the *Brut*, Laȝamon announced his intention to 'relate the noble origins of the English, what they were called and whence they came who first possessed the land of England' (7–9) and later outlines the history of the island in terms of its successive conquerors, who each changed its name and gave it their own. The sleight-of-mind by which Arthur becomes the Messianic hope of the Saxons who were his bitterest enemies was possible because the fundamental theme of the *Brut* is not culture but country, not race but land and the literary immortality of Britain's darling was to be the common inheritance of all who made the land their home.

Despite its imaginative qualities, Laȝamon's *Brut* was too localised in dialect, too archaic in idiom to be central to the English Arthurian tradition. Far more influential was to be another derivative of Geoffrey's *Historia*, less creative but enormously ramified and pervasive across the ages. Verse redactions of the *Historia*, predominantly Wace's *Roman*, were used to preface a similar paraphrase of the *Anglo-Saxon Chronicle*, introducing in turn contemporary records extended from reign to reign. Such composite chronicles appeared in all three literary languages; some 170 manuscripts preserve an English prose version covering, with many variations, events well into the fifteenth century when Caxton's *Chronicles of England* (1480) recognised its popular appeal as history for laymen. In the legendary prelude from Brutus to Arthur it is the king's dynastic role, his iconic status as one of the Nine Worthies featured in many a civic pageant, which mattered rather than any individuality of personality.[9]

But in parallel with his function as a popular icon, Arthur continued to serve as a focus of national aspirations and aristocratic values. As late as 1400 his dynastic role was celebrated in an alliterative line as rigid as anything in the Anglo-Saxon tradition, in a highly eclectic composition rooted in some version of Wace. In the Alliterative *Morte Arthure* the chronicle theme is concentrated in little more than a quarter of Laȝamon's extent (4346 lines), beginning four-fifths of the way through with Rome's demand for homage and structured in the epic manner, detailed, highly dramatic scenes grouped in six major sections, five beginning with messengers whose nature or news characterizes the following episode. The dynastic context is established by an initial catalogue of Arthur's conquests since his accession (26–47) and his Trojan ancestry is recalled in a brief epilogue (4342–46). Though often absent from the action, he is the moral and thematic focus of the poem, presented in terms of his role rather than any individual characteristics. As 'the conqueror' (*passim*) he takes counsel with his followers (243–413) who vow vengeance upon his opponents – recalling the competitive boasting of the *chansons de geste* but also the Anglo-Saxon *beot* – rejects with contempt imperial claims to his homage (417–42), sees his lieges fulfil their vows using his name as their battle-cry (*passim*), kills the emperor Lucius in single combat (2242–56), avenges Modred's treason with his own hand (4224–53) and commands his successor, Constantine, to extirpate the traitor's evil seed by killing his children (4316–23).

But Arthur's role in this *Morte Arthure* is dual, as both king and knight, called 'Sir Arthur' (*passim*), 'the knyghtlyeste creatoure in Cristyndome' (534),[10] magnificently armed (900–19), engaging the giant of Mont St Michel in a prolonged struggle which begins as sword against club and ends as all-in wrestling (840–1221). All the emphatic iteration and semantic elaboration of alliterative verse is exploited to convey the physical grotesquery and thematic complexity of the encounter. The giant is an abortion in nature, with the strength, ugliness and bestial qualities of the animals he resembles, an incubus, eater of baptised children, ravisher and murderer of noble women, who wears the beards of subject kings as trophies. In eliminating him, Arthur displays his prowess not just in chivalrous suppression of evil but as a Christian monarch defending his subjects against ungodly forces, Roland and Charlemagne in one.

The episode exemplifies in miniature the whole campaign against Rome, a tyranny which allies itself with 'Sowdanes and Sarezenes' and makes war with giants, witches and warlocks in its ranks. The king's role as the champion of

9 The enormous influence of the Prose *Brut*, rooted in its flexibility of form and medium, ensuring longevity and wide dissemination, was seconded by a variety of verse chronicles. For further details of both with relevant bibliography see, respectively, W.R.J. Barron and Lesley Johnson in Barron, ed., *Arthur of the English*, pp. 32–38 and pp. 38–46.

10 References and quotations are from the edition of the Alliterative *Morte Arthure* by Mary Hamel (New York, 1984).

Christendom is constantly emphasized by his personal piety (1218–21, 2410–16, 3212–17), by the prophetic dream which prefigures his victory over Lucius (756–831), the prayers of the giant's victims at the moment when the struggle turns in Arthur's favour (1136–39), and his final triumph 'thurghe þe crafte of Cryste' (1107). The ruse by which he conceals his solitary knight-errantry from his companions, a supposed pilgrimage to Mont St Michel as the shrine of a saint, relates the episode to the thematic structure of the romance in which war and pilgrimage are repeatedly opposed. Vowing commitment to the mission against Rome, his knights invoke the Vernicle (296–303, 308–15, 347–56), a symbol of Christian compassion and familiar object of Roman pilgrimage. Rome is the seat not only of imperial power but of the Christian pontiff, whose lands and clergy Arthur swears to protect (2410–15). But in the violence of his campaign churches are destroyed (3038–43) and the Papal state of Spoleto despoiled (3158–61). As Arthur's forces approach the Holy City, action and implication increasingly question the degree of violence appropriate to such a mission.

Arthur's conduct and motivation are not initially queried. Though he expels the Roman ambassadors, sumptuously entertained, with brutal threats should they delay or deviate from the prescribed route (443–78) and answers the Roman demand for tribute ironically, despatching treasure-chests charged with the bodies of the defeated emperor and sixty senators (2290–351), this may have seemed to contemporaries no more unfitting than the imperious temper, generous in giving but stern in doing justice, with which Laȝamon endows him. As the campaign approaches its climax there are signs of stress when Arthur orders a slaughter of prisoners in revenge for one of his knights (2261–77) and swears to kill his child hostages if Rome will not pay tribute (3587–90). And while the validity of his dynastic mission seems unchallenged, his attitude to the prowess of his chivalric comrades undergoes a change. Early in the war Cador displays reckless bravery in action and is reprimanded by Arthur for putting the lives of his companions in peril (1920–27). Later, in an episode borrowed from the romanticized epic of Fierabras (French or English), Gawain wins the help of the pagan knight Priamus against vastly superior Roman forces by defeating him in a duel of extreme, grotesque violence and is praised by Arthur. The contrast between dynastic warfare and the self-vaunting chivalry of romantic knight-errantry implies that courage and prowess are to be evaluated by the validity of the cause they serve.

The implications for Arthur's reputation appear in a second prophetic dream in which he sees himself raised upon Fortune's wheel in power and majesty only to be dashed down to destruction as it relentlessly turns. The philosophers who interpret it for him make explicit a moral commentary which has been implicit since the proem (1–25) in which the poet invokes divine grace for human misgovernment:

> 'Thow has schedde myche blode, and schalkes distroyede,
> Sakeles, in cirquytrie, in sere kynges landis.
> Schryfe the of thy schame and schape for thyn ende!
> Thow has a schewynge, sir Kynge, take kepe ȝif the lyke,
> For thow sall fersely fall within fyve wynters.' (3398–402)

['You have shed much blood and, in your arrogance, slaughtered many innocent men in various kingdoms. Confess your wickedness and prepare for your death. You have had a forewarning, sire; take heed if you choose, for within five years you shall perish violently.']

Against such a career at its apogee, the true goal of the pilgrimage of life is counterpointed by a passing pilgrim on his way to Rome, Cradoke, Arthur's chamberlain bringing news of Modred's usurpation and Guinevere's unfaithfulness (3468–590). The dynastic dream dissolves in tragedy rooted in Arthur's imperial obsession since, in his eagerness for conquest, he had appointed his nephew regent despite his protest at being deprived of his chance of military glory. As the Britons invade their own country, Gawain's reckless pursuit of glory brings his death at his cousin's hand. Arthur, too eager for vengeance to wait for reinforcements, is outnumbered in the final battle; he kills Modred but amidst the carnage recognises the desolate end of worldly glory:

'I may helples one hethe   house be myn one,
Alls a wafull wedowe   þat wanttes hir beryn;
I may werye and wepe   and wrynge myn handys,
For my wytt and my wirchipe   awaye es for euer!' (4284–87)

['I shall be left alone upon the field, all by myself, like a woeful widow deprived of her mate; I may well curse and weep and wring my hands, for my reason and my good repute is gone for ever.']

The tragedy of the Alliterative *Morte Arthure* is the failure of an heroic ideal embodied in a flawed character which the element of exemplum generalises beyond Arthur's personal failings. The presentation of his wars is so factually precise and concrete that some critics have identified episodes in the Continental campaigns of Edward III; but to a nation exhausted by the endless cruelties and losses of the Hundred Years War it was perhaps war itself which queried the validity of Arthur's imperial obsession. And his companions upon the wheel of Fortune – world conquerors of past (Alexander and Julius Caesar) and future (Charlemagne and Godfrey of Bouillon)[11] – suggest that his imperial ambitions are universal rather than personal delusions.[12]

The process by which Gawain, Arthur's kinsman and loyal lieutenant in the dynastic tradition, becomes his moral foil in the Alliterative *Morte Arthure* reflects the evolution of the *roman courtois* with Chrétien's adoption of the Round Table as the locus of courtly idealism, individual knights exemplifying aspects of the chivalric code, one superseding another in the progressive refinement of the code. Among the companions of Arthur's early adventures in Celtic folklore, the bold but arrogant Kay came to be unfavourably compared with

11 The poet may perhaps have had in mind Charlemagne's weary expectation after the triumphs and disasters of the *Chanson de Roland* that the struggle must continue and Godfrey's participation in the assault and massacre at Jerusalem in 1099.

12 Such a brief analysis does scant justice to a text whose complexity of theme and statement is still emerging. The Notes to Mary Hamel's edition (n. 10 above) and the Introduction to the partial edition by John Finlayson (London, 1967) contain many perceptive observations. For a recent assessment see Lesley Johnson in Barron, ed., *Arthur of the English*, pp. 90–100.

Gawain, perfect exponent of knightly valour but fatally susceptible to women, and so surpassed in constancy by Lancelot inspired by a unique love, but besotted by passion and so outdone in the Grail quest by Galahad, devoted to spiritual chivalry in the service of divine love. Arthur himself, debarred by dynastic duty from engaging in the knight errantry by which they sought a personal reputation as the supreme exponent of chivalry, was progressively confined to a prestigious but passive role as the embodiment of the state, arbiter in chivalric disputes, fountain of justice and honour, a *roi fainéant* undermined by inactivity.

The degenerative process is already far advanced in the near contemporary Stanzaic *Morte Arthur* in which the fall of the Round Table through challenge from abroad and treason at home derives from the *Mort Artu* of the Vulgate Cycle where it is combined with the inherent conflict between feudal duty and chivalric aspiration, so shifting the thematic focus from Arthur, representative of the nation, to Lancelot the embodiment of knighthood. The love between Lancelot and Guinevere, whose socially beneficial effects were celebrated in Chrétien's *Lancelot*, is here an apple of discord which, known to all but not openly acknowledged, distorts all relationships. Suspicion breeds constraint between the lovers, causing Lancelot to absent himself from court, his comrades resent the loss of his prowess and even Gawain, determinedly loyal, causes trouble by boasting of his friend's conquest of the Maid of Ascolot whose unrequited love, revealed at court, again drives Lancelot away. So when tragedy strikes in the death of a Scottish knight poisoned at the queen's table, none of Arthur's company will champion her against his accusing kinsmen until Lancelot returns to do so. When he is trapped in her bedroom by the sneaking Modred and, in snatching Guinevere, condemned for treasonous adultery, from the stake, kills three of Gawain's brothers, Gawain is driven by the ancient code of kinship vengeance to seek Lancelot's destruction.

The position of Arthur in all this is abject; the posture of the cuckold, never gracious, is further degraded by the fact that the adulterer is the glory of his court, tap-root of his regal power. But in the use of his power the king is not a free agent – 'Though Arthur were king the land to weld / He might not be again the right' (920–21);[13] constrained as the fount of justice to see a wife go to the stake, powerless to use his prowess in her defence, reluctantly compelled by the bonds of kinship to join Gawain in his blood-feud against a fellow knight. On the intervention of the pope, Lancelot restores the queen and retires to his lands in Brittany, besieged there by Arthur sickened by the insane fury with which Gawain pursues the feud. So Modred's treachery finds the Round Table fatally divided, father and illegitimate son kill each other and the Hope of the British lies buried with Arthur at Glastonbury. The lovers, voluntarily parted in quest of spiritual regeneration, recognise the high cost of their pursuit of self-fulfilment through love: ' "Our will hath be too sore bought sold" ' (3651). Their

[13] Quotations are from the edition of the Stanzaic *Morte Arthur* included in Larry D. Benson, ed., *King Arthur's Death* (Exeter, 1986). For a fuller analysis see Carole Weinberg in Barron, ed., *Arthur of the English*, pp. 100–11.

ideal nonetheless leaves them ennobled while Arthur is degraded by the extent to which the clash of codes has undermined the dynastic ideal he embodies.

Denigration of Arthur in both the Alliterative and Stanzaic *Morte* is oblique, implicit in the narrative situation rather than openly voiced. But outside the dynastic tradition it is increasingly explicit, especially where the chivalric romance is invaded by elements of exemplum reflecting the moral and social issues underlying contemporary chivalry. *The Awntyrs off Arthure* (north-west, c. 1400–30) consists of two episodes on a common theme of disregard of self and generosity to others, in both of which Gawain acts as Arthur's surrogate. In one he accompanies and comforts the queen when confronted by the ghost of her mother begging masses for the release of a guilty soul, implying condemnation of Guinevere's adultery. In the other, having fought a challenger to a standstill before the court, he restores his lands which had been conferred by the king upon Gawain himself, echoing the ghost's warning that territorial acquisitiveness would bring the downfall of the kingdom:

> 'Your king is to couetous, I warne þe sir kniȝt.
> May no man stere him with strength while þe whele stondes. *move, molest*
> Whan he is in his magesté, moost in his miȝt,
> He shal light ful lowe on þe sesondes. (265–68)[14] *seashore*

The allusion to the passing of Arthur's power in relation to the instability of Fortune's wheel and, in what follows, to his conquests in France (274–79) and Tuscany (284, 291–92), to Gawain's death on landing in Britain (298) and the slaughtering of his knights by Modred's forces (300–12) may well echo the Alliterative *Morte Arthure*. The alliterative tradition to which both texts belong may imply a somewhat provincial perspective from which the queen's adultery (with Lancelot in the Stanzaic and Modred in the Alliterative *Morte* (3549–52)) and Arthur's greed for the lands of others at home and abroad would appear to degrade the dynastic ideal through which the legend exercised most influence upon the English imagination.

But even in chivalric romance, superficially courtly in form and derived from French matter, Arthur is not always immune from implications of abuse of royal power. In *Golagros and Gawane* (Scots, c. 1500), radically re-structured and reinterpreted from the Chastel Orguelleus episode in the First Continuation of Chrétien's *Perceval*, Gawain, by putting his own reputation at risk, spares the honour and secures the independence of an opponent – a cipher in the original, whose worth is elaborately established by the redactor deploying all the tropes of romance – under the eyes of a rapacious, oppressive Arthur. Sighting the Chastel Orguelleus while starting on a pilgrimage to the Holy Land and learning that its lord, Golagros, owes allegiance to no one, Arthur vows to compel his homage: ' "Sall neuer my likame (*body*) be laid vnlaissit (*disarmed*) to sleip, / Quhill I haue gart (*made*) yone berne bow" ' (294–95).[15] The resultant

14 References and quotations are from the edition by Ralph Hanna III (Manchester, 1974). The complex of allusion and implication by which the condensed text conveys its theme is explored by Rosamund Allen in Barron, ed., *Arthur of the English*, pp. 150–55.

15 References and quotations are from the edition by F.J. Amours, ed., *Scottish Alliterative Poems*

series of encounters between his followers and members of the Round Table climaxes when Gawain engages Golagros, unhorses him and demands his surrender. He refuses to dishonour his ancestors, preferring to die unless Gawain will spare him public disgrace by accompanying him to his castle in apparent defeat. In the French version the demand is made to save the life of his *amie* watching from the walls, who will die with shame at his humiliation; Gawain is persuaded by what he has seen of the violence of their passion during a hunting interlude which has left no trace in the English redaction. His decision there must be based on his esteem for an opponent whose worth has been demonstrated in episodes almost entirely contrived by the redactor: an embassy during which Gawain has, with his renowned courtesy, presented the king's demand for homage only to have it rejected with equal courtesy but inflexible resolve (320–457); the magnificence of his armour and the loyalty of his lieges flocking to his support (884–902, 480–544); their impassioned prayers at his fall (1051–63); and, throughout, the laudatory commentary of a member of the Round Table whose prior knowledge of Golagros has made him keenly partisan. Within three lines Gawain sacrifices his reputation for the sake of a worthy opponent who, once reassured of his followers' continuing loyalty, admits his defeat and submits to Arthur. Where the French original compels him to membership of the Round Table, the English Arthur matches Gawain's magnanimity in restoring his independence: ' "I mak releisching of thin allegiance; . . . Fre as I the first fand" ' (1358, 1361).

The redactor has gone to enormous lengths not, it would seem, to denigrate Arthur but to write a conventional chapter in the hagiology of Gawain, omitting a lengthy episode in which his hero seduces the Damoisele de Lis, kills her father and brother and is only prevented from killing another by the intervention of his own love-child, who runs between father and uncle snatching at their shining swords.[16] But for Scots, such as James IV reading *Golagros and Gawane* as one of the first products of the Edinburgh press he had established in 1508, its key-note may well have been the antagonist's defiance:

> 'I will noght bow me ane bak for berne that is borne; *submit*
> Quhill I may my wit wald,
> I think my fredome to hald,
> As my eldaris of ald
> Has done me beforne.' (449–53)

May they not, on the eve of Flodden, have seen in Golagros the personification

in Riming Stanzas (Edinburgh, 1897). For a fuller analysis see W.R.J. Barron in Barron, ed., *Arthur of the English*, pp. 155–61 and in particular n. 198 which contrasts Arthur's ruthlessness towards Golagros (294–98) with his tears of distress for his embattled knights (693–94), calling out to Christ in fear when he sees Gawain hard pressed (953–59), moaning and weeping when he thinks him defeated (1129–41) and fearing attack when he sees the procession of submission approaching (1259–71).

16 It is a salutary reminder of the range of the audience for English romance and of Gawain's potential to be all things to all men that it was this discarded, discreditable episode which the author of *The Jeaste of Syr Gawayne* turned into a scabrous bar-room anecdote; see Maldwyn Mills in Barron, ed., *Arthur of the English*, pp. 162–64.

of Scotland defying the age-old enemy personified in Arthur, the dynastic tradition still resonating in a characteristic romance of individual chivalry?[17]

It is similarly tempting to see in the imperious Arthur of English chivalric romance echoes of tensions between crown and nobility in the later Middle Ages, in contrast to acceptance of his dynastic role – admittedly tempered by resentment of royal exactions for wasteful foreign wars – as a focus of national consciousness in the earlier post-Conquest centuries. But the most sophisticated of English romances uses established personalities to examine fundamental human values and question the very nature of romance. In *Sir Gawain and the Green Knight* (north-west Midlands, late-fourteenth century) roles and situations appear entirely formulaic: Arthur presiding over a seasonal assembly of the Round Table in celebration of Christian and courtly ceremonial; Gawain nominated by common consent to undertake a solitary adventure of knight errantry. But the adventure is evoked by the king's expectation, in fulfilment of royal usage, is undertaken by Gawain as Arthur's surrogate and seems to promise certain death. Throughout its complex evolution every convention of romance is employed – and controverted; every aspect of Gawain's chivalric reputation is evoked – and negated; and, contrary to all expectation, it ends in failure.

When his ambivalent expectation of adventure as either idealized fiction or deadly reality (90–99) brings a challenge to 'a Crystemas gomen' (283), a pluck-buffet exchange which promises to be fatal, the shocked silence of the court provokes Arthur to seize the proffered axe, a quasi-legal commitment (316–28) which moves Gawain to intervene with a calm self-abnegation contrasting with the king's traditional instability of temperament.[18] The court takes counsel and delivers its judgement in terms which, while echoing the playful pretext of the challenge, acknowledge the real threat to the realm: 'To ryd (*exempt*) þe kyng wyth croun, / And ȝif Gawan þe game' (364–65). The blow struck, the challenger's severed head names the place for the return contest a year later, to the horror of the court. But Arthur, who 'at hert hade wonder', laughingly dismisses the affair as a theatrical entertainment, fit sport for Christmas (467–80). Gawain is silent; but the poet suggests what may be in his mind, warning him not to shrink from pursuing the adventure because of its danger.

The year passes, fitt two prefaced by a passage of incoherent syntax and

17 The Scots, having their own foundation myth of origin from Athens, stressed in their national chronicles the enmity of Greeks and Trojans, mythical ancestors of the British, and treated Modred as a Scottish hero, lawful heir to the British throne, fighting for his birthright against an illegitimate Arthur. Against this background the imperialistic Arthur of the dynastic tradition was seen as an embodiment of the constant threat from English kings to Scottish independence, justifying the generally pejorative characterization of him in Scottish sources. See G.W.S. Barrow, *The Anglo-Norman Era in Scottish History* (Oxford, 1980) and S. Reynolds, 'Medieval "Origines Gentium" and the Community of the Realm', *History*, 68 (1983), 375–90.

18 The poet's critical presentation of the king, to be sharpened later, begins as no more than a comment on his restlessness as he refuses to take his place at the Christmas feast: 'Arthur would not eat until all had been served, he was so youthfully light-hearted, and rather boyish: he liked an active life, and was all the less willing either to lie idle or to sit still for long, his youthful blood and restless brain stirred him so' (vss 85–89). References and quotations are from my parallel text edition and translation of *Sir Gawain and the Green Knight* (Manchester, 2nd ed. rev., 1998).

ambivalent vocabulary on time and mutability (491–535) which challenges the reader's – and, contentiously, Gawain's – judgement of the events of fitt one: 'Gawan watȝ glad to begynne þose gomneȝ in halle, / Bot þaȝ þe ende be heuy haf ȝe no wonder' (vss 495–96). There follows another celebration of courtly solidarity in the ceremonial arming of Gawain whose heraldic blazon, the 'pure pentaungel', emblem of his *trawþe* (vs. 626) symbolises absolute integrity in faith, deeds and chivalric virtues (536–665). But the confident mood is undermined by consciousness that no armour, perhaps no chivalric virtue, can be proof against an undefended blow, by muttered regrets among the courtiers, feigning mirth though sad at heart. Arthur remains silent at Gawain's tight-lipped comment on his mission: ' "ȝe knowe þe cost of þis cace, kepe I no more / To telle yow teneȝ þereof, neuer bot trifel" ' ['You know the nature of this affair, and I do not care to speak to you further about the difficulties involved, it would only be a waste of breath" ', vss 546–57]. As he rides away – 'for ever, as he thought' – his comrades burst out in bitter rejection of the corporate decision in which they had been complicit: '"Who ever knew any king to take such counsel as knights give in quibbling over Christmas games!"' (vss 682–83). The solidarity of the Round Table has been undermined and the sincerity of its members is questioned by alliterative excess: 'Wel much watȝ þe warme water þat waltered of yȝen' (684). Yet when we meet them again these men are to be Gawain's judges!

The poem, whose structure is dominated by numerical patterns, ends with a third scene of communal celebration at Camelot, Gawain's ritual recapitulation of his mission with its overtones of public confession (vss 2489–521). He accuses himself of *vntrawþe*, manifold and fundamental breaches of his professed code governing his relationship to man and God, irremediable and unforgivable. And is answered by communal laughter, comforting words from Arthur and adoption of the penitential symbol of his sin as a badge of honour: 'For þat watȝ accorded þe renoun of þe Rounde Table, / And he honoured þat hit hade, euermore after' (vss 2519–20). The court's response has divided the critics: mature acceptance of human limitations or, in the light of their formal agreement to the original challenge and subsequent criticism of Arthur for its dubious outcome, superficial and escapist? Whatever the individual reader's judgement it must be set against the genre of the poem, only now declared a romance, and the dynastic tradition evoked in identical terms in the opening and closing lines (vss 1–19, 2524–28). The former suggests that a commemorative and celebratory mode has become a critical and questioning one in which the audience is induced by a complex dialectic to determine meaning on a personal basis. The latter implies that in a society rooted in the ambivalent culture of betrayed and fallen Troy, whose history is a record of 'blysse and blunder', the ultimate reality is human fallibility, against which aspiring idealism must appear profoundly comic.

The evolution of medieval romance reflects social and cultural change across the centuries: ideals undermined by shifting values, regal authority resented as tyranny, chivalry distorted by conflicting loyalties. But in English examples the dynastic tradition persists, despite the gradual deterioration of Arthur's iconic status. Malory used it to frame his compendium of chivalric romance, the Alliterative *Morte* as authority for the king's imperial conquests, the Stanzaic for the tragic collapse of the Round Table. The power of his work preserved the dynastic concept through the contempt and neglect of the Enlightenment until the Gothic Revival brought a gloss of historical romance to Victorian imperialism. The willing suspension of disbelief which made Arthur *Bruttene deorling* acceptable to the various races of post-Conquest Britain is still active as an imponderable element in the sporadic attempts of multi-racial, post-imperial Britain to define its national identity.

*King Arthur: From History to Fiction**

DENNIS GREEN

The two terms in my title, history and fiction, constitute a regular contrast in medieval poetics (between *historia* and *fabula*) which is often reflected in vernacular literature. Thus, in Old French the word *fable* can be contrasted with *la plus veraie estoire* which the author is about to begin, just as its antithesis *estoire*, for which truth is claimed, can be further defined by *sans nulle fable*.[1] In his characterisation of three contemporary types of narrative literature Jean Bodel describes the *chanson de geste* (the genre in which he is himself at work) as true (*voir*), as a trustworthy record of the historical past, whilst for him the Arthurian romance, the *matière de Bretagne*, is no more than untrue, merely entertaining.[2] That the same distinction was recognised in Germany is clear at one point in the *Tristan* of Gottfried von Strassburg, where the author refuses to be side-tracked into recounting Tristan's military exploits in Germany while in banishment. He dismisses tales of these adventures as mere fables (*fabelen*), chaff to be cast to the wind, since he has enough on his hands in presenting the truth (*wârheit*).[3] This contrast between fables and truth reflects the rhetorical distinction between *fabula* and *historia*, while the latter concept informs Gottfried's prologue, in which he describes his task as if he were a historian.[4] (Whether he meant this seriously and did not indulge in fables elsewhere when it suited his book is another matter.)

In literary practice, however, the distinction was not always so clear-cut, for there is no shortage of historical works that embody what we would regard as fictional embellishments, while conversely recognisably historical details can be found episodically in clearly fictional works. This blurring of the boundary between history and fiction may justify us in asking whether fiction, in the particular form of the Arthurian romance, may not have arisen from history. A

* This article is an abbreviated adaptation of part of ch. 6 of my book, *The Beginnings of Medieval Romance. Fact and Fiction, 1150–1220*, published by the Cambridge University Press in 2002 and reproduced in this form by permission.

1 *Aiol*, vss 1–9 (cf. Ulrich Mölk, *Französische Literarästhetik des 12. und 13. Jahrhunderts. Prologe/Exkurse/Epiloge* [Tübingen, 1969], p. 4); *L'Histoire ancienne jusqu'à César*, vss 251–59 (no modern edition, but cf. J.E. Singerman, *Under Clouds of Poesy. Poetry and Truth in French and English Reworkings of the Aeneid, 1160–1513* [New York, 1986], p. 154).

2 *Chanson des Saisnes*, vss 6–12 (cf. Mölk, *Literarästhetik*, pp. 6–7).

3 *Tristan*, ed. Peter Ganz (Wiesbaden, 1978), vss 18,467–70.

4 Cf. Mark Chinca, *History, Fiction, Verisimilitude. Studies in the Poetics of Gottfried's 'Tristan'* (London, 1993), pp. 49ff.

similar question has been raised in classical scholarship: did the Greek romance arise from historical writing? It has been suggested that it was within Greek historiography that the fictional contract between author and audience (central to my view of fictionality) was first applied to prose narrative, 'allowing fiction . . . to enter a new form and generate . . . fiction in the form of history'.[5] The impression is thereby created that the action of such works is located in gaps in real history, so that fiction emerges from such gaps or their supposed existence. A comparable suggestion has been made in general terms for French narrative literature of the twelfth century: Wolfzettel says that these narratives arose under the auspices of history and he talks of the transition from chronicle to utopian romance, of the emancipation of the romance from history.[6] It is this transition which I wish to consider in the specific case of literature devoted to King Arthur.

A modern scholar has drawn the cautious conclusion that there 'may have been a supreme British commander of genius in the late fifth century who bore the Roman-derived name of Arthur',[7] but no such caution was felt in the Middle Ages, when he was regarded as an undoubtedly historical figure. Although neither Gildas nor Bede refers to him by name as the leader of the Britons against the Saxons, they both mention the battle of Mount Badon with which he was later regularly associated.[8] Only in the ninth century does the *Historia Brittonum* connect this battle with a *dux bellorum* explicitly called Arthur.[9] This same named historical figure, now elevated to royal rank, recurs in the *Annales Cambriae* in connection with the same battle (given a date, 516), but also with a later battle, likewise dated, against Medraut, known in Arthurian literature as Mordred.[10] With William of Malmesbury this historiographical tradition about Arthur reaches the twelfth century.[11] This leading historian knows also of Arthur's nephew Gawain, but has moreover heard of fabulous tales (*fallaces fabulae*) circulating about Arthur amongst the Celts, which however he turns down in favour of the historical accounts (*veraces historiae*) which this figure richly deserves. William thus draws a line between untrustworthy accretions and the historical nucleus to which they have been attached. Even when Arthur may appear in a negative light, as in his episodic appearance in a number of Celtic saints' lives,[12] this is not detrimental to his historicity, for if the saints were

5 J.R. Morgan, 'Make-believe and Make Believe: The Fictionality of the Greek Romance', in Christopher Gill and T.P. Wiseman, eds, *Lies and Fiction in the Ancient World* (Exeter, 1993), pp. 186–87.

6 Friedrich Wolfzettel, 'Probleme der Geschichtskonstruktion im arthurischen Roman', in Hans-Werner Goetz, ed., *Hochmittelalterliches Geschichtsbewußtsein im Spiegel nicht-historiographischer Quellen* (Berlin, 1990), pp. 341, 345.

7 Kenneth Hurlstone Jackson, 'The Arthur of History', in Roger Sherman Loomis, ed., *Arthurian Literature in the Middle Ages: A Collaborative History* (Oxford, 1959), pp. 10–11.

8 Reto R. Bezzola, *Les Origines et la formation de la littérature courtoise en Occident (500–1200). Deuxième Partie: La société féodale et la transformation de la littérature de cour* (Paris, 1960), p. 529.

9 Bezzola, *Les Origines*, pp. 529–32.

10 Jackson, 'The Arthur of History', pp. 4–5.

11 Cf. Brigitte Burrichter, *Wahrheit und Fiktion. Der Status der Fiktionalität in der Artusliteratur des 12. Jahrhunderts* (Munich, 1996), pp. 34–35.

12 On these saints' lives see now Brynley F. Roberts, '*Culhwch ac Olwen*, the Triads, Saints' Lives', in Rachel Bromwich et al., eds, *The Arthur of the Welsh: The Arthurian Legend in Medieval Welsh Literature* (Cardiff, 1991), pp. 82–85.

regarded as historical figures and their lives as presenting events that had in fact taken place (the medieval saint's legend could be termed *historia*), then the same aura of historicity belongs to the Arthur with whom they had dealings.

This is the historiographical tradition into which Geoffrey of Monmouth, for all his unheard-of novelties and (to us) impossible fabrications, inserts his *Historia regum Britanniae* and to which he claims to conform. Like William of Malmesbury he seeks to join the Anglo-Saxon historical tradition, but also, as one writing for an Anglo-Norman audience, he appears to have been stimulated by Norman historiography.[13] By his very choice of title he ranks himself again with William of Malmesbury, but also with Henry of Huntingdon (both of whom composed a history of the kings of the English), to whom however he adds something new, namely a history of the kings of the Britons, reign by reign in correct chronological sequence and with Arthur as its focus. As a purportedly historical writer Geoffrey also takes care to synchronise details in his history with events in classical, biblical and Christian history.[14]

However, because of what we today recognise as the obvious falsification of history by Geoffrey (amounting to a pseudo-history) his work has at times been called a 'fiction' by some modern scholars. Improperly, I think, because fiction in the technical literary sense (as opposed to everyday usage, meaning 'deceit') presupposes complicity between author and recipients over what they know to be factually untrue. There is no sign that Geoffrey intended his work to be seen through. To be effective, propaganda has to be believed as true, and Geoffrey could not afford the counterproductive luxury of undermining the force of what he was providing for the high-ranking members of Anglo-Norman society to whom he dedicated his history, namely a survey of the past that legitimised their present position in Britain, but also vis-à-vis the French royal house. In the light of this we may take Geoffrey's work not as fiction but, as most of his contemporaries did, as claiming to present history.[15]

Accordingly, Geoffrey was judged in the twelfth century by historiographical criteria, accepted as reliable despite some doubts over details or (rarely) found wanting by historical standards. The main response was therefore to incorporate his *Historia* into wider surveys and to reconcile it with existing authorities, so that from 1200 his work provided the framework for early British history.[16] For example, Giraldus Cambrensis places Geoffrey's Merlin in the company of the biblical prophets and makes use of the *Historia* in his own work.[17] For his sketch

13 Burrichter, *Wahrheit*, p. 29; Francis Ingledew, 'The Book of Troy and the Genealogical Construction of History: The Case of Geoffrey of Monmouth's *Historia regum Britanniae*', *Speculum*, 69 (1994), 665–704, here 681–88.

14 Martin B. Shichtman and Laurie A. Finke, 'Profiting from the Past: History as Symbolic Capital in the *Historia Regum Britanniae*', *Arthurian Literature* XII (1993), 1–35, here 12; Chinca, *History*, p. 30; W.R.J. Barron, Françoise Le Saux and Lesley Johnson, 'Dynastic Chronicles', in W.R.J. Barron, ed., *The Arthur of the English: The Arthurian Legend in Medieval English Life and Literature* (Cardiff, 1999), p. 15.

15 Peter Johanek, 'König Arthur und die Plantagenets. Über den Zusammenhang von Historiographie und höfischer Epik in mittelalterlicher Propaganda', *Frühmittelalterliche Studien*, 21 (1987), 346–89, here 353.

16 R.W. Leckie, *The Passage of Dominion: Geoffrey of Monmouth and the Periodization of Insular History in the Twelfth Century* (Toronto, 1982), pp. 21–22, 27.

17 Ingledew, 'The Book', p. 679; Burrichter, *Wahrheit*, p. 61.

of the British past from Brutus onwards Gervase of Canterbury draws on Geoffrey and shows no awareness of any contradiction between what Geoffrey says of the Britons and what other sources report on the Anglo-Saxons. Both Geoffrey and William of Malmesbury are for him reliable authorities for two different strands of insular history.[18] Matthew Paris inserts a narrative, dependent on Geoffrey, on British history from the fall of Troy and the building of Troja Nova, the capital of Britain, into what is otherwise biblical history, alternating between Jewish and British history and attributing a comparable authority to each.[19]

However compressed and selective these examples of the reception of Geoffrey's work by Latin, largely historiographical scholarship of the twelfth century may be, they show that, although modern scholarship knows it to be fraudulent, Geoffrey's version of the Britons' past was regarded as credible, providing a framework in which the present could be understood, for his Anglo-Norman contemporaries, even for Latin historical scholarship. As a result, the figure of Arthur, as drawn by Geoffrey, was held to be historically true and, despite, say, an odd combat with giants, no figment of the imagination.[20] On the basis of this conviction English kings could henceforth legitimise their political claims to rule over Wales and Scotland.[21]

Where doubts about the truth of what is reported on Arthur come to the surface, it is telling that, with one exception, no mention is made of Geoffrey. This is obviously the case with William of Malmesbury's contrast between a historical Arthur and fabulous tales about him, since William wrote this before Geoffrey. Aelred of Rievaulx talks of made-up fables about Arthur, but his use of the word *vulgo* suggests popular, vernacular stories, not learned Latin historiography.[22] The same applies to Peter of Blois, who refers in a critical tone to the fabulous tales about Arthur, Gawein and Tristan recited by minstrels. The mention of Tristan takes us beyond the context of Geoffrey's *Historia*.[23]

Only one example is known to me from the twelfth century in which doubts are explicitly directed at Geoffrey's work. For William of Newburgh the Britons' idea that Arthur would return from Avalon was mere superstition (and Geoffrey could not be faulted on that score), but he goes further in denigrating the work as *fabula* and *figmenta*, and its author as a *fabulator*.[24] Despite his use of these terms this does not mean that the historian William is accusing Geoffrey of writing fiction (in the technical sense), since he is still judging him by the yardstick of historiography. Geoffrey is therefore at fault for including events attested in no other historical source, for violating established chronology, for bringing disgrace to history by putting forward British fables in Latin.[25] William

18 Leckie, *The Passage*, pp. 93–95.
19 Ingledew, 'The Book', pp. 696–98; Burrichter, *Wahrheit*, p. 61.
20 Johanek, 'König Arthur', p. 356.
21 Johanek, 'König Arthur', pp. 360–66.
22 Johanek, 'König Arthur', p. 378, n. 166.
23 Johanek, 'König Arthur', p. 378, n. 167.
24 *Historia rerum Anglicarum*, ed. R. Howlett (London, 1884), pp. 11, 12–13, 16, 18. Cf. Leckie, *The Passage*, p. 25.
25 Johanek, 'König Arthur', p. 377; Burrichter, *Wahrheit*, p. 62; Siân Echard, *Arthurian Narrative in the Latin Tradition* (Cambridge, 1988), pp. 75–79.

sums up his criticism by saying that Geoffrey raved against or deviated from the truth of history *(contra fidem historicae veritatis deliravit)*.[26]

The same conviction that Geoffrey's work was historiography (without the criticism of his historical ability voiced by William of Newburgh) underlies the first two translations of the *Historia* into the vernacular, by Gaimar and by Wace, both of whom see their versions as likewise belonging to historical writing. We know of two histories written by Gaimar in Anglo-Norman: a history of the English (based on the *Anglo-Saxon Chronicle*) and a history of the Britons, which has not survived, but was almost certainly translated from Geoffrey of Monmouth.[27] Together these two works constitute the first examples of vernacular historiography, keyed to the requirements of Anglo-Normans of the second generation, wishing to integrate themselves historically into their new land.[28] What characterises Gaimar's historical writing in his surviving work is therefore likely to be as true of the work that we have lost. He uses historiographical terms like *estoire* and *geste* to designate his own writing, he gives the dates when many of the events occurred, and takes care to comment on the sources he has consulted, investing his version with the reliability of verifiable authorities.[29] All this enables him to argue at the close of the history of the English that it presents historical truth (neither a lie nor a fable nor a dream, but drawn from true history),[30] a claim which can just as well be applied to his history of the Britons. If so, Gaimar differs markedly from William of Newburgh and aligns himself with those Latin writers of his day who accepted the outlines of Geoffrey's work as historically true.

Geoffrey's *Historia* was also the principal source for the *Roman de Brut* by Wace. He puts it forward at the start as a translation of what he regarded as a historical text, for this enables Wace to claim the truth of his own version.[31] He also follows his source and conforms to historiographical practice in presenting events in their correct chronological sequence (in the *ordo naturalis*) and agrees with Geoffrey again in synchronising events in his text with historical ones in biblical and classical antiquity.[32] In another work of his (the *Roman de Rou*, a history of the Normans) Wace distances himself from the fabulous accounts of

26 *Historia rerum Anglicarum*, p. 13.

27 Ian Short, 'Gaimar et les débuts de l'historiographie en langue française', in Danielle Buschinger, ed., *Chroniques nationales et chroniques universelles* (Göppingen, 1995), pp. 155–63; also Short, 'Gaimar's Epilogue and Geoffrey of Monmouth's *liber vetustissimus*', *Speculum*, 69 (1994), 323–43; D.R. Howlett 'The Literary Context of Geoffrey of Monmouth: An Essay on the Fabrication of Sources', *Arthuriana*, 5 (1995), 25–69, here 47–55; Peter Damian-Grint, *The New Historians of the Twelfth-Century Renaissance. Authorising History in the Vernacular Revolution* (Woodbridge, 1999), pp. 50–51.

28 Short, 'Gaimar's Epilogue', pp. 323–24.

29 Damian-Grint, *The New Historians*, pp. 255–56, 258; Burrichter, *Wahrheit*, pp. 72, 73; Damian-Grint, ' "*Estoire*" as Word and Genre: Meaning and Literary Usage in the Twelfth Century', *Medium Aevum*, 66 (1977), 189–206, here 191.

30 *L'Estoire des Engleis*, ed. A. Bell (Oxford, 1960), Appendix, vs. 15, p. 207.

31 Wace, *Roman de Brut*, ed. Judith Weiss (Exeter, 1999), vss 7–8.

32 Wace, *Brut*, vss 1–8. Cf. Burrichter, *Wahrheit*, pp. 119–22, Penny Eley, 'How Long is a Trojan War? Aspects of Time in the *Roman de Troie* and its Sources', in *Shifts and Transpositions in Medieval Narrative: A Festschrift for Dr. Elspeth Kennedy*, ed. Karen Pratt et al. (Cambridge, 1994), pp. 139–50, here 144–45.

mere *ioculatores*, thereby claiming the truth for himself.[33] He proceeds similarly in the *Roman de Brut*, occasionally voicing criticism of his sources, especially the tales that cluster around Arthur and his final disappearance.[34] Like William of Malmesbury he therefore distinguishes between the historical figure and the *fabulae* he has attracted. Presumably as a historian Wace was commissioned to write both his histories by Henry II so that past glory, incorporated in the figure of Arthur, was reflected in the Anglo-Norman present.[35] Even the embellished descriptions of courtly splendour in the twelve-year period of Arthurian peace (in which Wace largely goes beyond Geoffrey) serve a topical purpose, for the cultural leadership of Henry II's court was made possible, as it was for Arthur, by a period of peace (at the start of the king's reign).[36] Wace's courtly embellishments, although marking a pronounced change of emphasis from Geoffrey, are no mere fanciful touches grafted on history, for they serve as links between past and present. They concern episodic descriptions, they do not amount to a fictional refashioning of the course of the narrative.

With all this I seem to have boxed myself into a corner, for the more one stresses the historicity of Arthurian material, as it was seen in the twelfth century, the more difficult it becomes to imagine what kind of bridge led from such historical to fictional writing. We shall see that the adventures of the Round Table were later found a home in the twelve-year period of peace in Arthur's campaigning, but this gap was not filled by Geoffrey with any account of these adventures. Unintentionally he thereby provided an opportunity for later fiction, but not the fictional exploits themselves.

It might seem anomalous, in taking a first step across the bridge between historical and fictional writing, to revert to Wace in view of what I have just said of him. As a historian he did not practise fiction himself, as little as had Geoffrey of Monmouth, but at least Wace was aware of it in connection with Arthur, placing its genesis within his historical narrative. The stories about Arthur, dismissed by him as fables, neither true nor untrue, are located by him in the twelve-year period of peace which interrupts the widespread campaigning he takes over from Geoffrey's *Historia*, where they remained unexploited because an eventless period was of no interest to a medieval historian.[37] Whereas Geoffrey had had the figure of Cador speak up critically against the debilitating effects of too long a period of peace, Wace changes the emphasis by having Gauvain voice his disagreement with Cador in favour of the delights of peace, thereby granting a positive role to this interval within war-making.[38] For Gauvain this is a period in which knights are encouraged by love to accomplish individual adventures (by contrast with the collective wars of conquest

33 Wace, *Roman de Rou*, ed. A.J. Holden (Paris, 1970–73), vss 1355, 1371–72.

34 *Roman de Brut*, vss 13,275–84. Cf. Burrichter, *Wahrheit*, pp. 121–22, 125–26.

35 Burrichter, *Wahrheit*, pp. 130–31, but also 91–92; Barron, Le Saux and Johnson, 'Dynastic Chronicles', p. 18.

36 Burrichter, *Wahrheit*, pp. 90, 95–96.

37 *Roman de Brut*, vss 9787–98 (cf. Geoffrey of Monmouth, *Historia Regum Britannie*, ed. Neil Wright [Cambridge, 1984], p. 107). See also Burrichter, *Wahrheit*, pp. 96–99; Ad Putter, 'Finding Time for Romance: Mediaeval Arthurian Literary History', *Medium Aevum*, 63 (1994), 1–16.

38 Vss 10,765–72.

conducted by Arthur) on behalf of their ladies and in which Arthur's court is a focus for refined entertainment, including the recital of fables.[39] Both these adventures and the tales told about them are regarded by Wace as being non-historical, so that he omits them from his account while making it clear that he is referring to other works known, so he can assume, to his audience, directly or indirectly.[40] In other words, Wace recognises the existence of Arthurian fables without indulging in them himself, he places them chronologically in this pause in Geoffrey's *Historia* and provides a historiographical seedbed from which a fully developed Arthurian fiction sprang.

Although Wace provides a first link between Geoffrey's history and Arthurian fiction, it was only by Chrétien de Troyes that the decisive step was taken. First negatively, in that the 'historical' conquests of Arthur throughout Europe, of far greater importance to Geoffrey and Wace than any peaceful interlude, fade into the background with Chrétien and give way to a fictional depiction of individual adventures within the period of peace that had earlier been passed over. But also positively, since the *conteürs* rejected by Wace may also be criticised by Chrétien,[41] who is however ready to make use of their narrative material. He sees in the gap left by Wace an opportunity to create a fictional realm in which, 'freed from the constraints of history, he could address the concerns that occupied him and his audience'.[42] He does this by ignoring Wace's historical framework and by filling a gap in it with the *fabulae* dismissed by the historian. That these *fabulae* belong to this peaceful interlude was also recognised by the scribe of a thirteenth-century manuscript, who interrupts the *Roman de Brut* precisely at this point in order to insert Chrétien's romances before continuing his copying of Wace's text.[43] This scribe may 'historicise' Chrétien by placing his romances in their correct chronological position in a collective manuscript that runs sequentially from the *Roman de Troie* and the *Roman d'Enéas* through to the *Roman de Brut*, but I should hesitate to attribute this historicising concern to Chrétien as well. This scribe, writing at a time when historical truth was beginning to play a larger role than fictional truth, goes against Wace's view that these adventures are mere fables, but also against Chrétien's conception of non-historical literary fiction. But at least he confirms for us that it was at this point in Arthur's historical career, as Wace had presented it, that Chrétien's fiction originated.

To illustrate how Chrétien establishes the status of his fictional writing by explicitly differentiating it from historical writing I must confine myself to one example, from his *Yvain*. At a crucial opening point the author polemicises, on

39 Vss 10,749–50, 10,771–72 (where, following I.D.O. Arnold and M.M. Pelan, *La Partie arthurienne du Roman de Brut* [Paris, 1962], I read *fables* instead of *tables*).

40 Burrichter, *Wahrheit*, p. 127 and n. 2.

41 *Roman de Brut*, vss 9795–98; Chrétien de Troyes, *Erec*, ed. Wendelin Foerster (Halle, 1934), vss 20–22.

42 Putter, 'Finding Time', p. 5.

43 On the manuscript Bibl. nat. fr. 1450 see Lori Walters, 'Le Rôle du scribe dans l'organisation des manuscrits des romans de Chrétien de Troyes', *Romania*, 106 (1985), 303–25; Sylvia Huot, *From Song to Book. The Poetics of Writing in Old French Lyric and Lyrical Narrative Poetry* (Ithaca, 1987), pp. 27–32; Rosemary Morris 'Aspects of Time and Place in the French Arthurian Verse Romances', *French Studies*, 42 (1988), 257–77; Putter, 'Finding Time', pp. 5–9.

behalf of fictional writing, against the established view that the truth-claim of the historian rested on his status as an eyewitness of the events he reported. (In the Middle Ages this view went back to Isidore of Seville and informed, for example, the preference given to Dares rather than to Homer because of the former's claim to have participated in the Trojan War himself, as a kind of classical war-reporter.)[44] In this episode from *Yvain* Chrétien goes to work by means of intertextuality, referring to a detail in the *Roman de Rou* by Wace, *the* vernacular historian from whom Chrétien, in the act of launching Arthurian fiction, would most obviously have to distance himself. In his history of the Normans Wace had reported on the fables of the Bretons concerning a magic spring in the forest of Broceliande and had gone there to check their truthfulness in person, as an eyewitness.[45] He criticises himself for foolishly even entertaining the belief that these fables might conceivably be true, but thereby in reality he strengthens his claim to be a reliable historian, checking his sources and no longer a mere dupe of fables.[46] This is taken up, with verbal echoes, by Chrétien at the point when the Arthurian knight Calogrenant in his turn gives an account of his visit to a magic spring at Broceliande, which he has likewise seen for himself, together with the marvels that in his case did take place (disastrously for him, as it turned out).[47] The implication is that this account of an eyewitness, however fabulous, should be accepted as the truth. The wording with which Calogrenant upholds his truthfulness as an eyewitness (he has no intention of serving up talk of dreams or fables or lies, as many others have done, but will report on what he saw for himself)[48] is in fact the terminology with which historians such as William of Malmesbury, William of Newburgh and Aelred of Rievaulx conventionally established their reliability.[49] Behind the figure of Calogrenant, of course, there stands the author Chrétien who, in all this, as a writer of fiction rather than history, questions the eyewitness truth-claims of historiography. In having Calogrenant, in a work of fiction, contradict Wace's report on the non-marvellous nature of Broceliande Chrétien is appropriating the truth-claims of history for his own fable, thereby playing havoc with the conventional rhetorical distinction between *historia* and *fabula*.

After this lengthy detour through England and France I return to Germany, in the first place to the adaptation of Chrétien's romance by Hartmann von Aue in his *Iwein*. The German author was unable to make use of the example from the French work we have just looked at, for the simple reason that, since there

44 D.H. Green. *Medieval Listening and Reading. The Primary Reception of German Literature 800–1300* (Cambridge, 1994), pp. 237–38 (where on p. 238 'Dares' is to be read for 'Darius'!).

45 Vss 6374–420.

46 On the historian as an eyewitness in twelfth-century historical writing see Damian-Grint, *The New Historians*, pp. 68–84.

47 *Yvain*, ed. Wendelin Foerster (Halle, 1926), vss 175–580. On the intertextual connections between the passages in *Yvain* and the *Roman de Rou* see A. Wolf, '*Fol i allai – fol m'en revinc!* Der Roman vom Löwenritter zwischen *mançonge* und *maere*', in *Uf der mâze Pfat: Festschrift für Werner Hoffmann*, ed. Waltraud Fritsch-Rössler (Göppingen, 1991), pp. 205–25; Green, *Medieval Listening*, pp. 254–55.

48 Vss 171–74.

49 Green, *Medieval Listening*, p. 251. See also, in more general terms, Damian-Grint, *The New Historians*, pp. 114–17.

was no adaptation of the *Roman de Rou* in German, no intertextual play was possible. However, independently of Chrétien, Hartmann also makes clear the distinction between history and his fiction in the immediately following episode, in Iwein's repetition of Kalogreant's adventure at the spring. The episode may be a different one, but the use made of it by Hartmann is the same as with Chrétien: fiction is pointedly set against the truth-claim of the historian *qua* eyewitness.[50] In the combat between Iwein and Ascalon at the spring the narrator argues that he is unable to describe the encounter in detail because Iwein, the solitary survivor, was too well-bred to have boasted of his victory and also because no one else was present who could have acted as an eyewitness informant.[51] By stressing this absence of an eyewitness fully three times Hartmann brings it home how much importance he attaches to a detail irrelevant to the course of the action. The German author may well have had other reasons for not dwelling further on this encounter, but by making his point about eyewitnesses so emphatically he shows his deliberate distance from Isidore of Seville's definition of the historian as someone who had been present and seen for himself what was to be written up.[52] In thus rejecting any possible claim for historical veracity in this episode (could it not apply to other episodes as well?) Hartmann underlines the fictional nature of his work.

That this was no isolated position with the German author (perhaps occasioned by his wish to find a substitute for his inability to follow Chrétien's example with Calogrenant) can be shown from Hartmann's *Erec* where, independently of Chrétien, he again parodies eyewitness truth-claims for fictional purposes. In replying to an imaginary question about the dress worn by Mabonagrin's mistress he says that he did not see the dress himself because he never went there.[53] He then playfully refers his questioner to the lady's chamberlain for further details, as if self-referential confirmation from within a fiction enjoyed the same truth-status as the external referentiality of historical writing.

My other German example I take from the *Tristan* of Gottfried von Strassburg, admittedly no Arthurian romance but certainly belonging to the *matière de Bretagne*. I mentioned earlier that Gottfried presented his task in the prologue as if it were that of a historian. In arguing for the historical authenticity of his source, Thomas of Britain, whose version he claims to follow in place of any other Gottfried claims the same for his own version.[54] By suggesting historical sources for the Tristan story Gottfried implies that its figures existed in historical reality.[55] In opening the prologue with the need for remembrance he is employing a *topos* of historical writing (as, for example, at the beginning of the *Roman de Troie*),[56] but this dimension can also be insinuated by verbal details that must have struck a German audience the more forcibly for being new

50 Green, *Medieval Listening*, p. 256.
51 *Iwein*, ed. G.F. Benecke, K. Lachmann and L.Wolff (Berlin, 1968), vss 1032–34, 1035, 1068–70.
52 *Etymologiae*, ed. W.M. Lindsay (Oxford, 1910), I, p. 41.
53 *Erec*, ed. Albert Leitzmann (Tübingen, 1963), vss 8946–49.
54 *Tristan*, vss 146–54.
55 Chinca, *History*, p. 53.
56 Benoît de Sainte-Maure, *Roman de Troie*, ed. L. Constans (Paris, 1904ff.), vss 1–24. Cf. also Chinca, *History*, pp. 53–56.

coinages. Gottfried is the first to use in German such eminently historiographical terms as *istôrje* and *geste*: scattered throughout his work and referring to the background of the love-story, they suggest that this story is embedded in history.[57]

Gottfried's self-presentation as a *historiographus* is, however, only part of the picture, for more recently there has been talk of his 'imaginary historicity', of an appearance of being historical which is in fact a rhetorical ploy suggesting that *res fictae* are *res gestae*.[58] We may ask in his case what William of Malmesbury asked of the Arthurian material: whether the presence in a work of figures held to be historical makes of it a historical work. The implication that Tristan and Isold existed in historical time does not mean that the story based on them is historically true.[59] Gottfried's role as a critical historian rejecting fabulous elements in favour of the truth can be seen as a pose when we take into account other occasions where he is prepared to adopt fabulous, implausible details.[60] These details reveal that his historical stance is not an end in itself and that he makes use of history without historiographic intentions. For Gottfried the past is a point of departure for telling a love-story, not for reconstructing history.[61]

Like Chrétien and Hartmann, Gottfried is prepared to undermine the eyewitness truth-claim in order to differentiate his fictional from historical writing. At the close of his description of the love-grotto he maintains the truth of what he has said ('I know this to be so, because I was there'), a formulation with the same force of eyewitness attestation as Kalogreant's in *Iwein* ('It happened to me, therefore it is true').[62] The passage in *Tristan* has therefore been regarded as an attestation of what has been witnessed, conforming to Isidore's definition of historical writing.[63] This cannot be so, since the narrator also adds that he has known the grotto since his eleventh year even though he has never been to Cornwall.[64] This addition transposes the truth-affirmation from the sphere of historical, factual eyewitness testimony to that of the personal experience of love, meant figuratively[65] and divorced from time (history) as well as space (Cornwall). Moreover, we could apply here, too, what was true of Hartmann's Kalogreant. If in a written work of literature the narrator is a fictional figure,

57 On *istôrje* see Joachim Knape, *Historie in Mittelalter und Neuzeit. Begriffs- und gattungsgeschichtliche Untersuchungen im interdisziplinären Kontext* (Baden-Baden, 1984), pp. 110–34, and on the use of *geste* in Anglo-Norman historiography see Damian-Grint, *The New Historians*, pp. 221–25.

58 Karl Bertau, *Deutsche Literatur im europäischen Mittelalter, Band 1: 800–1197* (Munich, 1972), pp. 920–21; Fritz Peter Knapp, *Historie und Fiktion in der mittelalterlichen Gattungspoetik. Sieben Studien und ein Nachwort* (Heidelberg, 1997), p. 32; Samuel Jaffe, 'Gottfried von Strassburg and the rhetoric of history', in J.J. Murphy, ed., *Medieval Eloquence. Studies in the Theory and Practice of Medieval Rhetoric* (Berkeley, 1978), p. 302 ('historicizing posture'); Winfried Christ, *Rhetorik und Roman. Untersuchungen zu Gottfrieds von Straßburg 'Tristan und Isold'* (Meisenheim, 1977), p. 297 ('nur als Haltung'); Chinca, *History*, p. 89 ('allegedly historical').

59 Chinca, *History*, pp. 46–47.

60 Chinca, *History*, pp. 68–69.

61 Chinca, *History*, pp. 57, 58.

62 *Tristan*, vs. 17,104; *Iwein*, vs. 259.

63 Cf. the note to vs. 17,142 in Ganz's edition of *Tristan*, II, p. 330.

64 Vss 17,140–42.

65 Christ, *Rhetorik*, p. 314, interprets vs. 17,140 (*ich hân die fossiure erkant*) as meaning 'Ich kenne mich in der Liebe aus.'

then Gottfried's first-person narratorial *ich* is as fictional as Kalogreant. But only the witness standing outside a narrative can give historical testimony to its truth, its agreement with external reality, whereas this is denied anyone, be he Gottfried's narrator or Hartmann's Kalogreant, who is part of the fiction himself. With Gottfried, as with Chrétien and Hartmann, the historiographer's eyewitness gives way to a fictional creation.

In conclusion, considering Geoffrey, Wace and Chrétien (together with his German colleagues) in this light opens up a progressive move away from *historia* towards *fabula.* Geoffrey mentions a period of peace in the middle of a series of historical campaigns but, apart from the occasional reference to Arthur's court, this period is not treated in any detail. In his likewise historical work Wace also presents this period as an interval within Arthur's wars of conquest, but with noticeably more detail (the Round Table, court life more fully treated, the conjunction of love and chivalry, the fables dealing with this period, even if they are rejected as untruthful). Finally, with Chrétien we find ourselves exclusively within the period of peace, with no treatment at all of the framing campaigns and no depiction of Arthur as *dux bellorum.* What is left in Chrétien's romances corresponds to the gap in Geoffrey's account, but filled with the adventures that Geoffrey had not mentioned and Wace had rejected. With Chrétien we have made the move from the realm of history to that of fictional adventures.

Welsh Tradition in Calais: Elis Gruffydd and his Biography of King Arthur[1]

CERIDWEN LLOYD-MORGAN

Elis Gruffydd's Chronicle provides one of the most important Welsh Arthurian sources of the sixteenth century, but the lack of any published edition of his work has meant that it is still little known, even to those who can read Welsh.[2] This essay will concentrate on one small part of it which provides an account of the life and deeds of king Arthur, establishing which sources were used and how these were brought together to form a coherent narrative. The chronicler's depiction of Arthur and his attitude to him will be analysed and set in their contemporary context. First, however, a brief sketch of Elis Gruffydd's own career will be necessary, as his work cannot be divorced from the trajectory of his life.

He was born about 1490 at Gronant Uchaf in Flintshire, north-east Wales, a younger son of an impecunious cadet branch of a gentry family. Forced to work for his living, like many young Welshmen at this period he crossed the border and joined the English army. He spent most of the next eight years fighting on the continent and by around 1518 he was in Calais. It was most probably at this time that he met Sir Robert Wingfield, who took Elis Gruffydd into his employment. He may have been looking for someone with Elis's skills and experience, but the very distant family connections – both men were related to the Mostyn and Audley families – were perhaps an additional factor in his choice. Elis Gruffydd accompanied his new master on various diplomatic missions abroad, notably in France, which presumably accounts for his excellent command of French and familiarity with the culture and history of that country. Between 1524 and 1529, however, he was in London, looking after Sir Robert Wingfield's house in London. It was during those years that he worked on his earliest known manuscript, now Cardiff, Central Library, MS 3.4, a miscellany of Welsh

1 An earlier version of this paper was published as 'Portread Elis Gruffydd o'r Brenin Arthur' in *Ysgrifau Beirniadol* xxiii, ed. J.E. Caerwyn Williams (Denbigh, 1997), pp. 118–32.

2 A number of short extracts have been published during the last hundred years, and I am currently preparing an edition of the Arthurian section of the Chronicle. The most recent general survey of Elis Gruffydd's life and work is Ceridwen Lloyd-Morgan, 'Elis Gruffydd a thraddodiad Cymraeg Calais a Chlwyd', *Cof Cenedl*, 11 (1996), 29–58; for a study of the political and intellectual context of his Chronicle, see Jerry Hunter, *Soffestri'r Saeson. Hanesyddiaeth a hunaniaeth yn Oes y Tuduriaid* (Cardiff, 2000). For general accounts in English see Thomas Jones, 'A Welsh Chronicler in Tudor England', *Welsh History Review*, 1 (1960), 1–17; and Prys Morgan, 'Elis Gruffudd of Gronant – Tudor chronicler extraordinary', *Journal of the Flintshire Historical Society*, 25 (1971–72), 9–20.

poetry and traditional lore, completed in 1527.[3] His interest in Arthurian material is already reflected in this early project, for he included in the volume a version of the series of triads known as the *Pedwar Marchog a farnwyd yn gadarnaf* (the twenty-four knights judged to be the strongest).[4] Already he was showing himself to be a scholar as well as a man of action. From 1530 onwards, Elis Gruffydd was based in Calais, where Sir Robert Wingfield had been deputy-governor since 1526, and where the Welshman formed part of the royal retinue. From then on legal documents refer to him as 'the soldier of Calais', an epithet which he himself adopted. By January 1548/9 he had completed another manuscript compilation, now Aberystwyth, National Library of Wales, MS Cwrtmawr 1, containing his own translations into Welsh of five medical texts, working from French, English and Latin texts.[5]

He started writing the Chronicle almost immediately afterwards, though he must have been preparing the work for some years previously. He took as his model the medieval chronicle of the Six Ages, tracing the history of the known world from Creation to the author's own day. The final section recounts events of 1552 and we may suppose that he brought his work to an end soon afterwards. It is not known whether he lived on to witness or to survive the fall of Calais in 1558. The Chronicle is known from the unique holograph manuscript, now forming four substantial codices, National Library of Wales MSS NLW 5276Di–ii, covering the years from Creation until 1066, and NLW 3054Di–ii (*olim* Mostyn 158), which takes the narrative from the Norman Conquest until 1552. The biography of Arthur occupies MS NLW 5276Dii, fols 321r–42r. At least one leaf has been lost between fols 340 and 341, but most fortunately a later transcript of this section survives, in MS NLW 6209E (pp. 84–87) where Dafydd Parry (?1682–1714), assistant to the notable antiquarian and curator of the Ashmolean Museum, Edward Lhuyd, copied the missing portion of text from an earlier transcript, now lost, in the hand of one of the most notable collectors and copyists of the early modern period, John Jones (b. *c.* 1578x1583, d. ?1658) of Gellilyfdy in Flintshire. Despite Parry's notorious predilection for strong drink, which was to cause his untimely death, he seems to have been an accurate transcriber, judging by comparison of his work with the original manuscript in the hand of Elis Gruffydd.

Within his chosen framework of the *Sex Aetates Mundi*, Elis Gruffydd places Arthur's career in the Sixth Age, that which begins with the birth of Christ. The main influence on this section of his Chronicle was undoubtedly Geoffrey of Monmouth's *Historia Regum Britanniae*, on which he sometimes drew directly,

3 See description in J. Gwenogvryn Evans, *Reports on Manuscripts in the Welsh Language* (London, 1898–1910), I, p. 99, where it is listed as MS Cardiff 5. Elis Gruffydd notes on fol. 225: 'Elis Gruffydd . . . ai ysgrivenodd anno miiii, xxvij ynn llundain ymhalas Sir Robert Wyng[field] yn yr amser hwnw depeiti ynghaleis' (Elis Gruffydd . . . wrote this in the year 1427 in London in the mansion of Sir Robert Wingfield who was at that time deputy in Calais).

4 Edited by Peter C. Bartrum in *Études celtiques*, 12 (1968–69), 157–94.

5 See Delwyn Tibbott, 'Llawysgrif Cwrtmawr I', *National Library of Wales Journal*, 11 (1960), 276–83; S. Minwel Tibbott, *Castell yr Iechyd gan Elis Gruffydd* (Cardiff, 1969); and Mari Davies Evans, 'Astudiaeth o gyfieithiad Ellis [*sic*] Gruffydd o rannau o "The Boke of Children" ac o "The Regiment of Life" ' (unpublished MA dissertation, University of Wales [Aberystwyth], 1968).

but he also made considerable use of translations and adaptations into other languages, notably English and French. The story of Arthur is thus set in the familiar context of the flight of Brutus after the fall of Troy and the establishment of a new dynasty and a new nation in Britain, with Arthur's reign providing the glorious high point of this history, to be followed only by decline and disappointment.

Elis Gruffydd follows Geoffrey in his account of the reign of Arthur's father, Uthyr Pendragon, including the account of the conception of Arthur. But if Geoffrey provided the framework, much of the detail is derived from other texts, as we shall see. It is not always easy to identify the precise sources, however, because the chronicler tends to rephrase or to condense, an indication that he was working from notes, as we shall see below. Since he is often translating into Welsh from English, French or Latin, many significant textual variants disappear, and it is usually only when there are major differences in the account of a particular event that it is possible to identify his source with any confidence. It can be impossible to tell which of two or three possible sources he was using at a given point.

I take as the starting-point of the Arthurian section the feast held at Caer Ludd (London) to celebrate the coronation of Uthyr Pendragon, during which Uthyr falls in love with Eigyr, wife of Gwrliws, earl of Cornwall. This is followed by the well-known account of Uthyr, who has taken on the appearance of Gwrliws, visiting Eigyr at Tintagel castle, impregnating her whilst Gwrliws meets his death on the battlefield. Uthyr and Eigyr subsequently marry, but native Welsh tradition quickly asserts itself when Arthur is born for he is fostered with Cynnydd Cain Farfog. This section is derived mainly from *The Chronicles of England*, the English adaptation of Geoffrey's *Historia* published by William Caxton in 1480. But Elis Gruffydd has also drawn on *Y Pedwar Marchog a farnwyd yn gadarnaf*, a text which, as we have seen, he had himself copied in 1527, and also on the Welsh account of the birth of Arthur known to us from National Library of Wales, MS NLW 1A (*olim* Llanstephan 201), copied in the second half of the fifteenth century, and from a variant text copied in National Library of Wales, MS Peniarth 215B by John Jones of Gellilyfdy, completed in 1611.[6] After a brief account of Uthyr's final years and a brief excursus into the history of the Franks, Elis returns to his Arthurian narrative with the sudden death of Uthyr in suspicious circumstances and the problem of the succession. At this point the chronicler introduces the tale of the sword in the stone, following closely the account in MS NLW 1A, which itself has undergone some influence from the French *Prose Merlin*.

After Arthur's accession to the throne, he sets off on campaign in north Britain, at which point Elis Gruffydd incorporates in his narrative part of *Darogan yr Olew Bendigaid* (the prophecy of the holy oil), an early fifteenth-century Welsh prose tale which combines Arthurian material of Welsh, Latin and French origin, with the story of Thomas Becket and the ampoule of holy oil

6 For an edition of the Llanstephan version, see J.H. Davies, 'A Welsh Version of the Birth of Arthur', *Y Cymmrodor*, 24 (1913), 247–64; I hope to publish the Peniarth 215B text together with a discussion of the sources of both versions.

used to anoint the kings of France.[7] Here the chronicler jettisons the Becket material in order to focus entirely on Arthur, describing how an angel appears to archbishop Dyfrig (Dubricius) and orders him to consecrate Arthur as king by anointing him with the holy oil that was brought to Britain by Joseph son of Joseph of Arimathea, whilst the Virgin Mary presents Arthur with a golden cross, a detail used to explain Arthur's heraldic arms, which included a depiction of the Virgin holding her child, a tradition echoing the statement in the ninth-century *Historia Brittonum* that at one of his battles Arthur carried an image of the Virgin on his shoulders. The tradition that this became part of his heraldic arms was well-established amongst the Welsh long before Elis Gruffydd's time and was certainly current in the fourteenth and fifteenth centuries, being mentioned, for example, in the *Llyfr Arfau*, a Middle Welsh heraldic treatise attributed to one Sion Trefor (John Trevor).[8] It is worth noting that this text may be of north-eastern provenance. For the details of Arthur's coronation, however, Elis Gruffydd chooses an English rather than a Welsh source, the *New Chronicles of England and France* composed by Robert Fabian in 1504 and printed in 1516.[9] Fabian was himself drawing on several earlier chronicles, most notably Ranulf Higden's *Polychronicon*, but Elis Gruffydd remains sufficiently close to Fabian's sometimes idiosyncratic text for us to identify Fabian rather than Higden as his source.

Immediately after his coronation Arthur has to go to war against Colgrin and the Scots, who are supported by Sieldrig, king of Germany. Hywel, king of Llydaw (Brittany), comes to Arthur's assistance, and after a series of battles they succeed in vanquishing the enemy alliance, which includes Gwilmor, king of the Irish. Here the chronicler's debt is to Geoffrey of Monmouth, or more particularly Caxton's version of his account, but some details derive from another text, the Anglo-Norman *Roman de Brut* of Wace. But we soon return to indigenous Welsh traditions for the account of Arthur's marriage to Gwenhwyfar, who is presented as the daughter of Gogran Gawr (Gogran the giant).[10] Robert Fabian was the source for the list of Arthur's twelve major battles, as indeed for the next section, where Serdickws, king of the West Saxons, makes a treaty with Arthur after a war between them.

At this point Elis Gruffydd incorporated into his narrative a story that he must undoubtedly have acquired from oral tradition, the tale of Huail ap Caw.[11]

7 For texts and discussion see R. Wallis Evans, '*Darogan yr Olew Bendigaid* a *Hystdori yr Olew Bendigaid*', *Llên Cymru*, 14 (1981–82), 86–91, and Ceridwen Lloyd-Morgan, '*Darogan yr Olew Bendigaid*: chwedl o'r bymthegfed ganrif', *Llên Cymru*, 14 (1981–82), 64–85; see also Ceridwen Lloyd-Morgan, 'Prophecy and Welsh Nationhood in the Fifteenth Century', *Transactions of the Honourable Society of Cymmrodorion 1985*, 9–26.

8 *Medieval Heraldry. Some Fourteenth-Century Heraldic Works*, ed. by Evan J. Jones (Cardiff, 1943), pp. 2–94, especially pp. 86–89.

9 Ed. Henry Ellis (London, 1911).

10 For Welsh traditions of Gwenhwyfar, see *Trioedd Ynys Prydein*, ed. by Rachel Bromwich (2nd edn, Cardiff, 1978), pp. 363–64, 380–85, 551–52, 553.

11 For text and discussion, see Thomas Jones, 'Chwedl Huail ap Caw ac Arthur', in *Astudiaethau Amrywiol a gyflwynir i Syr Thomas Parry-Williams*, ed. Thomas Jones (Cardiff, 1968), pp. 48–66. For discussion of Elis Gruffydd's use of oral traditions, see Ceridwen Lloyd-Morgan, 'Oral et écrit dans la chronique d'Elis Gruffydd', *Kreiz 5, Études sur la Bretagne et les Pays Celtiques* (1996), 179–86.

This is an onomastic tale, explaining the name of Maen Huail (Huail's stone) which is still to be seen today in the centre of the town of Rhuthun in Denbighshire. The story relates how Arthur and Huail go drinking and womanising together but fall out and after Huail betrays Arthur, who has dressed as a woman in order to gain access to a particular young woman, Arthur has him beheaded on Maen Huail. From this traditional story, firmly localised in north-east Wales, the chronicler switches suddenly to a written source, this time to a French romance of the early thirteenth century, the *Prose Lancelot*. Elis Gruffydd refers to the romance as 'Ysdoria y Sang Reial' (the history of the holy grail), presumably because he viewed the *Lancelot* in the context of the Vulgate Cycle where the grail story is part and parcel of the history of the development and eventual decline of the Arthurian court. There can be no doubt that the *Prose Lancelot* was the source for the account of Arthur's strange dream that he had lost his hair, his fingers and toes.[12] After failing to gain any satisfactory explanation for this dream from the most learned men in the kingdom, Arthur goes hunting, and at this point the narrative returns to Welsh oral tradition as the king goes hunting in Denbighshire. What follows bears all the hallmarks of a folk-tale. Arthur is captured, imprisoned and humiliated by a family of giants and it is only after he has succeeded in a test, where he has to pronounce 'tri gair gwir'' [three true words] that he is finally released and able to return to his court. Inevitably this tale, like that of Huail ap Caw, is very different in character to those episodes in the Chronicle which can be shown to derive from specific, non-Welsh, written sources, but Elis Gruffydd has taken great pains to incorporate it neatly into the narrative by providing an explanation for it in terms echoing exactly the details of Arthur's dream.

After this excursus, Elis Gruffydd returns to the *Prose Lancelot* once more for the next episodes, where a hermit comes to Arthur's court to provide a different exegesis of the dream, and hostilities begin against a new enemy, king Gawns. With the help of his knight Lansilott, Arthur gains another victory, and Gawns not only becomes an ally but is also made a knight of the Round Table. This provides the context for an account of how the rules for the behaviour of the Round Table knights were drawn up, and how four clerks were appointed to record their adventures. At this point Elis Gruffydd abandons the French romance and returns to the Galfridian history, following William Caxton's account of Arthur's campaign in Ireland, where he defeats king Gwilmor before sailing to Iceland, which he soon brings under his sway. Arthur's renown throughout western Europe attracts countless knights to his court, and this brings us back to the history of the Round Table and how it was established, a section which seems to draw on more than one source. Some details could be taken from either Wace or Caxton, but the influence of another French romance, Robert de Boron's *Merlin*, can also be discerned. After a brief account, derived from the *Prose Lancelot*, of Arthur going to France to avenge the death of Lansilott's father, the Chronicle then follows Caxton once more for the tale of Arthur's killing of Ffrolo in Paris, and his further adventures in conquering the

12 *Lancelot do Lac. The Non-Cyclic Old French Prose Romance*, ed. Elspeth M. Kennedy (Oxford, 1980), i, 260.32–262.18.

peoples of Galia (Gaul). On his return home, a huge banquet is held at Caerllion-ar-Wysg so that Arthur may receive the homage of those who are now his vassals, and in describing these festivities Elis Gruffydd seems to have made as much use of Welsh traditions as of the work of Geoffrey of Monmouth and his successors. But it is Geoffrey and Caxton who provide details of the arrival during the banquet of messengers from Lushiws (Lucius), deputy to the emperor of Rome, demanding that Arthur pay tribute to the emperor. Arthur, having raised a huge army and left his nephew Morddred in charge of the kingdom, reaches Newsder (Normandy) where he hears that Elen, niece of Hywel, king of Llydaw, has been abducted by the giant Dinabws and is being kept a prisoner at Mont St Michel. Although both Geoffrey and Caxton include this episode, Elis Gruffydd seems to have borrowed most of his account from Wace, for it is only there that the more unpleasant details about the rape and killing of the young woman are found. With the help of his warriors Kai and Bedwyr (cf. Bedivere), however, Arthur succeeds in killing Dinabws, cutting off his head and carrying it back to the camp to show it to his men.

Elis Gruffydd seems to follow Caxton fairly closely over the next episodes, which relate how Arthur and his army with God's help defeat Lushiws and his pagan followers, and how Lushiws's body is sent to Rome in place of the tribute demanded by the emperor. Caxton is again the source for the account of Morddred's perfidy in making himself king and taking the queen as his mistress, once his uncle had crossed to the continent. He also allied himself to one of Arthur's old enemies, Serdickws, king of the west Saxons. Arthur returns to Britain and wins the first battle against Morddred, who retreats to Caer Wynt (Winchester). In the meantime, the queen, seeing which way the wind is blowing, flees from Caer Efrog (York) to Cernyw (Cornwall) and later to Caerllion, where she lives out her days in a convent. This narrative follows Caxton but with some details perhaps deriving from Geoffrey, whether directly or indirectly via Wace or possibly Laȝamon's English *Brut*.

The next section of the Chronicle again agrees with Caxton, Wace and Laȝamon, in recounting how Arthur besieges Caer Wynt and wins a battle against Morddred and Serdickws, who retreat to Cornwall. But for his account of the last battle, 'ar vaes eang ger mynachlog Lasenbri' [fol. 340r: on a broad field near the monastery of Glastonbury], Elis Gruffydd used a text which I have not been able to trace but appears to be closely related to the English *Stanzaic Morte Arthur* and to a Spanish chronicle, both composed during the fifteenth century.[13] The Welsh chronicle agrees with the English and Spanish narratives that the battle was started accidentally, for as the two armies were lined up Morddred sent a messenger to parly with Arthur, but when the former tried to

13 Traces of the same tradition can be found in Thomas Malory's *Morte Darthur*, where a knight draws his sword to kill a viper, an action misconstrued by the waiting, opposing armies, who take it as the sign to join battle: see *The Works of Sir Thomas Malory*, ed. E.Vinaver and P.J.C. Field (Oxford, 1990), III, p. 1235. See also Kirkland C. Jones, 'The Relationship Between the Versions of Arthur's Last Battle as they Appear in Malory and in the *Libro de las Generaciones*', *Bibliographical Bulletin of the International Arthurian Society*, 26 (1974), 197–205, and Richard Barber, 'The *Vera Historia de Morte Arthuri* and its Place in Arthurian Tradition', *Arthurian Literature* I (1981), 62–82 (here 74).

kill a snake – the Welsh term *pryf* is more ambiguous – which he saw threatening the king, the flash of his sword was misconstrued by the soldiers, who immediately joined battle. For the end of the battle Elis Gruffydd returns once again to the Galfridian model: Arthur kills his nephew, but not before Morddred has in turn mortally wounded him in the thigh. Feeling death approaching, Arthur formally presents his sceptre to Constantein son of Cadfor, earl of Cornwall. But the story does not end there. The chronicler turns next to another romance of the French Vulgate Cycle, *La Mort le roi Artu*, to pick up the account of how Arthur asked Constantein (here playing the role taken by Girflet in the French text) to throw his sword into the lake nearby. Constantein fails to do so the first time, but finally returns to carry out his task, and this time he sees a hand rise from out of the water to catch the sword and 'llu o ferched' (a host of women) appear on the lake shore to fetch Arthur's body. In the last sentence there is an echo of Thomas Malory, however, for Elis writes: 'ynny modd yma y newidiodd Arthur ei vowyd naturiol' (in this way did Arthur change his natural life), recalling the similar, ambiguous formula of the *Morte Darthur*: 'here in thys worlde he chaunged hys lyff'.[14] No similar phrase is found in the French *La Mort le roi Artu*, where Arthur's body is buried in a beautiful grave with his name upon it.

As this very brief outline shows, Elis Gruffydd's account of Arthur's biography can be summed up as one essentially derived from Geoffrey of Monmouth, albeit mainly indirectly, but a number of other sources have also been used, notably those themselves derived to varying degrees from the *Historia Regum Britanniae*, such as the English chronicles of William Caxton, Robert Fabian and perhaps Laȝamon and the Anglo-Norman *Brut* of Wace. But Elis Gruffydd also took material from Welsh texts occupying a position on the frontiers between story and history, as well as lifting virtually complete episodes from French romances, in particular the *Prose Lancelot*. There can be no doubt that the chronicler had read very widely before selecting the elements for his narrative and weaving them together, but he was well placed to have access to such a variety of texts. When he embarked on writing his chronicle around 1548–9, he had already spent eighteen years in Calais, a town which provided a wealth of opportunities for collecting the relevant material. The importance of the geographical, political and mercantile situation of Calais, which stood as a bridge between England and the continental countries, can not be overemphasised in this context. Many noblemen and officials spent periods in Calais in the service of the English king and some of them owned private libraries which would have contained a number of the very texts which would have been of interest to the Welsh writer. Elis Gruffydd himself refers in an earlier manuscript to gaining access to books owned by such people, in a comment in National Library of Wales, MS Cwrtmawr 1, the collection of medical texts which he translated into Welsh and which he completed immediately before commencing work on his Chronicle:

> . . . megis ac J gwelais J mewn henne lyuyr ynghalais, yr hwnn a viasai ymeddiant vi ne vii o hennafgwyr ac a viasai ynn gymeradwy am i pwyll a'i synwyr o vewn

14 Malory, *Works*, III, p. 1242.26–7.

y dref [p. 836: . . . such as I saw in an old book in Calais, which had been in the possession of six or seven elderly gentlemen who were respected in the town for their good sense and intelligence.]

One well known Calais resident to whose library Elis Gruffydd may well have gained access was John Bourchier, lord Berners, the English author and translator, who had arrived there as early as 1520, when he was first deputy-governor there. Berners was succeeded by Elis Gruffydd's master, Sir Robert Wingfield, and himself returned to England, but returned to resume his post in 1531, the year after the chronicler arrived in 1530. In view of the Welshman's position in the king's retinue and his closeness to Wingfield, it is scarcely possible that he and Berners did not meet. They certainly had much in common as authors, for it was whilst in Calais that Berners completed his English translation of Froissart's chronicle, as well as other translations from French, Spanish and Latin, including *Arthur of Lytell Brytayne*, *The Castell of Love*, and the Golden Book of Marcus Aurelius. The post-mortem inventory of lord Berners's goods lists some eighty books, many of them in Latin and French. Although specific titles are not given, it is clear that Berners's library, and more specifically the books he would have needed in composing his own works, would have been extremely useful to Elis Gruffydd in his own project and it is certainly possible that he had access to Berners's library at some point.[15]

It is tempting to speculate that the Welsh chronicler might also have come into contact with the antiquarian John Leland (?1506–52), who shared Elis Gruffydd's interest in king Arthur as well as his Protestant faith. In 1530, the year of the Welshman's arrival in Calais, Leland was appointed rector of the nearby parish of Pepeling, but unfortunately there is no firm evidence of his residence there. But another antiquarian, the chronicler Robert Turpin, was not only resident in Calais but must have known Elis Gruffydd well, for they belonged not only to the same regiment but also to the very same *vynteyne*, or company of twenty soldiers. Like his colleague, Robert Turpin was deeply interested in current affairs and recent history, and his *Chronicle of Calais* recounts the history of the English colony from 1485 to 1540.[16] His chronicle is shorter and more superficial than Elis Gruffydd's, but since he must have had to make use of written sources for the earlier part of his chronicle, it seems likely that the two men shared information and perhaps even books or other written materials.

Where it is possible to identify Elis Gruffydd's sources and compare them with his version, it quickly becomes evident that he did not simply lift entire sections of text and translate them faithfully and it seems more likely that he was working from notes he made as he worked through the texts, a process that may have continued over a long period; he may well have begun to assemble material in this way some years before he began to compose the Chronicle. In fact from the large number of texts to which he has had recourse it is impossible to believe that he could have had them all at his elbow as he worked on the

15 I am grateful to Professor James P. Carley for a useful discussion about Berners and for a chance to read before publication his entry on Berners in the *New Dictionary of National Biography*.

16 *The Chronicle of Calais, in the reigns of Henry VII and Henry VIII to the year 1540*, ed. by J.G. Nichols (London, 1846).

Chronicle. But he did not rely on these myriad texts alone. We have already noted that he included in the Arthurian section stories derived from orally-transmitted popular traditions from his native Wales, namely the onomastic tale of Huail ap Caw and the tale of Arthur being imprisoned by the three giants.[17] The structure and narrative techniques of these tales are indisputably characteristic of oral story-telling and it is significant that they are not attested in any written sources predating Elis Gruffydd's Chronicle or contemporary with it, and although such negative testimony on its own could be unreliable it is consistent with the internal evidence. These are only two examples: similar cases can be found in other sections of the Chronicle.[18] It is not only complete, self-contained narratives that are derived from such indigenous traditions, for the chronicler constantly reveals his extensive knowledge of Welsh story material, adding details which give his work a more strongly Welsh flavour, as, for example, when he defines Gwenhwyfar as the daughter of Gogran Gawr, or calls Arthur's hall by its native Welsh name of Hangwen.[19] At times Elis Gruffydd quotes traditions from his own native district in north-east Wales, such as that of Arthur building a court at Nannerch, this information being added at the end of the story of Huail ap Caw.[20]

The compilation of the Arthurian section and, indeed, of the Chronicle in its entirety, from so many written and non-written sources, originating in various countries and languages, can only be described as a creative process. Not only was it necessary for the author to select, arrange and splice together this disparate material, he had also to impose some kind of literary unity upon his work, which might otherwise have been no more than a badly sewn patchwork. By and large Elis Gruffydd succeeded in this task, mainly through the consistency of his approach and above all by imposing his own idiosyncratic style, and even persona, over the whole massive text. His narrative style is so energetic that it can read like a breathless gallop from one adventure to the next; in this constant movement he tends to lose control over the length of his sentences, which swoop ever on, as he adds still more clauses to which further subordinate

17 On Elis Gruffydd's use of oral traditions, see Thomas Jones, 'Chwedl Huail ap Caw ac Arthur', in *Astudiaethau Amrywiol a gyflwynir i Syr Thomas Parry-Williams*, ed. Thomas Jones (Cardiff, 1968), pp. 48–66, and id., 'A Sixteenth-Century Version of the Arthurian Cave Legend', in *Studies in Language and Literature in Honour of Margaret Schlauch*, ed. M. Brahmer, S. Helsztynski and J. Krzyzanowski (Warsaw, 1966), pp. 175–85; and Ceridwen Lloyd-Morgan, 'Oral et écrit dans la chronique d'Elis Gruffydd', *Kreiz. Études sur la Bretagne et les Pays Celtiques*, 5 (1996), 179–86.

18 See, e.g., Ceridwen Lloyd-Morgan, art. cit., *Ystorya Taliesin*, ed. Patrick K. Ford (Cardiff, 1992), esp. p. 46, and Thomas Jones, 'Hanes Llywelyn ap Iorweth a Chynwrig Goch o Drefriw', *National Library of Wales Journal*, 3 (1943–44), 151–57.

19 The same tradition is reflected in the tale of *Culhwch ac Olwen*: 'Ehangwen neuad Arthur', *Culhwch ac Olwen. An Edition and Study of the Oldest Arthurian Tale*, ed. Rachel Bromwich and D. Simon Evans (Cardiff, 1992), line 264; cf. *Yr Areithiau Pros*, ed. D. Gwenallt Jones (Cardiff, 1934), p. 80.

20 'Ac ynn yr amser yma, ynn ol hrai o'r ysdoriae, J gwnnaeth Arthur lys yn y lle heddiw a elwir Nannerch. Ac etto J gelwir y man Llys Arthur. Ac yvo a ddywedir mae J gappel ef ydoedd yr eglwys, yr hwnn a alwyd ynn hir o amser ynn ol y Kappel Gwial' [NLW MS 5276D, part ii, fol. 330r: And at that time, according to some of the stories, Arthur made a court in that place now called Nannerch. And even now the spot is called Llys Arthur. And it is said that the church was his chapel and was for long afterwards called the Wicker Chapel].

clauses are attached. He often uses forms drawn from oral rather than written use, in particular omitting unstressed vowels in unaccented syllables, so that often the orthography is not immediately transparent to the reader and not infrequently words need to be read aloud before they can be identified. These characteristics, together with his tendency to express his own opinion and address the reader directly, give his work a powerful immediacy whilst at the same time smoothing over transitions between material from different sources. Whilst these features make for a very readable text, they inevitably make it harder to identify the sources, where more than one text follows a broadly similar narrative.

If, then, the Chronicle as a whole, including the Arthurian section, can be regarded as a work of creative literature, the question arises as to how successful the author was in bringing together content from such varied sources, some of which expressed rather different views or even contradicted each other. Elis Gruffydd makes no attempt to conceal these differences: on the contrary, he periodically draws the reader's attention to disagreements between authorities, in an early exercise of textual criticism. But this often leads him to point out the areas of agreement between conflicting accounts, as in the following examples:

> Neithyr eraill o'r awdurion ysydd ynn dangos mae o'i gwir vodd J kymerssantt twy J helyntt o'r gogledd J Dottines, yr hyn sydd debycka J vod ynn wir, kanis J mae pawb o'r awdurion ynn kordio gymeryd ohonnaunt twy dir ynn hauyn Dodtines. [NLW MS 5276D, ii, fol. 237v: But other authors show that they deliberately took a course to the north of Totnes, which is more likely to be true, for all of the authors record that they landed in Totnes harbour.]

> Ac wrth opiniwn hrai o'r bobyl yvo a yroedd yr esdron genedyl oll allan [o]'r dyrnas, onid hrai eraill ysydd ynn dangos y gwrthwyneb. Onid y mae pawb o'r awdurion yn kordio gaffel ohonnaw ef xii o vatteloedd nodedig [NLW MS 5276D, ii, fol. 329r: And it is the belief of some people that he drove all of the foreign race out of the kingdom, but others show the opposite. But all of the authors record that he won twelve notable battles.]

In bringing together material from so many different sources, originating from Wales, England and France, the author needed to present a consistent picture of king Arthur, and on the whole he has succeeded in doing so. This consistency derives in part from his frequent reliance on the account of Geoffrey of Monmouth and his successors. Thus the focus throughout the Arthurian section of the Welsh chronicle is on the king as an imperial warrior and ruler, first subduing Britain's enemies before extending the bounds of his territory by conquest to Ireland, Iceland and the continent. He is defined as a Christian king, winning his battles as a direct result of his faith in God, even receiving instructions directly from the Virgin Mary, but he also belongs to an older world, far removed from the *merveilleux chrétien*. In this world Merddin (Merlin) casts his spell on Uthyr to allow him to visit Eigyr in her husband's form, and Arthur himself meets giants in Denbighshire and Normandy: the pagan supernatural coexists with Christianity, and it is worth noting that there is not the slightest hint of this causing any unease to Elis Gruffydd, an enthusiastic convert to Protestantism.

Although he concentrates on presenting a warlike image of Arthur, from time to time he presents him in a less than heroic light, and it is significant that this occurs only in those sections which are derived from French romances and from Welsh traditions. Of the French texts, it was the *Prose Lancelot* and other romances of the Vulgate Cycle which exerted the greatest influence on the Arthurian section, and in those romances the king's human weaknesses are revealed as well as the remarkable qualities as warrior and king which he possessed when in his prime. This view is in keeping with the material from Welsh tradition which surfaces in the Chronicle, for in those particular sources both the heroic and the courtly aspects of Arthur's character and deeds are less prominent. Thus in the tale of Huail ap Caw, for instance, Arthur is a great pursuer of women, competing with one of his warriors for the favours of one of his '[g]ordderchadon' (lovers, mistresses). In a burlesque portent of his wounding by Morddred in his last battle, Arthur is struck in the thigh by Huail; later, in an extraordinary scene, he goes to Rhuthun, to see a girl who has caught his fancy, and for this purpose dresses up in women's clothes ('wedi ymddinodi mewn dillad merch'). There Huail catches sight of him 'ynn chware dawns ymhlith merched' [NLW MS 5276D, part ii, fol. 330r: dancing among the women]. This must surely be one of the most undignified depictions of Arthur in European literature. Huail rashly makes fun of his lameness, which impairs his dancing ability, and Arthur's only recourse is to use his position as king to summon the mocker to his court and have him summarily sentenced to death for breaking his promise to keep silent about the the king's sexual peccadilloes.

This mixture of the kingly and the human is found in the following episode, Arthur's dream, imported from the *Prose Lancelot*. The king's dream causes him far more anxiety than facing his enemies in battle, but he makes use of his royal power and status to order the wise men to his court to explain the dream, and to throw them into prison when their attempts at exegesis fail to please. In the tale of the three giants, which follows on from this episode, Arthur finds himself entirely at the mercy of his jailers, who add to the insult of capture by forcing him to turn the spit over the fire, a most demeaning task. However, he manages to escape by a clever ruse and by flattering the chief giant.

These less than flattering, less than heroic images, where Arthur's authority lies not in his personal qualities but derives purely from the power that is invested him by virtue of his status as king, bring Elis Gruffydd's portrayal of Arthur close to that found in the early Welsh prose tale *Culhwch ac Olwen*. There too, Arthur is not always in control and he depends heavily on others, again without his royal status and authority being questioned. The account in *Culhwch* of Arthur killing the witch has a strong element of burlesque similar to that in the tale of Huail ap Caw in Elis Gruffydd's narrative.[21] Perhaps the Arthurian traditions which Elis Gruffydd first heard when he was a young man in Flintshire portrayed the king in such ambiguous terms; it is possible that even after the chronicler came across more honourable, more heroic tales about him later on, in written texts such as the *Historia Regum Britanniae*, he was unable to

21 *Culhwch ac Olwen*, ll, 1205–29.

rid himself of the more popular image familiar to him from the orally-transmitted stories in Welsh. In fact such tales seem to have held a considerable appeal for him, judging by the number which find their way into this section of his Chronicle. Even outside this account of Arthur's life, when describing events of his own lifetime, Elis Gruffydd could not always resist the temptation of introducing more of this material. In his account of the period from 1518 to 1524, for instance, he found an opportunity to repeat another story he had heard, presenting it as an example of the 'chwedle hryuedd' (strange tales) which were popular 'ymhlith kyffredin y dyrnas' (amongst the common people of the kingdom) at that time:

> 'Hrai a ddywedai weled ymrauaelion weledigaethau hryuedd, megis gweled gwyr ynn ymladd ynn ddwy vyddin ar serttein o veussudd ynn hran y gorllewin' [Some said that they had seen many strange visions, such as seeing men fighting in two armies in certain fields in the western part (of the country).]

With no more introduction than this he proceeds to relate a story from Gloucestershire about Arthur sleeping in a cave and a woman being brought there by one of his servants who had bought a horse from her. When the woman returned home she showed her husband the strange coins which had been paid her for the horse.[22] The chronicler insists that this story is not credible:

> kanis, wrth fy nhyb a'm hamkann, jr ydoedd y chwedl hwn kynn wiried a bod y kerig ynn dywedud ne'r moor yn llosgi' [for in my view and in my belief, this story was as true as that the stones should speak or the sea burn].

Nonetheless, he does not criticise those who do believe it. He hastens to add a further comment to soften the criticism:

> Neithyr val kynt ir ydoedd lawer gwr pwyllog o vewn llys y brenin ac o vewn y dyrnas yn koylio bod y chwedlav hynn kynn wiried a'r Pader [Yet as before many a judicious man within the kingdom believed that these stories were as true as the Lord's Prayer.]

These comments by Elis Gruffydd, and his Arthurian biography itself, must be set in the context of the fierce controversy about the historicity of Arthur which was raging in the first decades of the sixteenth century. It was around 1512–13 that Polydore Vergil's *Anglicana Historie*, the first serious attempt to undermine the Galfridian history, began to circulate in manuscript; it appeared in a printed edition in 1534. Many scholars rushed to defend Geoffrey of Monmouth's *Historia Regum Britanniae* against Polydore Vergil's contention that there was no historical foundation to the legends of Brutus and Arthur, which were no more than fictions.[23] One of the first to jump to the defence of Geoffrey

22 For text and discussion of this story, see Thomas Jones, 'A Sixteenth-Century Version of the Arthurian Cave Legend'.

23 See, e.g., Antonia Gransden, *Historical Writing in England II* (London, 1982), pp. 430–33, for an account of Polydore Vergil's life and work; for an account of the defence of the Galfridian history, see T.D. Kendrick, *British Antiquity* (London, 1950), pp. 78–98. On the Welsh response to the controversy, see Brynley F. Roberts, 'Ymagweddau at *Brut y Brenhinedd*', *Bulletin of the Board of Celtic Studies*, 24 (1970–72), 122–38.

was John Leland. Like Elis Gruffydd, he was a Protestant and loyal to the English crown;[24] as we have seen, he had been appointed rector of the parish of Pepeling, near Calais, in 1530, the year in which the Welsh chronicler arrived in the colony, although there is no firm evidence that Leland ever lived there. But it would not be unexpected for Ellis Gruffydd in Calais to hear, whether via Leland or through other Calais channels, of the great controversy and perhaps even to gain access to a copy of Polydore Vergil's work and read it for himself. In the circumstances, it is not surprising that he decided that an epilogue should be added to the Arthurian biography in his Chronicle, in order to address the thorny question of the authenticity of that narrative. It would scarcely be possible at that time for a chronicler with any pretentions of authority to relate the tale of Arthur without referring to the argument and perhaps taking sides.

After describing how Arthur's reign came to an end after he had reigned for twenty-six years, the Welsh chronicler adds (NLW MS 6209E, p. 85) that this accounts broadly agrees with that of 'y rhann fwyaf o'r awdurion' [the majority of authors], and with this phrase launches into a discussion of the veracity of Geoffrey's *Historia* and the works of authors in agreement with it. Some, he says, believe that Arthur was 'rhodd ne anrheg gan y Tad o'r Nef' [a grace or gift from the Father in Heaven], sent by God to punish people for their wicked conduct, whilst others 'dal tyb na bu ef farw etto ac y daw ef yn vyw i reoli yr dyrnnas hon drachefn' [hold the belief that he is not yet dead and that he will return alive to rule this kingdom again]. To reassure his readers that he is above such foolish beliefs, Elis Gruffydd adds immediately that they are 'yn anghyffelib i'r gwir' [far from the truth]. According to others, however, Arthur was killed in battle 'a chladdu ei gorff mewn ty o grefydd a oedd [m]ewn pannwl neu nant, yr hwnn a oedd yn gorwedd garllaw yr maes ac a elwid Glynn neu Nant y Gofalon' [and his body buried in a religious house in a hollow or river valley near the battle-field and which was called Glyn y Gofalon or Nant y Gofalon (the Valley of Care), NLW MS 6209E, p. 85]. Some sources, he continues, state that his wife Gwenhwyfar was first buried in the same place but that both their bodies were later moved to the abbey of 'Glassynberi' (Glastonbury), where they were 'discovered' around 1180 (NLW MS 6209E, pp. 85–86). The same account may be found in Robert Fabian's *New Chronicles*. But Elis Gruffydd then hastens to remind his readers that according to Merddin's prophecy, 'ei ddiwedd ef a vydd pedrys' [his end will be uncertain] – an exact translation of the words used by William Caxton in his chronicle: 'but certes this is the proficie of Merlyn he said that his deth shal be doubtous'.[25] This could be true, adds Elis Gruffydd, for some say that Arthur is dead whilst others claim that he is still alive, and furthermore he notes that 'mae llaweroedd o bobyl o bob nassiwn yn kymerud difyrwch a solas mawr yn darllain ac yn klywed ei darllaint wynt' [NLW MS 6209E, p. 86: many people of every nation take great delight and comfort in reading and hearing (them, i.e., these stories)].

This brings us to the heart of the problem. In spite of this common belief 'mae

24 See James P. Carley, 'Polydore Vergil and John Leland on King Arthur. The Battle of the Books', *Interpretations*, 15 (1984), 86–100.

25 Caxton, *Chronicles* [*STC* 9991], p. lxxxviii.

ymrafaelion awdurion wedi ysgrifennu ac wedi dangos yn gadarn na bu ermoed ddim o'r kyfriw wr ac Arthur ac y mae Galffreidus wedi ysgrifennu ohonaw' [NLW MS 6209E, p. 86: many authors have written and demonstrated forcefully that there never was such a man as Arthur as Geoffrey has written of him]. The chronicler then sums up the doubters' arguments: Bede does not mention Arthur in his *Historia ecclesiastica gentis Anglorum*, comprehensive though that history is; William of Malmesbury insists that the tales about him were 'ffuent' (sham) and 'enwiredd' (untruth), and there is no reference to Arthur in the Chronicle of the Francs nor in the works of Roman authors. Neither do the latter mention Lushiws (Lucius), Arthur's great enemy. For these reasons the English, says Elis Gruffydd, have chosen to refute Geoffrey of Monmouth's *Historia*, maintaining 'mae Jr klod a mawrhad a moliantt J'r Bryttaniaid Jr ysgriuenodd Galffreidws yr ysdori hon' [that Geoffrey wrote this history to glorify the Britons and praise them], since Geoffrey was himself a Welshman (NLW MS 5276Dii, fol. 341r).[26] At first sight, the reader might assume that this argument is the chronicler's own, but in fact it is lifted directly from a short chronicle in English, John Rastell's *Pastyme of People*, which was printed in 1530. Elis Gruffydd goes on to translate more or less word for word this section of Rastell's text (chapter ciii), where the argument centres on the authenticity of a document to which Arthur's seal was purportedly fixed and which was kept on the tomb of Edward the Confessor at Westminster Abbey.[27] Elis Gruffydd has to concede that both document and seal are probably forgeries, for the document purports to confirm that Arthur had granted property to the abbey, yet the abbey had not been founded until after his supposed lifetime, and it is well known, moreover, that the practise of attaching a seal to a document in order to authenticate it was not instituted until after the Norman Conquest. Despite this weight of evidence against Geoffrey's *Historia*, however, Elis Gruffydd could not bring himself to refute his work entirely. Leaving aside the consideration that Geoffrey was a Welshman like himself, if Elis Gruffydd were to reject the *Historia Regum Britanniae* he would inevitably undermine the authority of his own narrative. Although this section is deeply indebted to Rastell, he adds what appears to be a personal comment: 'nid ysgri[u]ennais ddim o'r llyuyr yma i hroddi kyssur a hryuig J ddyn ynn y bydd J amav ac J anghoelio ysdori Galffreidws' [NLW MS 527Dii, fol. 341v: I did not write any of this book to comfort and embolden anyone to doubt and disbelieve Geoffrey's history]. Nonetheless, he feels obliged to present a balanced view: 'ni roddaf annog a hryuig J neb J gredv yn sickyr wir J bood hi yn ysdorri gywir' [I shall not give

26 Earlier in his Chronicle Elis Gruffydd had stressed that Geoffrey was translating from Welsh sources: '. . . yr ysdori yma mewn hen lyuyr a viassai ysgriuenedig yn hen Jaith y bryttaniaid . . . ac J mae Galffreidws yn dangos a ddamunodd arno ef darllain y llyuyr a dangos . . . J ysdyr ef oblegid J vod ef yn Gymro [. . .] A'r llyuyr o'r ysdori hon a droes y Galffreidws yma o Gymraeg yn Lading' (NLW MS 5276Di, fol. 81r: . . . this history in an old book which was written in the old British tongue . . . and Geoffrey shows that he wished to read this old book and reveal its meaning because he was himself a Welshman [. . .] And the book of this history was translated by this Geoffrey from Welsh into Latin.].

27 William Caxton was also familiar with this supposed evidence, for he too discusses the seal (though more briefly than Rastell or Elis Gruffydd) in the preface to Malory's *Morte Darthur*. See *The Works of Sir Thomas Malory*, ed. by E. Vinaver and P.J.C. Field, I, p. cxliv.

anyone encouragement or boldness to believe in all certainty that it is a true story]. Each reader must decide whether or not to believe it, 'megis ac J bo kymwys a da gantho' [as it may seem suitable and good to him]. Elis Gruffydd could not, however, leave the matter there without taking the opportunity of serving a riposte to the English, the use of the personal pronouns making a clear distinction between 'them' (the English) and 'us' (the Welsh): his years in the service of English masters had clearly not diminished his patriotic fervour. He complains that the English criticise the Welsh 'am *ynn* hryuig *ni* am Arthur' [for *our* presumption about Arthur] (my emphasis), but in fact 'mae yn vwy *J* son *wyntt* amdano ef no nnyni' [NLW MS 527Dii, fol. 342r: *they* talk much more about him than we do] (my emphasis). He notes that it is the English themselves who believe that Arthur will return again to be king and insist that he is sleeping 'mewn googof dan vryn garllaw Glasynbri' [in a cave under a hill near Glastonbury], where he 'ymddangosodd ac a ymddiuanodd a lawer o bobyl mewn llawer modd hryuedd ers trychant o vylynyddoedd [NLW MS 527Dii, fol. 342r: appeared and conversed with many people in many strange ways three hundred years ago].

In the foreword to the second part of his Chronicle, Elis Gruffydd states that his intention was to

> dwynn llawer o bethav nodedig o ysdoriay ardderchion, dyledog, o barthe'r dwyrain, o'r hrain ni bu gyswyn amdanaunt o vewn Kymru ymysg y kyffredin Jrmoed ynn y blaen [NLW MS 3054Di, fol. 2r: convey many remarkable things from excellent, noble stories from the eastern parts, ones which have never before been recounted in Wales amongst the common people.]

But as his version of Arthur's biography shows, if he kept his word and presented his readers in Wales with new material from England and the Continent (these being the 'eastern parts' to which he refers), he did not, for all that, exclude Welsh traditions from his Chronicle. His decision to include them may reflect an attempt to find common ground between the tales that were circulating in other languages and those that were common in Welsh popular tradition. But it is more likely that it was his own interest in the stories which he had himself heard about Arthur that led him to include material from oral tradition. Elis Gruffydd succeeded in presenting to contemporary Welsh readers not only a convenient narrative of the tale of Arthur, based on major sources which were available in the cosmopolitan, urban *milieu* of Calais, but also a summary of the arguments that were being mustered on both sides of the debate about the authenticity of that account of British history. For us today his account is especially valuable because as well as giving a clear indication of which Arthurian texts were available and of contemporary attitudes, he also recorded a number of popular tales and traditions which are unattested elsewhere and which would otherwise have been lost.

The Ambiguous Fortunes of Arthur: The Lancelot-Grail and Beyond

NORRIS J. LACY

Any relatively brief discussion of the character or fate of King Arthur inevitably fails in one of two ways. Either it offers vast generalizations, with no space for demonstrations drawn from particular texts, or it concentrates on a few texts to the exclusion of many others that might either confirm or contradict its conclusions. Faced with these alternatives, I have here chosen the latter approach, believing it necessary to ground our discussions, to whatever extent possible, in textual realities. I will concentrate on French material but will also offer passing comments on some works in other languages.

The beginning of *Möttuls Saga* ('The Saga of the Mantle'), an Old Norse Arthurian text from the late twelfth or early thirteenth century, presents a portrait of Arthur that corresponds to the expectations of most readers:

> Artús kóngr var hinn frægasti höfðingi at hverskonar frækleik ok allskonar drengskap ok kurteisi með fullkomnu huggæði ok vinsælasta mildleik svá at fullkomliga varð eigi frægari ok vinsælli höfðingi um hans daga í heiminum. Var hann hinn vaskasti at vápnum, hinn mildasti at gjöfum, bliðasti í orðum, hagráð<a>sti í ráðagerðum, hinn góðgjarnasti í miskunnsemd, hinn siðugasti í góðum meðferðum, hinn tiguligasti í öllum kóngligum stjórnum, guðhræddr í verkum, mjúklyndr góðum, harðr illum, miskunnsamr þurftugum, beinisamr bjóðendum, svá fullkominn í öllum höfðingskap at engi illgirnd né öfund var með honum ok engi kunni at telja lofsfullri tungu virðuligan göfugleik ok sæmd ríkis hans.[1]

> [King Arthur was the most renowned ruler with regard to every aspect of valor and all kinds of manliness and chivalry, combined with perfect compassion and most appealing mildness, so that in every respect there was no ruler more renowned or blessed with friends in his day in the world. He was the most valiant man at arms, the most generous with gifts, the gentlest in words, the cleverest in his designs, the most benevolent in mercy, the most polished in good manners, the noblest in all kingly craft, godfearing in his undertakings, gentle to the good, harsh to the wicked, merciful to the needy, hospitable to the companionable, so perfect in his entire authority that neither ill will nor malice was found in him,

1 Marianne E. Kalinke, ed. and trans., *Norse Romance II: The Knights of the Round Table* (Cambridge, 1999), pp. 6–7.

and no one could adequately laud the splendid magnificence and honor of his realm.]

This praise, curiously, leads directly into a setting of the famous mantle test that reveals the infidelity of women and thus the fact that Arthur is not only a benevolent, noble, virtually perfect king, but also the court's most conspicuous cuckold. And despite the encomium of Arthur, the *Möttuls Saga* goes on to show that this work is, as Kalinke points out, 'in a class by itself because of its irreverent portrayal of courtly society'.[2]

Irreverent portrayals of courtly society may be rare (though this one is hardly unique), but we are by no means wanting for examples of irreverent or simply negative views of Arthur himself. A case in point occurs in the central romance, the Prose *Lancelot*, of the French Vulgate Cycle. There we find a striking passage in which a monk initially praises Arthur as the king who 'plus maintient chevalerie en grant honor et plus avés fait grans biens que nus rois' ['best maintains the honor of knighthood, and you have done more good, both spiritual and worldly, than any king']. But then, without pause, he launches into harsh criticism:

> 'Mais trop estes perecheus de vengier les grans hontes et les damages que l'en vous fait . . . . Vous honerés et doutés et servés chex qui desloiaument vous guerroient et courent sus, et cheus oubliés qui vous ont loiaument servi et sans fauser.'
>
> ['But you are too slow to avenge acts of shame and injury . . . You honor and fear and serve those who disloyally take up arms against you and attack you; and those who have served you loyally and faithfully, those you forget!'][3]

Thereupon he concludes audaciously that, for these reasons, Arthur is not the most worthy of men.

Hearing this, Arthur is embarrassed, and the people are astonished that someone would address the king in such an insulting manner. The monk then explains that Arthur has never avenged the death of King Ban, whose widow has been disinherited and has had one of her children taken from her. He adds, shockingly, 'C'est si laide chose et si vilaine a vostre oels qu'il est mervelle comment vous poés ne osés nul preudomme veoir en mi le vis' ['This matter so sullies your reputation that it is a wonder how you can dare look any honorable man in the face'].[4] We might expect Arthur to take umbrage at this stunning affront, but instead he meekly acknowledges that the monk is right, admitting that he, the king, did *hear about* the death and the injustices but objecting, lamely, that at that particular time there was really nothing he could do about it.[5]

2 Kalinke, ed. and trans., *Norse Romance II*, p. 3.

3 Alexandre Micha, ed., *Lancelot: Roman en prose du XIIIe siècle*, 9 vols (Geneva, 1978–83), VII, p. 97. The English translation is by Samuel N. Rosenberg in *Lancelot-Grail: The Old French Arthurian Vulgate and Post-Vulgate in Translation*, ed. Norris J. Lacy, 5 vols (New York, 1993–96), II, p. 24.

4 Micha, *Lancelot*, VII, p. 100; trans. by Rosenberg in Lacy, ed., *Lancelot-Grail*, II, p. 25.

5 Arthur does add that, for a long time thereafter, he had much to do, and he suggests that his attention was occupied by challenges to his authority. That may be a correct and acceptable

We could easily multiply examples, both of the criticism of Arthur and of the curious mix of unreserved praise and frank condemnation. One thinks, for instance, of the French *Yder*, the date of which is virtually the same as that of the Norse text (i.e., probably the very early thirteenth century).[6] An early passage of the romance has a character describe Arthur as

> 'Li preus, li sages, li cortois,
> Qui d'ennor ad passé les rois
> Cels qui furent e cels qui sunt:
> De cels qui emprés lui vendront
> N'en sera nuls ne vaille meins;
> N'en di pas trop ke tant est pleins
> De valur e de corteisie
> Ke nus n'en ment qui bien en die.'
>
> [renowned for his valour and his wisdom and his courtliness, whose honour surpasses all other things, past and present: all who come after him will be inferior to him; I am not exaggerating for he is so endowed with valour and courtliness that nobody who speaks well of him can lie.][7]

Yet, as Keith Busby points out, in this romance 'everything that has to do with Arthur and the court [is] evil, and everything non-Arthurian (especially the hero), good'.[8] Throughout this romance, and despite the praise of him, Arthur is negligent, indifferent to his duties and promises, sometimes devious or spiteful, and above all rabidly jealous of Yder. The latter, incidentally, is not remotely interested in the queen, but the opposite is not true, a fact that perhaps makes Arthur's jealousy understandable: Guenevere, one of literary history's most celebrated adulteresses, acknowledges when pressed that, if Arthur were dead, Yder is the man she would marry.[9]

As these examples suggest, unambiguous assessments of Arthur will not be common, and even the condemnation of the king and his court in *Yder* stands alongside the praise for him that was cited above. However, the customary combination of praise and reproach for the king suggests that extravagant encomia of Arthur have already, at a comparatively early stage, been established as a trope, a rhetorical imperative that routinely shapes even those characterizations of the king that are contradicted by narrative developments. In some instances, the encomium might reflect a deliberate narratorial strategy creating an ironic disparity between the Arthur who is praised and the one who is dramatized. More often, I believe, it is doubtless a mere convention, and the evocation of the Arthurian ideal does not necessarily hold any implications for

explanation, but my intent here is not to imply that Arthur neglected his duty, but to note that he sometimes exhibits serious flaws, that not everyone is hesitant to condemn him, and that he accepts the criticism with surprising meekness.

6 Alison Adams dates it between 1199 and 1216. See the introduction to her edition of *The Romance of Yder* (Cambridge, 1983), p. 13.

7 Adams, ed., *Yder*, pp. 28–29, vss 37–44. Translations from *Yder* are Adams's.

8 In Norris J. Lacy, ed., *The New Arthurian Encyclopedia* (New York, 1991), p. 529, s.v. *Yder*.

9 Adams, ed., *Yder*, pp. 191–92; vss 5216–20.

the human and fallible monarch who inhabits so many texts. The real and the ideal diverge, and their coexistence, without apparent discomfort (at least for the narrators), is one of several dichotomies that frequently shape Arthurian romance and the presentation of the king himself.

Dual or contradictory portraits of Arthur occur in all the medieval literatures, including early Welsh or Welsh-Latin material. From the earliest texts we find conflicting views of Arthur. As Padel notes, the ninth-century *Historia Brittonum*, sometimes attributed to Nennius, offers 'two different, seemingly contradictory, portrayals of Arthur'.[10] One involves the famous list of Arthur's battles, in which he is praised as a great military leader (a *dux bellorum*), though not as a king. The other emphasis in that work concerns the so-called Wonders of Britain, including two marvelous occurrences related to Arthur. How do we reconcile a pseudo-historical account of Arthur's military activities with accounts of wonders and miracles? Padel explains:

> [T]he continuing Arthurian tradition, in Welsh and other literatures, was itself often split between trying to fit [Arthur] into known history and acknowledging the magical and legendary quality of his world; so we may view this duality in the earliest Arthurian text as establishing the pattern for all later Arthurian literature.[11]

That pattern was widely adopted and exploited by authors on the continent. If the Welsh first offer a portrait of Arthur as military hero on one hand and as the subject of miraculous events on the other, we must still attribute much of the complexity of Arthur to the first great French author of Arthurian romance, Chrétien de Troyes. Beginning with Chrétien's first romance (*Erec et Enide*), Arthur, as Erich Köhler has suggested, is never the ideal king of an ideal realm.[12] The king himself is stubborn and petulant in *Erec*; incapable of preventing Guenevere's abduction, or even raising objections to it, in *Lancelot*; inclined to nod off at inappropriate times in *Yvain*; and so absorbed in sulking about problems in the *Perceval* that he is unable even to respond to a cheery greeting from the newly arrived Perceval. And Perceval, the naive Welsh boy who wants to become a knight but has no idea what that means and who knows only that Arthur is 'the king who makes knights' – insists that this brooding man before him cannot possibly be Arthur: 'Cis rois ne fist chevalier onques. / Coment porroit chevalier faire, / Quant on n'en puet parole traire?' ['This king never made knights. How could he make knights, when you can't even drag a word out of him?'].[13]

10 O.J. Padel, *Arthur in Medieval Welsh Literature* (Cardiff, 2000), p. 3.

11 Padel, *Arthur*, p. 9. Padel's words may remind us of a more dramatic statement by Tom Artin, writing not of Celtic materials but of the legend in general: Artin contends (with some slight exaggeration, in my view) that there were always two competing traditions of the king: 'In one, he is the great *dux bellorum*, the once and future king who is Britain's savior; in the other, he is a fool.' See Artin, *The Allegory of Adventure: Reading Chrétien's* Erec et Enide *and* Yvain (Lewisburg, PA, 1974), p. 65.

12 Erich Köhler, *Ideal und Wirklichkeit in der höfischer Epik* (Tübingen, 1956), passim. Köhler's title itself identifies succinctly the basic duality of Arthur in Chrétien's works.

13 Chrétien de Troyes, *Le Roman de Perceval ou Le Conte du Graal*, ed. Keith Busby (Tübingen, 1993), vss 928–30. Translations are mine except where otherwise indicated.

Beate Schmolke-Hasselmann has pointed out that Arthur was *consistently* characterized by the alternation of activity and extreme passivity, even lassitude.[14] Nowhere is this lassitude, which is suggested in *Yvain* and *Perceval*, more evident than in the very beginning of *Perlesvaus*. This anonymous text opens with a King Arthur who, ten years into his glorious reign, one day finds himself suddenly melancholy, deprived of will, ambition, and energy, uninterested in holding court and no longer given to generosity. This is not the only example of Arthur's distraction or lassitude, as witness the scene, mentioned above, from Chrétien's *Perceval*. In most instances, however, his failing is either a natural character trait or the effect of aging. That is not the case with *Perlesvaus*, where we learn that the cause of his depression and impotence, indeed the cause of all the world's woes, was Perlesvaus's failure to ask the necessary questions about the Grail.[15]

In the face of his apparent indifference, Arthur's knights begin to drift aimlessly away from court, until there remain only twenty-five of the original 370. Significantly, adventures cease to occur at court; and then other princes and nobles give up their quest for excellence. Guenevere is appalled by this state of affairs, and eventually she informs Arthur that she feels shame on account of his conduct and its effect on the court. She tells him of her fear that 'Dex ne vos ait mis en obli', that God has forgotten him. Arthur acknowledges his languor and lack of will to perform generous and honorable deeds; 'ainz m'est mes talenz muëz en floibece de cuer' ['rather, my will is transformed into weakness of heart' (or lack of resolve)].[16] At her bidding, he goes to the Chapel of St. Austin to seek spiritual renewal.

Later in this work we encounter a young woman who, we are told, symbolizes Fortune, and the cart she is pulling represents Fortune's wheel.[17] It would be difficult to overestimate the importance attributed by medieval authors to the figure of Fortune and, almost as much, to her wheel. Indeed, Jane H.M. Taylor describes the Wheel of Fortune as 'one of the dominant metaphors of the Middle Ages'.[18] The characteristics of the personified Fortune often vary from text to text. Frequently in romances of the time, she is described either as having two faces (one smiling, the other frowning) or, as in Chrétien's *Perceval*,[19] as bald in

14 See her *Der arthurische Versroman von Chrestien bis Froissart* (Tübingen, 1980), p. 52. She also discusses Arthur's insatiable territorial ambitions and other aspects of his character; see pp. 52–57.

15 *Le Haut Livre du Graal: Perlesvaus*; vol. I (Text, Variants, and Glossary), ed. William A. Nitze and T. Atkinson Jenkins; vol. II (Commentary and Notes), ed. William A. Nitze and Collaborators (Chicago, 1932, 1937); here citing I, pp. 37–38. However, it should be noted too that the hermit who explains this to Arthur has also spoken of the king's sin (I, p. 37), but we are apparently dealing here with multiple modes of causality, with Perlesvaus's failure leading or disposing Arthur to sin by not attending to his duties.

16 *Perlesvaus*, I, p. 26.

17 *Perlesvaus*; I, p. 110.

18 'Arthurian Cyclicity: The Construction of History in the Late French Prose Romances', *The Arthurian Yearbook*, ed. Keith Busby (New York, 1992), II, pp. 209–23; here citing p. 219. See Taylor's n. 35 for basic bibliography on the subject of Fortune. The standard if somewhat dated study of the subject is Howard R. Patch, *The Goddess Fortuna in Mediaeval Literature* (Cambridge, MA, 1927).

19 Busby, ed., *Perceval*, vss 4646–47.

back, with hair on the front of her head, the hair being a forelock that one could 'seize, like Opportunity' in order to pull oneself up.[20] But when Fortune turns her head (or her wheel), there is no escaping one's fate.

However, as is his wont, the anonymous *Perlesvaus* author does things his own way, and here we learn that the woman is entirely bald. The author explains that Fortune was bald before the Crucifixion and had hair only after Christ's death redeemed humanity. The particular details of Fortune's hair in this case imply not that we can save ourselves from Fortune by our own will and effort, but that we must be saved, by Christ's sacrifice, from the fate represented by Fortune and her wheel. The explicit connection between Arthur and Fortune will be reprised, under different circumstances, in a great many subsequent texts.

In the great French Vulgate Cycle, Arthur is a curious figure, especially toward the end. After proving himself a remarkable warrior and a relatively skilled ruler, he becomes something quite different. Particularly in the last romance of the cycle, *La Mort Artu*, we see another Arthur: one who is often weak, indecisive, and unable to overrule some of his own knights, especially Gauvain.

In the Vulgate Cycle, there is a very good reason for Arthur's apparent incapacity for action and decisiveness: the Grail quest. The beginning of the fourth romance, the *Queste del saint Graal*, introduces Galahad, whose destiny as the chosen Grail knight has repeatedly been announced. What we may not have anticipated – and Arthur certainly did not – is that when Galahad prepares to undertake the quest, Gauvain immediately leaps to his feet and swears to do so as well; and then all the best knights at court follow suit. Arthur foresees already the inevitable dissolution of his Round Table, with many of his best knights killed in the Quest, and with no further adventures, but only wars and destruction, awaiting those who survive:

> Et lors comença a resgarder monseignor Gauvain et li dist: 'Gauvain, Gauvain, vos m'avez trahi! Onques ma cort n'amenda tant de vos come ele en est ore empoiriee. Car ja mes ne sera honoree de si haute compaignie ne de si vaillant come vos en avez ostee par vostre esmuete. . . . Ha! Diex, je ne me cuidai ja mes desevrer de ceste compaignie que fortune m'avoit envoiee!'
>
> [Then, turning to Gawain, the king said, 'Gawain, Gawain, how you have betrayed me! All the good you have done for my court does not offset the harm you bring upon it today. Never again will this court be honored by knights as noble and valiant as those whom you have spirited away by your initiative. . . . God, I

20 For this detail, as well as for a brief but useful introduction to Fortune, see Richard Leighton Greene, 'Fortune', in *Dictionary of the Middle Ages*, ed. Joseph R. Strayer, 13 vols (New York, 1982–89), V, pp. 145–47; here citing 147. Greene also reminds us that Dante (*Inferno* VII) christianized Fortune, remaking her into one of God's ministers (p. 146). Concerning the personified Fortune, David F. Johnson and Geert H.M. Claassens note that this characteristic – Fortune is hairy in front and bald in back – represents a 'confusion of the roles of Fortune and *Occasio* (opportunity), but it is one common in medieval representations of the workings of Fortune'. See their *Dutch Romances II. Ferguut* (Cambridge, 2000), p. 251. The textual description of Fortune is located at vss 2406–10.

never thought I would be separated from this company of men whom good fortune has sent to me'.][21]

Even earlier in the Vulgate Cycle, however, Arthur often appears passionless and passive. He is already well established as warrior and ruler when he is betrothed to Guenevere, but the betrothal is not even his doing. Instead, Merlin happens to mention to Leodagan that he and others are seeking a wife for their leader. Leodagan responds that he has a candidate for the position, and when he mentions his daughter Guenevere, Merlin accepts the offer on behalf of Arthur.[22] Curiously, only after that does Merlin ask Leodagan, 'Sire ne sauries vous moult uolentiers qui nous somme et a qui vous aues doune vostre fille?' ['Wouldn't you like to know who we are and who the person is whom you have given your daughter to?'].[23] Leodagan and Guenevere are naturally pleased to learn that it is Arthur. Later, but only at Merlin's suggestion, Arthur and Guenevere kiss; and only now are we told that they are 'iouene gent qui moult sentramoient' [youthful and very much in love].[24] Nothing more. And when the marriage eventually takes place, Arthur's reactions to the event, if he has any, are not even reported. Later, following the tournament organized to celebrate the marriage, Merlin suggests that Arthur go to bed with his wife, 'car bien en estoit tans' [for it was time]. Thereupon, the king and queen, who 'moult s'entramoient' [loved each other deeply] 'si menerent toute nuit moult boine uie ensamble . . . et ne finerent iusqual iour quil sendormirent bras en bras' [all night they spent a most happy time together . . . and they did not stop until daybreak, when they fell asleep in each other's arms].[25] Of course, Arthur's public, political, and military exploits are the true subject of this portion of the *Merlin*, but this depiction of his first conjugal encounter with Guenevere is nonetheless conspicuous for its extraordinary brevity and almost casual tone. And then the subject changes.

As noted, the *Mort Artu* shows us a surprisingly bland Arthur. The end of the work offers an exception, more striking because it now seems uncharacteristic of Arthur: that is the king's grief at the death of his knights, and particularly Lucan's accidental death at Arthur's own hand. Only then is his sorrow profoundly felt or at least vividly portrayed. (Concerning his grief at these events, see below.) Elsewhere, his more customary impassivity is exemplified by his reactions when he discovers, in Morgan's castle, the set of wall paintings in which Lancelot had depicted all the major events of his and Guenevere's relationship. It is true that Arthur is described as 'touz esbahiz et touz trespansez'

21 Albert Pauphilet, ed., *La Queste del saint Graal* (Paris, 1921), pp. 21–22; trans. E. Jane Burns, in Lacy, ed., *Lancelot-Grail*, IV, p. 9. Here is one of the rare occurrences of 'fortune' used in a positive sense in the later portions of the Vulgate Cycle (whence Burns's translation as 'good fortune'); however, it refers to the earlier rise of Fortune's wheel, whereas Arthur and his court will henceforth be descending toward ruin.

22 H. Oskar Sommer, ed., *The Vulgate Version of the Arthurian Romances*, 8 vols (Washington, DC, 1908–16), II, p. 216; trans. Rupert T. Pickens, in Lacy, ed., *Lancelot-Grail*, I, pp. 285–86.

23 Sommer, ed., *Vulgate*, II, p. 217; trans. Pickens, in Lacy, ed., *Lancelot-Grail*, I, p. 286.

24 Sommer, ed., *Vulgate*, II, p. 219; trans. Pickens, in Lacy, ed., *Lancelot-Grail*, I, p. 287.

25 Sommer, ed., *Vulgate*, II, p. 310; trans. Pickens, in Lacy, ed., *Lancelot-Grail*, I, p. 339. I have modified the translation slightly for purely stylistic reasons.

[very astonished and pensive], and he says that 'se il est veritez . . . ce est la chose qui me metra au greigneur duel que ge onques eüsse' [and if that is true . . . this causes me more grief than I have ever known].[26] Yet his professed grief is neither explored nor particularly evident. He questions Morgan at length, but calmly. He refers to his dishonor and to Lancelot's treason. He swears to avenge this sin, *if* it is true[27] that Lancelot is sleeping with the queen – though he has just had incontrovertible proof of it. What is exceedingly curious about this passage is not that Arthur swears vengeance, but that his words belie his demeanor: he has no great rages, and he seems not even to raise his voice.

No less remarkable is a scene in which Agravain informs Arthur unambiguously that Lancelot and the queen are lovers. Arthur is silent for a moment, after which he says, 'Ce sont merveilles' ['that is remarkable'].[28] And he says no more.

Even where we would most expect passion, Arthur has none. In the Post-Vulgate, Arthur rapes a young woman and fathers a bastard son, Arthur le Petit. But this rape is narrated in a casual, almost cavalier manner, virtually without detail: it is just one event among many. After meeting and conversing with the attractive young woman,

> si la trouva le roy si sage et de si belles paroles qu'il en fut eschauffés si merveilleusement qu'il luy print volenté de gesir a luy. Il la print et lui fist a force et jut sans faille a luy, voulsist ou non, et la trouva pucelle. Celle . . . commença a crier endementres que le roy gisoit a luy, mais tout ce ne luy vault riens, car toutes voies jut le roy a luy et engendra dedens lui hoir masle. Quant il en eust fait sa volonté . . .
>
> [The king found her marvelously wise and well-spoken, and he was so pleased with her that he lay with her by force. She . . . began to cry out while he was lying with her, but it did her no good, for the king did what he wanted anyway, and at that time he made in her a son. After he had had his pleasure . . .][29]

Both here and in certain other passages, Arthur clearly has appetites; it is far less apparent that he has passions. In this case, the event in question is recounted from a viewpoint located outside the king, as if an observer were describing the action; we know nothing of Arthur's thoughts beyond the fact that the woman pleased him and aroused his desire.[30] The narrator is telling

26 Jean Frappier, ed., *La Mort Artu: Roman du XIIIe siècle*, 3rd ed. (Geneva, 1964), p. 61; trans. Norris J. Lacy in Lacy, ed., *Lancelot-Grail*, IV, p. 106. I have previously discussed some of these questions concerning Arthur's muted reactions; see 'The *Mort Artu* and Cyclic Closure', in *The Lancelot-Grail Cycle: Text and Transformations*, ed. William W. Kibler (Austin, 1994), pp. 85–97; for one of the specific examples I revisit here, see p. 89 of that article.

27 This is in fact the third time in the episode that Arthur has implied doubts, even though the images and words on the wall are unambiguous: *if* what he sees on the wall is true (p. 61), *if* it is the truth (p. 61), *if* it is so (p. 64).

28 Frappier, ed., *Mort Artu*, p. 109. My published translation of this line as 'I can't believe this!' now appears to me more emphatic than the Old French; see Lacy, ed., *Lancelot-Grail*, IV, p. 119.

29 Fanni Bogdanow, ed. *La Version Post-Vulgate de la* Queste del saint Graal *et de la* Mort Artu: *Troisième partie du* Roman du Graal (Paris, 1991), II, p. 473; trans. Martha Asher, in Lacy, ed., *Lancelot-Grail*, V, p. 215.

30 As Arthur is preparing to leave, the woman's father arrives; he informs Arthur that he would

rather than showing, and the result is a leveling effect in which a rape is as routine an event as a conversation or a casual meeting of knights.

In fact, it appears to be a common characteristic of the Arthurian romance (at least in French, but I believe it to be true of a good many works in other literatures as well) that, when an event occurs that should stir Arthur personally or arouse profound passions, the narrator, almost as a reflex, will remove the emotional center of the story to another character or else shift the point of view and resort to a purely descriptive method in order to avoid exploring any emotional depths – or even acknowledging that Arthur has any. Indeed, there seems to be almost an aversion, especially in scenes of potentially profound emotional import, to locating the romance's center of consciousness within the king, even when he is ostensibly the central figure of an episode or a romance. For whatever reason, when talking about Arthur himself, writers tend to step into a chronicle mode, recounting what happened but presenting Arthur not as a subjective presence but as the objective monarch whose reign serves primarily to provide the context for other adventures, for the stories of other knights.

The obvious question is *why* the removal of narrative focus from Arthur occurs so regularly. Authors rarely hesitate to give him flaws or even make him a ridiculous figure at times. So why should this great king and indomitable military leader seem to have passionate views concerning very few subjects, including his wife's love affair with one of his knights? That question must be left partially open at present: there can be no simple or satisfactory answer. However, we may speculate that motives and emotions of a powerful and passionate king are muted in order to sharpen the texts' focus on the rivalries, the conflicting loyalties, the flaws, and the passions of other characters at court and elsewhere.

A further response is suggested by Arthur's reactions to the deaths of Gauvain and his brothers, and to that of Lucan. In fact, were we to reread the Vulgate's full account of the king's life, we would find that his character is *not* constructed entirely without emotional depth, as my comments may have implied, but only that the narrators reserve those emotions (or at least their depiction) for Arthur's official, royal persona and particularly for his attachment to his knights and his antipathy toward his enemies. Thematically, Arthur's public and personal lives are inextricably related, since the adultery of Lancelot and Guenevere causes the downfall of Camelot, but only the former – the king's public life – is deemed appropriate material for emotional elaboration. His private life – his personal or domestic reactions as human being, husband, and veteran cuckold – can be described but not displayed. Surely it is this narrative split between the public and the private spheres that permits the simultaneous adulation and condemnation of Arthur in a great many texts.

In any event, concerning his betrayal by Guenevere and her lover, the Arthur of the *Mort Artu* is dispirited and weak. Even though we have witnessed his

kill him were he – Arthur – not king. The latter, who realizes that he has wronged, not the woman, but her father, offers to find her a suitable husband. Yet, he does not acknowledge that the rape was wrong except insofar as it constitutes, apparently, a crime against the father's property.

previous indecisiveness or distraction, his reactions here may surprise us, as in the scene to which I have already alluded: told that Lancelot is sleeping with the queen, his response is muted and almost perfunctory. And when Gauvain, on his own initiative, informs Lancelot that Arthur wants him, Lancelot, to leave his land, Lancelot asks the king to confirm this order. Arthur's feeble response is 'puis que Gauvains le velt . . . il me plest bien' ['since Gawain wishes it . . . so do I'].[31]

And yet this is the Arthur described by *Möttuls Saga* and many another text as 'the most renowned ruler with regard to every aspect of valor and all kinds of manliness and chivalry'. This is also the Arthur who will be listed and depicted regularly as one of the Nine Worthies – the Pantheon consisting of three pagans, three Christians, and three Jews who are considered worthy of respect and emulation. And he is often described as the first among the Christian Worthies (and thus more illustrious than Charlemagne and Godefroi de Bouillon). Clearly, there is an image of Arthur that is set and resistant to change; and then there is the real Arthur, a flawed and perhaps even tragic being. In different terms, there is, as I suggested, a public figure, and there is the private life of a largely unexceptional person with ordinary flaws. In a great many cases, these two figures do not coincide, and in any case the latter one *is* private: if he has strong reactions to the drama of his domestic and personal life, they are shared with us in only the briefest and most perfunctory way.

Of course, our assessment of Arthur has to move well past generalizations. In fact, the only generalizations about him that are reasonably reliable, especially in the Gallic tradition, concern reputation rather than reality. The reputation of Arthur's court itself is constant through most texts, and even Arthur himself generally, though with some exceptions, appears immune to criticism: he is almost invariably the greatest of kings, the sovereign whose court shines more brightly than any other and attracts to it the most talented and ambitious knights from the world over.

Yet the king himself – the man – as we have seen, may be feeble, stubborn, petulant, doddering, even in rare cases dishonorable. No matter: his court and his reputation appear not to suffer. Here is one of the great paradoxes of medieval Arthurian literature: the split between the Arthurian ideal (the image of the court, the glory of chivalry, the majesty of the throne) and the Arthur, a conspicuously imperfect human being, behind that image. This dichotomy, this dialogic relationship between two opposing conceptions of the king, appears to have been the work, initially, of Chrétien de Troyes, who must have understood that a flawless monarch had an inauspicious literary future. If Arthur were perfect, or as nearly so as a human can be, what might he offer a writer? What could such a person do other than win endless battles and sit magnanimously on his throne? (The best illustration of this literary dilemma is in fact Galahad: pure, pious, and perfect, he is also a character who engages the interest of very few readers.)

So Arthur is human, and at times, especially in the *Mort Artu*, he becomes a

31 Frappier, ed., *Mort Artu*, p. 158; trans. Lacy in *Lancelot-Grail*, IV, p. 132.

hapless if not a pathetic figure. One of the major instrumentalities of the king's decline is Fortune. Galahad and the Quest have long been anticipated, and Galahad, we are told more than once, was chosen by genealogy, by historical forces and by God to achieve the Grail Quest. But curiously, God virtually disappears from the final romance and, instead, emphasis is placed on Fortune. Dreams and visions are frequent, and a number of them concern Fortune. The most extended and remarkable of these is Arthur's dream of the Wheel of Fortune; the passage merits quotation *in extenso*:

> Quant il fu endormiz, il li fu avis que une dame venoit devant lui, la plus bele qu'il eüst onques mes veüe el monde, qui le levoit de terre et l'enportoit en la plus haute montiagne qu'il onques veïst; illuec l'asseoit seur une roe. En cele roe avoit sieges dont li un montoient et li autre avaloient; li rois regardoit en quel leu de la roe il estoit assis et voit que ses sieges estoit li plus hauz. . . . 'C'est, fet ele, la roe de Fortune.' Lors li demandoit: 'Artus, que voiz tu? – Dame, il me semble que ge voie tout le monde. – Voire, fet ele, tu le voiz, n'il n'i a granment chose dont tu n'aies esté sires jusques ci, et de toute la circuitude que tu voiz as tu esté li plus puissanz rois qui i fust. Mes tel sont li orgueil terrien qu'il n'i a nul si haut assiz qu'il ne le coviegne cheor de la poesté del monde.' Et lors le prenoit et le trebuschoit a terre si felenessement que au cheoir estoit avis au roi Artu qu'il estoit touz debrisiez et qu'il perdoit tout le pooir del cors et des menbres.

> [When Arthur had fallen asleep, it seemed to him that the most beautiful lady in the world appeared before him and lifted him up from the earth and took him up onto the highest mountain he had ever seen; and there she set him upon a wheel. The wheel had seats, some of which rose as others sank. The king saw that his seat was in the highest position. . . . She said . . . 'It's the Wheel of Fortune.' Then she asked him, 'Arthur, what do you see? – 'Lady, it seems to me that I see the whole world.' – 'Indeed', she said, 'you do see it, and in it there is little that you have not been lord of until now, and of all you see, you have been the most powerful king who ever was. But such are the effects of earthly pride that no one is so highly placed that he can avoid falling from worldly power.' And then she took him and dashed him to earth so cruelly that it seemed to King Arthur that he was crushed and that he lost all the strength of his body and its members.][32]

Fortune and her wheel are prominent and common fixtures in Arthurian romance, and even a catalogue of their occurrences would require a good deal of space. Yet, among the many Arthurian texts that feature this theme, few emphasize it in the same way as Heinrich von dem Türlin, in his *Diu Crône*. This German romance is remarkable for the ubiquity of fortune, which is sometimes but not always personified (as Vrou Saelde, Dame Fortune).[33] The work is even more remarkable for its distinctive interpretation of Fortune. In some cases, Fortune does have a wheel, and she also has a son, named Heil, 'Luck'. But the most striking facts are two. First, Fortune is said to favor those who merit it – suggesting that Fortune is not blind in this instance – and Arthur, in fact, is

32 Frappier, ed., *Mort Artu*, pp. 226–27; Lacy, trans., *Lancelot-Grail*, IV, p. 149–50.

33 For a study of fortune's role in this romance, see Karin R. Gürttler, *Kunec Artus der guote': Das Artusbild der höfischen Epik des 12. und 13. Jahrhunderts* (Bonn, 1976), esp. pp. 212–25. See also Neil Thomas, Diu Crône *and the Medieval Arthurian Cycle* (Cambridge, 2002), pp. 65–71 and passim.

called the child of Fortune. Second, Gawein is the dominant character of the romance, and *he* even dominates Fortune. We are told that, in rather conventional fashion, the wheel turns and reduces some to poverty while raising others to positions of wealth. However, in this untraditional view of Fortune, she and Luck sit upon the wheel along with others, and, like those others, they are sometimes happy and beautiful, sometimes ugly and sickly, depending on whether their place on the wheel is rising or falling. But as soon as Gawein arrives – occurring at the romance's mid-point, with the episode beginning at line 14,927 of the 30,001-line work[34] – the wheel stops and leaves Fortune, Luck, *and all who are on the wheel*, beautiful, healthy, and happy. So in this instance, Fortune does not rule Gawein but is ruled *by* him. He is the savior of Fortune and of those subject to her. As Neil Thomas puts it, 'Fortuna's boons are assimilated to the more practical qualities of human resourcefulness, daring and strength . . .'.[35]

I mention this text (which will be discussed in more detail in Neil Thomas's essay in the present volume) in order to suggest not only the prominence but also the versatility of Fortune, the endless interpretations that can be given to it/her. And it is surely significant that whereas Arthur is identified as the child of Fortune, when we encounter a text in which Fortune is subject to human power and virtue, the person who exercises that control is not Arthur himself, but one of his knights, Gawein; again Arthur is displaced. The king himself will resurface periodically as the central, active figure in romances, but there is still something indefinable in his character that tends either to move him from center-stage to the edge or to place him in the center but leave his thoughts, his motives, and especially his passions without the sharp definition that we would expect of the king routinely praised, as we saw at the beginning, as magnanimous and magnificent. Once and future king he may be, but when depicted in a textual *present*, he proves remarkably resistant to definition.

34 The edition is G.H.F. Scholl's *Diu Crône von Heinrich von dem Türlin* (Stuttgart, 1852).

35 Thomas, *Diu Crône*, p. 79.

Changing the Equation: The Impact of Tristan-Love on Arthur's Court in the Prose Tristan *and* La Tavola Ritonda

JOAN TASKER GRIMBERT

Elspeth Kennedy has traced throughout the Vulgate cycle the evolution of the attitude expressed toward the love of Lancelot and Guinevere and its effect on Arthur's realm.[1] In this huge Arthurian cycle comprising five romances completed between 1215 and 1235, the lovers first appear in the third romance, the Prose *Lancelot*, where their adulterous passion is viewed as a positive force, for it is through the love that Guinevere inspires in Lancelot that he brings Arthur's realm to its height. But the two successive romances reveal a negative attitude toward this passion. In the *Queste del Saint Graal*, the affair is seen as sinful, and, although Lancelot repents and does penance, he is prevented from seeing the Grail. In the *Mort Artu*, where Lancelot has reverted to his carnal obsession and Arthur is informed of the affair, the resulting rivalry sets in motion the events leading to the destruction of Arthur's realm.[2]

Despite this clear downward spiral in his fortunes, Lancelot's characterization is quite complex, and Kennedy warns against the tendency to simplify it and stresses the importance of inter- and intratextual allusions:

> The thirteenth-century romance was never meant to be isolated from the existing twelfth-century literature, and Lancelot's role within the cycle can be properly appreciated only if account is taken of the importance of intertextuality and intratextuality as it is manifested in the system of pairing Lancelot with other Arthurian heroes both within and without the text. Such pairings and such resonances help to structure a romance where authorial intervention or comment is rare. The interplay with existing texts serves to create links with past knights and lovers and with the familiar themes associated with them; it underlines two main themes, the quest for identity and the relationship between love and chivalry, both of which are already typical of twelfth-century Arthurian romance in general and of the earlier Lancelot tradition in particular.[3]

1 Elspeth Kennedy, 'The Figure of Lancelot in the *Lancelot-Graal*', in *Lancelot and Guinevere: A Casebook*, ed. and with an introduction by Lori J. Walters (New York, 1996), pp. 79–104.

2 Fanni Bogdanow, 'La Chute du Royaume d'Arthur – Evolution du thème', *Romania*, 107 (1986), 508–09, points out, however, that the author of the *Mort Artu* attempts to exonerate Lancelot by transferring almost the whole responsibility for Artus's fall onto the internal conflict and also by implying that Artus was wrong to condemn his wife to death.

3 Kennedy, 'The Figure of Lancelot', p. 81.

When evaluating the influence of the Tristan legend on the positive and negative attitudes toward the love of Lancelot and Guinevere, Kennedy refers only to the twelfth-century verse romances, the only versions known by the authors of the *Lancelot-Graal* cycle. My aim in this essay is to extend Kennedy's study by exploring how Lancelot and Guinevere's passion appears when they are paired with Tristan and Yseut in two important subsequent romances, the mid-thirteenth-century French Prose *Tristan* and the early fourteenth-century Italian romance *La Tavola Ritonda*. How does the equation change when Tristan and Yseut do not figure just as the literary allusions they constitute in the Vulgate cycle but as major players equal in importance to Lancelot and Guinevere? And what is the impact of that change on the depiction of Arthur's court?

I. The French Prose Tristan

The French Prose *Tristan* was one of the most popular romances of the Middle Ages.[4] Composed shortly after the *Lancelot-Graal* cycle, it is exceedingly lengthy and complex, in part because the authors grafted the Tristan legend as found in the verse romances onto the scheme provided by the *Lancelot-Graal* cycle and made the necessary adjustments.[5] The most striking change in relation to the verse *Tristan*s is that the hero's love for Yselt[6] is intimately linked with chivalry. He actually falls in love with her while witnessing the deeds of a rival knight, Palamedes, whose prowess is inspired by his love for her.[7] Once Tristan's love has been transmuted by the potion, it becomes the actual source of his prowess.

No wonder, then, that Tristan appears early on as a double for Lancelot, whom he soon rivals as the consummate lover and knight. According to Merlin, he is destined from birth not only to know great sorrow but also to join Galaad and Lancelot as one of the three best knights. The love story that is central to the verse *Tristan*s becomes somewhat obscured after Tristan is banned from Cornwall and begins the existence of a knight-errant, seeking the *compagnonnage* not just of Lancelot, but also of Sagremor, Dinadan, Kahedin and Palamedes. He will eventually become a knight of the Round Table, filling the place left vacant by Morholt, the Irish champion whom he slays in the verse versions. His induction into the Round Table occurs after he has fought incognito against Lancelot and has proven himself to be the equal of this near contemporary who has himself just joined Artus's fellowship. From then on, Lancelot's involvement in Tristan's life is total: he plays a major role in his difficult dealings with Marc,

4 It had a decisive influence on the development of the Tristan legend in Spain, Italy and England. Several Italian prose romances derive from it, the most famous (and most innovative) being the *La Tavola Ritonda*, and Malory drew on it extensively for his *Morte Dartur*. The Prose *Tristan* is preserved in over eighty manuscripts and fragments and eight early printed editions dating from 1489–1533.

5 On the origins and development of the Tristan legend, see my *Tristan and Isolde: A Casebook*, ed. with an introduction by Joan Tasker Grimbert (New York, 1995; repr. 2002), pp. xiii–c1.

6 When referring to the characters in the various primary works, I use the spellings that predominate in those works.

7 This character, whose passion for Yselt remains constant throughout this romance, was created by the authors of this romance.

rescuing him a few times from Marc's confinement and providing a convenient refuge for the lovers in Joiouse Garde, where they actually live for a couple of years. Both Lancelot and Artus are instrumental in forcing Marc to lift the ban on Tristan so that he can return to Cornwall.

Naturally, the decision to place the Tristan legend in a space contiguous with the Arthurian kingdom of Logres in its heyday inevitably invites comparison and contrast between not just Tristan and Lancelot but also Yselt and Genevre. Their contemporaries are constantly comparing them, speculating on which knight is the more valiant and which queen the more beautiful. As readers, we are meant as well to savor this parallelism, the point at which the ideology of the Tristan legend confronts that of the Arthurian legend.

The intersection of these two legends had been anticipated in Chrétien de Troyes's *Chevalier de la Charrete*. In a famous article published in 1973,[8] Jean-Charles Payen described how certain authors had attempted to mute the subversive impact of the Tristan legend. In the *Charrete*, Chrétien presents Lancelot in a situation analogous to Tristan's: he falls passionately in love with his lord's wife and has an affair with her.[9] But Chrétien defuses the situation in two important ways. First, he has the consummation of the affair occur in the Kingdom of Gorre, far from Artus's view, which effectively keeps the noble monarch away from the action and spares him the ridiculous role of cuckold. More importantly, Lancelot is endowed with a crucial social function: the Queen has been abducted by Meleagant who is holding other people from Artus's kingdom, and Lancelot is presented as the rescuer, as the savior not only of the woman he loves but also of Artus's kingdom.

If the Lancelot/Guinevere affair seems somehow more acceptable in a chivalric context, the threat constituted by its antisocial character comes to the fore in the latter part of the Vulgate cycle – in the *Queste*, where religious values predominate over secular ones, and in the *Mort Artu* where the affair is an indirect cause of the anarchy leading to Artus's downfall. But throughout the Prose *Lancelot*, Lancelot is celebrated as Artus's greatest champion. In an analogous way, the Prose *Tristan*, by placing the Tristan legend in the Arthurian context and establishing a parallel between Lancelot and Tristan and Genevre and Yselt, manages to endow Tristan with the same sort of social function as Lancelot, thereby muting the subversive impact of both men's adulterous affairs.

The parallel, which is established both explicitly and implicitly, has ideological implications. The first *implicit* link occurs when Tristan defends the Irish King Anguin at Artus's court in a judicial duel by which he both wins Yselt's hand in marriage to Marc and displays his strength, prowess and generosity. At this very point appears the episode of the split-shield, which predicts – as in the Prose *Lancelot* – the consummation of Lancelot and Genevre's love (I, §411–12).[10] This conjunction is significant since Tristan is at that moment both establishing

8 'Lancelot contre Tristan: la conjuration d'un mythe subversif (Réflexions sur l'idéologie romanesque au moyen âge)', in *Mélanges de langue et de littérature médiévales offerts à Pierre Le Gentil* (Paris, 1973), pp. 617–32.

9 Chrétien is said to have created Lancelot from the Fair Unknown paradigm that he had previously incarnated. See Walters, 'Introduction', in *Lancelot and Guinevere*, p. xiv.

10 References to the Prose *Tristan* are to two separate sets of editions. The abbreviations 'I', 'II',

his chivalric reputation and fighting to gain possession of Yselt, albeit for his uncle.

The first *explicit* connection between the two couples is made by Galahot, who informs Genevre that Tristan has lifted the enchantment of the Chastel de Plor. He affirms that there are only two knights and two ladies in the world: Lancelot and Tristan, and Genevre and Yselt. The men are unequaled in chivalry and the ladies have no equal in beauty (II, §482).

When Yselt becomes aware that she and Tristan are being compared to the Logrian lovers, she actually feels a certain rivalry. She instructs Palamedes to tell Genevre that there are only two knights and two ladies in the world, and that if she could arrange a meeting she would have judgment passed on the two women's beauty and on the two knights' strength and valor (II, §511). This episode anticipates the last major tournament, that of Louvezerp, where indeed Tristan and Yselt will establish their parity with – and even their superiority over – Lancelot and Genevre.

The essential link between love and prowess reveals a somewhat paradoxical attitude toward these illicit loves. When the narrator recounts how Tristan and Yselt come to consume the love potion, he identifies what he considers to be the most tragic element of Tristan's story, stating that this 'misadventure' will prove to be the downfall of a knight who was so valiant that in Artus's time there were few better knights in the world (II, §448). Over and over, this sentiment will be expressed – by the narrator, by Artus's knights and by Marc himself, who is acutely aware that Tristan has always brought great honor to Cornwall.

On the other hand, because Tristan's illicit passion, like Lancelot's, actually increases his prowess, it can be excused. When Yselt first learns about Genevre's affair with Lancelot, she exclaims that the Queen's conduct is base, given Artus's great worth. Her informant, a girl from Logres, retorts that no one should reproach the Queen, since she has bestowed her heart on the superior knight, while other ladies have chosen inferior ones. Clearly, the worthiest knight deserves the love of the most beautiful woman, and vice versa.[11] Moreover, when Marc reproaches Tristan for letting his passion for Yselt tarnish his chivalry and wreck the lives of all three of them, Tristan tells him he is proud to be both a valiant knight and one destined to die of love: it puts him in the company of many great men, including Absalom, Samson, Soloman, Achilles and Merlin (II, §539).

'III', followed by the section number (§), refer to: Renée L. Curtis, *Le Roman de Tristan en prose*, vol. I (Munich, 1963); vol. II (Leiden, 1976); and vol. III (Cambridge, 1985). The split-shield episode occurs in I, §411–12. The abbreviations 'I', 'II', etc., followed by the page number, refer to the series of nine volumes edited under the direction of Philippe Ménard, *Le Roman de Tristan en prose*, I, ed. Philippe Ménard (Geneva, 1987), II, ed. Marie-Luce Chênerie and Thierry Delcourt (1990), III, ed. Gilles Roussineau (1991), IV, by Jean-Claude Faucon (1991), V, by Denis Lalande and Thierry Delcourt (1992), VI, ed. Emmanuèle Baumgartner and Michèle Szkinik (1993), VII, ed. Danielle Queruel and Monique Santucci (1994), VIII, ed. Bernard Guidot and Jean Subrenat (1995) and IX, ed. Laurence Harf-Lancner (1997). On the split-shield episode in the Prose *Lancelot*, see Carol Dover, 'The Split-Shield Motif in the Old French Prose *Lancelot*', *The Arthurian Yearbook* I (1991), 43–61.

11 Significantly, Yselt is irritated by this answer and retorts that Tristan is better than Lancelot, to which the girl answers that Tristan is very handsome but as yet quite unknown compared to Lancelot (II, §513).

This is courtly ideology at its purest, but conventional morality occasionally competes with it. For example, when Tristan decides to marry Yselt of the White Hands, he claims that it is the preferable route for his honor and happiness and admits that his relationship with the Queen was wrong in the eyes of both God and the law. He should never have slept with his uncle's wife, and any worthy man who learned the truth would consider him treacherous and disloyal (II, §561).[12] Since this view is hardly the dominant one, news of Tristan's marriage is not well received in Logres by either Genevre or Lancelot, who both find Tristan's breach of faith shocking. Yselt easily finds empathy when she writes to Genevre to complain that Tristan has destroyed her by his base and cruel betrayal, whereas she had given her all to Love – faith, hope and service more than to God or any man. She laments that she has been ill-rewarded for her service, whereas Genevre has been lucky in love and well rewarded (II, §572).[13]

Despite the very deliberate parallels established between the two sets of lovers, the difference in their situations in their respective realms causes a certain divergence in how their passions are viewed. Lancelot, despite his love for Genevre, does not spend much time at Artus's court: indeed, the need to conceal his passion almost necessitates frequent absences, during which he engages in countless adventures that enhance his reputation. Although his affair is well known to some and the lovers are even denounced in court, Artus's esteem and respect for his best knight make him loath to punish them, and when he condemns Genevre to death, Lancelot defends her, and his peers take the lovers' side, blaming Artus for his cruelty.

The situation in Cornwall is quite different. Marc's evil nephew Audret denounces the lovers early in the Prose *Tristan*, and the enmity between Marc and Tristan is manifest even before Tristan wins Yselt for his uncle. From the moment Tristan is banished from Cornwall, he embarks on another kind of double life. Although most of it is spent as a knight-errant in Logres and as a member of Artus's fellowship, there are long periods when he and Yselt live together outside of both communities, and it is at these times that their contrast with Lancelot and Genevre seems greatest, especially during their extended stay in the Morroiz Forest, where they live in splendid isolation, with Tristan even forsaking chivalry entirely. The narrator laments that he had utterly forgotten everyone, including Marc, Artus and Lancelot, so intent was he on cherishing his lady and rejoicing in her company (II, §553).

The two years that Tristan and Yselt spend intermittently at Joiouse Garde, on the other hand, seem to offer the perfect *modus vivendi* for adulterous lovers in the universe portrayed in the Prose *Tristan*. They have escaped from Marc's surveillance and can live freely and happily together in a beautiful setting, but

12 The ambiguous oath in the conversation under the pine tree preserved in Béroul's version is replaced in the Prose *Tristan* by bald-faced lies. Tristan says, for the benefit of his uncle hiding in the tree, that God knows he never had any thought of committing adultery with Yselt and never would, to which Yselt answers that if he loved her as wrongfully as Marc thinks Tristan would be the most disloyal knight in the world.

13 The more experienced woman tells her that she cannot always expect joy, for love is a human condition and subject to the vagaries of Fortune. When one is most unhappy, one knows great joy will follow. Genevre herself fears the converse movement (II, §581).

they are hardly isolated from society. Other knights drop in for more or less extended periods of time, and Tristan uses Joiouse Garde as a base from which he can set out to enhance his reputation by engaging in adventures and tournaments. In essence, they are fully integrated into Arthurian society, such as it is. They enjoy all the pleasures and entertainments and challenges that that life has to offer.

The parallel established in the Prose *Tristan* between the Cornish lovers and their Logrian counterparts is generally positive, and whereas the narrator and others state occasionally that Tristan's immoderate love for Yselt tarnishes his chivalry, the same is not true of Lancelot's passion for Genevre, a phenomenon owing in large part to the chronological links between the events recounted in the Prose *Tristan* and those in the *Lancelot-Graal* cycle. Although the compilers of many manuscripts containing the Prose *Tristan* incorporate whole episodes of the *Queste*[14] and then simply append the *Mort Artu* as a kind of epilogue to Tristan's story, Tristan and Yselt actually die before the Grail Quest ends and well before the tragic events recounted in the *Mort Artu* that pit Lancelot against Artus and Gauven. Moreover, because the Grail Quest appears in this romance as a predominantly secular adventure, there is no reason to stigmatize either Lancelot or Tristan for their obsession with carnal love. Their love continues to inspire them in their numerous adventures where as knights-errant who incarnate the best values of their society they actually replace the king as the pivotal figure. As Emmanuèle Baumgartner notes, this phenomenon, already apparent in the Prose *Lancelot*, is more marked in the Prose *Tristan* for, although a large place is given to Lancelot's exploits in the Prose *Lancelot*, the *Lancelot-Graal* cycle as a whole is in many ways a chronicle of Artus's entire reign, whereas in the Prose *Tristan* Artus's main function seems to be to organize tournaments and preside over festive courts.[15]

Artus is still, nevertheless, a powerful symbol, for Marc is considerably more villainous in the Prose *Tristan* than he was in the verse romances, and his villainy is underscored by contrast with Artus, who is altogether a more sympathetic figure than in the Prose *Lancelot*.[16] From one end of the Prose *Tristan* to the other, Marc, though he is actually Artus's vassal, behaves as his implacable enemy, waging through ruse a relentless crusade against him and all that his

14 On the interpolation of the *Queste* and its effects, see Colette-Anne Van Coolput, *Aventures quérant et le sens du monde: Aspects de la réception productive des premiers romans du Graal cycliques dans le Tristan en prose* (Leuven, 1986). On intertextuality in the Prose *Tristan*, see Janina P. Traxler, 'The Use and Abuse of the Grail Quest: Ironic Juxtaposition in the *Tristan en prose*', *Tristania*, 15 (1994), 23–32, and her 'Ironic Juxtaposition as Intertextuality in the Prose *Tristan*', in *Text and Intertext in Medieval Arthurian Literature*, ed. Norris J. Lacy (New York, 1996), pp. 147–63.

15 Emmanuèle Baumgartner, *Le 'Tristan en Prose' – Essai d'interprétation d'un roman médiéval* (Geneva, 1976), p. 176.

16 Because Marc is so disloyal and the Cornish knights so craven (a fact that is underscored by sheer repetition), it is easier to justify the lovers' failure to respect the old loyalties. They are clearly on a plane so far above everyone else in Cornwall that they can only be compared with the most superlative members of the Arthurian realm: Tristan is the only knight whose prowess can rival Lancelot's, and Yselt is the only lady whose beauty can rival Genevre's. Of course, one might think that the contrast between Marc and Artus would make Lancelot's affair seem even less acceptable than in the later parts of the Lancelot-Grail cycle, but actually

realm and the elite corps of knights-errant represent. Though he models his court on Artus's, he surrounds himself with knights as vile as he is and heeds the counsel of his evil nephew Audret. Once Tristan has joined the Round Table and his celebrity spreads far and wide, Marc's enmity is felt as a personal affront in Artus's realm. A consummate coward, Marc leads a massive force to invade Logres at the very moment that it has been destabilized by the ravages of the Grail Quest. After abducting Yselt from Joiouse Garde, he lays siege to Camaalot, wounding Artus grievously. Only Galaad's last-minute intervention prevents the king from falling into Marc's hands.[17]

The reverence in which Tristan is held in Logres can be seen especially in the way Artus and his knights react to his death. In most manuscripts of the Prose *Tristan*, the hero dies by Marc's hand while he is harping to Yselt, stabbed in the back with a poisonous sword supplied by Morgain. He bids a fervent adieu to chivalry and entrusts his arms to Sagremor, asking him to present his sword to his dearest companions, Palamedes, Dinadan and Lancelot, and to bid them farewell, begging them to honor his sword since he loved them and did his best to uphold the glory of the Round Table. Distraught that he must die in this dishonorable way, he laments that the world is shamefully debased by it and all chivalry dishonored. Then he asks Yselt to die with him so that their souls will leave their bodies together, embracing her so hard that they expire together. The news of the lovers' demise – of their queen and their champion – shocks the Cornish. Marc, suddenly remorseful, buries them with great pomp in an elaborate sepulcher (IX, pp. 186–203).

In Logres, the level of grief is without precedent when Sagremor announces the news at Artus's court, where he finds his companions already reeling from the death of so many Grail questors – forty knights of the Round Table in all, including Palamedes, King Bademagu and Erec, son of Lac. Although Lancelot, Hestor and Blioberis do return from the Quest, the news of Tristan's death is so devastating that Artus yearns to die and claims that he will never again feel joy. Lancelot, whose sorrow is boundless, declares that the whole world should come to an end; for him Tristan's death means the death of all chivalry. Everyone dons black robes, and mourning is maintained in the court for a whole year. Artus, Genevre, Lancelot and others compose lays in memory of the lovers (IX, pp. 278–82).

In some manuscripts the Prose *Tristan* ends at this point, but in others the compiler has interpolated, at the point before Sagremor arrives at Artus's court, an episode from the *Queste* that recounts the deaths of Palamedes and his father Esclabor, Galaad and Perceval. More material from the *Queste* is inserted after the mention of the court's mourning for Tristan, and it is here that Artus is informed of Lancelot's resumption of his affair with the Queen, and Agravain is charged with spying on them. The reader is then referred to the *Mort Artu* for the tragic events that follow.

But according to Baumgartner, at least one compiler seized on the impor-

the parallel established between Cornwall and Logres seems to exalt both couples and Artus as well.

17 Baumgartner, *Le 'Tristan en Prose'*, pp. 192–93.

tance of the theme of Marc's enmity and added an original episode, preserved in a single manuscript.[18] BN fr. 340 records that after the battle of Salisbury and the death of Lancelot, Marc invades Logres one last time to inflict a posthumous revenge on the kingdom that had humiliated him all his life. Burning and ravaging everything in his path, he desecrates the tombs of Lancelot and Galahot and destroys Camaalot, including the Round Table. He then storms the hermitage where Bohort and the archbishop of Canterbury have withdrawn and kills the archbishop before being slain by an obscure knight from Ban's lineage.[19]

II. La Tavola Ritonda

Now that we have seen the impact of the Tristan legend on the depiction of the Arthurian court in the Prose *Tristan*, we are in a position to appreciate the surprising changes introduced by the anonymous author of the Italian prose romance *La Tavola Ritonda*.[20] Although it is the only complete Arthurian cycle in Italian, it is primarily a Tristan romance, despite the title and the stated intention of the author, whose narrator proposes in the prologue to tell the fine adventures, great deeds of chivalry and noble tournaments of the knights both of Uter Pandragon's Tavola Vecchia and of Artù's Tavola Nuova. By the second chapter, he has abandoned this grandiose design, narrowing his focus to the Tavola Nuova and especially to the birth, life and death of Tristano and Lancilotto.[21] Stating that he will begin with Tristano, who was the source and foundation of all chivalry, he sets out the different parts of the story – his most noble lineage and birth, his perfect love and his cruel death, and then the great lament that was made for this death, and the very great vengeance that was taken on his behalf.

Although this outline sounds very much like that of the Prose *Tristan*, *La Tavola Ritonda* actually has a strikingly different emphasis. While it duly underscores Tristano's commitment to chivalry, it also features some radical changes and additions clearly designed to refocus attention on a love portrayed as both overpowering and exemplary.[22] The narrator laments the corrosive effects of inordinate love in general but has consistently high praise for the Cornish lovers and their 'loyal love', and he exploits the parallel offered by Lancilotto and

18 According to Bogdanow, it also appears in the Post-Vulgate cycle ('La Chute du royaume d'Arthur', p. 516).

19 Baumgartner, *Le 'Tristan en Prose'*, p. 192.

20 The standard edition of this romance is Filippo-Luigi Polidori, ed. *La Tavola Ritonda o l'historia di Tristano*, 2 vols (Bologna, 1864–65). See also Anne Shaver, *Tristan and the Round Table. A Translation of* La Tavola Ritonda (Binghamton, NY, 1983). References are to the chapter numbers.

21 Daniela [Delcorno] Branca, *I Romanzi italiani di Tristano e la 'Tavola Ritonda'* (Florence, 1968), p. 90, speculates that he reduced the scope of his project because the initial one seemed too daunting.

22 See Branca, *I Romanzi italiani*, pp. 47–61 for an episode-by-episode chart comparing the *Tavola* with the Prose *Tristan* and its other sources.

Ginevara primarily in order to demonstrate the unmistakable superiority of Tristano and Isotta.[23]

The *Tavola* author underscores Tristano's status as exemplary lover by reducing drastically the number and length of the chivalric adventures recounted in the Prose *Tristan* and by recasting and reordering the events of the hero's life. Close ties with Artù and Lancilotto enhance his prestige, as Marco is demoted from maternal to paternal uncle, and Tristano's mother becomes both Artù's niece and the cousin of Lancilotto's father. The marriage of Tristano's parents, arranged in part to make peace between his father and Artù, is negotiated by Lancilotto, who in this romance is a generation older than Tristano. Tristano's birth is artfully framed by the consummation of Lancilotto and Ginevara's love, on the one hand, and, on the other, by the discovery of the stone erected by Merlino marking the future meeting there of Lancilotto, Tristano and Galeotto.[24] The narrator explains that all three had the first foundation for being a noble knight – a heart in love – as well as the requisite qualities of honesty, courtesy and loyalty, but he laments that they were neither secret nor wise in their loves; rather, they loved like wild beasts, seeking their delight inordinately and thinking only of themselves (XIII).

The issue of *willful excess* is key in this romance, and the narrator singles out Tristano as one whose inordinate love was excused by the potion. Lancilotto and Ginevara's immoderate passion was conceived when they first set eyes on each other and their decision to consummate their love was a conscious one, whereas Tristano and Isotta first came to love each other with a 'loyal love', like brother and sister, and their love became carnal only after they had unwittingly consumed the potion.

Tristano and Isotta's superiority is first demonstrated in the way the split-shield episode has been reworked and its meaning totally transformed. The episode occurs, as in the Prose *Tristan* just after Tristano has won Isotta from the Irish king, but here the shield is sent not as a warning that the Logrian lovers will soon consummate their love (for they had done so before Tristano's birth), but rather as notice to Lancilotto and Ginevara that they have been surpassed both in beauty and in the quality of their love by a couple bound by a loyal love that is faultless. This couple will soon enjoy great delight through a mistake; the shield will then resolder itself, only to fall apart again when they die. Since love is the foundation of noble knighthood, and Lancilotto's love is no longer the most perfect or loyal, he is no longer the noblest knight (XXVIII). In the Prose *Tristan*, Tristan joins the Round Table much later, but in the *Tavola* his induction occurs, significantly, just after the split-shield incident identifying him as a loyal lover and before that love is contaminated by his unwitting consumption of the potion (XXXI).[25] Moreover, in this romance, the lovers actually marry before

23 I do not subscribe to the view held by Branca and other scholars that the author sees Tristano's virtue as tarnished by his obsessive love for Isotta. See my article 'Translating Tristan-Love from the Prose *Tristan* to the *Tavola Ritonda*', *RLA: Romance Languages Annual*, 6 (1994), 92–97, on which I have drawn for part of this study.

24 The trio so-named in the Prose *Tristan* comprises Lancelot, Tristan and Galaad.

25 Artù, having received a letter describing Tristano's triumph over Lancilotto's cousin Brunoro

Tristano hands Isotta over to Marco upon their arrival in Cornovaglia (XXXVII).[26]

Tristano's subsequent adventures stress chivalry and reinforce the links already established between him and Lancilotto, Artù and Marco, but they also underscore his status as a perfect lover. He dominates every chapter from his birth in XII to his death in CXXIX, and except for the brief time he is in Brittany (LI–LIV) and wandering as a knight errant (LV–LXII), Isotta is rarely separated from him: she is with him in Ireland, Cornwall, and then at Gioiso Guardia (XC–CXXII).

Although Tristano consistently proves himself superior to Lancilotto, their *compagnonnage* ensures total reciprocity in matters of both love and chivalry: at one point, Lancilotto intervenes to obtain Marco's pardon of the Cornish lovers, and Tristano reciprocates by securing Artù's pardon of Lancilotto and Ginevara. At the tournament at Verzeppe, held in honor of Isotta, Tristano defeats Lancilotto and Artù and then engages in a bitter duel with Lancilotto incognito until their ladies make peace between them (XCIV–XCIX). This encounter is only one of many where Tristano is stopped before he can defeat Lancilotto. The two knights are virtually equal, but the narrator always underscores Tristano's superiority, and, at Tristano's death, he states that he was a bolder knight than the Tavola Vecchia knights, Lancilotto, or Galasso (CXXVIII). Although Galasso's birth introduces the kind of mystical love seen in the *Queste* (but not in the Prose *Tristan*), the narrator refuses to vaunt unequivocally his superiority. If Galasso was the most noble knight because he was touched by God's grace, Tristano was the best secular knight, the source and foundation of all chivalry, of which the cornerstone is a heart in love.[27]

The tournament at Verzeppe marks the definitive triumph of Tristano and Isotta over their rivals for prowess and beauty. Isotta bewitches even Artù, who has proclaimed the tournament so that he can judge if she is as beautiful as he has heard. Duly impressed, he offers Ginevara and Verzeppe to Tristano in exchange for Isotta! Eventually, he gives the castle to Isotta because the tournament was called by him and won by Tristano for love of her. He orders the construction in the meadow of statues representing Tristano, Lancilotto, Palamidesso, Amoroldo and eventually Galasso. After the destruction of the Round Table, their swords are suspended from their images. They were there when Carlo Magno rode into Logres and upon seeing them proclaimed that Artù deserved his dolorous death, for with five such barons he should have had all Christendom and the Saracens in his thrall. In a scene reminiscent of Charlemagne's praise of Roland and Durendal on his arrival at Rencesvals, the

the Red, inscribes Tristano's name in the Tavola book, although he will not actually meet him until much later.

26 Little is made of this union, which is forced on the lovers by the custom of the Castello del Proro, and the narrator makes no further reference to it.

27 Galasso is chaste, but significantly Tristano is at various points also referred to as 'chaste' because his love, unlike Lancilotto's, was a 'loyal love' that became carnal as well through no fault of his own. The narrator's insistence on this point is, to me, far more important than Dinadano's emphasis on the importance of chastity. In any case, I am not convinced that Dinadano is, as Christopher Kleinhenz contends, the author's spokesman; see his 'Tristan in Italy: The Death or Rebirth of a Legend', *Studies in Medieval Culture*, 6 (1975), 155.

Frankish king praises the beauty and quality of Tristano's image and judges his sword to be heavier and better tempered than the others (XCIX).[28]

The ending of *La Tavola Ritonda* offers final proof of the superiority of Tristano and Isotta. As in the Prose *Tristan*, Tristano dies through Marco's base treachery and pleads that his arms be presented to Artù and Lancilotto, but the moment is infused with intense religious fervor as he prays to God, expressing remorse for his sinful preoccupation with worldly matters (though not with his adulterous passion!) and begs humbly that Christ's precious blood be the price and payment for his sins. Isotta expresses confidence that they will obtain forgiveness for their sins.[29] After confessing, Tristano enjoins Isotta to accompany him in death, and their souls leave their bodies simultaneously.[30]

The apocalyptic aftermath of the lovers' death confirms the christological overtones of this passage. Tristano's death (at 33) plunges Artù and his knights into gloom. Lancilotto claims that the world has ended, and Artù must relinquish his dream of rebuilding the Round Table with his two best knights (CXXXIII). A high vendetta is announced against Marco, whom they capture and imprison in a tower across from the lovers' tombs, where he will die a victim of gluttony. Artù's knights also give in to excess. The destruction of the Round Table occurs in large part because Lancilotto's lust for Ginevara becomes so obsessive that he can no longer conceal their affair. Although the narrator laments Tristano's death as an irreparable loss to chivalry and to the Round Table, he blames the destruction of Artù's society not on Tristano's love for Isotta – which was beyond his control – but rather on Marco's treachery and on other instances of *willful excess*, including Lancilotto's lust.[31]

In *La Tavola Ritonda*, then, the Tristan legend has an impact on the depiction of Lancelot and Guinevere's love in relation to Arthur's realm that is totally different from that seen in the Prose *Tristan*. In the earlier romance, where Tristan is Lancelot's contemporary, the passion shared by the two couples is viewed in a generally positive light. Although Tristan's love is at times explicitly condemned as tarnishing his chivalry, by and large it is shown to be exemplary, as is Lancelot's love for Genevre. The Cornish lovers' death causes great mourning in Logres as Artus, Lancelot, Genevre and others remember the consummate knight-lover and his beautiful wife.

28 The parallel with the *Chanson de Roland* is enhanced as the narrator names the other swords: Galasso's 'Gioioso' is none other than Charlemagne's 'Joiuse', and Lancilotto's 'Altaclara' is Olivier's 'Halteclere'.

29 Moreover, Artù has Tristano's armor placed in the church, an honor reserved for him alone, and the pope offers indulgences to all who pray for the lovers' souls.

30 For a love now explicitly described as exemplary, the description of the vine that roots in each of the lovers' hearts and grows out of their tombs is accompanied by an unexpected allegorization (CXXXI) that according to Donald Hoffman 'invites an ecstatic exegesis that blends Dionysian celebration with eucharistic devotion, recreating Tristan as the patron of a new communion of lovers who will drink the wine transubstantiated from his body and blood'. Donald L. Hoffman, 'The Arthurian Tradition in Italy', in *King Arthur Through the Ages*, ed. Valerie M. Lagorio and Mildred Leake Day, 2 vols (New York, 1990), I, p. 177. See also his 'Radix amoris: The *Tavola Ritonda* and its Response to Dante's Paolo and Francesca', in Grimbert, ed., *Tristan and Isolde*, pp. 207–22.

31 Unlike Joan Ferrante, I do not think Tristano's love was responsible for the final disaster. See her book *The Conflict of Love and Honor. The Medieval Tristan Legend in France* (The Hague, 1973), p. 106.

La Tavola Ritonda, by contrast, exploits the parallel between the two couples in order to demonstrate the distinct superiority of Tristano and Isotta, who were joined by a 'loyal love' before the consumption of the potion forced them to commit adultery. Lancilotto and Ginevara are more worthy of condemnation because they made a conscious decision to betray Artù. In this romance, the impact of Tristano and Isotta's death on Artù's realm is nothing short of devastating. Once this exemplary couple, the flower of chivalry and beauty and the most loyal of lovers, is gone, it seems that nothing can hold. Artù and his knights indulge in various kinds of excess, including that exemplified by the behavior of Lancilotto and Ginevara, and it is precisely *willful excess* that undermines Arthurian ideals and wreaks havoc on Artù's realm.

Illustration and the Fortunes of Arthur

ALISON STONES

It is towards the end of the *Mort Artu* that the goddess Fortuna appears to King Arthur in a dream. She is the most beautiful woman he has ever seen. She takes him up the highest mountain and at the top she sits him on a wheel whose seats rise and fall; he sees that his seat is at the top. There follows a dialogue in which Fortuna questions Arthur, as though prompting him to realize for himself the meaning of the wheel and of the view of the whole world he sees from his place on high; but it is Fortuna who evokes the lordship that Arthur up till then has held over all this land – he has been the most powerful king to ever rule, she tells him. She goes on to say that the ways of the world are such that there is none who does not deserve to fall. Matching action to words, she dashes him cruelly to the ground; he then feels as though every bone in his body has been broken and he has lost all his strength in body and limbs; and he has understood this portent of the evil to come.

> . . . quant il fu endormis si li fu auis que vne dame vint deuant lui la plus bele quil eust onques ueu el monde . Ele le leuoit de terre si le portoit en la plus haute montaigne quil onques veist . Et illueques lasseoit en vne roe . et cele roe auoit sieges dont li un montoi[en]t et l[i] autre aualoi[en]t . Et li rois se regardoit en quel lieu de la roe il estoit assis . et il veoit que ses sieges estoit li plus haus . Et la dame li demandoit . Artus ou es tu . et il li respondi. dame ie sui en .j. haut roe mais ie ne sai que ce est ne quele senefie . Saces fait ele que cest la roe de fortune . Lors li redemandoit . Artus que vois tu . Dame fait il me semble que ie voie tot le monde. voirs est fait ele que tu le vois . Ne il ni a mie grantment de chose dont tu naies este sires iusques chi . Et de toute la circuite que tu vois as tu este li plus poissans rois qui i fust . Mais tel sont li eur[1] terrien quil ni a nul si haut assis quil ne le couiegne chaioir de la poeste del monde . et tu ten aparcheuras bien temprement . Lors faisoit la roe torner et le trebuchoit a terre si felenessement que al chaio[i]r li estoit bien auis quil estoit tos debrisies . et quil eust perdu tot le pooir del cors et des menbres.
> Einsi vit li rois artus les mescheances qui li estoient a auenir . . .[2]

> [. . . when he was asleep it seemed to him that a lady came before him, the most beautiful he had ever seen in the world. She lifted him up from the ground and

1 Other manuscripts give the variant 'orgueil' here (S VI 361, n. 11).

2 *La Mort le Roi Artus*, in H. Oskar Sommer, *The Vulgate Version of the Arthurian Romances*, 8 vols (Washington, D.C., 1908–16), VI, p. 361. Translations are my own.

carried him to the highest mountain that he had ever seen. And there she sat him on a wheel, and the wheel had seats, some of which went up and others went down. And the king looked to see where abouts on the wheel he was sitting, and he saw that his seat was the topmost one. And the lady asked him, 'Arthur, where are you?' and he replied, 'My lady, I am on a high wheel but I do not know what it means'. 'You know', she said, 'it is the Wheel of Fortune.' Then she asked him again, 'Arthur, what do you see?' 'My lady, it seems as if I can see the whole world.' 'Truly', she said, 'that is what you see. There is hardly anything over which you have not been lord up to now. And of all the length and breadth of what you see you have been the most powerful king there ever was. But such is earthly fortune that no one sits so high that it is not fitting that he fall from worldly power and you will see this in due course.' Then she made the wheel turn and cast him to the ground so wickedly that he felt as if the fall had dashed him to pieces and sapped all the strength in his body and limbs.
In this way King Arthur saw the evils that were yet to befall him . . .]

In the British Library Additional 10294 manuscript of the *Mort Artu*, part of the complete Short Version of the *Lancelot-Grail* romance and the base manuscript of Sommer's edition, this arresting passage is preceded by a single-column miniature, showing Arthur sitting at the top of Fortune's wheel, with Fortuna (her eyes covered with a transparent blindfold) at the centre (fig. 1).[3] The image, in many ways, is much simpler than the subtle textual account of Arthur's encounter with Fortuna; the artist has omitted the mountain and the vista of the world over which Arthur had held sway, nor is the dialogue between Arthur and Fortuna expressed in the miniature, let alone Arthur's crashing fall and his understanding of what all this was really about.[4] But the image is an important one, as by its very presence on the page it underlines visually the significance of the passage and links it to the entire series of highlights singled out, marked, and given special emphasis, by the pictorial component of the manuscript as a whole. The Additional copy is important in the illustrative tradition of the cycle in general, as it preserves more pictures – 748 in all – than any other surviving copy of the *Lancelot-Grail* romance – although it is also the case that other copies have illustrations for episodes and subjects that the makers of Add., or whoever put its programme of pictures together, chose not to illustrate, so that the dynamics of illustration across the cycle as a whole are highly fluid and by no means static. Add. also contains a date, 12 February 1316 (1317 ns),[5] carved on one of the Tombs of Judgement commissioned by Duchess Flegentine for Nabor, the seigneur de Karabel, and the giant, in the *Estoire del*

3 The miniature is placed at S VI 360. 1. It was first reproduced in Roger Sherman Loomis and Laura Hibbard Loomis, *Arthurian Legends in Medieval Art* (New York, 1938), fig. 245.

4 Fortuna is evoked on numerous occasions in the *Mort Artu*, and by different people, as Norris Lacy has pointed out; but this is the only occasion where Fortuna appears in person with her wheel, and it is the only illustration. For Fortuna in the text, see Norris J. Lacy, 'The *Mort Artu* and Cyclic Closure', in *The Lancelot-Grail Cycle, Text and Transformations*, ed. William W. Kibler (Austin, TX, 1994), pp. 85–97, especially 90–91. See also Karl Josef Höltgen, 'König Arthur und Fortuna', *Anglia*, 75 (1957), 35–54, trans. by Edward Donald Kennedy as 'King Arthur and Fortuna', in *King Arthur: A Casebook*, ed. Edward Donald Kennedy (New York, 1996), pp. 121–37.

5 In this period the New Year began on March 25, so dates given between Jan. 1 and March 24 refer to the following calendar year in modern reckoning, known as 'new style' (ns).

saint Graal, which is most likely the actual date when that miniature was painted (Add. 10292, f. 55v, left column).[6] And although no names of scribes, artists, or patrons, are given in the manuscript, Add. and its two sisters can be confidently attributed to the region of eastern Artois or western Flanders (most likely Saint-Omer, Tournai, or Ghent – but its artists may have come there from further east), in the early years of the fourteenth century.[7] At least six scribes, three or more pen-flourishers, two or more champie initial painters, and three major illuminators participated in the production of these copies, and one set also has pictures that were added in the late fourteenth century. These are some of the reasons why Add. and its related copies were selected for the Lancelot-Grail Project, and this essay draws in large measure upon the collaborative work of this project.[8]

What is also notable about the Fortuna image in Add. is that, so far as I know, it is the only depiction of the subject in the entire illustrative tradition of the *Lancelot-Grail* romance.[9] That is not to say that similar images of Fortuna did not appear in other contexts in this period and earlier.[10] There is even another

6 One could argue this otherwise, as with dates occurring in colophons – which were often simply copied, with their preceding text, into a later copy – so that manuscripts of the *Image du monde*, for instance, often carry the date of the 1265 redaction even though they were copied later; but in this case, 1317 is quite reasonable on paleographical and stylistic grounds by comparison with other manuscripts. The image was first reproduced in Loomis (cit. n. 3) fig. 248, and in colour on the cover of vol. 3 of *Artistes, artisans et production artistique* (Actes du colloque, Rennes, 1983), ed. X. Barral i Altet, 3 vols (Paris, 1986–90).

7 The sister manuscripts are London, British Library, MS Royal 14.E.III, containing *Estoire*, *Queste* and *Mort Artu*, lacking *Merlin* and *Lancelot* (hereafter Royal); 3) Amsterdam, Bibliotheca Philosophica Hermetica, MS 1, in 3 vols, containing *Estoire*, *Merlin* and *Lancelot* up to the beginning of the *Agravain* section (hereafter Amst.); the *Agravain*, *Queste* and *Mort Artu* are found, interleaved, and with lacunae, in Oxford, Bodleian Library, MS Douce 215 (hereafter Douce), and Manchester, The John Rylands University Library, MS French 1, bound in 2 volumes but foliated continuously (hereafter Rylands). The major artist was, in all probability, the chief painter in all three copies (assuming a certain evolution in his stylistic mode over a period of some years). An assistant did large parts of Add. 10292 and Add. 10293; another assistant did parts of Douce and Rylands. All of them can be found working on other books, see Alison Stones, 'Another Short Note on Rylands French 1', in *Romanesque and Gothic, Essays for George Zarnecki*, ed. Neil Stratford (Woodbridge, 1989), pp. 185–92.

8 See <http://www.pitt.edu/~medart> and <http://ltl22/sis.pitt.edu/lancelot/lancelot.html>.

9 So unusual is the subject that I managed to omit it from my comparative investigation of the iconography of the *Mort Artu*: 'Some Aspects of Arthur's Death in Medieval Art', in *The Passing of Arthur*, ed. Christopher Baswell and William Sharpe (New York, 1988), pp. 52–101. The subject is notably absent too in the manuscripts of Jacques d'Armagnac (d. 1477), of the early fourteenth and third quarter of the fifteenth century, Paris, Bibliothèque nationale de France, MSS français 112, 113–116, 117–120 (the last is the one made c. 1400 and inherited by Jacques from his great-grandfather, Jean de Berry); see Susan Blackman in 'A Pictorial Synopsis of Arthurian Episodes for Jacques d'Armagnac, Duke of Nemours', *Word and Image in Arthurian Literature*, ed. Keith Busby (New York, 1996), pp. 3–49, at 13–47; and, for fuller descriptions, Blackman, 'The Manuscripts and Patronage of Jacques d'Armagnac, Duke of Nemours (1433–1477)', Ph.D. dissertation, University of Pittsburgh, 1993, Ann Arbor, MI, University Microfilms, 1994, pp. 182–245. French manuscripts in the Bibliothèque Nationale de France are hereafter referred to as Paris, BNF fr. followed by their shelf number.

10 Of course images of Fortuna and her wheel had by then enjoyed a considerable vogue, in such distinguished contexts as the late twelfth-century *Hortus deliciarum* and Peter of Eboli's *Sicilian Chronicle*; the early thirteenth-century *Carmina Burana*, where the opening poem is about Fortune, and the *Roman de la Poire*, of shortly after 1270, where the image is referred to in the text and placed second in the series of full-page portraits of famous lovers, unusually showing the lady of the couple seated at the top (in her unidentified heraldic robes), pulling up her fallen lover, naked except for his braies and cale, while the huge figure of Fortuna,

example that may possibly be by the major artist of Add., illustrating the Preface to Brunetto Latini's *Trésor* in Paris, BNF fr. 566 (MS K), f. 10 (fig. 2).[11] There is heraldry in MS K, which I think may point to the patronage or at least the entourage of Henry IV, Count of Luxemburg from 1288, Holy Roman Emperor (1312–13), and his wife Marguerite de Brabant (m. 1292, d. 1311).[12] In the context of Brunetto Latini's *Trésor*, too, the Fortuna image is not at all common: to the best of my knowledge, MS K stands out as the only Brunetto Latini manuscript to use a Fortuna image for the preface, and the rest of K's iconography, apart from its saints, prophets, and animal pictures, is in general unrelated to the main clusters of the Brunetto Latini tradition. A small group of earlier copies of the *Trésor* shows that the subject of Fortuna and her wheel enjoyed a brief moment of interest elsewhere in the pictorial cycle, and in its earliest manuscripts: at Book II, Ch. 115, entitled *Des biens de fortune*, four copies, all made in or around Douai between about 1275 and 1290, include a Fortuna image: Paris, BNF fr. 1110 (fig. 3); Brussels, BR 10228; Vatican, lat. 3203 (fig. 4), and, at some distance stylistically, Arras, BM 182 (1060). These are related to two Douai manuscripts, the martyrology of Notre-Dame-des-Près, O. Cist., Douai, now Valenciennes, BM 838, and the psalter-hours of Saint-Amé, OSB, Douai, now Brussels, BR 9391; and a large number of other manuscripts can be attributed to the major artist,

crowned, holds the wheel (Paris, BNF fr. 2186, f. 2v). For the Fortuna motif see particularly F.P. Pickering, *Literature and Art in the Middle Ages* (London, 1970; first published in German in 1966); and for fr. 2186, Sylvia J. Huot, *From Song to Book* (Ithaca, NY, 1987), pp. 174–93, fig. 15, and for the date, Hans-Erich Keller, 'La Structure du Roman de la Poire', *Conjunctures: Medieval Studies in Honor of Douglas Kelly*, ed. Keith Busby and Norris J. Lacy (Amsterdam, 1994), pp. 205–17, at 213. For Fortuna depicted in some other literary contexts, see Alison Stones, 'Seeing the Walls of Troy', in *Manuscripts in Transition: Recycling Manuscripts, Texts, and Images*, ed. Brigitte Dekeyzer and Jan van der Stock (Leuven, 2005), 161–78, and Jean Wirth, 'L'Iconographie médiévale de la roue de fortune', in *La Fortune: thèmes, représentations, discours*, ed. Yasmina Foehr-Janssens and Emmanuelle Métry (Geneva, 2003), pp. 105–29.

11 Brunetto Latini, *Le Trésor*, ed. Francis J. Carmody, ed. (Berkeley, 1948) (based on Paris, BNF fr. 1110, MS T, supplemented by Chantilly, Musée Condé 288, MS C5); Paris, BNF fr. 566 is MS K, and transmits the First Redaction of the text; Julia Bolton Holloway, *Brunetto Latini: An Analytic Bibliography* (Research Bibliographies and Checklists 44) (London, 1986), no. 33. The manuscript has been connected with the Add. group by Judith Oliver and attributed to Liège, and indeed, our major artist would appear to have executed works for people living outside his region of eastern Artois and western Flanders; see Julia H. Oliver, *Gothic Manuscript Illumination in the Diocese of Liège (c. 1250–c. 1330)*, 2 vols (Leuven, 1988), I, pp. 187–89, pl. 195–97, noting that the text includes interpolations of Aegidius de Columna's *De regimine principum* in the translation of Henri de Gauchi, canon of Liège, composed c. 1296. The most recent list of Brunetto Latini manuscripts is Françoise Vielliard, 'La Tradition manuscrite du *Livre dou Trésor* de Brunet Latin: Mise au point', *Romania*, 111 (1990), 141–52. I thank Julia Bolton Holloway and Brigitte Roux for helpful discussion of Brunetto Latini issues at the *Città e libro II* conference in Florence in September, 2002.

12 On f. 205, an initial E shows a king and bishop seated together, the king flanked by knight in heraldic robe quarterly 1 and 4 argent [white] a lion gules (Limburg), 2 and 3 sable a lion or (Brabant), the arms adopted by Jean I de Brabant on acquiring the Duchy of Limburg in 1287; the bishop is flanked by knight in heraldic robe barry argent [white] and azure, a lion gules overall (Luxemburg); on f. 249 is an emperor wearing chain-mail and surcoat or an eagle sable, holding sword, between two knights, one with surcoat or three besants voided sable, holding a club; the other in grey surcoat, holding a buckler and club; the latter arms are unidentified and it is to be noted that the couple depicted before Christ on f. 116 are not in heraldic robes, so that the question of direct patronage by the Henri and Marguerite is not quite certain. For the family, see *Europäische Stammtafeln*, ed. Detlev Schwennicke, 21 vols (Frankfurt, 1998–), Neue Folge, I. 1, Taf. 82 and I. 2, Taf. 238.

called the Master of Valenciennes 838 after his most fully illustrated book.[13] But this chapter is not illustrated at all in any of the later Brunetto Latini manuscripts, and Fortuna did not appear there again.[14]

How was King Arthur otherwise treated in pictures?[15] I limit my investigation to manuscripts, and especially the *Lancelot-Grail* cycle in French and made in France, for it is there that the major corpus of Arthurian illustration, and illustrations of King Arthur, are to be found.[16] I survey briefly some of the important aspects of Arthur's rôle in the four branches in which he appears, and then I focus on a few comparative examples of his treatment in the pictures, selecting examples which I hope are telling ones. As more descriptions and sets of illustrations become available, this survey will undoubtedly be supplemented; for the time being only relatively few manuscripts are fully described, reproduced, or on line complete, and the comparative work has been done only in part. I will take my examples mainly from manuscripts for which full subject-lists exist, and from the one case where all the illustrations are on line.[17]

A full understanding of the ways in which the images reinforce, embellish or

13 I listed some of these in 'Illustrations of the French Prose Lancelot, 1260–1320', University of London, Ph.D. dissertation, 1970/71, ch. 3, and have made several additions in other publications. The fullest list is in *Illuminated Manuscripts Made in France, 1260–1320* (London and Turnhout, forthcoming). Devotional books: Franciscan psalter of Saint-Omer, Oxford, Christ Church College 98, written before the death of Eleanor of Castile in 1290, including an opening Beatus initial by the artist of the Saint-Omer literary compendium of 1268, Paris, Bibl. de l'Arsenal 3516; psalter-hours of Amiens use, Philadelphia Free Library, Widener 9, Hours part; fragmentary legendary, St Petersburg State Lib. FN 403; *Estoire del saint Graal*, Le Mans MM 354, written by Walterus de Kayo who may also be the person who copied an *Image du monde*, Paris, BNF fr. 14962, in 1282 (to which Terry Nixon kindly drew my attention); *Estoire, Merlin, Histoire d'outre-mer et du roi Saladin, La fille du Comte de Ponthieu, Ordre de chevalerie*, Paris, BNF fr. 770; *Agravain, Queste, Mort Artu*, Oxford, Bodl. Digby 223; *Prophécies de Merlin*, London, BL Harley 1629; two copies of *Marques* and *Laurin*, with other *Sept sages* texts: Paris, Ars. 3355 and Cambridge, Fitzwilliam, McClean 179; a Crusading compendium, Paris, BNF fr. 12203; *Enfances Godefroi*, Paris, BNF fr. 795 (in collaboration with the artist of the psalter part of Widener 9); Vincent of Beauvais's *Speculum Doctrinale*, owned by Ter Doest (O. Cist., diocese of Thérouanne), Bruges, SB 251. The well-known *Agravain, Queste* and *Mort Artu*, Paris BNF fr. 342, written by a female scribe in 1274, is also related, but less closely.

14 For my comparative table, see *Illuminated Manuscripts Made in France* (cit. in previous note), and the *Città e libro* web site <http://www.florin.ms/beth5.html>. See also, Brigitte Roux, 'L'iconographie du *Livre du trésor* de Brunetto Latini' (diss., Université de Genève, 2004).

15 The fundamental study is still Loomis, *Arthurian Legends in Art*, and I surveyed the literature up to about 1990 in 'Arthurian Art since Loomis', *Arturus Rex*, II (Acta Conventus Lovaniensis 1987), ed. Willy Van Hoecke, Gilbert Tournoy, Werner Verbeke (Leuven, 1991), pp. 21–78. It is time for another update.

16 Arthur figures also in various of the Chronicle traditions, as noted by Loomis, *Arthurian Legends in Art*; further study is needed.

17 It is hoped that the manuscripts of the Lancelot-Grail Project may soon be posted on the web, pending copyright agreements; subject-lists are also forthcoming in print. New Haven, Yale University, Beinecke Library, MS 229 is on line with a subject-list at <http://webtext.library.yale.edu/beinflat/pre1600.MS229.htm>; a subject-list for Paris, BNF fr. 95 is available on the BNF site <http://www.bnf.fr> under the rubric 'mandragore', soon to be supplemented by images, and more BNF manuscripts are shortly to be made available; the *Lancelot, Queste* and *Mort Artu* sections of BNF fr. 112, 113–116, 117–120 are published as a comparative table by Susan Blackman, 1994 and 1996, with full descriptions of all the illustrations in ead., 1994 (cit. n. 9); Bonn UB 526 is on microfiche; Morgan M 805–6 is described in brief (no subject list) on the Morgan Library web site <http://www.morganlibrary.org>; Morgan Library images are available (for a fee) through the Index of Christian Art, Princeton University <http://ica.princeton.edu>.

detract from the presentation of Arthur in the text would require both a diachronic and a synchronic approach that would examine on the one hand the Arthur images in a particular manuscript in relation to all the other illustrations in that manuscript; and on the other hand, it would compare particular Arthur-images across the manuscript tradition.[18] Then all this would need to be examined in relation to a detailed reading of the text in each manuscript (because of variants that turn out to critically affect what is in the picture) to consider questions of placing and treatment of the images and sequences of images, including build-up and follow-on[19] – and finally there is the question of artistic context: what else these artists illustrated and to what extent they used and re-used the same artistic models in different textual contexts.[20] And all discussion of images must be accompanied by a reproduction of the actual image – words alone simply will not do. It would require the best of all possible worlds to achieve all this, and here we are limited by space, time, and resources – so what follows is necessarily fragmentary.

Arthur makes his appearance in the second branch of the cycle, the *Merlin*, where his conception and birth, his selection as King of Britain and his success as a peaceful king are related.[21] Thereafter Arthur's rule is not quite so peaceful, and what follows (usually without a break),[22] the *Suite Vulgate*, is largely concerned with Arthur's military activities, but also includes his marriage to Guinevere and some other amorous adventures.[23] The focus in the *Lancelot* branch is of course the eponymous hero, but Arthur is an important foil and is depicted amidst the adventures of his knights, exercising the duties of kingship or failing to exercise them, in ways that are interesting pictorially.[24] Similarly in *Queste*, Arthur's place is in the background, but it is at his court and in his presence that the Grail makes its first appearance and the Grail Quest is launched;[25]

18 An effort in this direction is 'Some Aspects of Arthur's Death in Medieval Art', in *The Passing of Arthur*, ed. Christopher Baswell and William Sharpe (New York, 1988), pp. 52–101.

19 This is the approach Elspeth Kennedy and I have evolved in our examination of text and picture in the three early fourteenth-century copies. A collection of essays is in preparation, and the present analysis owes much to our research sessions in Oxford, Cambridge and Upper Bucklebury from 1999–2003.

20 I looked into this in 'Sacred and Profane Art: Secular and Liturgical Book Illumination in the Thirteenth Century', in *The Epic in Medieval Society, Aesthetic and Moral Values*, ed. Harald Scholler (Tübingen, 1977), pp. 100–12; and an essay by Martine Meuwese, 'Recycling Sacred Iconography', is forthcoming in the Lancelot-Grail Project.

21 Editions are S II, 3–88.19; Alexandre Micha, ed., *Merlin, roman du XIIIe siècle* (Geneva, 1979), (MM) based on Paris, Bibliothèque nationale de France, MS français 747 (Long Version); *Le Livre du Graal*, vol. I, ed. Daniel Poirion, Philippe Walter, et al. (Paris, 2001), pp. 571–774, based on Bonn, Universitätsbibliothek 526. Very regrettably, this edition does not list the illustrations nor place them in the text.

22 See Alexandre Micha, 'Les Manuscrits du *Merlin* en prose', *Romania*, 79 (1958), 78–94, 145–74.

23 Not to be confused with the *Huth Merlin* version. For *Suite Vulgate*, see S II, 88.19–466. 7, based on Add. 10292; and Poirion and Walter, 809–1662. An edition of the Short Version is in preparation by Richard Trachsler.

24 S III–V, based on Add. 10293; *Lancelot do Lac: The Non-Cyclic Old French Prose Romance*, ed. Elspeth Kennedy, 2 vols (Oxford, 1980), Pre-Cyclic Version (hereafter LK), based on Paris, BNF fr. 768 (siglum Ao in Kennedy's edition); Alexandre Micha, *Lancelot, roman en prose du XIIIe siècle* (TLF), 9 vols (Paris, 1978–83), based on a number of manuscripts of Long and Short Versions (hereafter LM).

25 S VI 3–199 and *La Queste del Saint Graal*, ed. Albert Pauphilet (Paris, 1923) (different page

and at the beginning of *Mort Artu* he instructs his scribes to record the account of it that Boort gives on his return to court. Arthur's failures, the destruction of his court and kingdom, the deaths of his cherished knights and eventually his own end, are recounted in the *Mort Artu*.[26]

Sword-Drawing

It is by successfully drawing a sword from an anvil in a stone that Arthur's right to the throne of Britain is affirmed in the *Merlin*, which ends with his coronation;[27] later in the text, as Arthur draws his sword to defeat the rebel kings, we learn that it is called Excalibur, and it is referred to by name again as Arthur prepares to defeat the giant King Rion.[28] The sword-drawing motif occurs again in relation to Galaad in the *Queste* – not the same sword, of course, and Galaad's sword remains nameless. Among the most poignant moments at the end of *Mort Artu* is Arthur returning Excalibur to the lake.[29]

Many manuscripts of the *Merlin* branch, however, have only a single opening illustration, showing the Harrowing of Hell, often in conjunction with the council of the devils – even if other branches in the same set of volumes are fully illustrated. Thus, for instance the Amsterdam/Douce/Rylands copy, and the manuscripts of Jacques d'Armagnac: Paris, BNF fr. 112, 113–116, and 117–120 (the latter inherited from Jean de Berry, and a twin to Paris, Bibliothèque de l'Arsenal 3479–80), have only an opening initial for their *Merlin*, even though their copies of *Lancelot, Queste* and *Mort Artu* have a sequence of miniatures.[30]

numbers in the 1965 edition), based on Lyon, BM, Palais des Arts MS 77 (siglum K in Pauphilet's edition).

26 S VI 203–391 and *La Mort le Roi Artu, Roman du XIIIe siècle*, ed. Jean Frappier (Paris, 1936, 3rd ed., Geneva, 1964), based on Paris, Ars. 3347 (siglum A in Frappier's edition); henceforth *Mort Artu*.

27 '. . . ou milieu de cele piere auoit vne englume de fer de demi piet de haut largement. et parmi cele englume auoit vne espee fichie ius quau perron outre . . .' (S II 81. 20) [. . . in the middle of this stone there was an anvil made of iron, easily half a foot high, and in the middle of this anvil there was a sword stuck right through to the stone.]

28 Quant li rois artus fu desestordis si traist lespee du feure qui ieta ausi grant clarte comme se doi chierge i eussent este alumees. et ce fu cele espee quil ot prinse el perron. Et les letters qui estoient escrites en lespee disoient quele auoit non escalibor et cest .j. non ebrieu qui dist en franchois trenche de fer et achier et fust si disent les lettres voir si comme vous orres el conte cha en arriere . . . (S II 94. 26–31) [When King Arthur had recovered, he drew from the scabbard the sword that shone as brightly as if two candles had been lit there. And this was the sword that he had drawn from the stone. And the letters written on the sword said that its name was Excalibur, and this is a Hebrew name that means in French 'cutting with iron and steel and wood', and the letters were correct, as you will see in the story to come.]
And '. . . escalibor sa boine espee que il traist del perron . . .' (S II 230. 22–23) [Excalibur, his good sword that he had drawn from the stone]. When Arthur knights Gauvain he girds him with 'sa boine espee quil osta del perron' (S II 253. 31) [his good word that he had drawn from the stone]. King Rion's sword is also distinguished: it was forged by Vulcan and used by Hercules (S II 230. 33–43); it is won by Arthur when Rions is put to flight (S II 235. 40), and successfully used by Arthur in his fight against the Saxons (S II 239).

29 For a note on which manuscripts illustrate this, see Stones, 'Some Aspects of Arthur's Death' at 99–100.

30 There is no published list of the illustrations in Ars. 3479–80. This is much needed. For the others, see Blackman 1994 and 1996 (cit. n. 9).

The case of Amsterdam/Douce/Rylands is especially interesting as its sister manuscript, Add., has a fully illustrated *Merlin* and *Suite Vulgate*; not only does Amst. lack *Merlin* pictures (apart from the opening scene), it also omits the *Suite Vulgate* text and starts the *Lancelot* on the same page as the end of the *Merlin*. The copy now in Bonn, Universitätsbibliothek 526, written by Arnulphus de Kayo in 1286,[31] on the other hand, has only two pictures in its *Merlin* but a full set of illustrations for its *Suite Vulgate*. So I here compare Add. with the important and slightly earlier copy that contains a fully illustrated *Merlin*: Paris, BNF fr. 95, made c. 1290–1300.[32] It has no rubrics, and the miniatures are either large, mostly in two registers, with borders, or small, and in a single register (sm); and it transmits the Long Version. I tabulate the sword-drawing episode in BNF fr. 95 and Add. in Appendix, Table A.

What is surprising is the difference in placing and emphasis between the two sets of pictures: BNF fr. 95 concerned to emphasize pictorially Arthur's repeated success at the sword-drawing activity, Add. depicting it a single time only, preceded by discussion of the issue and a failed attempt by another knight, and a demonstration of Arthur's approach to the administrative issues of governing the country; only then do the pictures proceed to the successful sword-drawing, in combination with the coronation which marks the conclusion of the sequence, and the end of the *Merlin* text (fig. 5). By comparison, BNF fr. 95 seems to reflect a mentality that is more concerned with decorative effect than logical progression, and which uses a multiplicity of pictures to reinforce essentially the same point – the legitimacy of Arthur's right to the throne. As in Add., the final scene is a combination of the coronation and the sword – not by having Arthur draw it again, but place it on the altar (fig. 6). Perhaps the profusion of male and female heads and naked figures in the margins is an indication of amorous events to follow – and possibly the heraldry indicates a patron in the circle of the counts of Flanders or Hainaut,[33] and maybe the drinking from vessels is a reference to the Grail; but these are also common motifs in the work of this artist and I think they, too, are primarily used here as decorative embellishments to liven the appearance of a very large page – which is not to say that elsewhere in the manuscript there are not instances of a close correlation between marginal motif and main illustration. The marginalia are indeed the hall-marks of BNF fr. 95 and Yale 229, which are the only extant *Lancelot-Grail* manuscripts to include such a profusion of secondary illustration (Add. and its sister manuscripts

31 Hereafter Bonn 526. For Arnulphus to say that he wrote it in Amiens most likely means that he was normally based elsewhere, a point not taken in most references to this colophon; also of interest is that the colophon is written in Latin, not French. There is an interesting confluence of name between Arnulphus and the Walterus mentioned above, suggesting they were possibly related to each other. See Bénédictins du Bouveret, *Colophons*, I, Fribourg, 1965, no. 1437 and *Colophons* V, 1979, no. 18579; there is no reference in *Colophons* to the Wautiers dou Kai who copied the *Image du monde*, Paris, BNF fr. 14692, in 1282.

32 For its artistic context and date, see Stones, 'The Illustrations in BN fr 95 and Yale 229, Prolegomena to a Comparative Study', in Busby, ed., *Word and Image*, pp. 206–83.

33 At one time I thought Guillaume de Termonde, son of Guy de Dampierre, Count of Flanders; now I am less sure that the Yale marginal image really refers to him; but if not him personally, then someone in the entourage of the counts of Flanders or Hainaut, is the most likely candidate (both counts bore arms *or a lion sable*).

reserve marginalia for opening pages of branches only, see Appendices F and I) – and the commonest occurrence of the sword motif in BNF fr. 95 is also in the context of these marginalia.

The Sword, the Round Table, and the Grail

In *Queste*, the sword-drawing test is part of the lead-in to the appearance of the Holy Grail before King Arthur and his knights at the Round Table at which the future Grail-Winner Galaad, son of Lancelot and of King Pelles's daughter, takes his place in the Perilous Seat reserved for him. The manuscripts in which this episode is depicted are not the same as those that included Arthur's triumphant retrieval of the sword in the *Merlin*. So, for instance, Bonn 526 (written in 1286) and Yale 229 (the latter most likely the continuation of BNF fr. 95), have no illustration for any of this sequence in *Queste*, giving only the opening visit of the damsel and the knighting of Galaad; while BNF fr. 342 (written by the female scribe in 1274),[34] has only Gauvain's failure (f. 61v), and no images of Galaad's success or of the Grail's appearance; Florence, Laur. Ash. 121, perhaps made for, or at least for someone in the entourage of, Pope John XXII in 1319, has Galaad's successful sword-drawing followed by the Grail's appearance (ff. 5 and 6 respectively).[35] A few other manuscripts also manifest an interest in the sword-drawing episode in *Queste*, including Jacques d'Armagnac's books; but what is especially interesting about the comparative choices made in these manuscripts, is that Add., where Arthur's sword-sequence is so prominent in *Merlin*, is not among those that depict Galaad's success, nor does Add. depict the Grail's appearance at the Round Table. Royal, on the other hand, combined the sword-drawing success of Galaad with the damsel appearing to tell Lancelot that he is no longer the greatest knight in the world (fig. 7). In Rylands the damsel is not shown at this point. Notable in the sequence in Rylands is the rôle of Guinevere in this sequence: Rylands is notable for including Guinevere at Arthur's side, as in the text (S VI 10. 33, P 11, fig. 8) watching the success of Galaad at drawing the sword (but she is not included for Gauvain's failure), and for being shown at table with Arthur both when Galaad takes his seat there and also at the Grail's appearance (fig. 9). In neither of those instances is she present in the text, and the corresponding miniatures in Royal omit her as well. The table at which she and Arthur sit in Rylands is not the Round Table, more like a High Table and separate from the Table (shown as rectangular) at which sit the knights[36] – but the depiction is important for the pictorial prominence it gives to

34 Mentioned above in the context of the Brunetto Latini manuscripts.

35 This is not an exhaustive list. I compare copies of *Queste* made up to c. 1320 in 'The Illustrations of the French Prose Lancelot, 1260–1320', Ph.D., University of London, 1970–71, at 307–36. On Florence, Laur. Ash. 121, see Lori Walters, 'Wonders and Illuminations: Pierart dou Thielt and the Quest del saint Graal', in Busby, ed., *Word and Image*, pp. 339–72, at 357–58; Stones, 'The Illustrations of BN fr. 95 and Yale 229', in Busby, ed., *Word and Image*, 213, 218–19; 'Seeing the Grail', in *The Grail: A Casebook*, ed. Dhira Mahoney (New York, 2000), pp. 301–66 at 322, 327, 331; and ead., 'Illustrations in the Manuscripts of Pope Clement V and John XXII', in *Avignon under the Papal Captivity*, ed. Susan Noakes and F.R.P. Akehurst (forthcoming).

36 The Round Table is regularly depicted as rectangular until the advent of interest in spatial

Guinevere, unmatched elsewhere at this point in the story, so far as I know, and therefore suggesting, perhaps, that this copy was made for a female patron.[37] Jacques d'Armagnac's manuscripts tell an equally interesting story: the success of Galaad is omitted in BNF fr. 112 and 116 in favour of the failure of Gauvain or Perceval (fig. 10). In BNF fr. 120, made for Jean de Berry, Galaad's success is shown as part of a sequential narrative – it can be seen happening in the distance, through the doorway of the room in which the Grail makes its appearance to King Arthur and the knights of the Round Table – thus underlining pictorially the important relationship between Galaad as chosen Grail Winner and the Grail itself and its physical presence at Arthur's court (fig. 11). D'Armagnac's other two copies of course also include the Grail at the Round Table, but without the emphasis on Galaad's rôle in that appearance. I tabulate this episode in Add. and its sister manuscripts and in Jacques d'Armagnac's books in Appendix, Table B.

The final sword episode – Arthur returning Excalibur to the lake – is illustrated, so far as I know, in only three manuscripts: Yale 229, f. 359 (probably the continuation of BNF fr. 95 and certainly produced by the same craftsmen), where a two-register miniature shows Arthur in the Noire Chapele with Lucan le Bouteillier and Girflet and, below, Girflet throwing Excalibur into the lake, to be received by an outstretched hand; Add. 10294, f. 94, showing Arthur deep in thought, seated head on hand, while Girflet throws Excalibur into the lake where it is received by the hand; and BNF fr. 112, Jacques d'Armagnac's Special Version, f. 229v, where Girflet, standing at the edge of the lake, holds Excalibur and debates what he should do.[38]

Arthur and Guinevere

The amorous adventures of Arthur are various, beginning in the *Suite Vulgate* with his brief liaison with King Lot's wife – his half-sister, Morgause, unbeknownst to both – in which Mordred is conceived (S II 128. 13–129. 33). This is depicted in Add. (f. 113, fig. 12) and Bonn (f. 88, fig. 13), both of which manifest a great deal of interest, in general, in depicting scenes of couples in bed – whether engaged in sexual intercourse or sleeping, dreaming, and discussing the meaning of a dream. In BNF fr. 95, the conception of Mordred is avoided altogether, so that the beginning of this episode in the text is marked, unusually, by

depth in painting in the fifteenth century, cf. Jean de Berry's and Jacques d'Armagnac's manuscripts; the phenomenon is excellently analysed by Emmanuèle Baumgartner, 'La couronne et le cercle: Arthur et la Table Ronde dans les manuscrits du *Lancelot-Graal*', *Texte et Image*, Actes du Colloque international de Chantilly 13 au 15 octobre 1982 (Paris, 1984), pp. 191–200.

37 It may be significant that the first twelve miniatures, including this opening sequence in Rylands/Douce are illustrated by a second artist. There are other instances where Guinevere and the knights eat together, for instance at the opening of *Queste* where the damsel arrives to disturb a meal in most manuscripts, and later, during the poison apple episode in *Mort Artu*. For the latter, see Stones, 'Images of Temptation, Seduction, and Discovery in the Prose *Lancelot*', *Wiener Jahrbuch für Kunstgeschichte*, 46–47 (1994), 725–35, at 733–35 and figs 16–21.

38 S VI 380. 14, F 248. 75. Listed in Stones, 'Some Aspects of Arthur's Death', pp. 99–100.

a historiated initial O, showing King Lot and his men riding back to Orcanie (f. 181); it is during Lot's absence that Arthur sleeps with Morgause. There is a parallel instance of the use of a small historiated initial, distinct from the usual miniatures, large or small, in Yale 229 (probably the companion volume to BNF fr. 95) for Lancelot's discovery of his deception with King Pelles's daughter in the *Agravain* (f. 50); I have suggested this choice of format was a deliberate effort to de-emphasize the subject, perhaps with a juvenile audience in mind.[39]

In Bonn there is even the extraordinary depiction of the two royal couples, Kings Ban and Boors and their wives, re-united after the battle of Trebes, in foot-to-foot beds (f. 122v, S II 273. 15, corresponding to the text at 277–78); and a double wedding at the end – of Caesar and Avenable, and her brother Patrice and Caesar's daughter.[40] I tabulate this sequence in Bonn, BNF fr. 95, and Add. in Appendix, Table C. The bed scene marks, for Ban and Elaine, the conception of Lancelot, which is followed by Elaine's dream about the two herds each headed by a crowned lion, of which Merlin will give an explanation that is not fully understood. That dream-sequence is paralleled by Caesar's dream of a sow with a band of gold on her head, and its explanation. In BNF fr. 95 and Add. this sequence is also illustrated, but differently. BNF fr. 95 omits the bed scene altogether and plays down Elaine's dream by compressing its explanation into a historiated initial, while Add. omits the queens on the battlements of Trebes, does give Ban and Elaine in bed (fig. 14), and Caesar and his wife, but above all emphasizes Merlin's role as interpreter of dreams – first Elaine's, then Caesar's, the latter played out across five scenes as against the three in Bonn and BNF fr. 95. Add. also omits Avenable, to say nothing of the weddings that conclude the sequence in Bonn, including instead Merlin, not just shown once in disguise, but acting out his explanations, and his disguises, as a narrative sequence, ending with a written version of the explanation, posted above the door in Caesar's palace.

The events leading up to the marriage of Arthur and Guinevere, and her presence at court following the marriage (tabulated in Appendix, Table D), are pictorially de-emphasized in Add., but there is an important scene of Arthur's first encounter with Guinevere in which she tends to him by washing his face (Add. f. 122, S II 156. 7, fig. 15) that is not illustrated in Bonn or BNF fr. 95. At that place in the text they give a battle, the feasting at Leodegan's castle, or (as also in Add.'s second miniature) news about Gauvain transmitted by Merlin. Later, Bonn and BNF fr. 95 both depict the marriage of Arthur and Guinevere (figs. 16, 17) – an event best known from the splendid wedding scene in the *Chroniques de Hainaut*, begun for Philip the Bold, duke of Burgundy, in 1449 and illustrated in 1468 by Willem Vrelant and others;[41] while in Add. it is only when Arthur establishes his court at Logres that the presence of Guinevere, as queen,

39 See Stones, 'The Illustrations in BN fr. 95 and Yale 229', p. 36.

40 At the end of the *En la marche de Gaulle* section of *Lancelot* (S III 339. 15, f. 254), there is another double bed scene with two couples depicted in two beds, a sequence not matched in Add., which marks the same place in the text, unusually, with a champie initial (Add. 10293, f. 119v); and in Amst there is no marker at all. The text in Bonn appears to diverge at this point to recount an amorous episode between King Arthur and the enchantress Camille, and between Gaheriet and a damsel. This section of the text is not yet covered in the edition by Poirion et al.

41 Loomis, *Arthurian Legends in Art*, 125–26, fig. 343 (Brussels, Bibliothèque Royale Albert 1er, 9243, f. 39v).

already married to Arthur, is shown, in scenes which are also paralleled in Bonn and BNF fr. 95. Thereafter Guinevere weathers numerous challenges to her legitimacy as Arthur's lawful wife, notably from the False Guinevere (also the daughter of King Leodegan by the wife of his senechal Cleodalis, conceived on the same night as the True Guinevere, S II 149, not illustrated in Add.), and her champion Bertholais, who plots to dispose of the True Guinevere and substitute the False Guinevere in her place. In *Merlin*, this plot is quickly defeated thanks to Merlin's intervention (S II 301–312, Appendix, Table D below), but it is much more serious a threat in the *Lancelot*, where Arthur renounces the True Guinevere for a time in favour of the impostor, even leaving the kingdom in such disarray that the barons elect Gauvain to replace Arthur, a scene depicted in Bonn, Add. and Amst. (Appendix, Table E). The champions of the True Guinevere, Lancelot and Galehot, finally prevail, and the sequence ends with the Queen begging Lancelot to rejoin the Round Table. This episode is treated pictorially at enormous length in Add. The entire sequence was clearly of very great interest, and extends in subtle detail over no fewer than twenty-four scenes, compared with what is done in Amst., where there are only five illustrations in the corresponding text. Both Amst. and Add. have an opening scene depicting the appearance of Bertholais and the False Guinevere's messenger at court – treated with much more attention to detail in Amst. (fig. 18), where, for instance, the scarf flung on the ground and the box containing the letter are both clearly shown; and the setting, with its splendid tiled floor, is also shown in more detail than in Add. (fig. 19). Once again (cf. Arthur's sword-drawing), Add. displays a concern to lay out over many scenes a long and complicated legal issue. Significant is its placing of the death of the False Guinevere (fig. 20), not at the place it is given in the text by Bonn (fig. 21) and Amst. (fig. 22), but preceded and followed by additional scenes exploring numerous aspects of the legal situation faced by Arthur's barons, the fate of Bertholais, the intervention of the pope, and concluding with the penitence of the barons of Sorelois, the repentance of Arthur, and the Queen handed back, and her begging Lancelot to remain at court. Royal lacks the *Lancelot* altogether, and the BNF fr. 95/Yale 229 volumes lack the *Lancelot* except for the *Agravain* section (at the beginning of Yale 229), so no comparisons are possible; but it is noteworthy that Bonn aligns with Amst. here, giving only four scenes at corresponding places in the text, making even more striking the exceptional detail given to this sequence in Add.

The treatment of the False Guinevere episode in Jean de Berry's and Jacques d'Armagnac's manuscripts is also interesting as scenes from it are spread out, as it were, among the three copies, no single copy giving as minute a pictorial account of the sequence as Add., and not always at quite the same places in the text, but a fuller account than those in Bonn and Amst. (Appendix, Table E).

Arthur's Prowess

Much of Arthur's reputation as king derives from the military victories in which he leads his army, depicted *passim* in many scenes of mounted combat with lances or swords, from his early defeat of the rebel barons with the help of

Merlin, accompanied by the splendid fire-breathing dragon standard, to his valiant combats against Saxons, Romans, and Irish, extending to the end of the *Mort Artu*. There are also individual victories where Arthur triumphs, as does each of the knights, over particular persons in one-to-one combat on horseback or on foot. Two of Arthur's battles are especially noteworthy, and both occur towards the end of *Merlin*: Arthur's defeat of the giant of Mont-Saint-Michel (S II 429. 36) and his killing of the Cat of Lausanne (S II 442. 21). Both are part of Arthur's campaign against Roman Emperor Lucius who attempts to make Arthur do homage and pay tribute; and in both, Merlin has an important part to play – assisting King Arthur for the last time before he succumbs to the wiles of Viviane and is imprisoned in a cave for the rest of the *Merlin*, to reappear no more in the *Lancelot-Grail*. As Arthur crosses the Channel, he has a dream about a dragon attacking a bear and killing it. In Merlin's interpretation, Arthur is the dragon and a terrible giant is the bear. It is the giant of Mont-Saint-Michel, responsible for killing many people. Arthur kills it single-handed and has Bediver cut off its head, whose size suitably impresses Arthur's knights. BNF fr. 95 omits the combat with the giant altogether, giving at this place in the text a two-part miniature of Merlin advising Arthur and Arthur and his men sailing across the Channel (f. 334v). In Add. (f. 205v) and Bonn (f. 160v), the combat with the giant is compressed into a single scene, but differently placed: Bonn's at S II 427. 9 (fig. 23), where in Add. (f. 204v) there is a lead-in miniature for the campaign against the Romans as a whole, depicting Merlin advising Arthur to prepare for war. The combat in Bonn shows Arthur with sword and shield standing on the top of Mont-Saint-Michel (shown as a bare hill), with the giant placed further forwards in the picture-plane but turning back and raising his club, his ugly face and curly hair shown in profile. In Add. (f. 205v, fig. 24), the giant, also clad in armour, is on the ground being pierced by Arthur's sword; on the right is a blazing fire in which a chicken is roasting on a spit; and three of Arthur's knights on the left are witnesses to their leader's victory.

Arthur defeating the giant of Mont-Saint-Michel was a subject popular in the chronicles, beginning with the earliest known depiction of Arthur altogether, in the well-known historiated initial in the twelfth-century copy of the *Historia regum britanniae* of Geoffrey of Monmouth, owned by the Abbey of Anchin (OSB, dioc. Arras), Douai, BM 880, f. 66;[42] and the combat figures splendidly later too, for instance in the *Chroniques de Hainaut* mentioned above.[43] It is also taken over into the *Alliterative Mort Arthur* as its only illustration, added at some later stage on the blank leaf preceding the text opening.[44] There, King Arthur is shown bearing a shield with the three crowns – which in Add. and its sister manuscripts is just beginning to be used consistently for the first time (although

42 Loomis, *Arthurian Legends in Art*, fig. 340.

43 Brussels, Bibliothèque Royale Albert 1er, 9243, f. 49v, and Loomis, ed., *Arthurian Legends in Art*, fig. 347.

44 *The Thornton Manuscript (Lincoln Cathedral MS 91)*, eds D.S. Brewer and A.E.B. Owen (London, 1975), on f. 52v. For more on the heraldry of Arthur and his knights, see Michel Pastoureau, *Armorial des chevaliers de la table ronde* (Paris, 1983), and Alison Stones, 'Les Débuts de l'héraldique dans l'illustration des romans arthuriens', in *Les Armoriaux*, ed. Hélène Loyau and Michel Pastoureau, *Cahiers du léopard d'or*, 8 (1998), 395–420.

often there are only two crowns, and painted in white for argent instead of yellow for or) – and the giant, who holds a mace, is also shown in armour, with three mask-heads 2 and 1 on his breastplate. In view of these parallels, it is surprising there are so few representations of Arthur's combat with the giant of Mont-Saint-Michel in *Suite Vulgate* manuscripts.

As for Arthur's defeat of the Cat of Lausanne, the subject is still rarer: so far as I know it appears only in Add. (f. 209v, fig. 25). One might have expected this 'cat-as-devil' motif to have enjoyed a more robust tradition of representation in the *Suite Vulgate*, particularly as, around the time that the *Lancelot-Grail* was being written and the earliest copies made c. 1210–20,[45] the cat motif symbolising heresy (cf. the etymology of 'Cathar') was depicted in connection with the Jews and infidels in the two earliest copies of the *Bible moralisée*, Vienna ÖNB1179 (with captions in Latin) and ÖNB 2554 (with captions in French), made in Parisian royal circles for Louis VIII and his family.[46] The Rennes manuscript, I have argued, was also made in these circles.

Arthur as Chronicler

If Arthur plays an active rôle in much of the *Merlin*, *Suite Vulgat*e and *Mort Artu*, he is also portrayed in what might be described as a passive rôle as well, as listener and as chronicler of the adventures related orally to him by his knights on their return from adventures. In *Merlin* and *Suite Vulgate*, the chronicler of events is Blaise, the 'preudom' confessor of Merlin's mother, to whom Merlin recounts his adventures and tells his prophecies, and who commits them to writing, beginning with Merlin's account of the events in *Estoire*. There, the story is itself the one written in the book given to the hermit-narrator by Christ (S I 5, 8, 11, 12), and the sequence of the hermit-narrator receiving the book and writing his own copy is popular in *Estoire* iconography – but not universal, as, for instance, there is no depiction of either hermit or book in BNF fr. 95; and in Bonn two of these events – Christ giving the book to the hermit-narrator, and the latter writing – are included as second and fourth in the six-part opening minia-

45 For a date c. 1220 for Rennes BM 255 (*Estoire, Merlin, Lancelot* to S IV, 220. 33, ending incomplete and with a huge lacuna before the last leaf), made in Paris, see Stones, 'The Earliest Illustrated Prose *Lancelot* Manuscript?' *Reading Medieval Studies*, 3 (1977), 3–44; and I think there is every chance that the Modena copy, Bibl. Estense E 39, containing a prose version of Robert de Boron's *Joseph* and *Merlin*, followed by the Didot-*Perceval*, and *Lapidaire* is earlier (c. 1210?) and perhaps made in Champagne or the north of France. This dating means, of course, that the composition of the entire cycle is earlier than most scholars admit, as is the date of the pre-cyclic version; BNF fr. 768, the base manuscript of Kennedy's edition, could well support a date c. 1210. For the text of *Joseph*, see *Robert de Boron, Joseph d'Arimathie: A Critical Edition of the Verse and Prose Versions*, ed. Richard O'Gorman (Toronto, 1995).

46 The literature on these is enormous. For Vienna, ÖNB 2554 see the facsimile and commentary by Reiner Haussherr, *Bible moralisée, Faksimile-Ausgabe im Originalformat des Codex Vindobonensis 2554 der Österreichische Nationalbibliothek* (Graz, 1973), and his numerous articles; ÖNB 2554 was edited a second time (despite the continued absence of a facsimile of the no less important ÖNB 1179) by G. Guest, *Bible moralisée: Codex Vindobonensis 2554, Vienna, Österreichische Nationalbibliothek*, Manuscripts in Miniature 2 (London, 1995). On the cat motif, see Sara Lipton, 'Jews, Heretics, and the Sign of the Cat in the *Bible moralisée*', *Word and Image*, 8 (1992), 362–77. I thank Sarah Bromberg for stimulating discussion of the cat issue.

tures, but not at their place in the narrative account. I compare Add. and its sister manuscripts with the Jean de Berry/Jacques d'Armagnac set in Appendix F. It will be seen that in terms of the placing of the hermit-narrator's writing activities, there is overlap with the subject narrated, namely the Crucifixion which in Add. displaces the writing activity altogether: in Royal the copying is given much more prominence – both model and copy are depicted on the hermit-narrator's desk in the image – and it is the Crucifixion which is displaced to a position corresponding to the actual account of it given in the text. In Amst., the use of a champie to mark the corresponding point is noteworthy – as in Add., the Crucifixion is given pride of place, but like Royal at its place in the narrative. Of Jacques d'Armagnac's manuscripts, the only one with a narrative cycle for *Estoire* is BNF fr. 113–116, in which the opening composite miniature (f. 1) includes in the top left quadrant a displaced image of Walter Map/Arthur's clerk presenting his book to King Henry/King Arthur; and the second miniature (f. 1v) shows Christ appearing to the hermit but without a book: it is a vision of the Trinity (but one that lacks a depiction of the other two Persons).[47]

This is the background against which Blaise's written account of Merlin's activities should be read, a point that Blaise himself makes explicit:

> 'si sera li liures ioseph adiouste au tien et quant tu auras ta paine achieuee et tu seras tels com tu dois estre en la compaignie del graal lors sera tes liures aioins al liure ioseph si sera la chose bien esprouee de ma paine et de la toie se en aura dieus merci sil li plaist et cil qui lorront proieront nostre seignor por nous. Et quant li doi livre seront ensamble si i aura .j. biau livre. et li doi seront .j. misme chose . . .' (S II 20. 5–10)
>
> ['. . . and Joseph's book will be joined to yours, and when you have completed your toils as you should in the company of the Grail then your book will be joined to Joseph's and the task will bear witness to your work and mine and God will be merciful if it pleases him and those who hear it will pray Our Lord for us. And when the two books come together there will be a single fine book and the two shall be one . . .']

Indeed, the narrative of *Merlin* and *Suite Vulgate* is punctuated at intervals with Merlin's visits to Blaise in order for his account of the events to be recorded. At first Blaise is not eager to undertake the task of writing down what Merlin tells him because he knows the Merlin was conceived by the devil; but, in this version of the text, Merlin has been baptized, as he himself makes clear, convincing Blaise of the virtue of the writing enterprise:

> . . . Et merlins dist il est coustume de tous maluais cuers que il notent plustost le mal que le bien ensi com tu ois dire que iestoie conceus del diable . ensi mois tu dire que nostre sires mauoit donne sens et memoire de sauoir les choses qui estoient a uenir et por ce se tu fuses sages deuses tu esprouer et sauoir al quel iou me uoldroie tenir . . . (S II 18. 27–32)
>
> [. . . And Merlin said wicked hearts are accustomed to attribute to me evil rather than good, just as you have heard tell that I was conceived by the devil, and you

47 See Blackman, *The Manuscripts and Patronage of Jacques d'Armagnac*, p. 505.

hear me say that Our Lord gave me reasoning and memory so that I should know the things that are to come and because of that if you were wise you ought to test me and to know to what I would adhere . . .]

Blaise finally agrees to what Merlin asks, to write down what Merlin tells him – provided it is done in the name of the Trinity. Merlin promises not to do anything that is against the will of Jesus Christ his Saviour;

> . . . et blayses respont ore me di ce que tu vels car ie ferai des ore mais tout ce que tu me commanderas de bien. Et merlins li dist ore quier encre et parchemin ades que iou te dirai moult de choses ce que tu quideroies que nus hon ne te peust dire. (S II 19. 11–14)

> [and Blaise replied now tell me what you want for from now on I will do all such good works as you command me. And Merlin said to him now fetch ink and parchment here so that I may tell you many things which you would think no man could tell . . .]

This is followed by the first of several miniatures – and the only one in the *Merlin* – in which Merlin is shown dictating to Blaise. In this instance, which is the sequel to Merlin's clearing of his mother's name at the tender age of only two and a half years old, he is shown as a child – an interesting reversal of the usual teaching or dictating situation common in so many didactic texts (Add. f. 80v, S II 19. 15, fig. 26).[48] An element of this reversal is preserved in subsequent depictions in Add. (illustrating *Suite Vulgate*), since Blaise is depicted as the older of the two men, as he is in the text; but in Bonn and BNF fr. 95, Merlin and Blaise are both shown as grey-haired, bearded men. In Add. f. 80v, Blaise is seated in an elaborate chair with tracery on the back and side, and a movable lectern attached; he sits wearing a hooded robe and writing, while Merlin holds the desk with one hand and points with the other. Comparisons for this image at this place in the text are not forthcoming: this is not one of the two miniatures that illustrate *Merlin* in Bonn, and it is also omitted from the picture cycle in BNF fr. 95 although the trial of Merlin's mother is shown (f. 120). In *Suite Vulgate*, Bonn and Add. each give three more pictures of Merlin and Blaise, and BNF fr. 95 gives four; in two instances (at S II 292. 38, figs. 27, 28, 29; and S II 375. 3) all three copies place an illustration at the same line in the text; in one other case, BNF fr. 95 and Add. align (at S II 206. 16); and BNF fr. 95 and Bonn each have one additional Merlin and Blaise miniature placed, respectively at S II 180. 12 and 300. 38. These are tabulated in Appendix. Table G.

In all Add.'s miniatures, great interest is shown in depicting the details of Blaise's chair and its lectern attachment, and in the appearance of the page on which he is writing – sometimes shown as a folded leaf, sometimes as a single tall leaf; and Blaise himself is tonsured and wearing a hooded robe, regardless of which illustrator is at work. And Blaise's sole activity, in Add. is to write. In BNF fr. 95 and Bonn, on the other hand, there are several instances where Blaise is

48 Such as Brunetto Latini, *Le Trésor*; Vincent of Beauvais, *Speculum historiale*; Aristotle; Medical treatises; Thomas of Cantimpré, *De rerum natura*; Bartholomeus Anglicus, *De proprietatibus rerum*; Papias, *Vocabularium*, and the like.

shown listening to what is being said by Merlin rather than writing it down, and, in these cases, he is shown either standing like Merlin (Bonn f. 127v, 147), or sitting (BNF fr. 95, f. 309, 268; fig. 28); in one case (BNF fr. 95, f. 268), he is even holding head on hand and resting his elbow and other hand on the written pages of his book as he listens. In BNF fr. 95 his lectern is a separate desk, not an attachment to the chair as in Add., while in Bonn, the one occasion on which he is shown actually writing is on a scroll held on his knee (f. 129v; fig. 27). In Bonn, Blaise is always shown wearing a hat, and on two occasions also in BNF fr. 95 (ff. 210, 268); it is of a type that is in general reserved for academics or for lawyers,[49] thus endowing Blaise and his activities with an official status not accorded to Arthur's scribes. In Add., the structure of Blaise's seating arrangements is notable, as is the care and attention paid to the format of his writing on the page; fig. 29.

Not every textual mention of Merlin relating his adventures to Blaise is illustrated, for on occasion what is shown instead is the actual fulfilment of Merlin's prophecy. A case in point in Add. is at f. 87, S II 41 (not illustrated elsewhere, so far as I know), where the miniature shows the brothers Uther and Pendragon riding together; the text that follows gives the context: Pendragon has just met up with his brother Uther, and asks him whether the death of Augis had occurred in the way in which Merlin had prophesied to Pendragon that it would; to which Uther answers in the affirmative. The miniature underlines the textual confirmation that Merlin's prophecies are to be believed; and for the reader too, they are authenticated by Blaise's writing them down:

> Lors prinst merlins congie al roy pandragon et sen ala a blayse si li dist ces choses. Et blayses les mist tout en escrit et par ce le sauons nous enore. Et pandragons chevalcha tant par ses iournees quil troua uter son frere. Et quant il virent lun lautre si entre fisent grant ioie et pandragons trait son frere a une part si li conta la mort augis si come merlins li auoit conte si li demanda sil fu ensi et uter li respond sire se dieus mait vous maves tel chose dite que iou ne quidoie mie que nus hons leust seu fors que diex et uns viex hons qui en conselle me dist . . . (S II 41. 5–12)
>
> [Then Merlin took leave of King Pandragon and went off to Blaise and told him these things. And Blaise wrote all of them down and because of that we know them still. And Pandragon rode for many days till he found Uter his brother. And when they saw each other they rejoiced and Pandragon drew his brother aside and told him about the death of Augis just as Merlin had related it and asked him if it was so and Uter replied Sire, as God is my help, you have told me something that I would never have thought any man would know except for God himself and an old man telling me privately . . .]

Subsequent images of Merlin telling and Blaise writing will thereafter carry these associations of authenticity and authority in the transmission of the narrative in its written form.

In the remainder of the *Lancelot-Grail*, the person responsible for having events committed to writing is King Arthur. The methods he employs are more

49 It is commonly found, for instance, in the illustrations of Gratian's *Decretum*, see A. Melnikas, *The Corpus of the Miniatures in the Manuscripts of Decretum Gratiani*, 3 vols (Rome, 1975).

properly those of history writing, in that what is being recorded, and by Arthur's court scribes, are the events that have taken place during Arthur's reign. At the same time, the source of the information is the oral account each knight tells in turn – not information copied from written documents. In addition to providing the primary source for Arthur's written chronicle, these oral witnesses to events also serve to inform the entire community of the court, directly and at first hand, about what they have accomplished. All this is different from the one-to-one accounting that Merlin gave to Blaise, to which Arthur and his court are not party. What is surprising about Arthur's chronicling activities is the relative absence of illustrations depicting these important moments in the recording of the knights' adventures. Much more attention is paid, in the illustrations in general, to another kind of communication – that of letter-writing, sending, and the reading of letters – a still more urgent and immediate means of relating events when the letter-writer is far away, since the reader need not wait for the writer's return to learn what has happened, still less for the events to be officially chronicled. The rôle of letters, letter-writing, and the reading of letters, is an enormous topic that merits a study of its own, and I leave it aside here. In relation to the recounting and recording of the knights' adventures, what is most often depicted is a scene from the adventure itself, not of its writing down: so at S V 191. 34, Add. is unusual in including an image showing Gauvain relating his adventures to King Arthur and the court, without a scribe present in the picture (f. 315v, fig. 30). This is preceded and followed by textual reference to adventures being written down – those of Lancelot, who had told his just before Gauvain, then the other knights. What is critical here is Arthur's insistance that the oral accounts be true and complete – to the point that the knights must swear an oath on relics to that effect. First Arthur summons all the knights, and his clerks, and relics of saints on which oaths were to be sworn, and Lancelot must swear that what he will say is a complete account of all the adventures he has had since leaving court, omitting nothing; to which he swears (but in fact omits mention of his affair with King Pelles's daughter).

> Celui iour apres disner fist li roys uenir tous lez compaignons de la table roonde . Et quant il furent tout uenu deuant lui. si les fist asseoir ou renc . Lors apela ses clers qui metoient en escrit lez auentures de laiens et toutez lez auentures qui auenoient as cheualiers errans Et on aporta lez sains sor coi on faisoit le sairement Si dis li roys a lancelot oiant tous ceuls de laiens. lancelot il est ensi que vous partesistes de chaiens sans faire sairement . Et pour ce volons nous que vous iures. que vous nous conteres orendroit toutes les auentures qui auenues vous sont puis que vous uous partesistes de chaiens. Et que vous pour honte ne le laires a dire qui auenues vous soit . Ei il le iure tout ensi comme li roys li ot deuise . . . (S V 190. 15–24)

> [That day after dinner the king summoned all the companions of the Round Table. And when all had come before him, he had them sit down. Then he summoned his clerks to write down their adventures and all the adventures of the errant knights. And the relics of saints were brought forth on which they were to make their oaths. Then the king said to Lancelot in the hearing of all, Lancelot, is it true that you would leave this place without swearing an oath? For this reason

we wish you to swear that from now on you will tell all the adventures you have had since you left here, and that you would be ashamed not to tell about any of the adventures that have happened to you. And he swore it just as the king had asked . . .]

Lancelot's adventures were so much more voluminous than anyone else's that they had to be put in a special book all by themselves, which was found at Salisbury after Arthur's death:

> . . . Ensi comme lancelot disoit sez auentures furent elles mises en escrit Et pour ce que si fait estoient greignor que nus de ceuls de laiens . lez fist li roys mettre par lui seul . Si que dez fais lancelot troua len .j. grant liure en lanmaire [*not* laumaire *as S*] le roy artu Apres ce quil fu naures a mort en la bataille de salebieres . Si come cils contes le deuisera cha auant . . . (S V 191. 29–33)

> [. . . Lancelot's adventures were written down just as he had told them. And because they were greater than those of anyone else the king had them written separately. This is how it came about that the deeds of Lancelot were found in a big book in the [library] cupboard of King Arthur after he was mortally wounded at the Battle of Salisbury as this story already told . . .]

But, regrettably, neither Add. nor, so far as I know, any other manuscript, depicts any of Lancelot's narration. What follows this passage is a picture of Gauvain's account, the only one to depict the act of telling in the *Lancelot*; and again, Arthur has the events committed to writing immediately: 'Quant les auentures lancelot furent mises en escrit ensi com vous poes oir . Si conta me sires Gauuain lez soies apres . . .' (S V 191. 34–35) [When Lancelot's adventure had been written down as you have heard, my lord Gauvain told his next . . .]. And 'Quant mesires Gauuain ot toutes contees lez auentures qui li estoient uenues Si lez first li roys mettre en escrit . . .' (S V 192 12–13) [When my lord Gauvain had told all his adventures the king had them written down . . .]

The rest of the illustrations surrounding these accounts depict, as was the case on occasion in *Merlin*, the actual adventures – so Add. gives Lancelot playing against the magic chessboard in the preceding miniature (f. 315), and Guinevere giving Lancelot her enchanted ring in the miniature that follows (f. 316v). This scene was also chosen for Bonn (f. 382) and BNF fr. 95 (f. 85v), but none of it was included in the Jacques d'Armagnac manuscripts, whose only image of writing is at the opening of *Mort Artu*, and where even the chess and ring scenes are lacking.

The opening of *Mort Artu* is most often illustrated with a scene depicting a king ordering a scribe to write (Bonn is exceptional in offering two different subjects; see Appendix, Table I). Sometimes the king and the scribe are alone, as in Rylands (f. 212, fig. 31) and Royal (f. 140); more usually others are present (Yale 229, f. 272v; Add. 10294, f. 53). The 'historical context' in which King Henry II and Walter Map are invoked at the beginning of the text suggests, of course, that it is they who are represented in the pictures; but it is equally likely that another obvious overlay of meaning is to be understood here – King Arthur and his scribe. In the case of Add., the seated king is clearly Arthur, and he is listening and even commenting (by pointing his finger) upon what his knights are recounting. The one speaking is likely to show Boort recounting the adventures of the *Queste del saint Graal*, as Arthur asks him to – but the miniature could also, or instead, depict what the rubric says it does, namely Arthur asking Gauvain how many knights he killed in the quest. I suggest these kinds of ambiguities are deliberate, allowing for a multi-valent reading in which the viewer could decide or weigh the alternatives. The same kinds of multiple readings may be found in Jacques d'Armagnac's two copies; with the added dimension of a foretaste of what is to come, if indeed one of the miniatures shows Agravain telling Arthur about the adultery. The inclusion of a second miniature showing this subject, in BNF fr. 112 (f. 183) makes it all the more likely that this is how the right-hand component of the miniature in BNF fr. 116, f. 1 (fig. 32), should be interpreted (see Appendix, Table I). Here it is of interest to note that Jean de Berry's copy, BNF fr. 120, has only two miniatures for its *Mort Artu*, and there is no scene at the opening, so that the preferences expressed in the choices in BNF fr. 112 and 116 are likely to be those of d'Armagnac himself.

Conclusions

What has been learned from this rapid survey? First and foremost, that the reception of this text was a highly complex matter. The long episodic narrative was read, and interpreted, with enormous care – comparable to the beautiful handwriting, careful corrections, the paragraphing marked with penflourished initials in colours and sometimes also in gold, that could not be examined here. No two copies transmit the same pictorial emphasis, even when we know they were produced by the same or closely related craftsmen (perhaps women too, but we know that only in the case of BNF fr. 342, which has been barely touched upon here); and there is no clear case of direct and precise copying. Comparisons within the same copy and between copies show that patrons and makers (or both) followed highly divergent paths as to which episodes and sequences they preferred, and in what ways they wished the selection, placing, and treatment of the illustrations to convey those preferences. The results show a mesh of complicated interrelationships whose significance only emerges in a comparative examination – and even then, only with difficulty, for we cannot always be clear as to just what the differences mean. Yet the manuscripts, and the images, have much to tell about what it was people found interesting and important in these stories. They are likely to fascinate us for some time to come, as they clearly did their medieval audience.

APPENDIX[1]

Table A. *Merlin*: Arthur draws the sword

Text	Paris, BNF fr. 95	London, BL Add. 10292 illustrations by two hands
S II 80. 21 MM 264. 52		Add. f. 99r Rubric: *Ensi que vns archeuesques reuestus por canter messe parla a Antor par deuant le puple.* The archbishop addresses the people about the sword in the stone; the stone is inscribed 'ki cheste/espee hors/tria. roy sera/de la terre.' (hand 1). L, champie initial Text: *Lors dist li uns a lautre que cest li mieudres consaus que nus i puisse metre . . .*
S II 81. 23 MM 268. 8		Add. f. 99r Rubric: *Ensi que Artu assaie por sakier lespee hors de lenglume de le perron.* (a knight; not Arthur) A knight tries to draw the sword from the stone (hand 1). Q, champie initial Text: *Quant cil le virent qui del moustier furent issu si en orent moult grant merueille . . .*
S II 81.28 +var MM 273 +var	BNF fr. 95 f. 156v Sword in the anvil: bishop and crowds look at it; sword removed by Arthur, who rides up past watching knights on horseback (one shield Flanders or Hainaut: or a lion sable) and takes sword; top border: two sets of embracing male and female head terminals, entwined; bottom: hare holding banner or a cross sable. Text: *Lors le comanderent a garder a .x. homes . . .*	
S II 82. 30 MM 272. 4		Add. f. 99v Rubric: *Ensi que Antor fist iurer le roy Artu sor sains quil tenra loyaument conuenenche a Keus son fil.* Arthur pledges to Antor to appoint Keu his seneschal: he lays his hand on a book inscribed 'puer natus est nobis'; the sword is in the background, the stone inscribed 'ki cheste/espee trete/ hors roy/ sera de la tere'(hand 1). L, champie initial Text: *Lors si assaierent tuit li vns apres lautre . . .*

S II 84. 23 MM 278. 31		Add. f. 100r Rubric: *Ensi que li archeuesques bailla lespee a Artu par deuant le puple.* (Arthur hands over the sword, not the opposite) Arthur hands the sword he has drawn to the archbishop; the stone is inscribed 'ki cheste es/pee hors oste/roy sera del/tere' (hand 1). S, champie initial Text: *Sire vees chi .j. mien enfant fait Antor qui nest mie cheualiers . . .*
S II 84. 28 MM 280	BNF fr. 95 f. 157v sm: Arthur, on foot, removing the sword again, watched by bishop and men; dragon terminal. Text: *Ensi le portent au moustier . . .*	
S II 86. 17, MM 285	BNF fr. 95 f. 158v Sword removed from anvil again by Arthur, watched by bishop and crowd; top border: naked man chinchucks male and female head terminals; hooded male terminals; bottom: naked man sitting in border terminals. Text: *Et lors le prisent et le leverent . . .*	
S II 87. 21 MM 287. 24		Add. f. 101r Rubric: *Ensi que vns archeuesques tient .j. coronne dor pour donner au roi Artu qui sasaioit a lespee trere* The archbishop holds a crown; Arthur draws the sword again; the stone inscribed 'ki cheste/espee traira/hors roy/sara' (hand 1). E, champie initial Text: *Ensi assaierent Artu si quen mile maniere ne porent en lui trouer nule maluaise teche . . .*

1 The selections from Add., Royal, and Rylands, are adapted from the Tables of the Lancelot-Grail Project and include both rubric and text incipit below the miniatures; Bonn also has rubrics, as do BNF fr. 112, 113–116, 117–120, but full transcriptions have yet to be made, as for the text below the miniatures in those manuscripts and in BNF fr. 95/Yale 229 (which lack rubrics). In the transcriptions, proper names have been capitalized for ease of reading. We retain u and v, i and j, and do not supply the apostrophe or modern accents. Tironian 'et' and ampersand are transcribed as 'et'. We note discrepancies between what the rubric says and what is accurate according to the text that follows. Miniatures in BNF fr. 95/Yale 229 are large unless otherwise stated (sm=small miniature, or historiated initial).

Text	Paris, BNF fr. 95	London, BL Add. 10292 illustrations by two hands
S II 88. 14 MM 290	BNF fr. 95 f. 159v Arthur draws the Sword again, in the presences of bishop, clerics, and people; Coronation of Arthur: he places the sword on the altar, on which is a covered chalice, and is crowned by a bishop; top border: 2 stork terminals hold jugs and drink from bowls; bottom: 4 biting dragon terminals. Text: *Et quant il li ot mise si le sacrerent . . .*	
S II 88.18 MM 290. 57		Add. f. 101v col. d, line 3 Expl. . . .*Ensi fu Artus esleus a roy e tint la terre et le regne de Logres lonc tans en pais.*

Table B. *Queste del saint Graal:* Galaad draws the sword

	Additional 10294 (miniatures by hand 1 throughout)	Royal 14.E.III	Rylands Fr. 1 illustrations by two hands
S VI 3. 1 Pau 1. 2	(f. 1r bound separately) Add. 10294, f.1r. No rubric Banquet at Camelot; damsel summons Lancelot (to knight Galaad). A, foliate initial containing human hybrid Text: *A la veille de Pentecoste . . .*	Royal f. 89r. No rubric Banquet at Camelot; damsel summons Lancelot (to knight Galaad). A, initial containing mitred head Text: *A la veille de la Pentecouste . . .*	missing
S VI 4. 31 Pau 3. 11		Royal f. 89r, col. c Space for rubric left blank Galaad knighted at the White Abbey by Lancelot. Q, undecorated ink capital Text: *Quant il ot fait tout chou qui apartient a y estre fait a cheualier . . .*	missing
S VI 7. 6 Pau 6. 21			Ryl. f. 182r No rubric Gauvain or Perceval tries in vain to draw the sword from the stone that floats in the river (hand 2). Q, undecorated ink capital Text: *Quant li rois oi cheste parole si se repent de che que me sires G. a fait . . .*

S VI 8. 14 Pau 8. 15			Ryl. f. 182v No rubric The preudome shows Galaad to the Perilous Seat (hand 2). S, undecorated ink capital Text: *Sire cheuvaliers asseez vos ci, car cist sieges est vostres . . .*
S VI 8. 15 Pau 8. 18		Royal f. 90r Space for rubric left blank The preudome seats Galaad in the Perilous Seat. E, undecorated ink capital Text: *Et salues moi tous chiaus del saint hostel . . .*	
S VI 11. 1 Pau 12. 15		Royal f. 91r Space for rubric left blank Galaad draws the sword from the stone; the damsel appears, telling Lancelot he is no longer the greatest knight. L, penflourished initial Text: *Lors met main a lespee et le trait ausi legierement de la pierre comme se elle ni tenist point . . .*	Ryl. f. 183v No rubric Galaad draws the sword from the stone, watched by Arthur, Guinevere, and courtiers (hand 2). L, undecorated ink capital Text: *Lors met la main a lespee et le trait ausi legierement de la perre comme se elle ni tenist point . . .*
S VI 13. 11 Pau 15. 19		Royal f. 91v Space for rubric left blank The Grail appears to King Arthur and his knights at the Round Table. L, penflourished initial Text: *Lors entra laiens li sains Graaus. Couers dur blanc samit . . .*	
S VI 13. 13 Pau 15. 22			Ryl. f. 184v Rubric: *Chi aporte on le saint Graal devant la Taule Reonde* The Grail appears to King Arthur, Queen Guinevere, and the knights at the Round Table (hand 2). E, undecorated ink capital Text: *Et maintenant quil i fu entres fu li palais raemplis de si boines oudours ke se toutes les espisces del monde y fuissent entrees . . .*

	BNF fr. 117–120	BNF fr. 112	BNF fr. 113–116
S VI 7. 6		BNF fr. 112 f. 3 Gauvain or Perceval trying to remove the sword from the stone.	BNF fr. 116 f. 608v Gauvain or Perceval trying to remove the sword from the stone.
S VI 8. 13		BNF fr. 112 f. 3v The preudome shows Galaad to the Perilous Seat.	BNF fr. 116 f. 609 The preudome shows Galaad to the Perilous Seat.
S VI 11. 1	BNF fr. 120 f. 524v Galaad drawing the sword from the stone and the Grail appearing to King Arthur and his knights.		
S VI 11. 6			BNF fr. 116 f. 610 A damsel tells Lancelot he is no longer the best knight in the world.
S VI 13. 11		BNF fr. 112 f. 5 The Grail appears to King Arthur and his knights.	
S VI 13. 13			BNF fr. 116 f. 610v The Grail appears to King Arthur and his knights.

Table C. *Merlin:* Kings Ban and Boors reunited with their wives; the dream of Elaine and of Caesar and their interpretations

	Bonn 526	BNF fr. 95	Add. 10292
S II 260. 18	f. 119 Battle of Trebes: King Arthur and his knights in mounted combat with swords.	f. 251 King Arthur and his army riding; battle of Trebes: mounted combat with lances; top border: hare, dog.	Add. f. 153v Rubric: *Ensi com li roys Artus cheualche et sa gent tout ordene et rengie.* King Arthur's army on horseback holding banners (hand 2). C, champie initial Text: *Chi endroit dist li contes que quant Merlins sen fu partis du roy Artu. si fist li rois Artus monter toutes ses gens . . .*
S II 262. 31			Add. f. 154v Rubric: *Ensi com Claudas se combat au roy Ban. et li a li roys Bans ocis son cheual desous lui.* King Ban fights in mounted combat with swords against Claudas; he kills Claudas' horse under him (hand 2). D, champie initial Text: *De lautre part se recombat li rois Bans as gens le roy Claudas . . .*

S II 265. 13	Bonn f. 120v Battle of Trebes: mounted combat with lances and swords.		
S II 268. 10	Bonn f. 121v Queens Elaine and Evaine watch Arthur's knights set out from Trebes.	BNF fr. 95 f. 254 King Arthur (dragon standard) and his forces defend the castle of Trebes in which are the two queens, the sisters Elaine and Evaine, wives of kings Ban and Boors; battle of Trebes: mounted combat with lances; top border: hare mounting dog; beaked hybrid pecks rear of man playing pipe and tabor; bottom: woman with garland on her loose hair offers wreath to man in academic hat seated at desk, who turns back to look at her.	Add. f. 156r Rubric: *Ensi que on se combat deuant .i. castel et .i. valles demande quel gent ce sont* A messenger inquires who are the knights fighting against Claudas at Trebes; the two queens and their ladies watch from the battlements (hand 2). L, champie initial Text: *Li contes dist chi endroit que chil del chastel de Trebes uirent le cri et le huee des gens dehors . . .*
S II 270. 6	Bonn f. 122 Battle of Trebes, mounted combat with swords.	BNF fr. 95 f. 255 sm: Battle of Trebes: mounted combat with swords.	Add. f. 156v Rubric: *Ensi com lez batailles sont asamblees de ceuls de Benoyc. et de la gent au duc Frolles dAlemaigne.* The people of Benoyc fighting in mounted combat with swords (hand 2). E, champie initial Text: *En ceste partie dist li contes que moult fu fiere la bataille et li estours mortels . . .*
S II 273. 15	Bonn f. 122v Kings Ban and Boort with their wives, Queen Elaine and Queen Evaine, lying in two beds placed feet-to-feet.		
S II 275. 21			Add. f. 158r Rubric: *Ensi com Gauuains abat le roy Claudas de cop de lance a terre ius de son cheval.* Gauvain wounds Claudas and beats him to the ground in mounted combat with swords (hand 2). L, champie initial Text: *Lors se met en la cache apres les autres si fu la cache moult grans . . .*

	Bonn 526	BNF fr. 95	Add. 10292
S II 278. 39			Add. f. 159r Rubric: *Ensi com li rois Bans gist avec sa femme et songa .i. songe dont il ot grant paor.* Queen Elaine tells King Ban in bed about her strange dream (hand 2). E, champie initial Text: *En cel soigne ou li rois Bans estoit li fu auis que quant la uois qui chou li ot dit sen parti . . .*
S II 279. 22	Bonn f. 124 Merlin explains Queen Elaine's dream to the seated King and Queen.	BNF fr. 95 f. 255 C initial, Merlin explaining Queen Elaine's dream to King Ban of Benoic.	Add. f. 159v-1 Rubric: *Ensi comme li roys Bans parole a Merlin et li conte sa vision de son songe.* King Ban asks Merlin what his wife's dream signifies (hand 2). C, champie initial Text: *Chi endroit dist li contes que a .j. iour uint li rois Bans a Merlin et li dist . . .*
S II 280. 16			Add. f. 159v–2 Rubric: *Ensi com Merlins a dit la senefiance dez so[n]ges et prent congie as trois rois.* Merlin interprets the dream and takes his leave of the three kings (hand 2). A, champie initial Text: *A tant sen parti Merlins des .iij. rois et sen ala a samie ki latendoit . . .*
S II 281. 15	Bonn f. 124v–1 King Arthur and his knights at sea in a sailboat.	BNF fr. 95 f. 261 Gauvain and his knights ride up to Benoic; King Arthur and his knights at sea in 2 sailboats; top border: double-headed trumpeter terminal, hybrid creature; bottom: bagpiper turns back to look at mummer peeping out of tall hairy body with stag's head; long-beaked bird; hybrid terminal with long horns.	

S II 281. 31	Bonn f. 124v–2 Emperor Julius Caesar lying in bed (alone), dreaming: by the bed are lions attacking a sow with a gold crown on her head.	BNF fr. 95 f. 261v Merlin as an old man in the forest; Julius Caesar in bed, dreaming: a hairy sow wearing a gold crown is by the bed; top: two men fight over a gaming board; bottom: falconer holding bird and lure; hybrid long-beaked terminal.	Add. f. 160r Rubric: *Ensi com lenpereris gist avec lempereor* Julius Caesar, lying in bed with his wife, has a strange dream (about a sow with a circle of gold on her head, not shown) (hand 2). O, champie initial Text: *Ore dist li contes que quant Merlins se fu departis del roy Artu quil sen ala es fores de Romenie . . .*
S II 283. 1	Bonn f. 125 Emperor Julius Caesar sits (no table) and listens to Merlin in the guise of a stag.	BNF fr. 95 f. 262 Merlin in the guise of a stag before Caesar's table at which sit Caesar, his empress and a courtier (Avenable disguised as Grisoledes ?); top border: bird, hybrid; bottom: female acrobat, hooded trumpeter.	Add. f. 160v Rubric: *Ensi com li rois sist au manger et Merlins y uint en samblance dun cherf.* Merlin in the guise of a stag on the table tells Julius Caesar, who is at table, that only the wild man can explain his dream (hand 2). C, champie initial Text: *Chi endroit dist li contes que quant li emperreres seoit si pensis al mangier . . .*
S II 284. 7			Hand 1 resumes from f. 161r–184v Add. f. 161r Rubric: *Ensi com vns homs salvages est venus a vn fu ou len rostisoit vne haste. et il tolt au garchon le haste.* Merlin in the semblance of a wild giant snatches a spit of roast meat from a man sitting by a table, watched by three hooded figures (hand 1). E, champie initial Text: *Ensi pense Grisandoles et deuise en son cuer tout cheualchant . . .*
S II 287. 12			Add. f. 162r Rubric: *Ensi com li homs saluages est leues en estant et espont al empereour son songe.* Merlin as an old man interprets Caesar's dream (hand 1). Q, champie initial Text: *Qvant vint al quart jor apres ce que li saluages hom fu uenus . . .*

	Bonn 526	BNF fr. 95	Add. 10292
S II 292. 1	Bonn f. 127 Double wedding: two bishops marry Emperor Julius Caesar to Avenable, and Caesar's daughter to Avenable's brother Patrice.	BNF fr. 95 f. 267v Avenable reunited with her parents, in the presence of Caesar and his men; Caesar receives a messenger from Greece; top border: female terminals tearing their hair.	Add. f. 163r Rubric: *Ensi que li emperes siet au mangier et vns messages est a genouls deuant le roi et parole a li.* A messenger from Greece kneels before Caesar and his wife at table; seeing the inscription above door (written by Merlin, it relates the previous events and explains his part in them) (hand 1). C, champie initial Text: *Chi endroit dist li contes que quant li homs saluages sen fu partis del empereor de Romme . . .*

Table D. *Merlin:* King Arthur's First Encounter with Guinevere and her threatened abduction

	Bonn 526	BNF fr. 95	Add. 10292 illustrations by two hands
S II 156. 7	Bonn f. 94v King Leodegan of Carmelide and four courtiers at table, a servant hands the king a cup.	BNF fr. 95 f. 196v sm: Battle of Carohaise: rout of the Saxons.	Add. f. 122r Rubric: *Ensi com la fille le roy Leodegan a laue le viaire et le col le roy Artu et puis lessue dun doublier.* Guinevere washes Arthur's face and neck (hand 2). E, champie initial Text: *En ceste partie dist li contes que moult furent lie et joiant cil del roialme de Carmelide . . .*
S II 159. 36	Bonn f. 95v Merlin informs King Arthur about Gauvain and his two companions who stand on the right.	BNF fr. 95 f. 198v sm: Banquet at King Leodegan's castle.	Add. f. 123r Rubric: *Ensi com Merlins a trait a vne part lez trois rois et parole a euls a conseil.* Merlin talks to the three kings privately (hand 2). O, champie initial Text: *Ore dist li contes que moult furent bien assis al souper et serui de viandes et de uins . . .*

S II 298. 37	Bonn f. 129 King Arthur and three knights ride into Carmelide where they are greeted by King Leodegan.	BNF fr. 95 f. 272 sm: King Arthur sails back to England .	Add. f. 165v Rubric: *Ensi que li rois Artus et si baron sont en une nef en mer.* Arthur and his barons return to England in boats (hand 1). C, champie initial Text: *Chi endroit dist li contes que quant li rois Artu et li haut baron furent entre es nes. si siglerent tant.quil vindrent en la Bloie Bertaigne . . .*
S II 300. 1	Bonn f. 129 The rebel kings receive news of Arthur's return from a man wearing an academic hat.	BNF fr. 95 f. 272v sm: Armies of the 10 kings separate; top border: bagpiper.	Add. f. 165v Rubric: *Ensi que pluisor prince cheualchent et nouveles lor uienent del roy Artu.* The rebel kings receive news of Arthur's return (hand 1). O, champie initial Text: *Ore dist li contes que quant li .xij. prinche furent desconfit et furent repairiet cascuns a son repaire . . .*
S II 300. 38	Bonn f. 129v–1 Merlin as an old man relates his adventures to Blaise (wearing academic hat) who sits by trees, writing them down on a scroll.		
S II 301. 4	Bonn f. 129v–2 The archbishop of Brice marries King Arthur and Guinevere, in the presence of King Leodegan.	BNF fr. 95 f. 273 The archbishop of Brice marries King Arthur and Guinevere, in the presence of King Leodegan; knights tilting at quintain; top border: frontal hare between pairs of dragons; bottom: man balancing on one leg, playing portative organ.	Add. f. 166r Rubric: *Ensi com vns parlemens est pris et Merlins traist a vne part Ulfin et Bretelet.* Merlin tells Ulfin and Bretel about plans to substitute the false Guinevere for Arthur's wife (hand 1). O, champie initial Text: *Ore dist li contes ke Genieure le fillastre Cleodalis avoit de moult rices parens de par sa mere . . .*

	Bonn 526	BNF fr. 95	Add. 10292 illustrations by two hands
S II 303. 35			Add. f. 167r Rubric: *Ensi com vne bataille sentresamble si y fait mesires Gavain meruelles darmes.* Gauvain's brilliant feats of arms at a tournament (hand 1). Q, champie initial Text: *Quant chil furent monte et atourne si en vindrent les vns contre les autres . . .*
S II 307. 34	Bonn f. 131 A group of six traitors sieze Queen Guinevere in the garden.	BNF fr. 95 f. 277 King Arthur, Queen Guinevere, and courtiers at banqueting table; Ulfin and Bretel defend Guinevere in foot combat with swords; she is roped to a tree.	Add. f. 168r Rubric: *Ensi com mesires Gauain et pluiseur autre chevalier sieent a table. et parolent de moult de cosez* The knights sitting at the Round Table (hand 1). C, champie initial Text: *Chi endroit dist li contes que quant li rois Artus en ot mene monsegnor Gauain el palais . . .*
S II 309. 3			Add. f. 168v Rubric: *Ensi com Ulfins et Bretel se combatent pour rescourre la royne.* Ulfin and Bretel attack the traitors who seized Queen Guinevere (hand 1). Q, champie initial Text: *Qvant Ulfins et Bretel uoent cels que il tant desiroient a ueoir . . .*
S II 312. 14	Bonn f. 132 King Leodegan calls upon kings Arthur, Ban, Bors, and 7 knights (four kings and one man are shown) to pass judgement on Bertholais for having attempted to abduct Queen Guinevere: he will be sentenced to be banished and disinherited.	BNF fr. 95 f. 279v Bertolais and his men before King Leodegan and his courtiers; top border: dog.	Add. f. 169v–1 Rubric: *Ensi com li rois Artus li rois Bans et li rois Bohors. et lor baron. sont a vn iugement. et li rois Bans rent le iugement* Bertholais is judged to be disinherited and banished by an assembly of knights (hand 1). C, champie initial Text: *Chi endroit dist li contes que quant li rois Leodegans ot commande a son senescal quil menast sa fillastre hors du roialme de Carmelide . . .*

S II 313. 26	Bonn f. 132v–1 King Arthur tells his barons to prepare for the journey to Logres.	BNF fr. 95 f. 280v sm: Gauvain and his followers riding; border: hybrid lion creature holding banner sable a lion or (Brabant).	Add. f. 169v–2 Rubric: *Ensi que li rois Artus traist monseignor Gauain a consel a vne part ensus des autres barons. et parole a lui.* King Arthur bids Gauvain to ride to Logres and make preparations to receive the court (hand 1). E, champie initial Text: *En cheste partie dist li contes que moult demena li rois Artus boine vie il et sa feme . . .*
S II 314. 21	Bonn f. 132v–2 King Arthur and Queen Guinevere (loose hair, crowned, holding lapdog) ride with three followers.	BNF fr. 95 f. 281 sm: King Arthur (shield or) and Queen Guinevere (gold robe) riding with followers.	Add. f. 170r Rubric: *Ensi com li rois Artus et sa feme et doi autre roy et lor compaignie cheualchent tout arme vers vne chite.* King Arthur, Guinevere and their company follow Gauvain three days later (hand 1). O, champie initial Text: *Ore dist li contes que al tierch iour apres que messires Gauvain sen fu partis del roy Artu . . .*
S II 315. 8	Bonn f. 133 King Arthur and Queen Guinevere (veiled head, crowned, no lapdog) ride with three knights.	BNF fr. 95 f. 281v King Arthur and Queen Guinevere (holding lapdog) ride with army; battle of the forest of Sarpeine; top border: dragon terminal bites rear of naked man with lion's head wielding sword.	Add. f. 170r Rubric: *Ensi que lez gens le roy Artu et le gent le roy Loth se combatent et li rois Artus iouste au roi Loth.* King Lot and his army attack Arthur and his company; Arthur and Lot in mounted combat with lances (hand 1). L, champie initial Text: *Li contes dist chi endroit que quant li rois Artus se fu partis del roy Leodegan . . .*
S II 316. 34			Add. f. 170v Rubric: *Ensi que li roys Loth est a genouls deuant le roi Artu et li rent sespee.* King Lot surrenders to King Arthur, hands him his sword by the pommel, and asks him for mercy (hand 1). Q, champie initial Text: *Qvant li rois Artus uoit son neueu si fierement uenir . . .*

	Bonn 526	BNF fr. 95	Add. 10292 illustrations by two hands
S II 322. 5			Add. f. 172r Rubric: *Ensi que li roys a disne et il regarde volentiers sez gens qui menoient grant ioie.* King Arthur greeted by his barons (no table) (hand 1). A, champie initial Text: *A tant furent les napes ostees et les dois si commencha la ioie par laiens . . .*
S II 325. 14			Add. f. 173r Rubric: *Ensi comme on tornoie deuant vn castel et la roine estoit as fenestres.* A tournament is held in the meadows before Logres; Guinevere and her lady watch from windows (hand 1). Q, champie initial Text: *Qvant li compaignon de la Table Roonde uirent quil estoient tourne a la desconfiture . . .*
S II 327. 19			Add. f. 173v–174r Rubric: *Ensi com vns tornoiemens est commenchies crueuls et felenes. ou Gauain faisoit meruelles darmes.* f. 174r Gauvain in mounted combat with swords (hand 1). Q, champie initial. Text: *Qvant li chevalier la roine entendirent monsignor Gauvain ensi parler et il uirent la bele route des cheualiers qui al dos le sieuent . . .*
S II 334. 7			Add. f. 175v Rubric: *Ensi que li rois Artus sist entre sez barons et illueques virent chevalier et sagenoillent et ploient le pan de lor mantel par ame[n]de.* A knight of the Round Table kneels and holds out the hem of his garment to Gauvain, Queen Guinevere and King Arthur, watched by other knights (hand 1). A, champie initial Text: *A tant vindrent li compaignon de la Table Roonde devant le roy . . .*

S II 335. 21	Bonn f. 137v King Lot and his sons riding (wrongly placed ? cf. S II 339. 7).	BNF fr. 95 f. 291 King Ban (or King Lot), accompanied by falconers, debates with King Arthur, supported by Queen Guinevere (holding lapdog) and courtiers; top border: affronted centaurs holding swords and shields or fretty azure and or; bottom: knights, one wielding sword, the other drawing sword, wearing circular cusped ailettes.	Add. f. 176r Rubric: *Ensi que .iiij. roy sont assis a vne table. et de lautre part sont li compaignon de la Table Roonde.* King Arthur, King Ban, King Bohort and King Lot being served at one table and the Knights of the Round Table at another (hand 1). O, champie initial Text: *Ore dist li contes que moult furent li compaignon de la Table Roonde lie quant il furent acorde a monsignor Gauain . . .*

Table E: The False Quinevere episode in *Lancelot*

	Bonn 526	Add. 10293	Amsterdam 1, vol. ii
S IV 10. 14 LM I 18	Bonn f. 260v King Arthur's wise men (maistre) explain Galehot's dream to him and Lancelot.	Add. f. 131r. Rubric: *Ensi que li roys Artus et ses barons a cheles vne damoisele i vint qui avoit vestu cote et mantel de soie et si fu ele bien trechie et si amenoit cheualiers plusors.* A lady (the False Guinevere's damsel messenger), accompanied by an old knight (Bertholais), addresses King Arthur (having flung her veil to the ground and brought a letter for Arthur, not shown) (hand 1). O, champie initial Text: *Or dist li contes que quant li message Gaieholt se furent parti de lui quil errerent tant quil vindrenat au roy Artu en la cite de Camaaloth . . .*	Amst ii, f. 202r. Rubric: *Chi aporte vne damoisiele et .vn chevalier lettres au roy Artu de grans merueilles.* A lady (the False Guinevere's damsel messenger), having flung her veil to the ground, accompanied by an old knight (Bertholais), brings a letter to King Arthur and Queen Guinevere, having flung down her veil which lies on the ground, and holding a box (which contains the letter). C, champie initial Text: *Chi endroit dist li contes que quant li message Galeholt furent venu au roy Artu en la cite de Camaaloth . . .*

	Bonn 526	Add. 10293	Amsterdam 1, vol. ii
S IV 11. 1 LM I 19		Add. f. 131v. Rubric: *Ensi que li prestres list les lettres par deuant le baronnie que li fause roine enuoia a le roi Artu* A clerk reads the unfurled letter to King Arthur, Queen Guinevere, and the assembled court (hand 1). Q, champie initial Text: *Quant li roys ot dit tout son plaisir a la damoisele si li respont et dist au roy en ceste maniere . . .*	

S IV 18–45 The Helias episode follows here, illustrated by 9 miniatures in Add.

S IV 45. 19 LM I 96		Add. f. 143r. Rubric: *Ensi que vne damoisele ot .xiiij. pucheles vint parler au roy Artu.* The False Guinevere and her ladies received by King Arthur, Queen Guinevere, and the court (hand 1). E, champie initial Text: *En ceste maniere vint la damoisele a court au ior de la Candelier . . .*	
S IV 47. 29 LM I 102		Add. f. 143v. Rubric: *Ensi comme Tholomes prent le roi Artu et ses veneours en .j. forest.* King Arthur seized by King Tholomer's knights in a forest (hand 1). Q, champie initial Text: *Quant li roys Artus qui de riens ne se parchut que cil le uolsist deceuoir . . .*	

S IV 50. 1 LM I 107	Bonn f. 268v The False Guinevere (in hair net and veil) talks to King Arthur who looks out of his prison window and swears to acknowledge her.	Add. f. 144v. Rubric: *Ensi que une damoisele qui tenoit le roy Artu en sa prison et ele parole a lui en le prison.* King Arthur shown with the False Guinevere in the window of her prison, swearing to acknowledge her (hand 1). O, champie initial Text: *Or dist li contes que quant la damoisele fu au roy uenue Si li dist sire or vous ai iou en ma prison si ne isteres iamais . . .*	Amst ii, f. 218r. Rubric: *Chi est li roys Artus en prison et iure a la damoisiele samour* King Arthur, imprisoned by the False Guinevere, sits with her on a bench and swears to acknowledge her, watched by barons. O, penflourished initial Text: *Or dist li contes que quant la demoisele fu reuenue en son pais . . .*
S IV 51. 15 LM I 110	Bonn f. 269 Arthur's knighs, bereft of their king, begin to fight: Mounted combat beween two knights armed with swords, both facing right, one grasping the other round the waist, both raising swords.	Add. f. 145r. Rubric: *Ensi comme li roys Galehot conseille a Gauuain que il recoiue lonneur de la coroune par devant le royne Genieure.* Queen Guinevere and King Galehot debate, and the barons offer the crown to Gauvain because of Arthur's continued absence (hand 1). C, champie initial Text: *Ce dist li contes que quant li baron de Bertaigne se virent sans seignour si commenchierent a guerroier li vn encontre lautre . . .*	Amst ii, f. 219r. Rubric: *Chi presentent chil du pais couronne a monseigneur Gauvain pour chou que li roys Artus nestoit mie ou pais.* The barons offer the crown to Gauvain because of Arthur's continued absence. O, penflourished initial Text: *Or dist li contes que tantdemora li roys en prison el royaume de Carmelide que li baron de Bertaigne quidoient quil fust mors. Et quant il virent quil estoient sans seignor si commencherent a guerroier li vn encontre lautre . . .*
S IV 54. 31 LM I 118		Add. f. 146r. Rubric: *Ensi que li rois Galaad [sic] blame au roi Artu de chou kil a laissiet se femme pour vn autre* King Galehot (not Galaad) reproaches King Arthur for condemning Queen Guinevere without proving her guilty (hand 1). E, champie initial Text: *Ensi conforte Galehot la royne . . .*	

	Bonn 526	Add. 10293	Amsterdam 1, vol. ii
S IV 56. 37 LM I 123		Add. f. 146v. Rubric: *Ensi comme Lancelot sest desuestus et demande le roy Artu ki le iugement auoit fait sour la royne Genieure* Supported by King Galehot and the barons, Lancelot takes off his cloak and asks King Arthur who had brought judgement against Queen Guinevere (hand 1). E, champie initial Text: *Ensi demoura la royne en le garde monseignor Gauuain dusques au ior de Pentecoste . . .*	
S IV 59. 21 LM I 129		Add. f. 147v. Rubric: *Ensi que que li rois Artus rechoit les gages de Lancelot et de Bertelai le Vieus par devant lor baronie.* Lancelot pledges to fight for the Queen's innocence, and Bertholais pledges to uphold the False Guinevere's claims; both hand a glove to King Arthur (hand 1). Q, champie initial Textr: *Quant Lancelot ot gete ius son mantel ensi com vous poes oir si li auint moult bien quil estoit en cote . . .*	
S IV 61. 1 LM I 132		Add. f. 148r. Rubric: *Ensi que li rois Galehot parole au roy Artu et deuise la bataille comment Lancelot le fera par deuant lor baronie encontre Bertelai le Vieus.* King Galehot persuades King Arthur that it would be unfair for Lancelot to fight all three knights at once, but rather one by one (hand 1). E, champie initial Text: *Ensi furent li gage donne dune part et dautre apres dist Galehot que che nest pas drois de combatre .i. chevalier en contre iij . . . .*	

S IV 62. 1 LM I 135		Add. f. 148v. No rubric; hoardings of castle in rubric space. Lancelot is mounted for the duel on Galehot's horse; King Arthur orders knights to guard the field. Onlookers, including Queen Guinevere, watch from the upper hoardings of the castle behind (hand 1). Q, champie initial Text: *Quant Lancelot fu armes si monta sor .i. cheual qui fu moult boins et estoit a Galehot son compaignon . . .*	
S IV 63. 37 LM III 72		Add. f. 149r. No rubric, no space Having defeated Aglodas in front of crowds outside and at the castle windows and battlements, Lancelot has taken off Aglodas's helmet and flung it away, holding his sword by the pommel on Aglodas's head (hand 1). L, champie initial Text: *Lors descent Lancelot de son cheual et latache a .i. arbre. Et oste la guiche de son escu de son col . . .*	
S IV 66. 15 LM III 77		Add. f. 150r. No rubric Lancelot holds Aglodas at his mercy; Queen Guinevere, from the battlements, begs Lancelot to spare his life (hand 1). Q, champie initial Text: *Quant Galehot et les autres gardes uirent le chevalier a si grant meschief si en orent pitie . . .*	

	Bonn 526	Add. 10293	Amsterdam 1, vol. ii
S IV 68. 1 LM III 80		Add. f. 150v. Rubric: *Ensi que li parlemens del roy Artu et Gauvain parla au roy son onkle por la royne acheles et Bertelai li Vieus parole a lui et faisoit samblant de plorer* King Arthur, King Galehot, Bertholais and the court debate the fate of Queen Guinevere; Gauvain urges King Arthur to treat her well, while Bertholais, feigning tears, insists she be exiled (hand 1). Q, champie initial Text: *Quant li roys ot la royne ensi parler si li demande Dame et ou gist cele terre . . .*	
S IV 69. 17 LM III 83		Add. f. 151r. Rubric: *Ensi que li rois Artus tint la roine Genieure par le main et la bailla a garder le roi Galehot par deuant lor baronie. et les barons en orent grant pitie.* King Arthur entrusts Queen Guinevere to King Galehot, witnessed by the barons (hand 1). L, champie initial Text: *Lors prent li roys la royne et en uait a Galehot et li liure par le main . . .*	
S IV 72. 9+ var in Bonn LM III 89	Bonn f. 273v The False Guinevere, who lies dying with Bertholais at her side, makes her confession to King Arthur. Text: *Or dist li contes que a lentree des auensque li rois Artus ot une court tenu a Kalion . . .*	Add. f. 152r. Rubric: *Ensi que on gete sentence sour le roy Artu.* The pope enjoins King Arthur to leave his new wife and take the old one back (hand 1). O, champie initial Text: *Oor* [sic] *dist li contes que ensi est li roys Arthus departis de sa femme par le desloiaute de lautre Genieure . . .*	Amst ii, f. 227v. Rubric: *Chi gist malade de meselerie li fausse royne et li roys Artus le vint veir.* The False Guinevere, who lies dying with Bertolais at her side, repeats her confession to King Arthur and the barons. O, penflourished initial Text: *Or dist li contes que ensi est li rois Artus partis de sa femme par le desoiaute de lautre Genieure . . .*

S IV 75. 16 LM III 94		Add. f. 153r. Rubric: *Ensi comme li rois Artu se fist confesser dun hermite en son hermitage* King Arthur confessing to the hermit Amustans in his church-like hermitage (hand 1). T, champie initial Text: *Tant dist mestres Gauvain au roy Artus son oncle . . .*	
S IV 76. 37 LM III 97		Add. f. 153v. Rubric: *Ensi que li roys Artu et se baronie oirent messe en .j. hermitage* King Arthur and his men hear mass in an elaborate, Gothic, hermitage where a priest elevates the host (hand 1). Q, champie initial Text: *Quant li roys ot ensi parler lermite si giete vn souspir . . .*	
S IV 79. 4 LM III 101		Add. f. 154r. Rubric: *Ensi que li fause Genieure gist mesele et si uo vint li rois Artu parler a li.* The False Guinevere, who lies dying with Bertolais at her side, repeats her confession to King Arthur and the barons (hand 1). D, champie initial Text: *Dame vous gisies en si dolereuse carire comme cele qui a tout le pooir du cors perdu . . .*	
S IV 80. 6 LM III 103		Add. f. 154v. Rubric: *Ensi que li rois Galehot et Lancelot parolent a le royne et li conseillent le millor quil peuent.* Queen Guinevere sits with Lancelot and King Galehot and asks them to advise her (hand 1). L, champie initial Text: *Li roys se seigne moult durement et a moult grant meruelle li vient . . .*	

	Bonn 526	Add. 10293	Amsterdam 1, vol. ii
S IV 81. 23 LM III 106		Add. f. 155r. Rubric: *Ensi que les gens de Carmelide prient merci a leur droite dame en peur les chemises.* The barons of Sorelois, dressed in their undershirts as humble sinners, ask Queen Guinevere for mercy, in the presence of bishops and the court (hand 1). Q, champie initial Text: *Quant li baron de Carmelyde orent pris conseil ensamble comment il yroient a la royne lor dame . . .*	
S IV 82. 34 LM III 108		Add. f. 155v. Rubric: *Ensi que li roy Artu donna en garde la royne Genieure au roy Galeholt* King Galehot hands Queen Guinevere back to King Arthur (hand 1) (not the opposite, as in the rubric). Text: *Lors saparelle pres ce la royne et sa compaignie et si monterent et sen vont en la Grant Bertaigne . . .*	
S IV 84. 12 LM III 111		Add. f. 156r. Rubric: *Ensi que Galehot et Lancelot parolent a la roine en sa chambre.* Queen Guinevere talking to Lancelot and King Galehot in her chamber (hand 1). E, champie initial Text: *En ceste partie dist li contes que li roys Artus est rassanbles a sa femme . . .*	Amst ii, f. 232r. Rubric: *Chi baise li roys Lancelot* King Arthur embracing Lancelot. C, penflourished initial Text: *Chi endroit dist li contes que li rois Artus est rasambles a sa feme . . .*

S IV 85. 29 LM III 114		Add. f. 156v. Rubric: *Ensi que Lancelot relieve la roine qui estoit agenoillie par deuant les barounes.* Lancelot raises up Queen Guinevere, who knelt and begged him to rejoin the Round Table, watched by King Arthur, King Galehot, and the barons (hand 1). L, champie initial Text: *Lors se met la royne a genouls deuant lui . . .*	

	BNF fr. 117–120	BNF fr. 112	BNF fr. 113–116
S IV 10. 14 LM I 18	BNF fr. 118 f. 264 The False Guinevere's female messenger, accompanied by Bertholais le Vieux, gives a letter to King Arthur		BNF fr. 114 f. 300 The False Guinevere's female messenger before King Arthur's court
S IV 11. 1 LM I 19			
S IV 13. 12 LM I 15		BNF fr. 112 f. 158v Galehot talking to wise clerks	
S IV 32. 1 LM I 66	BNF fr. 118 f. 269–1 Helias of Toulouse expounding Galehot's dream		
S IV 33. 26	BNF fr. 118 f. 269–2 Helias and Galehot in a chapel see an arm holding a bloody sword		
S IV 40		BNF fr. 112 f. 164 A knight standing between the 'Pont d'espée' and the 'Pont dessous l'eau'	
S IV 49. 25			BNF fr. 114 f. 313v King Arthur addressing the False Guinevere from his prison window and promising fidelity
S IV 51. 15 LM I 110		BNF fr. 112 f. 167 King Arthur handing a letter to a messenger	BNF fr. 114 f. 314 King Arthur's barons electing Gauvain king

	BNF fr. 117–120	BNF fr. 112	BNF fr. 113–116
S IV 56. 37 LM I 123	BNF fr. 118 f. 275v Bertholais le Vieux swearing on behalf of the False Guinevere	BNF fr. 112 f. 171 The barons of Carmelide rejecting the True Guinevere as Arthur's lawful wife	
S IV 63. 37 LM III 72		BNF fr. 112 f. 172 Lancelot defeating the barons	
S IV 72. 9+ var in Bonn LM III 89			BNF fr. 114 f. 321v The False Guinevere on her deathbed makes her confession to Arthur and Gauvain
S IV 82. 34 LM III 108		BNF fr. 112 f. 211v Queen Guinevere returning from Sorelois	
S IV 83. 19	BNF fr. 118 f. 283 Lancelot, Galehot, Guinevere and an attendant talking		
S IV 84. 12 LM III 111			BNF fr. 114 f. 325v Guinevere kneels before Lancelot, begging him to remain at court

Table F. Narrating, Writing, and the Book in *Estoire*

	Add. 10292 illustrations by hand 1	Royal 14.E.III	Amsterdam BPH 1 illustrations by hand 1
S I 3. 1 Pon 1. 3. 1	Add. f.1r No rubric. Miniature in 2 cols., left: Priest-narrator saying the night office at an altar with a chalice on it; blessed by Hand of God; right: Christ in a cloud gives book to priest narrator in bed; C, woman playing rebec (badly rubbed); border (badly rubbed): left: hooded male terminal playing bagpipes; a blessing hand on the end of the point of his hood holds a crozier; top: mitred head terminal holds portative organ; right: 2 bells on a long robe pulled by creature (ape ? – cut off) wearing a sword (?), a moth (?) below; bottom: a duck in a cage is attached (?) to the bar of the cage by a youth, watched by another youth; a man embraces a woman who holds a falcon on her gloved hand; 2 youths wrestle over a gaming board with pieces on it; below border: an ape hybrid blows a trumpet; another ape rides on the shoulders of a man (?) and aims a lance at a backturned ape holding buckler and raised sword; snail terminal (?). Text: *Chil ki se tient et iuge au plus petit et au plus peceor du monde . . .*	Royal f. 3r No rubric Priest-narrator saying the night office at an altar with a chalice on it; blessed by Hand of God; C, youth holding dog; in adjacent space: 2 fighting monkeys with heraldic cloaks: paly of 6, gules and checky argent and azure; and argent a cross moline azure semé of lis argent, overall a bendlet gules; left border: bird hybrid terminal plays a gold and silver portative organ; bagpiper and female dancer; ape playing portative harp; hare; stork in cloak; bottom: in border: hare, hunter spearing boar, 2 dogs chasing hare; below: mounted hunter blowing horn, greyhound, hunter on foot with spear; long-eared owl, stag (cut); on border: trumpeter with banner argent a cross moline azure semé of lis argent, overall a bendlet gules; youth playing pipe and tabor; trumpeter with banner gules a chevron vert [sic] between 3 mullets or; trumpeter (holding bagpipes) and banner (indecipherable); a herald in party az and or tunic holds 2 banners: gules a chevron vert [sic] between 3 mullets or (on the left) and (badly rubbed) sable bendways 3 allerions or between 2 bendlets argent, between 2 knights riding, on left in housing, surcoat azure with white dots around a central boss and around the	Amst. i f.1r No rubric The priest-narrator-hermit saying the night office in a church at an altar with a crucifix on it; borders: left: ape terminal juggling with sticks; bottom: figure (human ?) sitting by bird cage; animal terminal; hybrid with sword-tail; later shield of La Rochefoucauld barruly argent (rubbed) and azure, 3 chevrons gules overall, topped by a helmet and crest of a peacock's tail; right: bishop/hybrid holding portative organ; bird; man on very tall stilts (badly rubbed); C, champie initial. Text: *Chil ki la hauteche et la signourie de si haute estoire com est chele du graal . . .*

		border; ailette overpainted; right knight in surcoat and housing or, shield and ailette or in dexter chief a mullet (star) gules, an eagle sable; right border: a three-storey arched structure with tall pinnacles: (bottom) a frontal-facing angel in gold dalmatic playing a gold psaltery; (middle) the Virgin and Child; and angel playing a rebec and looking over to the adjacent scene in col. c; top: woman in knotted headscarf, tucked-up robes, and heavy buttoned boots, carrying a distaff over her shoulder; a knight in white housing lined with red, pink surcoat, shield and ailette argent a cross crosslet gules (badly corroded) raises his sword to fight a bat-winged horse/human/hybrid wearing a knotted headscarf, holding a basket of eggs and raising a scimitar. Text: *Chil ki la hauteche et la signourie de si haute estoire comme est chele du graal . . .*	
S I 4. 12; Pon 2. 4. 3		Royal f. 3r–2 col. c. Rubric: *Ensi que Dieus en une nue parole a i hermite qui est devant son autel* At an altar with a draped chalice on it, Christ standing in a cloud gives book to priest-narrator in bed. D, one-line ink capital Text: *De trois coses vne et dune cose trois . . .*	Amst. i f.1v Rubric: *Chi endroit parole Dieus en une nue au saint ermite* Christ appearing in a flaming cloud to the priest-narrator-hermit outside his 'petit habitacle'. D, one-line ink capital Text: *De trois coses une et dune cose trois . . .*
S I 12. 30 Pon 22. 31. 1	Add. f. 3v Rubric: *Ensi que Ioseph recuelle les goutes de sanc en .j. esquiele* Crucifixion with Mary and John, two thieves, their souls taken by an angel and a devil, and Joseph collecting Christ's blood in the Grail (as a silver bowl). A, champie initial Text: *Au ior que li salueres du monde souffri mort . . .*	Royal f. 6v Space for rubric left blank Before a draped altar, the priest-narrator copies the book. A, penflourished initial Text: *Av iour que li sauueres du monde souffri mort . . .*	Amst. i f. 5v Rubric: *Chi parole comment Joseph saprocha de Jhesucrist* No miniature f. 6 A, champie initial (hand 1) Text: *Av iour ke li sauveres du monde souffri mort . . .*

S I 14. 5 Pon 25. 35. 6		Royal f. 7r Rubric: E, penflourished initial; *Ensi que Josephs recoilli le degout du sanc qui issoit des plaiies Nostre Seigneur qui puis fu apeles li saint Graalz.* Crucifixion with Mary, John, two thieves, and Joseph collecting Christ's blood in the Grail (as a sliver bowl). E, penflourished initial Text: *Et quant il vint au cors si conquelli le degout du sanc . . .*	Amst. i f. 6v Rubric: *Chi est ensi que Joseph rechut le sanc Nostre Seignour qui puis fu apeleis Graalz* Crucifixion with sun and moon, Mary and John, and Joseph collecting Christ's blood in the Grail (as a silver bowl). E, one-line ink capital Text: *Et quant il vint au cors si concuelli le degout du sanc . . .*

Table G. Narrating and Writing in *Merlin* and *Suite Vulgate*: Merlin and Blaise

	Bonn UB 526	Paris, BNF fr. 95	Add. 10292
S II 19. 15 MM 60. 9			Add. f. 80v Rubric: *Ensi que Merlins fait escrire .i. livre plain de merveilles a Blase sen clerc.* Merlin as a child dictates to his clerk Blaise (hand 1). L, champie initial Text: *Lors quist Blaises ce que mestier li fu . . .*
S II 180. 12		BNF fr. 95 f. 210 C initial: Merlin as old man relating his adventures to Blaise, wearing an academic hat and sitting, listening, in his doorway. Border: bat-winged tonsured male terminal.	
S II 206. 16		BNF fr. 95 f. 223 sm: Merlin as old man in a hooded robe stands and dictates to Blaise, bareheaded, who sits in his doorway, writing in a book on a lectern; top border: affronted knight terminals fight with lances; bottom: hooded dragon terminal.	Add. f. 137r Rubric: *Ensi que Gauain est deuant maistre Blaise et li conte lez auentures et il les mist en escrit* (Merlin, not Gauvain) Merlin (young) dictates to Blaise who writes in vertical columns (hand 2). E, champie initial Text: *En cheste partie dist li contes que quant Gauuain et si compaignon se furent melle a Thaurus . . .*

	Bonn UB 526	Paris, BNF fr. 95	Add. 10292
S II 292. 38	Bonn f. 127v Merlin as an old man recounts his adventures to Blaise, who stands listening, wearing an academic hat and holding a book.	BNF fr. 95 f. 268 sm: Merlin as old man recounts his adventures to Blaise, sitting in his doorway, wearing academic hat, listening with his hand on his chin, his elbow and his other hand resting on the open, written, pages of the book on his lectern; top border: ape eating bread; centaur wielding sword, holding shield gironny or and azure; bottom: archer aims at knight who holds up tall tabernacle.	Add. f. 163v Rubric: *Ensi com Merlins est deuant maistre Blaise et li fait mettre lez auentures en escrit.* Merlin as young man dictates to Blaise who sits writing in a book at a desk with movable lectern attached (hand 1). E, champie initial Text: *En cheste partie dist li contes que ausi tost ke Merlins fu departis de Iulius Cesar kil se mist au chemin vers la Grant Bertaigne a Blaise son maistre . . .*
S II 300. 38	Bonn f. 129v Merlin as old man dictating to Blaise, who wears an academic hat and sits by trees, writing on a scroll.		
S II 375. 3	Bonn f. 147–2 Merlin as old man recounting his adventures to Blaise who stands listening, wearing academic hat, both hands raised.	BNF fr. 95 f. 309–2 sm: Merlin as old man, hooded, and Blaise, bareheaded, sitting in his doorway, one hand on chin, the other on lap, listening.	Add. f. 188r Rubric: *Ensi com Merlins conte a maistre Blaise lez auentures et il les mist en escript.* Blaise, tonsured and wearing a hood, sits in profile at his desk with a movable lectern writing in an open book. Merlin also sits, opposite, pointing on his hand (hand 2). C, champie initial Text: *Chi dist li contes que a leure que Merlins se fu partis del roy Artu . . .*

Table H. Telling and Writing in *Lancelot*

	Bonn 526	Yale 229	Add. 10293
S V 190. 8 LM IV 393			Add. f. 315r Rubric: *Ensi que Lancelot joua as esches ou palais le roy a la royne.* Lancelot plays against the magic chess-board and wins the game, watched by Queen Guinevere, King Baudemagus and a courtier (hand 2). Q, champie initial Text: *Quant Lancelot ot dit au roy Bandemagu [sic] que ia pour paour destre mates . . .*
S V 191. 34 LM IV 397			Add. f. 315v Rubric: *Ensi ke Gauuain conte au roy et as autres cheualiers ses auentures.* Gauvain relating his adventures to King Arthur and his court (hand 2). Q, champie initial Text: *Quant les auentures. Lancelot furent mises en escrit . . .*
S V 192. 29 LM V 1	Bonn f. 382 Leaning out of her window, Queen Guinevere hands a ring to Lancelot who stands outside.	Yale f. 85v Top: Gauvain in bed (?) attended by Bohort; Gauvain, Bohort and Gaheriet annouce their departure to King Arthur, who sits on a throne covered with a green knotted cloth. Bottom: In her chamber, Queen Guinevere hands Lancelot the ring given her by the Lady of the Lake. Top border, left: woman terminal wearing hair net carries swaddled baby (the Lady of the Lake and Lancelot ?); right: donkey. Bottom, left: man with an arrow sticking out of his shoulder cranks a crossbow; right: centaur aims an arrow. Text: *Or dist li contes que quant cil qui compaignon orent este de la queste orent contes lor auentures . . .*	

	Bonn 526	Yale 229	Add. 10293
S V 194. 6 LM V 4			Add. f. 316v Rubric: *Ensi ke Lancelot et la royne sont a .j. fenestre et la royne li donna .j. anel d'or.* Queen Guinevere gives Lancelot a ring that has the power of disclosing enchantments to its wearer (hand 2). L, champie initial Text: *Longement deuiserent ensi ensamble entre Lancelot et la royne . . .*

Table I. Telling and Writing at the opening of *Mort Artu*

	Bonn 526	Yale 229
S VI 203. 1 F 1936:3.1; 1964: 1.1	Bonn f. 445 Left: The Demoiselle d'Escalot gives Lancelot a sleeve; right: Lancelot triumphs at the Tournament of Winchester in mounted combat with sword.	Yale f. 272v Top: A clerk (Arthur's scribe/Walter Map) sits at a desk, writing, knife in one hand, pen in the other. King Arthur/King Henry II, seated on a faldstool holding a sceptre, raises a pointed finger towards the scribe and turns towards a group of standing courtiers. Below: King Arthur, wearing a grey robe and holding a whip, rides out from Camelot (portcullis gate, rose window on side facade), accompanied by his knights (surcoat and housing or; surcoat and ailettes orange, shield pink, housing pink with cross-hatching in a darker shade of pink; surcoat orange, shield and housing grey, the housing drawn back in a knot behind the horse's ears). Top border: a frontal-facing knight on horseback (surcoat orange, housing or) brandishes sword and shield against two ape terminals, one with a shield and sword, the other raising an axe. Bottom: a hooded man riding bareback and brandishing a whip (left); a horse-head terminal (right).

	Add. 10294 illustration by hand 1	Royal 14.E.III	Rylands Fr. 1 illustration by hand 1
S VI 203. 1 F 1936:3.1; 1964: 1.1	*Queste* ends complete f. 53 col. b, *Mort Artu* follows after the Explicit. Add. f. 53r Rubric: *Ensi que li roy Artu enquiert a mon signeur Gauain quans chevaliers il auoit ochis en len queste.* King Arthur asks Gauvain how many knights he has killed in the quest. no borders A, champie initial Text: *Apres che que maistres Gautiers Map ot traitie des auentures del saint Graal asses souffisaument si comme il fu auis al roi* Henr*i son signor que ce quil auoit fait ne deuoit pas souffire . . .*	Royal f. 140r No rubric King Henry commands Walter Map to write the *Mort Artu*/King Arthur, enthroned, holding green sheep's head (? devil) sceptre, commands his scribe to write down the story of the *Queste*. borders: long-eared owl ape in hat blowing trumpet, holding club, riding border terminal; greyhound chasing 2 hares; fox, 2 heralds, a herald-hybrid and a hedgehog watch 2 men fight with swords and bucklers; bird; snail. A, historiated initial containing hooded head Text: *Apres che que maistres Gautiers Map ot traitie des auentures del saint Graal asses souffissaument si come il fu auis au roi Henri son seignor ke che quil auoit fait nen deuoit pas souffrir . . .*	Ryl. f. 212r Rubric: *Chi commenche li liures des mors Artus Gauain et tous les autres compaignons de la Taule Reonde et toute la fins.* A, historiated initial: King Henry/King Arthur stands before a seated scribe/Walter Map holding a book, the king points to what has been written borders: woman holding baby, ape eating and scratching rear; archer aiming at hybrid; bird of prey; nun nursing ape; ape in hat pruning border foliage; birds, hybrids, embracing couple; figure holding urine flask (part cut). Text: *Apres che que maistres Gautiers Map ot traitie des auentures del saint Graal asses souffissaument si comme il fu auis au roi Henri son signour ke che quil auoit fait nen deuoit pas souffrir [sic] . . .*

	BNF fr. 117–120	BNF fr. 112	BNF fr. 113–116
S VI 203. 1 F 1936:3.1; 1964: 1.1		BNF fr. 112 f. 182 Boort recounting the adventures of the Queste to King Arthur and his court, or King Arthur asking Gauvain how many knights he had killed.	BNF fr. 113, f. 1 (S III 3. 1), Left quadrant: King Arthur receiving the book of his knight's adventures/King Henry II receiving Walter Map's translation of the *Queste* (or his version of *Mort Artu*) BNF fr. 116, f. 678 Left: Boort recounting the adventures of the Queste to King Arthur and his court, or King Arthur asking Gauvain how many knights he had killed; right: King Arthur asking Gauvain how many knights he had killed, or Agravain telling King Arthur about the adultery of Lancelot and Guinevere.
S VI 205		BNF fr. 112 f. 183 Agravain telling King Arthur about the adultery of Lancelot and Guinevere.	

1. King Arthur on Fortune's wheel

2. Brunetto Latini, *Le Trésor*, Wheel of Fortune

3. Brunetto Latini, *Le Trésor*, Wheel of Fortune

4. Wheel of Fortune, from Brunetto Latini's *Trésor*

5. Arthur draws the sword and the bishop holds out his crown

6. Arthur draws the sword and lays it on the altar as he is crowned

7. Arthur and Guinevere watch Galahad draw the sword from the stone and the damsel tells Lancelot he is no longer the greatest knight in the world

les. Car li auenture est moie si nest pas
leur. Et p la seurte q ion auoie en ceste
nre aportage port acort si come v poes veoir.

Lors met main a lespee & le trait ausi
legierement de la pierre come se elle ni
tenist point puis prent le fuerre & la met
dedens. Maintenant la chaint entour

8. Arthur and Guinevere watch Galahad draw the sword from the stone

9. The Grail is brought before Arthur, Guinevere and the knights

10. The failure of Gauvain or Perceval to draw the sword

11. The Grail appears before Arthur and the knights of the Round Table

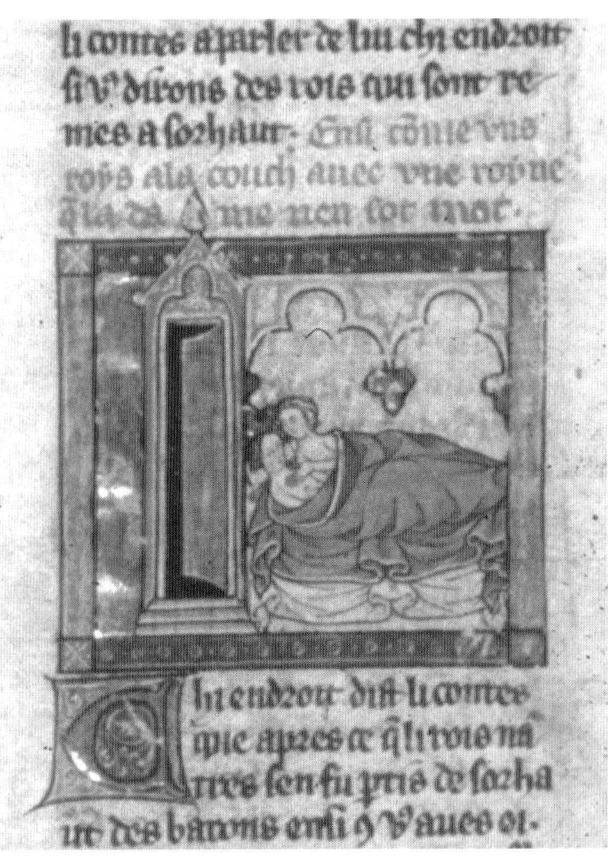

12. Conception of Mordred

13. Conception of Mordred

14. Ban and Elaine in bed

15. Guinevere washes Arthur's face

16. Marriage of Arthur and Guinevere

17. Marriage of Arthur and Guinevere

18. Bertholais and the False Guinevere's messenger challenge Guinevere's ligitimate status as Arthur's wife

19. Bertholais and the False Guinevere's messenger challenge Guinevere's ligitimate status as Arthur's wife

20. Death of the False Guinevere

21. Death of the False Guinevere

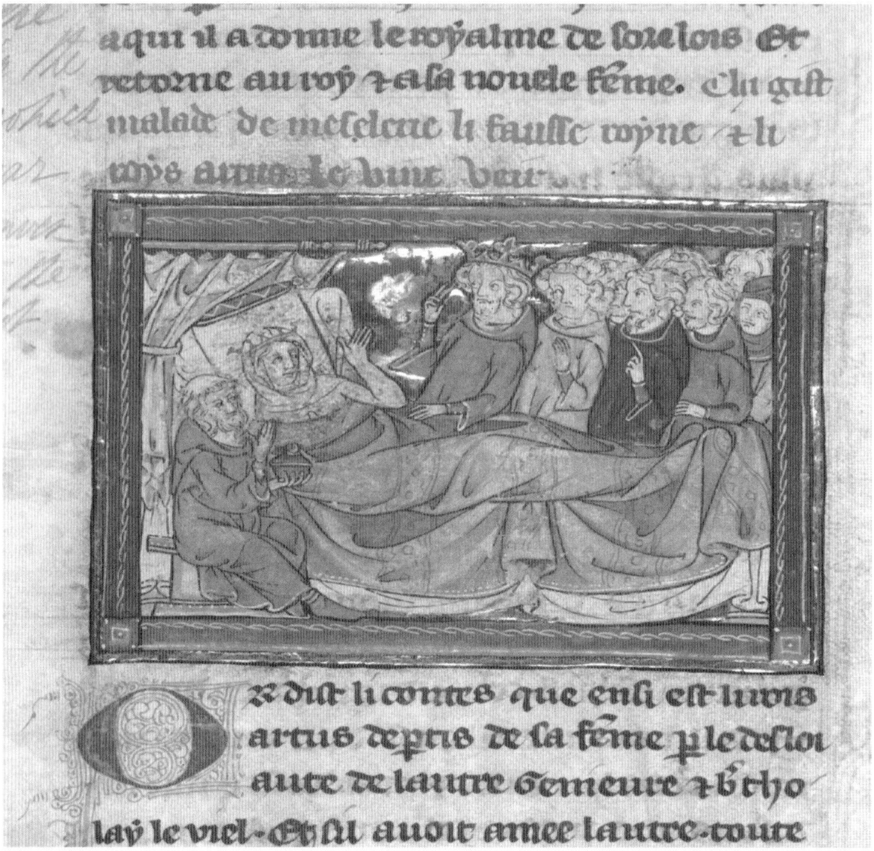

22. Death of the False Guinevere

ne a parler del roi artu qui mlt fu pen
sis del mandement que luces li empe
reres li fist.
Or dist li contes que quant
li .xii. message se furent p
ti del roi artu que li rois re
mest entre lui & sa baronie
mlt durement courecies del mandemt
que li empereres luces li avoit mande

23. Arthur's combat with the giant of Mont-Saint-Michel

24. Arthur kills the giant of Mont-Saint-Michel

25. Arthur's battle with the Cat of Lausanne

26. The child Merlin dictating to Blaise

27. Merlin dictating to Blaise

28. Blaise listening to Merlin

29. Merlin dictating to Blaise

30. Gauvain relating his adventures to Arthur and the court

31. King Henry commanding Walter Map to write the *Mort Artu*

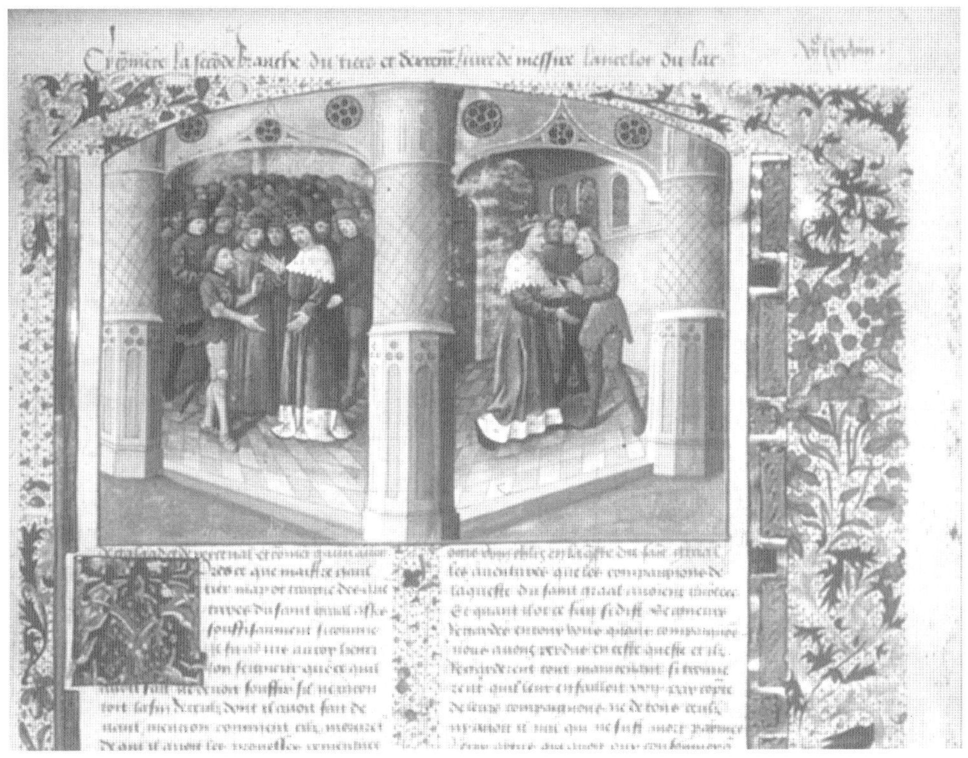

32. Boort recounting his adventures to Arthur or Arthur asking Gauvain how many knights he killed in the Queste; Agravain telling Arthur about Guinevere's adultery (?)

The Fortunes of Arthur in the Later German Romances

NEIL THOMAS

Unlike the more heroic Arthur fighting alongside his troops represented in the twelfth-century chronicles of Geoffrey and Wace, the Arthur of the 'classical' German romances becomes (as in the French tradition which the German authors adapt) a largely symbolic figurehead whose legend, detached from its insular origins, is borne along by moral concerns unrelated to his putative historical identity as an embattled British chieftain threatened by Saxons and other indigenous Britons. Arthur's regal qualities, now pertaining largely to feudal representation, are at this stage typically evidenced not through individualistic exploits but within the collective context of a knightly fellowship (to which Arthur contributes in an 'executive' capacity). When his name is invoked it is normally in a proverbial, metonymic sense referring not only to the person but also to the whole, chivalric culture of 'Camelot' (understood as the apotheosis of the feudal-courtly ideal).

This stage of legendary evolution introduced the image of the Court as a chivalric academy from which an individual knight would detach himself and be confronted with a moral challenge, this being in Hartmann's romances the resolution of a conflict between the protagonists' obligations to their wives and the wider chivalric society as symbolised by the Court as their moral centre. In Hartmann's *Erec* and *Iwein* two major framing scenes at Arthur's Court of Karidol (Camelot) are so positioned as to lend symbolic weight to the launch of the knight's career and to give regal validation to his later accomplishments. Arthur functions as a model against whom the efforts of individual knights may be measured rather than as a King whose values and political legitimacy are foregrounded or problematised. Although in Wolfram von Eschenbach's *Parzival* the denunciation of the loathly damsel (Cundrie) is first directed to the whole Court for bearing responsibility for Parzival's sins of omission, this wider accusation remains unexplored in the event and the onus comes to rest on Parzival to correct his *individual* sin.

Despite Arthur's seeming moral impunity, the theme of a flawed hero inaugurated by Chrétien and developed by Hartmann and Wolfram implicitly drew attention to potential tensions in the knightly system of values, and a critical audience would have been led to ponder the problems to which adherence to 'Arthurian' values gave rise. Although he is eulogised in narratorial asides, there is already in Chrétien's works a remarkable disparity between the author's formal panegyrics of the King and his actual conduct.[1] The King's ill-judged conduct at the beginning of *Erec* (where he persists with arranging a beauty contest despite Gauvain's warnings that this could cause invidious divisions at Court) together with his bizarre conduct in making a 'rash boon' in *Le Chevalier de la Charrete* (letting himself be manoeuvered by Keu into allowing the seneschal to escort Guinevere to his enemy, Meleagant) may be cited as somewhat anomalous images of a lauded king. Such ambiguous evocations suggest that depictions of Arthur were beginning to draw on the negative tradition of the *rex inutilis*.[2] The result of this trend was that the figure of the King underwent considerable epic degeneration, and an alternative source of authority was often located in the figure of Gawein (who models as the King's foremost advisor in many romances).[3] Meanwhile the creation of a further source of authority in *Yvain/Iwein* in the shape of Laudine's realm (to which the eponymous hero finally resorts) has often been read as a formal herald of the Grail realm[4] and the consequential demotion of the Arthurian Court: when in *Parzival* Wolfram depicts the hero's pagan half-brother Feirefiz accompaning Parzival to the Grail, he makes no mention of Parzival's confrère, Gawan, the Arthurian knight par excellence, and the impression arises of an overshadowing of the Arthurian realm by that of the Grail. Hence that small group of writers commonly termed 'classical' left a powerful yet ambivalent legacy to the disparate group of 'post-classical' authors who took over the mantle of Hartmann and Wolfram in the same way that the writers of the 'deuxième époque' continued the tradition inaugurated by Chrétien in France.[5]

It was once commonly supposed that the literary modus operandi of these 'epigonal' authors consisted in the more or less arbitrary reintegration of predecessors' motifs into their own work (the frequent roll-calls of admired literary models being taken as evidence that later authors had little of substance to add to their predecessors' achievements). Yet a unidirectional understanding of an evolving literary tradition does less than justice to the healthy spirit of emulation which reigned among many medieval poets. Behind the numerous pro forma humility formulae often lurked a competitive edge eager to circumvent the medieval shibboleth of *auctoritas* to enter the lists with renowned literary predesssors. This was *a fortiori* the case when works of the classical generation were adjudged problematical.

Tandareis und Flordibel, by the Salzburg writer Der Pleier (c. 1260/80),[6]

1 Hugh Sacker, 'An Interpretation of Hartmann's *Iwein*', *The Germanic Review*, 36 (1961), 5–26.

2 Edward Peters, *The Shadow King. Rex Inutilis in Medieval Law and Literature* (New Haven, CT, 1970), esp. pp. 170–209.

3 See for instance Neil Thomas, 'The Politics of Romance: Some Observations on the Political Content of the *Roman d'Yder*', in *The Formation of Culture in Medieval Britain* (Festschrift for Constance Bullock-Davies) (Lewiston, ME, 1994), pp. 171–81.

4 Hildegard Emmel, *Formprobleme des Artusromans und der Graldichtung. Die Bedeutung des Artuskreises fur das Gefüge des Romans im 12. und 13 Jahrhundert in Frankreich, Deutschland und den Niederlanden* (Berne, 1951), p. 39.

5 For an overview of all the later Arthurian romances and fragments see Matthias Meyer, 'Intertextuality in the Later Thirteenth Century: *Wigamur, Gauriel, Lohengrin* and the Fragments of Arthurian Romances', in *The Arthur of the Germans: The Arthurian Legend in Medieval German and Dutch Literature*, ed. W.H. Jackson and S.A. Ranawake (Cardiff, 2000), pp. 98–114.

6 Der Pleier, *Tandareis und Flordibel*, ed. Ferdinand Khull (Graz, 1885). See also *The Arthurian Romances of Der Pleier*, trans. J.W. Thomas (New York, 1992), Introduction.

problematises the motif of the King's rash boon (a common motif which recurs in the abduction incident in *Iwein*) when the Indian princess Flordibel gains from Arthur the undertaking that he will execute anybody who should sue for her favours. When the young and blameless Tandareis does so with the maiden's approval, Arthur still refuses to go back on his original word. Tandareis is supported by Gawan as his legal advocate and by Kei who places the blame on the King for his intransigence (opining that the King bears responsibility for the imbroglio). It is finally Arthur, rather than Tandareis, who has to yield by acknowledging the futility of trying to legislate in affairs of the heart, so resolving a tension which the King had failed to master in many previous romances, namely, how to strike a proper balance between stern absolutism and regal magnanimity.

If *Tandareis und Flordibel* is concerned with but a single regal foible, a more considerable moral aporia for many contemporary readers appears to have been the ostensibly negative conclusion of Hartmann's *Iwein* (c. 1205), where the eponymous hero finally deserts his Arthurian peers to rejoin his supernatural *dompna*, Laudine.[7] In the later thirteenth century the Hegau poet, Konrad von Stoffeln, may have attempted to supply a corrective to this disquieting ending in his *Gauriel von Muntabel* (c. 1280).[8] In a reprise of the 'fairy-mistress' tradition underlying *Yvain/Iwein*, *Gauriel* tells of how the love-sick hero is so taken with his Otherworldly consort (the unnamed queen of Fluratrône) that he performs acts against the interests of his Arthurian peers at her behest. At the conclusion of the work, on the other hand, Konrad brings his errant hero and his fairy spouse back into the Arthurian circle, opposing the implication that the affections of an Arthurian knight could be alienated by a foreign amazon such as Laudine. Gauriel thereupon takes his colleague's advice, convinces his inamorata of the courtly doctrine of the Golden Mean and tells her that he must repair his relationship with the knightly world in order to be able to appreciate their sexual union in a broader perspective.The two lovers then forsake their enclosed domain and return to Court, Gauriel to perform penance for Guinevere for having abducted his brother knights, his mistress symbolically renouncing her opposition to Arthurian chivalry, leaving us to infer that she will henceforth defer to Guinevere's command.

The term 'epigonal' as applied to Konrad von Stoffeln or Der Pleier is inappropriate since their works are aimed not at a respectful imitation of older works but at a creative confrontation with them. Nevertheless, by limiting themselves to an exploration of the pragmatics of the (fictional) chivalric value-system, both authors remained within the discursive parameters laid down by Hartmann. They thereby failed to exploit the opportunity to explore further the greatest dilemma of the courtly era, namely the Arthurian/Grail dichotomy left unresolved by Wolfram's idiosyncratic development of the Grail theme in

7 See Christoph Gerhardt, 'Iwein-Schlüsse', *Literaturwissenschaftliches Jahrbuch der Görres Gesellschaft*, 13 (1972), 13–39.

8 *Der Ritter mit dem Bock. Konrads von Stoffeln 'Gauriel von Muntabel'*, ed. Wolfgang Achnitz (Tübingen, 1997). See further Neil Thomas, 'Konrad von Stoffeln's *Gauriel von Muntabel*: A Comment on Hartmann's *Iwein*?', *Oxford German Studies*, 17 (1988), 1–9.

Parzival. My main concern is with two romances which, although they are often linked in literary histories, show very different approaches to the Wolframian legacy, namely, *Diu Crône* by Heinrich von dem Türlin, an Austro-Bavarian work written around 1225/1230[9] and *Wigalois* by Wirnt von Gravenberg (c. 1210/17).[10] *Diu Crône* presents its material in the following, quasi-chronicle form with the acquisition of the 'grail' (I use the lower-case since this is a largely secular boon in the context of Heinrich's romance) as the zenith of its narrative teleology).

Diu Crône opens with a somewhat dismal account of the humiliations, defections and schisms scarring the Arthurian Court whose tarnished honour Gawein eventually sets out to remedy (despite on one occasion having forsaken the Court himself). The grail action comes only towards the end of the work as the crowning achievement of a series of chivalric interventions in which Gawein returns to sustain the honour of his liege lord by negotiating numberless crises. One of the more notable of these is his peaceful resolution of a sexual challenge to Arthur made by a stranger knight (Gasozein) who claims that Guinevere had been his betrothed before Arthur had met her. After preventing what would have been the worst possible defection (for Guinevere shows some covert signs of attachment to the pretender) Gawein's quest for the grail is initiated in a sequence based on the Gawan adventures of Wolfram's *Parzival*. Here he is sworn to quest for the grail as a penance laid upon him for the (accidental) killing of the brother of Angaras of Karamphi. In this endeavour he is helped by the magician, Gansguoter (a benign version of Wolfram's Clinschor whose 'magic' often consists in expertise in castle construction and military tactics). Gansguoter helps Gawein to gain entry to the grail kingdom where he is given further advice by Manbur, Gansguoter's sister and *châtelaine* of the grail castle. At that castle, the old Grail king (*altherre*) explains the origins of the grail curse and its associated 'wonders' as being due to the sin of Cain having been committed by one of Parzival's kinsmen, resulting in a curse on the family which had 'spread' its fatal influence far and wide (the *altherre* himself is a walking corpse). After Gawein has asked the requisite question of the spectre (as to the meaning of the strange sights he witnesses), he receives a special sword from the *altherre* as acknowledgement that he is the long-awaited deliverer, after which the old king and his retinue of 'undead' retainers are by miraculous means granted release from the terminal sufferings of their present limbo. The

9 Werner Schröder, 'Zur Chronologie der drei grossen mittelhochdeutschen Epiker', *DVLG*, 31 (1957), 264–302, and 'Zur Literaturverarbeitung durch Heinrich von dem Türlin in seinem Gawein-Roman, *Diu Crône*', *Zeitschrift für deutsches Altertum*, 121 (1992), 131–74. The only complete edition is that by G.H.F. Scholl, *Diu Crône von Heinrich von dem Türlin* (Stuttgart, 1852, repr. Amsterdam, 1966). There is a newer edition based on the best manuscript: *Die Krone (Verse 1–12281) nach der Handschrift 2779 der Österreichischen Nationalbibliothek* (Altdeutsche Textbibliothek 112), ed. Fritz Peter Knapp and Manuela Niesner (Tübingen, 2000).

10 *Wigalois. Der Ritter mit dem Rade*, ed. J.M.N. Kapteyn (Bonn, 1926), trans. with Introduction by J.W. Thomas, *Wigalois: The Knight of Fortune's Wheel* (Lincoln, NE, 1977). Nothing certain is known of the author of *Wigalois* beyond his given name, the information that *Wigalois* was the author's first work (vs. 140) and his connection with Gravenberg (the modern Gräfenberg north-east of Nuremberg and Bayreuth).

grieving Angaras, who originally imposed the quest upon Gawein as a penitential office for the loss of his brother, is conciliated by the successful Grail quest – to the extent of agreeing to enter the Arthurian ranks. This is the last we hear of the 'grail' since, after Gawein's successful quest, he does not assume kingship in the grail lands but returns to the Arthurian ranks.

In the opening section of the romance, in verses alluding to the demise of the legendary kingdom, we are told that Arthur, however well blessed he had once been by Fortuna and the Fates, could not finally resist indefinitely the unwelcome ministrations of that celestial power, Atropos:

> Daz het im vrawe Chloto
> So ertailet allen *weis*,
> Daz er werltleichen *preis*
> Vor alr der werlde truog.
> Ouch was vil gefuog
> Vrou Lachesis dar an,
> Daz sie den vadem lanch span.
> Jch clag aber, daz Atropos
> Disen vadem niht verchos
> Vnd in so schier abe prach.
> Da an der werlt geschach
> Ein unverträgeleicher schad.
> Nv sitzet ein auf ei*m* rat
> An erben vrowe Fortune.[11]

> [Lady Clotho had bestowed this upon him (sc. the gift of making people happy) so that he might enjoy greater worldly renown than all his peers. Lady Lachesis, too, was very generous to him in the way she span out the thread of his life. But I lament the fact that Atropos did not drop that thread, thereby causing this world an insupportable loss, for now Fortuna sits alone on her Wheel without an heir.]

It is probable that the story of Arthur's terminal loss of Fortuna's favour in the Lancelot-Grail cycle[12] was known to Heinrich (who possessed a knowledge of French tradition unmatched by other German authors).[13] However, the theme of the Downfall of Camelot appears to have kindled in the German author the determination to plan a more constructive literary experiment. In *Diu Crône*, in which a considerable preoccupation with the Wheel of Fortune motif is evident, Gawein metaphorically 'regains' for his King the favour of Fortuna which Arthur lost in the course of the Old French prose cycle.[14] In place of a variant on the Destruction theme, Heinrich creates a more secure moral genealogy for the Arthurian world by developing the story of the youth who, we are told, had lost the father who was to educate him at the age of six (vss 313–15) and who has the

11 *Crône*, ed. Knapp and Niesner, vss 286–99.

12 *La Mort le roi Artu: roman du XIIIe siècle*, ed. Jean Frappier (Geneva, 3rd ed. 1959), esp. sections 176 and 177 for the Wheel of Fortune image.

13 Christine Zach, *Die Erzählmotive der 'Crône' Heinrichs von dem Türlin und ihre altfranzösischen Quellen. Ein kommentiertes Register* (Passau, 1990).

14 See Elizabeth Andersen, 'Heinrich von dem Türlin's *Diu Crône* and the Prose *Lancelot*; an Intertextual Study', *Arthurian Studies VII* (1987), pp. 23–49.

responsibilities of a crown and a wife to contend with 'after fifteen years' (vs. 422). Those twin rites of passage, we are repeatedly told (vss 4807, 10,777, 10,933) had taken place 'seven years ago', which would make the Arthur of *Diu Crône* a man in his early twenties. This young King becomes a fallible figure beset by both sexual and political difficulties, his funerary oration for his father revealing the profound feelings of inadequacy felt by a son who sees his father as the great conqueror of many lands which have now fallen rather too effortlessly under his jurisdiction. 'How could he, Arthur, ever come up to the standard of such an all-conquering forbear?' he asks himself in anxious tones.[15]

To remedy these initial images of regal weakness, the narrator assigns Arthur a messianic protector in the shape of Gawein, a knight Heinrich sets out to rehabilitate from his initial status of feckless renegade in order to prepare him for the impending grail quest. This he does not by making him a knight of superlative spiritual distinction but a loyal, *Arthurian* knight who single-handedly redeems his lord's fortunes.

When Gawein arrests the motion of Fortuna's notorious wheel and receives the goddess's assurance of prosperity for the Arthurian Court we might suppose that a signal benediction were taking place. Yet strangely the encounter would seem to point rather to that goddess's powerlessness and the consequential futility of attempting to conciliate her. Before he even departs her realm, Gawein encounters a form of volcanic storm which threatens to engulf him and against which he requires the additional help of a third party. Fortuna cannot apparently guarantee that her blessings will hold good even as far as the bourne of her own kingdom. There remains widespread accord amongst a number of characters (these including Gawein himself) about the fickleness of Fortuna, demonstrated most clearly in the Colloquy on Fortune between Gawein and Riwalin, Gawein's ally. The latter opines that Fortune is 'circular' and therefore untrustworthy (vss 5965–67), an opinion amply supported by his interlocutor who agrees that Fortuna is constant only in her inconstancy (vss 6033–34).

Despite initial appearances to the contrary, Gawein's seemingly successful treating with Frou Saelde issues in a bathetic sequel and Fortuna in *Diu Crône* remains the 'two-faced' *fortuna anceps* of Antiquity. For Riwalin it is axiomatic that, since luck invariably favours the brave, Gawein will win Fortune's favours (vss 6089–94). Hence the term 'fortune' as it occurs in *Diu Crône* frequently has a metonymic relationship with 'knightly prowess', so that Gawein himself, ostensibly a protégé of Saelde/Fortuna, must in fact become the *faber fortunae suae*.

The goddess Fortuna was to fall victim to further ironic strokes of misfortune in the high and later Middle Ages, culminating in a signal demotion by Dante. The latter, whose 'systemisation of the cosmology of the otherworld seems to have ended the speculation of the medieval mind on the topic',[16] made Fortuna somewhat tautologous in the metaphysical scale of things through his description of her as acting under God's jurisdiction in her adjudication of events

15 *Crône*, ed. Knapp and Niesner, vss 398–411.

16 Eileen Gardner, ed., *Visions of Heaven and Hell before Dante* (New York, 1989), Introduction, p. vii. See also on this point Tony Hunt, 'The Christianisation of Fortune', *Nottingham French Studies*, 38 (1999), 95–113.

restricted to the terrestrial sphere. Such a conception appears to have been partly anticipated by Heinrich von dem Türlin where Frou Saelde is portrayed not as a figure of towering transcendence but as one whose supposed supernatural authority is in fact fatally subverted by the circular logic of the dictum of Terence undergirding that romance: 'Fortune favours the brave' (*fortes fortuna adiuvat*).[17] Although Christian and pre-Christian mythological conceptions are frequently syncretised in locutions expressing faith in the joint sovereignty of Fortuna and the Christian God,[18] Heinrich's faith lay ultimately neither in Fortuna's boons nor Christian soteriology but in the strength of the chivalric order embodied in a knight who finally triumphs 'not through magic but by his own strength'.[19]

Against notions of the Grail quester as one in possession of a special, *spiritual* power, Heinrich gives a provocative encore to the Arthurian knight par excellence (in contradistinction to Perceval or Galahad whose elect status in other traditions tended to dissociate them from their knightly peers). After achieving the grail quest, Gawein returns to Arthur's court and sets up no independent kingdom of his own. Heinrich's narrator's observations about not spoiling his 'well-wrought crown' with gratuitous additions provide indications of a desire to place a 'copyright' over his chosen form of closure. This would have prevented a continuator following the example of Wolfram and adding an account of an exotic form of kingship detrimental to the *Arthurian* crown. The fabled court is not demoted to the status of a transitional stage of cultural development whose purpose is to point toward a higher realm. After the curse on the *altherre* is lifted there are no regal entailments and Gawein returns to Arthur to report the benefits of what from the point of view of himself and his peers is primarily a famous victory for the Round Table. Heinrich's title lends itself to a metonymic reading as being about the perpetuation of *Arthur*'s crown[20] (a number of sharp criticisms of Parzival and, by implication, of the concept of Grail kingship, pepper Heinrich's narrative).[21] In that respect the work may be regarded as a 're-Arthurianisation' of the Wolframian legacy back in the direction set by Hartmann.[22]

A more constructive revision of Wolframian ethics is offered by Wirnt von Gravenberg in his *Wigalois* whose eponymous hero is also at first a knight of Fortune's Wheel (vss 1362–77). This romance is preceded by an account of Gawein's marriage to Florie in a wondrous kingdom where the goddess Fortuna resides as the tutelary deity. The story of Gawein's son begins after his father (who receives a magic belt bestowing good fortune whilst in the wondrous kingdom) has ridden back to Camelot (omitting to take with him the girdle of

17 F.-P. Knapp, 'Virtus und Fortuna in der *Krone*: Zur Herkunft der ethischen Grundthese Heinrichs von dem Türlin', *Zeitschrift für deutsches Altertum*, 106 (1977), 253–65.

18 Gawein trusts that he is guarded over by God and Lady Fortuna alike (ed. Knapp and Niesner, vss 7111–12; 7285–89).

19 (durch) 'kein zoubar wan des mannes kraft' (ed. Scholl vs. 27,787).

20 The term crown is used metonymically to mean kingship and queenship respectively in vss 10,350 and 11,330.

21 See Ralph Read, 'Heinrich von dem Türlin's *Diu Krône* and Wolfram's *Parzival*', *Modern Language Quarterly*, 35 (1974), 129–39.

22 See further Neil Thomas, *'Diu Crône' and the Medieval Arthurian Cycle* (Cambridge, 2002).

Fortune, which is later inherited by his son). Bearing the belt left by his father, in early manhood the son seeks out his father at the Arthurian Court where Gawein (whom, we are told, the son does not recognise) is appointed as his chivalric mentor. In an initial series of skirmishes with sundry adversaries under the censorious gaze of a female emissary (Nereja), he persuades his sceptical guide that he is the equal of his father (whose services she had explicitly requested in preference to those of the youth). He thereby wins the qualification to proceed to the major challenge of defeating the Mohammedan necromancer, Roaz of Glois, Lar's murderer, and so releases the unquiet soul of Lar. This task he accompanies with the aid of an abundance of holy objects (not with the belt of Fortune, which has in the meantime been stolen). The work of salvation completed, he marries the old king's daughter, Larie, and rules over the now restored land of Korntin. In an extensive sequel he is joined by his father (whose identity has in the interim been formally revealed to him) and other Arthurian knights in his campaign against a second malefactor, Lion of Namur. The siege of Namur successfully accomplished, Wigalois pays a 'state visit' to Arthur at Nantes before resuming kingship in the land of Korntin where his rule maintains standards of statesmanship and Christian compassion inaugurated by the late King Lar.

The belt of Fortune at first appears to possess a material efficacy when the loss of it makes it impossible for Gawein to regain his wife's realm. Once the magical properties of Fortune's belt have been invoked as a prop to launch the narrative, however, it is not the specifically *magic* power of the belt which is foregrounded but rather its metaphorical properties as 'a symbol of knightly fortune and valour',[23] the concepts of good fortune and knightly prowess being effectively conflated according to contemporary usage. The emblematic association of the eponymous hero and his father with Saelde, a 'worldly' goddess comparable with the allegorical character Lady World (Frou Werlt),[24] indicates the fitness of both men to win the world's approbation through knightly prowess (after the sequence of exploits done in possession of the belt, Wigalois's female guide judges that he has won 'the plaudits of the world' in the same way as Gauvain wins the graces of the Proud Lady [Wolfram's Orgeluse] in the *Conte du Graal*).[25] Hence the subsequent loss of the belt heralds a new stage in the son's biography which goes beyond Gawein's customary limits which he can confront only by placing his faith in the Christian God:

> Des begunde er got genâde sagen,
> dar under tougenlîche klagen

23 'ein Symbol für ritterliche *saelde* und Sieghaftigkeit' (Max Wehrli, '*Wigalois*', in M.W., *Formen Mitelalterlicher Erzählung. Aufsätze* [Zurich, 1969], pp. 223–41, citing 231). In *Wigalois* Saelde undergoes a further attenuation since she appears not in person as in *Diu Crône* but only in effigy in Joram's great hall (vss 1046–52).

24 On German-speaking terrritory in the Middle Ages Fortuna's role as an autonomous metaphysical power was somewhat weakened for being conflated with her 'allegorical double', Frou Werlt, whose sphere of influence was likewise restricted to the sublunary sphere. See Marianne Skowronek, 'Fortuna und Frau Welt. Zwei allegorische Doppelgängerinnen des Mittelalters' (diss., Freie Universität Berlin, 1964).

25 'der werlte lop' (vss 3827ff.; cf. also vss 1355–57).

den gürtel und sîn îsengwant.
Er gedâhte 'nu sol ich zehant
Gegen der âventiure varn;
Wâ mit sol ich mich bewarn
Sît ich den gürtel han verlorn
Den ich ze trôste hêt erkorn
Zallen mînen dingen?
Noch muoz mir gelingen
Zer selben âventiure;
Sin ist nie sô ungehiure
Ichn welle dâ tot geligen,
Od mit der gotes kraft gesigen.' (vss 5990–6005)

[So he thanked God but secretly mourned the loss of the belt and his armour. He thought, 'I will meet my challenge without delay (but) how shall I defend myself since I have lost the belt which I always chose as my aid in all my straits? Yet I *will* prevail in this adventure, and, however terrifying it may turn out to be, I will triumph with God's aid or die in the attempt.]

The implication is that, although knightly fortune (*saelde*) has its place whilst the protagonist is establishing parity with his father, he requires higher aid for future, spiritual challenges, and in the infernal underworld awaiting him lurk adversaries taken not from from the chivalric personnel of the *matière de Bretagne* sequences but from Christian apocalyptic[26] and that large corpus of traditions termed 'The Divine Comedy before Dante'[27] (of which the best-known German example is the *Vision of Tundalus*).[28] Amongst the descendants of this race of Cain are Ruel, called 'the devil's consort' (line 6452, a figure whom later centuries would have termed a 'witch');[29] Karrioz (whose mother 'was a wild woman' – historically identifiable with Ruel herself in the manner of Beowulf and his dam);[30] a devilish dragon, a centaur and the heathen necromancer Roaz. Against such forces of cosmic evil no magic belt or other token of *saelde* can prevail, hence Wigalois's prayer of thanksgiving for apotropaic objects given him (such as the consecrated bread and the bough from the Tree of Paradise given over to

26 Ingeborg Henderson, 'Dark Figures and Eschatological Imagery in Wirnt von Gravenberg's *Wigalois*', in *The Dark Figure in Medieval German and Germanic Literature*, ed. Edward R. Haymes and Stephanie Cain Van d'Elden (Göppingen, 1986), pp. 99–113.

27 See Aron Gurevich, *Medieval Popular Culture: Problems of Belief and Perception*, trans. Janos M. Bak and Paul A. Hollingsworth (Cambridge, 1988), pp. 104–52.

28 See Nigel Palmer, '*Visio Tnugdali': The German and Dutch Translations and their Circulation in the Later Middle Ages* (Munich, 1982). For the extensive geographical distribution of the vernacular versions see the diagrams in Palmer, pp. 370–71, and on the reception of the genre up to 1520 see pp. 376–81. For conspectuses of this genre in the modern vernaculars see Eileen Gardner, *Visions of Heaven and Hell Before Dante*, and Peter Dinzelbacher, *Mittelalterliche Visionsliteratur*, Eine Anthologie (Darmstadt, 1989).

29 'The wild woman is a libidinous hag and it would seem entirely appropriate to use the term used for centuries for her kind by calling her a 'witch' (Richard Bernheimer, *Wild Men in the Middle Ages* [Cambridge, MA, 1952], p. 34).

30 'Es gereicht zu keiner geringen bestärkung der teuflischen natur Grendels in *Beovulf* (*sic*), dass ihm zur seite seine mutter steht, noch riesenhafter aufgefasst als er selbst, dass sie seinen tod rächen will, und erst durch ihre besiegung die heldenthat vollendet wird' (Jacob Grimm, *Deutsche Mythologie*, 2 vols [Göttingen, 1854], II, p. 841.

Lar as the place of his purgatorial remission, vss. 5842–49). At the heart of Wigalois's spiritual mission is the notion of a *katabasis* based on Christ's descent into Hell to redeem the just, the typological link supplied by Lar's surviving subjects in their equation of Wigalois's impending liberation with that of him 'who brought back so many a soul from hell with his divine power' (vss 3990–91).[31]

That Wigalois surpasses his father's moral standard is already apparent in his ability to touch Arthur's Stone of Virtue (in contradistinction to Gawein who was unable to do so because of a past sexual misdemeanour):

> her Gâwein der reichte dar
> mit der hant, und niht baz;
> ich sagiu wie er verworhte daz
> er dem steine niht moht komen,
> als ichz ofte hân vernomen:
> eine maget wol getân
> die greif er über ir willen an,
> sô daz si weinde unde schrê.
> deheiner slahte untugent mê
> er von sîner kintheit nie
> unz an sînen tôt begie;
> diu selbe in zuo dem steine niht lie. (vss 1501–17)

> [Sir Gawein was able to touch it with his hand, but he was able to do no better than that. I will tell you how he forfeited his right to approach the stone (as I have often heard tell): he once grabbed a beautiful maiden against her will, so causing her to shout out and scream. He committed no other offence for the rest of his life, but it was this which disallowed his approach to the stone.]

The tendency to sexual exploitation is a less noble part of Gawein's legendary reputation which the narrator condemns in broad terms in his frequent praise of noblewomen.[32] Meanwhile, the negative implication of Gawein's desertion of Florie would have been clear enough to an audience with knowledge of the similar narrative pattern occurring in Hartmann's *Iwein*. Nevertheless, the father is not used tendentiously as a negative *exemplum* as is the fate of the Gauvain of the Lancelot-Grail cycle where he conspicuously fails to grasp the moral imperatives issued by the Grail and suffers from the invidious implied comparison with Galahad.[33] Wirnt's Gawein is given the Grace to show insight into his fail-

31 See M.R. James, *The Apocryphal New Testament* (Oxford, 1972), pp. 134–35; and for the motif in the visual arts, George Henderson, *Early Medieval* (Harmondsworth, 1972), p. 87, plate 1.

32 Cf. vss 2355–69, 2388–94; 5408–12; 9696–715. Even in *Diu Crône*, which presents the most positive depiction of Gawein in medieval verse, Gawein is described as having committed a form of sexual harassment. On Gawein's legendary reputation see Keith Busby, 'Diverging Traditions of Gauvain in Some of the Later Old French Verse Romances', in *The Legacy of Chrétien de Troyes*, ed. Norris J. Lacy, Douglas Kelly and Keith Busby, 2 vols (Amsterdam, 1987–88), II, pp. 93–109, and Ute Schiessl, 'Die Gawangestalt im *Wigalois* des Wirnt von Gravenberc' (diss., University of Munich, 1968), esp. pp. 156–74.

33 Arthur himself appears as an anti-hero in the latter stages of the French cycle, offending the eirenic standards of Cistercian spirituality informing this cycle by pursuing his destructive feud with Guinevere and Lancelot *à outrance*.

ings and thereby achieve moral rehabilitation. His self-denying ordinance of abjuring knighthhood on hearing of his wife's death implies contrition for once having too zealously pursued knightly goals at Florie's expense:

> sô sprach her Gâwein der degen,
> 'wan daz mîn vreude sî gelegen
> mit ir hiute vür disen tac
> der ich mit hôhem muote ie pflac.
> ichn wil konlîcher ê
> mit staete gepflegen nimmer mê,
> noch rîterschaft, michn twinges nôt.' (vss 11,380–86)
>
> [The spirited Gawein said, 'From this time forward my joy is no more on account of (the death of) her to whom I was always devoted. I will never again seek such a union, nor will I practise deeds of arms, unless compelled to do so by dire necessity.]

Wirnt even attempts to save Gawein's face by glossing his breaches of faith as peccadilloes he has put behind him in his heady youth.[34] In this way he is able to safeguard the patronymic, Lifort Gawanides (vs. 11,639), for Wigalois's future son, the grandfather's legacy being valued highly enough to be thus projected into the future. It is doubtless because of the respect due to the family name that there is a special emphasis on the legitimacy of Gawein's son which is unique among the Fair Unknown romances.

The Middle English derivative of Renaut de Bâgé's *Le Bel Inconnu* memorably describes Gawain's son as being 'begotten be a forest side', the swift desertion by Gawain and consequential bastardy of his son being part of the original tradition according to the earliest known version of the Gauvain/Floree story in the Old French *Livre d'Artus* (where Gauvain's son is likewise the illegitimate issue of a fleeting sexual encounter).[35] By contrast, the hero of the German version is the scion of a formal (albeit brief) marriage. Wigalois is even permitted to enjoy the substance of a father-son relationship when he arrives at the Arthurian Court (the reunion between father and son serving to offset the effects of Gawein's original desertion):

> Er (sc. Arthur) sprach 'juncherre, sît gewert
> aller iuwer bete hie.'
> in sîn genâde er in enpfie
> und bevalch in an der stet,
> nâch der küniginne bet,
> sînem vater, dem herren Gawein.
> dô was under in zwein
> diu grôze triuwe unbekant
> die kint ze vater vant:

34 On attempts to play down Gawein's baser features in *Wigalois* and elsewhere see Maldwyn Mills, 'Christian Significance and Romance Tradition in *Sir Gawain and the Green Knight*', in *Critical Studies of Sir Gawain and the Green Knight*, ed. Donald R. Howard and Christian Zacher (Notre Dame, IN, 1968), pp. 85–105.

35 *The Vulgate Version of the Arthurian Romances*, ed. H.O. Sommer, 8 vols (Washington, DC, 1908–16), VII, pp. 109–11.

ir deweder erkante den andern dâ.
her Gâwein underwant sich sâ
des knaben mit sîner lêre;
des gewan er vrum und êre. (vss 1591–603)

[Arthur said: 'Young noble, all your petitions shall be granted.' He took the young man under his wing and, acceding to the preferences of his queen, handed him over to his father, Sir Gawein. At this time their strong filial bond was unknown to either man, for neither recognised the other. Sir Gawein undertook to be the youth's tutor – from which his charge acquired much knightly prowess and esteem.]

A consequential difference between *Wigalois* and other works within the same cycle is that the protagonist is transformed into a knight desiring not merely to find but also emulate his father:

ich wil benamen hinnen varn,
in mîner jugent erwerben daz
daz man mich von rehte
baz erkenne danne ein andern man,
als mîn vater hât getân. (vss 1294–98)

[I will go forth to ensure that whilst I am still young people will acknowledge *me* before all other knights – just as my father was able to achieve in his time.]

The Fair Unknown motif to be sure traditionally rests on a nice ambiguity – providing a demonstration of an upward social ascent but allaying aristocratic misgivings when the supposed 'new man' turns out to be an aristocratic scion after all,[36] but Wirnt's treatment leaves no room for even this much ambiguity. The possibility that the protagonist might be an unsuitable *parvenu* is ruled out from the start – a reactionary treatment which is consistent with the author's ideological preferences as expressed through a number of narratorial asides in which 'degree' is praised in favour of the 'mere oppugnancy' said to ensue when the ill-bred are able to assume knightly rank.[37] It is in that sense that the revenant king Lar assures the protagonist that any successful knight must be 'chosen' ('erwelt'):[38] Du solt von rehte sîn ein helt, / Wan dîn vater ist erwelt, / Der süeze her Gâwein [vss 4792–94: 'You may justly account yourself a hero since your father, the noble Sir Gawain, is one of the elect.'].

The importance of Gawein's legacy becomes particularly evident in the final four thousand verses of the romance. Although in the course of his previous *katabasis* the hero is obliged to draw on spiritual resources for which there is

36 In the Fair Unknown narrative pattern (*Le Bel Inconnu*, the Middle English *Libeaus Desconus*, the Italian *Carduino*) the knight 'becomes known, and it is revealed that he is not the incursionary thug that his presentation has implied, but in fact a member of the aristocracy' (Stephen Knight, 'The Social Function of the Middle English Romances', in David Aers, ed., *Medieval Literature. Criticism, Ideology and History* [Brighton, 1986], pp. 99–112, citing 105).

37 Cf. vss 2146–57, 2339–48, 10,254–79.

38 Cf. also 'Dâ von muoz er sîn erwelt/der zem besten wirt gezelt;/daz bejagt her Gwîgâlois der helt' (vss 2964–66).

little precedent in Gawein's legendary biography, there is nevertheless no narratorial attempt to demote Gawein who plays a signal role in the final campaign (including the dispatching of Lion himself). Gawein even bestows on his son a 'third education' where he instructs him in the obligations of regal office (vss 11,521–65). The integrative function performed by Gawein's residence at the new king's court may have been meant as a corrective to Wolfram's concept of a Grail kingship remote from Arthurian regulation. Wirnt gives an encore to Wolfram's neglected deuteragonist (as well as to the accompanying Erec, Iwein and Lanzelet). The inclusion of the Arthurian knights in the new king's regime (which is anything but accidental since the new king had sent a letter to summon his father) gives concrete shape to a harmonisation of Arthurian and spiritual elements to which Wolfram alludes in his final narrator's aside (*Parzival*, section 827, vss 19–24) but which he fails to realise in concrete terms at the end of his work.[39] Against Wolfram's enigmatic closure, Wirnt shows in the protracted Lion campaign (in which the lack of romance stylisation suggests narratorial improvisation) how Arthurian knights might comport themselves in a narrative world beyond that of the romance.[40] He thereby demonstrates the relevance of 'Arthurian' standards to a quasi-historical situation[41] appropriately described according to the conventions of the *chanson de geste* rather than those of the romance form.[42]

Although Wigalois's kingship (which aspires to renew the rule of the pious spirit king) undoubtedly pays greater attention to almsgiving and the plight of the poor than was customary in romance representations of Arthurian rule,[43] the hero's rule is at the same time a part-restoration of that of Arthur whom he continues to honour through continuing expressions of homage functioning as an 'Arthurian' frame and hence as an echo of the 'classical' structure found in *Erec*.[44] It is significant that Ulrich Füetrer, a primary recipient of the romance,

39 Parzival finally remains an open text at whose conclusion the son, Loherangrin, is plunged into the same compulsive behaviour of question-asking as his father before him, so that 'the fact that Parzival's good fortune does not extend to all the worthy characters serves as a reminder that the world has not changed in any fundamental way' (Annette Volfing, '*Parzival* and *Willehalm*: Narrative Continuity?' In *Wolfram's 'Willehalm': Fifteen Essays*, ed. Martin H. Jones and Timothy McFarland [New York, 2002], pp. 45–59, citing 59).

40 The provocation for the Lion conflict arises unheralded in the midst of the festivities surrounding the protagonist's marriage, nuptials which had appeared to form the natural conclusion of the work: 'Hie ist diu âventiure geholt / wâ ist nu der minne solt, / Des wunsches âmie / Diu schoene Larie?' (vss 7904–07).

41 The other Arthurian knights are allocated practical duties in keeping with the new tone of military realism: Erec gives advice on strategy (vss 9994ff.), Iwein and Erec are made responsible for the safe escort of Larie (vss 10,645ff.).

42 There is an analogy here with the French *Durmart le Gallois*, another 'mirror for princes written in the form of an Arthurian romance', according to Friedrich Wolfzettel, 'Doppelweg und Biographie', in *Erzählstrukturen der Artusliteratur*, ed. Friedrich Wolfzettel (Tübingen, 1999), pp. 119–41, citing 138. Wolfzettel (p. 138, n. 2) points out that Wendelin Foerster once termed this work a combination of the romance and *chanson de geste* forms. See Neil Thomas, 'The Old French *Durmart le Gallois*: A Demystified Version of the Perceval Story?' *Parergon*, n.s. 13 (1995), 117–28.

43 Although Gawein too points out to his son the importance of almsgiving to the poor and of alleviating their suffering wherever possible (vss 11,540–41).

44 Wigalois expresses loyalty to Arthur at the beginning of his career (vss 1607–09) and at the end at Nantes (Nantasan) where Arthur and Guinevere come forward to greet the hero and

glosses the final part of Wirnt's narrative as implying a moral equation of Wigalois's kingship with that of Arthur in his late fifteenth-century adaptation, *Wigoleis*: 'Korotin ward der frewden zil genennet, / an den vogt von Pritone / ward zu seinr zeit nye pesser chünig erchennet' [Korntin became known as the crown of joy. Apart from the Leader of The Britons (sc. Arthur) no better king (than Wigalois) was ever witnessed in those times].[45]

Similar assimilative impulses are observable in the terms of the campaign against Lion which, although it has recently been likened to an (internal) Crusade, and even claimed to represent a literary stimulus to Crusading activity,[46] is in fact not a crusade at all. The *casus belli* is the murder by the Western European Lion of Namur of the innocent Amire of Libya in order to procure Amire's wife. The hero's army unites figures from both sides of the sectarian divide in what is a bipartisan civil action made on legal and ethical, not confessional grounds (the non-Christians Zaradech and Panschavar are notable co-signatories to the formal declaration of hostilities, vss 10,074–88). A remarkable spirit of tolerance reigns at the new king's court where 'the explicit condemnation of paganism (vss 8180ff.) seems to be all but forgotten'.[47]

It is conspicuous that Roaz is not condemned for his faith but as a repository of evil ('valsches slôz', 'untriuwen zil', vs. 7625) and that his equally non-Christian wife, Japhite, is virtuous 'except that she is unbaptised' (vs. 7465). Like Wolfram's Belakane and Gyburg, her unfeigned compassion is deemed the equivalent of baptism.[48] The criterion that Wirnt takes to judge his fellows is a moral rather than sectarian one. In the case of the hero's ally, Adan, baptism is not the precondition of virtue but its symbol, for as Adan says on the eve of his baptismal ceremony, he had always been an *anima naturaliter christiana*:[49] 'Swie gar ich sî ein heiden, / von dem gedanke kom ich nie / ichn minnet iedoch den got ie / der uns geschuof von nihte' [vss 8199–202: 'Notwithstanding the fact that I am a heathen through and through, I never wavered from love of the God who created us from nothing'].

The new battle line in which combatants on both sides of the medieval religious divide join forces to punish a miscreant for non-sectarian reasons is a better evocation of an ecumenical vision than that found in *Parzival* or in *Willehalm* (which, being a commissioned work depending on some version of the *Bataille d'Aliscans*, was vitiated by interfererence from a source which stylised Muslims as the enemy). The narrator's disinclination to think in binary terms by creating a false division between men and women of good will is reflected in his attitude to Gawein. Although the son's 'great adventure' clearly

Arthur takes him by the hand (vss 11,394ff), Wigalois swearing to Arthur 'nu wizzet daz ich immer wil/iu dienstes wesen undertân' (vss 11,506ff).

45 Ulrich Füetrer, *Wigoleis*, ed. Heribert A. Hilgers (Tübingen, 1975), stanza 315.

46 Claudia Brinker, 'Hie ist diu âventiure geholt! Die Jenseitsreise im *Wigalois* des Wirnt von Gravenberg: Kreuzzugspropaganda und unterhaltsame Glaubenslehre?', in *Contemplata aliis tradere. Studien zum Verhältnis von Literatur und Spiritualität*, ed.Claudia Brinker (Berne, 1995), pp. 87–110.

47 Ingeborg Henderson, 'Eschatological Imagery', p. 108, n. 19.

48 'wâre riuwe ist gewesen/ir touf an ir ende' (vss 8023–24).

49 The ecumenical thrust of his convictions may also be reflected in his name (the Biblical Adam counts as the first man for Christians, Jews and Muslims).

requires messianic resources equal to his *imitatio Christi*, the redeemer is nevertheless obliged to acquire a 'normal' chivalric background resembling that of his father (rather than remain an ineffectual Galahad figure whose life inheres in the spirit alone). As a practical moralist Wirnt will have wished to create a hero capable of putting spiritual experience to practical effect, squaring the quintessentially medieval circle of making *imperium* and *sacerdotium* work in unison. Wirnt's hero presents a more compelling image of a 'priest king' than the somewhat tenuous evocations of such a person we encounter in Wolfram's 'Prester John'.[50]

[50] On this figure and his association with Wolfram's Oriental Grail realm see Ulrich Knefelkamp, *Die Suche nach dem Reich des Priesterkönigs Johannes, dargestellt anhand von Reiseberichten und anderen ethnographischen Quellen des 12. bis 17. Jahrhunderts* (Gelsenkirchen, 1986).

The Knight and the Parrot: Writing the Quest at the End of the Middle Ages

JANE H.M. TAYLOR

There is a rather telling moment in a short, quirky, late-medieval prose romance – author unknown, date at the end of the fourteenth century or the beginning of the fifteenth – called *Le Chevalier du Papegau*.[1] The hero – the young King Arthur himself, as it happens, just after his coronation – has slain a monstrous knight who is terrorising the surrounding countryside. After the knight is dead, they find the corpse lying on the ground, still on his horse. Intrigued, they try to separate horse and man – and find, to their amazement, that under the armour horse and man are one flesh;[2] the lady in whose name Arthur has acted asks that this monstrous being be skinned and the hide kept in her fiefdom, the *Amoureuse Cité*, as a remarkable tourist attraction, a *merveille* ('ou il soit toujours veu pour *merveille*' [CP, 24]). We may, the *romancier* concedes, be a bit sceptical – but no: on the contrary,

> l'en trouve en livre qui s'appelle *Mapemundi* qu'il est un monstre qui en mer a sa conversion que l'en clame Poisson Chevalier, qui semble avoir destrier, heaulme et haubert et lance et escu et espee, mais il est tout de luy mesmes, et tel estoit celluy [CP, 24: we find in a book called *Mappa Mundi* that there is a monster that makes its home in the sea, and which is called a Fish Knight; it looks as if it has a horse and a helmet and a hauberk, and a lance and shield and a sword – but in fact, all these things are part of its actual body].

And indeed, it does turn out, when Arthur and his companions retrace the odd hybrid's route, that he comes from the sea and is called the Poisson Chevalier. Now this is very intriguing – for all sorts of reasons and in particular of course for this human-animal fusion: it is this aspect that Nathaniel Smith examines, in an interesting article which adopts an anthropological stance.[3] But what I want

1 I shall quote from the only critical edition of the text, by Ferdinand Heuckenkamp (Halle, 1896); refs. henceforward in text, prefixed CP. The romance also exists in two modern translations, into English by Thomas Vesce, *The Knight of the Parrot* (New York, 1986), and into French in Danielle Régnier-Böhler, *La Légende arthurienne: le Graal et la Table Ronde* (Paris, 1989), pp. 1079–162. A new edition of the text, *Le Conte du Papegau*, edited and translated by Hélène Charpentier and Patricia Victorin (Paris, 2004), appeared too late for me to take account of it in this chapter.

2 'Et quant il l'ot fait escourchier, si ne trouva fors ung cuir, de destrier et du chevalier' (CP, 24/l. 5–7).

3 'The Man on a Horse and the Horse-Man: Constructions of Human and Animal in *The Knight of the Parrot*', in *Literary Aspects of Courtly Culture*, ed. Donald Maddox and Sara Sturm-Maddox (Cambridge, 1994), pp. 241–48.

to focus on here is the way in which the *romancier* supports what he says by that confident reference to a *Mapemundi* – and by the fleeting, tantalising vision of the Poisson Chevalier's hide hung in the city as a *merveille*. Nathaniel Smith assumes that our *romancier* is citing what he, Smith, describes as a thirteenth-century *Bestiary* by Pierre de Beauvais, often indeed called *Mappemundi*[4] – which, as he says, does include a couple of man-animal hybrids, mermaids and centaurs; I am less sure that Pierre's is indeed the authority to which our author is referring (unless, of course, we imagine that he was fusing two of Pierre's curiosities) – and there would be a number of other, different candidates, also often called *Mappemundi*, out of whom, admittedly, I have been unable to identify one in particular. What I want to suggest in this essay, however, has to do not so much with *identifying* our author's *Mapemundi* – satisfying though that would be – but rather with ways in which, it seems to me, the author is, quite unwittingly, drawing attention to a new conception of the quest at the end of the Middle Ages: what I shall argue is that where once the quest was, typically, a *Bildungsreise* in the course of which a knight established his reputation by deeds of valour in pursuit of a moral obligation – in which, in other words, the focus was on the quester and the quest – now, in late-medieval romances, it serves, like the proliferating 'journey-tales' of the period, as a frame for episodes and images which celebrate the exotic, the Other, rather than subduing it as a means of demonstrating chivalric maturity.

Let me start with a few more of the proliferating *merveilles* of *Le Chevalier du Papegau* – because it is not just *poissons-chevaliers* of whom we should take account. The eponymous hero is so-called, in fact, because of another remarkable animal: a parrot which Arthur wins as a prize (rather as Chrétien's Erec, much less exotically, wins a sparrow-hawk). The parrot is a remarkably vocal bird, but easily cowed – and much of the charm of the romance derives from its cries of terror whenever any threat of danger looms, and its scepticism (rather like Dinadan's) as to the *point* of chivalry. As his quest continues, moreover, Arthur is led across a featureless desert by a hybrid animal with a bull's body, a stag's head, a red pelt, and luminous golden horns (CP, 64–65); he shelters under a marvellous tree from an army of ghosts (CP, 66–67); he comes across a dragon (CP, 68) and a *wild woman* (CP, 72); and finally, he is shipwrecked on an island – rather like Prospero's – where there lives a dwarf driven to despair by his monstrous giant-son who was suckled by a unicorn and whose appetites cannot be assuaged (CP, 84–85).

All, of course, pleasingly baroque.[5] And perhaps all we need to imagine is an

4 A reference which puzzles me: Pierre's *Mappemonde*, written in the early thirteenth century, seems not to have circulated widely (see the edition by A. Angremy, *Romania*, 104 [1983], 316–50, 457–98, and a translation by Guy Mermier: *Le Bestiaire de Pierre de Beauvais* [Paris, 1977]), and although there are some possible analogues, they are not especially compelling. One who does mention, specifically, something rather like them is Barthélémy l'Anglais, in his *De Proprietatibus rerum*: see *On the Properties of Things: Trevisa's translation of De Proprietatibus Rerum*, ed. M.C. Seymour et al., 3 vols (Oxford, 1975–88), I, p. 681 (*ypotamus*). But there is, as we shall see, a far more compelling analogue, Thomas de Cantimpré's *zytiron*, details of which correspond very closely to the *chevaliers de la mer* in a romance I shall discuss below, the *Roman de Perceforest*.

5 On 'monsters', see David Williams, *Deformed Discourse: The Function of the Monster in Mediaeval Thought and Literature* (Exeter, 1996).

inventive writer with a jaded audience for whom dramatic duels and chivalric self-development are no longer titillation enough. But this does not seem to me sufficient explanation – not least because this is by no means the only one of the very late prose romances where this sort of *merveille* is on offer. Take another, this time the *Roman de Perceforest* – probably dating, in its original form, from around the middle of the fourteenth century, but especially popular, rather later, in the fifteenth century at the court of Burgundy, where all the surviving manuscript copies originate. In the course of this quite extraordinarily long romance – it is longer by far than the Vulgate cycle, longer than the prose *Tristan* – the heroes also come across a swarm of adventures; I shall concentrate, however, on just two, which both have affinities with the *merveilles* we have been looking at in the *Papegau*. The first adventure of which I am thinking, indeed, has to do with more Poissons Chevaliers.[6] One of the heroes of this vast romance, the *Blanc Chevalier*, is marooned on an island – where he watches astonished as a shoal of monstrous fish emerges from the sea and starts to graze. Some of them are huge, rather like bulls; some are smaller, horned, with furry pelts, looking a little like sheep; others again look rather like bears, or stags. More menacingly, the following morning, by which time the *Blanc Chevalier* is hungry enough to have been tempted to eat some of the fish, there emerges from the sea a contingent of much larger fish:

> Au dessus du comble de leurs testes, ilz avoient chascun une longue pointe, longue de une brasse et demie, en maniere d'espee. Et sus le dos, ilz avoient comme ung escu qui toute l'eschine leur couvroit depuis la teste jusques a la queue, et estoit ce a maniere de poisson [RP, III, p. 274: on the crowns of their heads, they each had a long spike, about a yard and a half long, which looked like a sword. And on their backs, they each had something that looked like a shield, which covered the whole length of their spines from their heads to their tails. And yet they were all still fish].

There are, it turns out, many of them, so it is fortunate that they seem to possess enough of the rudiments of chivalry to understand that it is wrong to attack an adversary other than one by one. Equally fortunately – since the Blanc Chevalier is starving – they taste good. . . . Other little details emerge: the great fish have short legs (so when the knight makes a run for it to a nearby spring, they can't keep up with him), and webbed feet; they can survive for a couple of hours, no more, on land; they blow, like whales, 'faisoient saillir [l'eaue] par leurs narines plus hault que la haulteur d'un homme' [RP, III, p. 278: they blew water out of their noses to the height of a man]; their *pointes* (spears) consist of a long bone emerging from their foreheads, and they have another which lies along the spine

6 The *Roman de Perceforest* has not yet been completely edited. The first part was edited by Jane H.M. Taylor (Geneva, 1979); Gilles Roussineau has been pursuing the remainder of the text, as follows: Book II, of which two volumes have so far appeared (Geneva, 1999–2001); Book III (Geneva, 1988–93); Book IV (Geneva, 1987). This episode is to be found in Book III, vol. II, pp. 273–85; refs. henceforward in the text, prefixed RP, III. In a fascinating, and beautifully researched, paper given at the conference of the International Arthurian Society, Bangor 2002, Janet van der Meulen reports that she has discovered a description of a *car* commissioned by someone close to the court of Hainaut, and which was decorated with images of *chevaliers de mer*.

like a shield (RP, III, p. 280); they can swim through the waves more swiftly than a speeding arrow (RP, III, p. 283); their king, at any rate, can communicate by signs so that the Blanc Chevalier is made to understand that he wants an honorable and chivalric duel to the death[7] – at the end of which the king of the Fish ('roy des poissons') is so overcome by admiration[8] for the chivalry of his adversary that he, the king, supplies the Blanc Chevalier with a little red fish which, when eaten, heals all the latter's wounds (RP, III, p. 282). Our author, here, is clearly fascinated by his exotic creatures: the images of the Blanc Chevalier and the king of the Poissons-Chevaliers sitting amicably sharing a fish or two, in perfect courtesy,[9] or of the king taking the Blanc Chevalier's sleeve politely in its teeth and inviting him to join in a tournament with the Fish, are particularly alluring.[10]

I shall come back to all these later, but for the moment, I just want to consider

7 When the Blanc Chevalier says he must drink first, 'le roy des poissons, qui avoit franc couraige, baissa la teste en signe qu'il en estoit content, puis se sist sus sa queue' [RP, III, p. 279: the king of the fish, who had a noble soul, bowed his head to show that he agreed, and sat back on his tail].

8 'le roy des poissons lui commença a faire moult d'amiracions en signe de humilité et de paix . . .' [RP, III, p. 282: the king of the fish began to make admiring movements as a sign of submission and peaceful intent].

9 'Et vous prommés que ce roy aloit autant discretement avecq lui comme s'il eust eu sens et conduite d'homme humain' [RP, III, p. 282: and I assure you that this king dealt as properly with him as if he had the mind and behavior of a human].

10 The best analogue for this description of the *chevaliers de mer* is in Thomas de Cantimpré, *Liber de natura rerum*: '*De zytirone, hoc est milite marino*: Zytiron monstrum est marinum quod vulgus vocat maris militem, sicut dicit Liber rerum, et est ingens ac fortissimum. Huiusmodi dispositionem habere dicitur: in parte anteriori quasi formam armati militis prefert et caput quasi casside galeatum ex cute rugosa ac dura et firma nimis. A collo eius dependet scutum longum et latum et magnum et cavum interius, ut in eo possit monstrum contra ictus pugnantium more defendi. Vene quedam ac nervi fortissimi de collo eius et de spondilibus protenduntur in humerum, et hiis quidem predictum scutum dependet in scapula. Est autem ipsum scutum forma triangulare, duritia ac firmitate tam validum, ut vix unquam possit iaculo penetrari. Brachia habet fortia nimis et loco manus quasi manum bisulcam, cum qua ita validissime percutit, ut frustra temptet homo eius posse ictus sine maximo discrimine sustinere. Unde fit, ut difficulter nimis capi possit ab homine. Et si captus fuerit, difficulter potest etiam necari nisi cum malleis. Huius animalis genus humani generis discordiam imitari videtur, quod utique inter se bella commovet; et tantam turbationem maris faciunt in pugnando, ut in loco certaminum tempestas quedam exsurgere videatur. In mari Britannico hec monstra habentur' [*Of zytiron, that is sea-knights*: The *zytiron* is a marine monster which the unlearned call the knight of the sea, as the *Liber rerum* tells us, and it is cunning and extremely strong. I shall explain its characteristics: its front part in form makes it look very like an armed man, and on its head is a helmet made of skin which is rough and hard and very strong. From its neck hangs a shield that is long and broad and thick and hollow within, so that the monster can use it to defend itself against blows from attackers. The veins and nerves of its neck are particularly strong and a hard spur of bone protrudes from its shoulders; the shield I mentioned earlier hangs from its collar-bone. This shield is triangular, particularly hard and strong, so that it is almost impossible for a weapon thrown at it to penetrate it. Its arms are remarkably strong and it has hands like cloven hooves, so that it can land very effective blows, and no man can wound it unless the blow is especially carefully aimed. As a result, it can only with the greatest difficulty be captured, and, if it is captured, it can be killed only with blows from a mace or a hammer. These beasts seem to imitate the conflicts of the human race, so they wage war among themselves, and their battles under the sea cause such a commotion and such turbulence, that it is sometimes supposed that there is a violent storm. And these monsters are to be found in the British Sea]. See Thomas de Cantimpré, *Liber de natura rerum* (Berlin, 1973), I, p. 249.

a final one in this series of *merveilles*,[11] also in the *Roman de Perceforest*, this time in the fourth book (the *Perceforest* is, among many other things, a sort of romance encyclopedia). This time, the marvel is . . . monkeys.[12] One of the more remarkable characters in the romance is a grotesquely deformed knight named Le Bossu, who – most unusually – is treated with the greatest sympathy and understanding.[13] This particular adventure of his, however, is, it has to be said, somewhat grotesque. Le Bossu finds himself, for complicated reasons, on yet another desert island, the *Isles aux Singesses* inhabited by flocks of vicious apes[14] who chatter and shriek and grimace (and 'aucuns . . . me monstroient leurs bulles'; RP, IV, p. 64). Among the apes is one much larger than the rest, a female, *une merveilleuse singesse, grande et laide sans comparoison* [RP, IV, p. 65: a remarkable female monkey, incomparably large and ugly], which, to Le Bossu's amazement, fights off the other apes. But there is a downside: the ape, he says, 'me monstroit signe d'amour . . .' [RP, IV, p. 66: showed every sign of love]. She takes him into her *caverne* [cave], feeds him on *petites nois et autres fruis* – and finally, 'par la convoitise qu'elle avoit en ma personne tant seullement . . .', gives birth to four *petitz singes qui . . . me ressambloyent assés bien* [RP IV, p. 66: little nuts and fruits and finally 'from no more than her sexual longing for me', gives birth to four 'little monkeys which looked considerably like me'], and to whom she is devoted.[15] Alas, the idyll is not to last: one day Le Bossu sees a ship by the shore and begs to be taken off – and as he is rowed out to sea, he catches a last glimpse of the great *singesse*, like a Medea, tearing one of her young limb from limb, 'et sambloit qu'elle vouloit dire: "Haa! faulz homme, comment puez tu laissier celle quy t'a fais tant de biens comme de toy avoir preservé de mort?" ' [RP, IV, p. 68: and I felt that what she meant to say by that was 'Ah! traitor, how can you leave the one who has done you the great favour of saving you from death?'].

Now although both of these little incidents are told with considerable verve, what lies at their root is not necessarily especially original – or even impossibly exotic. The idea of sexual union between man and monkey goes back to antiquity, and indeed to Eastern folklore,[16] and there are persistent legends of human/fish hybrids, of which the most widespread is the mermaid; the fact that the hybrids of the *Roman de Perceforest* can survive on land, Gilles Roussineau remarks (RP, III, intro., pp. xxiv–xxv), might suggest that our author had heard,

11 The word is a *leitmotiv*: the fish are *tresmerveilleux* (RP, III, p. 273); the Blanc Chevalier is overcome with *merveilles* (RP, III, pp. 274, 275); he *s'esmerveilla* (RP, III, p. 275); the fish are *merveilleusement* large (RP, III, p. 279), and so on.

12 The adventure appears in Book IV, vol. I, pp. 63–69; refs. henceforward in the text prefixed RP, IV.

13 See, for instance, Le Bossu's long and sympathetic 'autobiography' in Book I of the romance: ms. BNF, fr. 345, ff. 210v–218v.

14 'Qui faisoient contenance en leurs patois de moy mettre a mort' [RP, IV, p. 65: which in their own dialect gave every impression that they would put me to death].

15 All bestiaries emphasise the outstanding ugliness of monkeys – but a number note, interestingly, their devotion to their young: see Charles Cahier, *Mélanges d'archéologie, d'histoire et de littérature* (Paris, 1853), III, pp. 230–33.

16 See H.W. Janson, *Apes and Ape Lore in the Middle Ages and the Renaissance* (London, 1952), p. 280. Barthélémy l'Anglais is interesting also on apes: see *On the Properties of Things: Trevisa's translation of De Proprietatibus Rerum*, ed. M.C. Seymour et al., 3 vols (Oxford, 1975–88), II, pp. 1246–47.

vaguely, stories about a sea mammal like the narwhal, which has a tusk that can sometimes grow to something like six feet long. But again, my prime interest is not the origins of these different marvels, nor the degree to which they are geographically 'real': rather, I'd like to think about what the inclusion of these marvels says about the ways in which the structure and focus of late-medieval romances differs from those of the more canonical prose romances, like the Vulgate *Lancelot-Graal* cycle, or the *Tristan en prose* – and I shall start by thinking about that archetypical structural device, the quest.

Take a random selection of these quests, in all their variety. In the *Lancelot*, for instance: to the Queen's great grief – she is *molt mate et molt pensive* [very downcast and very thoughtful] – and the court's dismay, Lancelot has disappeared, and Gauvain swears to search him out: 'dist oiant tos qu'il movra le matin sans plus atendre ne jamés ne finera d'aler tant qu'il sache verraies noveles s'il est mors ou s'il est vis' [he said in the hearing of all the court that he would leave early the following morning, with no further delay, and that he would not abandon the search until he had found out reliably if he (Lancelot) was dead or alive].[17] Or, this time in the *Tristan en prose*, an occasion on which Gauvain, again, swears a quest

> 'en tele maniere que je le maintenrai un an et un jour et plus encore, se mestiers est, ne ne revenrai jamais a court pour cose qu'il m'aviengne devant que je l'aie veü [sc. the Grail] plus apertement qu'il ne m'a ci esté moustrés, s'il puet estre en nule maniere que je le puisse veoir ne ne doie. Et se il ne puet estre, jou m'en retournerai ariere ci endroit' [such that I shall maintain my search for a year and a day, or even more if necessary, nor shall I ever return to court, whatever happens to me, until I have seen the Grail more clearly than it has so far been shown to me, always supposing, of course, that I am to be able or permitted to see it. And if I am unable, or forbidden, I shall come back to this very place].[18]

What these examples, show, tellingly, is how far a quest is a *purposeful* activity. It has a specific and precise objective, something to achieve – and how fundamental this is is shown, for instance, by Arthur's melancholy when he discovers that a group of his knights has failed to achieve precisely the objective that they have set themselves: they are, he says, *faillis et recreant et parjurs* [failed and cowardly]:

> 'vous jurastes tout .XL. que vous ne venriés sans le chevalier ou sans vraies enseignes de lui: si vous en revenistes tout .XL. que onques le chevalier ne m'amenastes ne enseignes vraies n'en aportastes' ['You swore, all forty of you, that you would not return without the knight or at least certain knowledge of him – and yet you have returned, all forty of you, without bringing me the knight or giving me true report of him'].[19]

This moral dimension drives the quest: to undertake one is to assume a duty

17 *Lancelot: roman en prose du XIIIe siècle*, ed. Alexandre Micha, 9 vols (Geneva, 1978–83), II, pp. 318–19.

18 *Le Roman de Tristan en prose, publié sous la direction de Philippe Ménard*, vol. VI, ed. Danielle Quéruel and Monique Santucci (Geneva, 1994), p. 265.

19 *Lancelot, roman en prose*, VIII, p. 137.

which is clearly defined – and whose terms must therefore be chosen with the greatest care;[20] its achievement is also an index of knighthood, a sort of qualification. More important from my current point of view, it is this moral imperative that structures the quest since, as sworn, its achievement is its narrative closure. The quest narrative, in other words, provides textual coherence and unity: the questing knight may occasionally allow himself to be distracted, or his particular strand of the story may be laid aside for a moment in the process that is usually called *entrelacement* – but we know that the fulfilment of the objective, and the hero's own fulfilment, will in turn bring about narrative fulfilment, closure.

This is not, however, the sort of structure into which there fit the baroque adventures from the *Papegau* and the *Perceforest* that I discussed earlier. In a residual way, true, a conventional quest does underpin the former, at least in so far as the Poisson Chevalier is concerned: as so often, Arthur is in Camelot on the day of Pentecost, when a lone damsel bursts into the great hall (nothing could be more stereotyped: 'atant ez vous une damoiselle' [CP, p. 1: and suddenly, in came a damsel] and demands help for her anonymous lady against a *chevalier qui converse en la mer* [knight whose abode is in the sea] – that is, presumably, the Poisson Chevalier whom we have already met. Arthur himself claims the adventure, 'car c'est la premiere qui est avenue en ma court, et, puis que je suis roy nouveaux, ne veux je que autre voise . . .' [CP, p. 2: for it's the first adventure to present itself at my court and, given that I am newly crowned, I do not want anyone else to undertake it]. But even if the objective is clear – help for an anonymous *dame* – there is none of the legalistic solemnity that usually accompanies the quest: Arthur gives himself no specific objective, he sets no time-limit. And that acceptance of a specific quest is visibly not the focus of the romance is shown by how difficult it is to bear in mind what exactly was the task that Arthur undertook: what he achieves first is help against the Poisson Chevalier, on behalf of a lady called the Dame aux Cheveux Blonds, and that, as we have seen, he fulfils. But lo and behold: when once Arthur has killed that adversary, yet another damsel appears to say that actually there is a quite different task: to help yet another lady, Flor de Mont, against a quite different adversary: in other words, these are serial quests, with very few formalities and, if the ostensible objectives are indeed put in place, the emphasis of the romance is, virtually, on journey as an end in itself, only perfunctorily directed towards a goal. When, for instance, Arthur meets the dwarf with the monstrous son, it is a matter of pure accident: this is a shipwreck, the archetypical framework for random adventure.

This process is even further advanced in the *Roman de Perceforest*. If the Blanc Chevalier, for instance, is marooned on an island with the Poissons Chevaliers, it is not in pursuit of any particular objective: in other words, it is not that he has stumbled over the island while on the way to some other, more worthy target for his sword. On the contrary, he has been transported there by the spirits

20 Lisa Jefferson has a lot of interesting material on this topic in her *Oaths, Vows and Promises in the First Part of the French Prose Lancelot Romance* (Frankfurt am Main, 1993).

which proliferate in Britain.[21] As indeed has Le Bossu arrived in the *Isle aux Singesses*: not in pursuit of any particular quest, but brought there, implausibly enough, impaled on the lance of an evil spirit called Malaquin.[22] We learn of his adventure much later – indeed a whole Book of the romance later – when he is invited by Arthur to tell his story, as a sort of traveller's tale for diversion after dinner, and not in any way in which it could be construed as a step on the way to glory or maturity: it is, he says, and Arthur concurs, nothing more purposeful – that word again – than an *adventure merveilleuse* (RP, IV, p. 68).

But I have just – deliberately, of course – used an expression which introduces what I want to argue here: the phrase *traveller's tale*. As I said in the preamble to this essay, I want to suggest that as late-medieval Arthurian romance develops, the *journey* becomes the structuring narrative envelope, rather than the *quest* proper with its properly defined objective: the focus is more on serendipity, the chance discoveries of the journey, than on the process of self-testing or self-validation that was the usual focus of the conventional romance quest. I am encouraged in this contention by the extraordinary flowering of journey-literature at the end of the Middle Ages.[23] Travel narratives proliferate: Michèle Guéret-Laferté, for instance, has identified 40 or more surviving narratives. Some of them are of no particular distinction: a couple of Burgundians, for instance, Ghillebert de Lannoy[24] and Bertrandon de La Broquière,[25] who make their way to the East and return with detailed accounts of their voyages. And of course, more particularly, there are the best-sellers – both, incidentally, and for different reasons, written in French:[26] at a conservative estimate, there are something like 150 manuscripts of Marco Polo's account of his travels,[27] and well over 250 of Sir John Mandeville's, in different European languages.[28] There is, in other words, a thirst at every level for geographical

21 RP, III, vol. II, p. 20.

22 RP, IV, vol. I, p. 64.

23 See for instance the exhaustive bibliography in Michèle Guéret-Laferté, *Sur les routes de l'empire mongol* (Paris, 1994), and cf. Michel Mollat, *Les Explorateurs du XIIIe au XVIe siècles* (Paris, 1984).

24 *Œuvres de Ghillebert de Lannoy, voyageur, diplomate et moraliste*, ed. Charles Potvin (Louvain, 1878).

25 See most recently Bertrandon de La Brocquière, *The Voyage d'Outremer*, ed. and trans. Galen R. Kline (New York, 1988), replacing *Le Voyage d'Outremer de Bertrandon de La Broquière*, ed. Ch. Schefer (Paris, 1972).

26 Marco Polo's account was, it seems, written in conjunction with Rusticien de Pise (see *The Book of Ser Marco Polo, the Venetian*, ed. and trans. Henry Yule [London, 1903], I), and modern scholarship agrees that Sir John Mandeville, who was long thought to have written his original in Latin, in fact composed in French (see *Mandeville's Travels: Texts and Translations*, ed. Malcolm Letts, 2 vols [London, 1953], I, pp. xxviii–xxix).

27 See Paul Zumthor, 'The Medieval Travel Narrative', *New Literary History*, 25 (1994), 809–24 (809).

28 On Mandeville's quite extraordinary popularity, see two wonderfully informative and interesting recent books: Christiane Deluz, *Le Livre de Jehan de Mandeville: Une 'géographie' au XIVe siècle* (Louvain-la-Neuve, 1988), pp. 271–82 (with a complete list of manuscripts, pp. 371–82), and Iain Macleod Higgins, *Writing East: The 'Travels' of Sir John Mandeville* (Philadelphia, 1997). Mandeville's book, usually if wrongly called the *Travels*, seems to have been written in 1356–57; the earliest dated manuscript, BNF naf 4515, was commissioned in 1371 for Charles V of France by his physician. By the mid-fifteenth century, the *Travels* were circulating in translations in eight languages; there are more than seventy manuscripts in French; there were sixty printings, in eight languages, by 1600.

imaginings: as Sir John Mandeville tells us, 'Men covet to hear speak of [the Holy Land] and of divers countries there about and thereof they have of that great solace and comfort.'[29]

And what attracted so vast a readership? Well, some readers may have been attracted by the allure of a pilgrimage to the *Holy Land* and to *diverse contries*, and merchants, perhaps, might be tempted to follow in the tracks of the Polos. But what Marco Polo's readers, and Sir John Mandeville's, really want to explore is marvels, *mirabilia*. The prologue to Marco Polo's *Devisament* (probably due to Rusticien de Pise) promises *les grandismes merveilles . . . de la grant Hermenie*, and *des diverses parties du monde des grans merveilles* [the greatest of marvels of Greater Armenia and the great marvels of all the diverse parts of the world], and the word studs the narrative[30] – and Mandeville, as he says, is catering for a demand for *choses nouvelles*. Marco Polo's book, for instance, is called not *The Travels*, but *Devisament dou monde*, the description of the world – and that is indeed its nature: it is a *descriptio*, a book of wonders, on an astonishing, and quite unprecedented, scale.[31] As, in point of fact, is Mandeville's: he starts off, convincingly enough, by promising what amounts to a guidebook for the journey to Jerusalem, *la terre de promission*:

> pour ceuls qui volente ont de visiter la noble cite de Ierusalem et les sains lieux qui la entour sont; et leur deuiseray et domonsterray quel chemin ilz pourroient tenir, car ien ay par maint passe et cheuauchie [for all those who desire to visit the noble city of Jerusalem, and all the holy places that surround the city; and I shall describe and explain which routes they should take, for I have myself followed many of them on horseback].[32]

But he abandons this round about the midpoint and veers off eastwards in pursuit of rich marvels and marvellous anecdote,[33] with some rather disingenuous remarks about the timeliness of such an enterprise: now, he says, that he has told us all about the Holy Land, and although this is scarcely *le droit chemin pur aler es parties qe iay desus nomez* [p. 312: the most direct route to the countries I have mentioned above], it is time for him to 'parler des marches des illes, des diuerses gens et de diuerses bestes qui sont entre ces marches' [talk about the shape and outline of the islands, and the remarkable peoples and beasts that inhabit them].[34] And from that point we lose all trace of any purpose in a welter of *dames fees* [fairy women] in *petite Iermenie* [p. 311: lesser Armenia], and

29 *Mandeville's Travels: Texts and Translations*, ed. Malcolm Letts, 2 vols (London, 1953), I, p. 2.

30 For the most recent edition of the French text, with a facing-page translation into modern French, see Marco Polo, *La Description du monde*, ed. Pierre-Yves Badel (Paris, 1998), pp. 50, 80, 88, 106, etc. In the more widely available edition, that done by M.G. Pauthier (Paris, 1865), see pp. 3, 4, 42, 52, 81 and passim.

31 On this topic, see Linda Lomperis's article 'Medieval Travel Writing and the Question of Race', *Journal of Medieval and Early Modern Studies*, 31 (2001), 147–64, and *Métamorphoses du récit de voyage*, ed. F. Moureau (Paris, 1986).

32 I use the so-called Paris text of the *Travels*, ed. Letts, II, 226–413; the present citation is on p. 231. Christiane Deluz has recently produced a handsome edition of a rival text, the so-called *version insulaire: Le Livre des merveilles du monde* (Paris, 2000).

33 See Stephen Greenblatt, *Marvelous Possessions: The Wonder of the New World* (Chicago, 1991), ch. 1, pp. 26–51.

34 *Mandeville's Travels*, ed. Letts, p. 309.

monopods in Ethiopia (p. 318), and naked women lounging in the Nile (p. 322), and cannibals, and Amazons (p. 330), and crocodiles (p. 341). And, it turns out, apes:

> Et vne autre maniere de gens il y a, qui vont sur leurs mains et sus leurs piez comme bestes, et sont tous velus et rampent legierement sur les arbres et aussi tost comme vn singe [p. 344: and there is another variety of people there, who walk on their feet and hands like animals, and are covered with hair and scramble easily up trees, as easily as do apes].[35]

and parrots:

> Et si a grant plante de papions, ce sont signes sauuages, et grant foison de papegais, quil appellent en leur langaige priscat, dont il y a de telz qui bien parollent de leur nature et qui saluent les gens qui vont par my le desert et parlent aussi parfaittement comme feroit vns homs [and there are great numbers of *papions*, that is wild swans, and great flocks of parrots, known in the language of that country as priscat; some of them are able to speak naturally, and they call to men crossing the desert, and indeed speak as well as might a man].[36]

I am not, let me emphasise, suggesting that our romance authors based what they say on Mandeville's *Book* or Marco Polo's *Devisament* – although it is interesting that the Burgundian ducal library seems to have contained more than one copy of each of them.[37] What I am drawing attention to is what we might call the lure of the exotic: as Mandeville says, several times, he may not be explaining the most direct or convenient way to reach Jerusalem, *mes qi vorroit veoir celles merueilles* [the key word again], *il [le] purroit faire* [but if anyone wanted to witness these marvels, he could easily do so].[38]

My argument has to do, in fact, precisely with the key word in that last quotation: *celles merveilles*. What the late-medieval travel narrative increasingly becomes is a particularly capacious and flexible vehicle for the marvellous. I am not suggesting – on the contrary – that these late-medieval texts are the first to deal in wonders:[39] we have only to think of Pliny the Elder's *Natural History*, or the so-called *Wonders of the East*[40] – or, indeed, any number of medieval 'encyclopaedias'[41] – with all of which Mandeville, and Marco Polo share some details. But what differentiates our later medieval travel narratives from these

35 Which also figure in Marco Polo's travels: see Yule, II, pp. 382, 431.

36 Ibid., p. 385; for *priscat* here, read *psytakes* in ms. BL Harley 4383; see *The Buke of John Mandeville*, ed. G.F. Warner (London, 1889). Parrots, of course, also figure in Marco Polo's *œuvre*: see Yule, II, p. 376.

37 One of the most magnificent of the manuscripts to give Mandeville's Book has it copied, significantly enough, along with Marco Polo's *Liure des Merueilles du Monde*: this is BNF, fr. 2810, which John Duke of Burgundy had copied as a gift for his uncle Jean de Berry (see Deluz, *Le Livre de Jehan de Mandeville*, pp. 286–87).

38 Ibid., p. 312.

39 See, for instance, Mary B. Campbell, *The Witness and the Other World: Exotic European Travel Writing, 400–1600* (Ithaca, NY, 1988), esp. ch. 2: 'The Fabulous East: "Wonder Books" and Grotesque Facts' (pp. 47–86).

40 Discussed ibid., pp. 57–75.

41 Like, among others, Isidore of Seville's – which Jean Céard calls a *sottisier*; see his *La Nature et les prodiges* (Geneva, 1977), p. 45.

older (and very widely-read) tracts is the fact that in the later narratives it is an experiencing narrator – whose roots are, however distantly, in pilgrimage accounts and pilgrim guides – who meets the fabulous and the exotic. The fantasies of predecessors are turned into 'geography' and 'history' – and 'autobiography'[42] – and the marvels are set along a narrative vector which demands that, as readers, we participate in the pleasure of the journey, and that, as judges, we suspend disbelief because of the presence of the observing eye.

That said, the dividing-line between geographical marvel and fictional marvel is a fluid and shifting one: the factual exotic is indistinguishable from, and no more plausible than, the fictional. Modern readers are accustomed to thinking of Mandeville's travels as entirely fictional (a 'travel liar', as Percy Adams would have it[43]) – but it is worth remembering that when the *Santa Cruz* swept into the New World in 1492, what lay to hand in Christopher Columbus's day-room was a copy of Mandeville's *Book*.[44] Conversely, modern readers are accustomed to thinking of Marco Polo's account as astonishingly faithful, in contradistinction to Mandeville's, but contemporaries were distinctly sceptical – to put it mildly – about how far Marco Polo was to be believed: legend says that when the great traveller was on his deathbed, many of his friends begged him to retract his book because they were much afraid it was a tissue of lies from start to finish. And the fact that so many manuscripts call Marco Polo's *Devisament* something like *Le livre des merueilles du monde*,[45] and that the word *merveille*, as we saw, punctuates the book as a whole, cannot but have made contemporaries as sceptical of Marco's voyage as they justifiably were of John Mandeville's. After all – as Pliny points out, with justice, in his *Historia naturalis*, and I use a rather nice seventeenth-century translation:

> Qui jamais eust pensé que les Ethiopiens fussent noirs, si on ne les eust vus tels? Et je vous prie comment furent-ils regardez, quand on les vid premierement? D'ailleurs, combien y a-t-il de choses qu'on estime impossibles avant qu'on les voye faites? Et de fait, la force et la majesté de Nature se rend incredible à chaque moment, quand on la considere par ses particularitez seulement, et non en son tout [Who would ever have imagined that the Ethiopians could be black, unless he had seen them? And how indeed were they thought of, when they were first seen? Moreover, are there not a multitude of things which would have been thought impossible had they not been seen? And indeed, the power and majesty

42 For Leonardo Olschki, for instance, Marco Polo's *Devisament* is 'a guide book and a doctrinal work, fused into a literary combination so successful that it is impossible to tell the one from the other'. (See his *Marco Polo's Asia: An Introduction to His 'Description of the World' Called 'Il Milione'*, trans. John A. Scott [Berkeley, 1960]).

43 *Travelers and Travel Liars 1660–1800* (repr. New York, 1980). Although at least one writer, interestingly enough, has argued that John's travels were perfectly real: Giles Milton, *The Riddle and the Knight: In Search of Sir John Mandeville* (London, 1996).

44 See *Mandeville's Travels*, ed. M. C. Seymour (Oxford, 1967), pp. xx; and cf., for instance, Campbell, *The Witness and the Other World*, pp. 122–61.

45 See the list of 'Manuscripts of Marco Polo's Book so far as they are known', published as Appendix F in *The Book of Ser Marco Polo*, ed. Yule, II, pp. 526–52: no 18, ms BNF fr. 2810 (signed by Nicolas Flamel) – and cf. ibid., no. 49, *El libro de le cosse mirabile vedue per lo nobile homo Messer MP, and no. 52 De mirabilibus Mundi*, etc. etc. For other examples relating to Mandeville's Travels, version *insulaire*, see ed. Deluz, pp. 36–58: *Le Geste de sire Jehan Mandevylle de mervailles de monde*, etc.

of Nature are a source of permanent astonishment, when we think of her specific manifestations only, and not of her totality].[46]

The point is relevant, I think, because if I am right in seeing fictional quest stories and (purportedly) factual travel narratives as mutually contaminating, or more precisely mutually enriching, then it is no doubt the blurring of boundaries in each genre which is responsible.[47] A travel narrative is, after all, not dissimilar to a quest narrative: to quote E.M. Forster,[48] both of them are 'baggy monsters' which absorb digressions and sub-plots which delay the conclusion and acquire an attraction and validity of their own, both of them skip from sensational incident to sensational incident in what Derek Pearsall calls 'unbuttoned style'.[49] But the difference is that whereas the true quest narrative consists, ultimately, as we saw, of a series of tests which prove the worth of the hero by allowing him to destroy what he finds, the travel narrative is designed to showcase marvels, to celebrate the exotic.[50] What happens, it seems, towards the end of the Middle Ages, is that this 'showcase' function comes to predominate over the 'probatory' function: what we are seeing is an interchangeability of two genres, the travel text and the quest.

That there is some interchange between the two genres cannot be doubted. Henry Yule, long ago, pointed out[51] that *Baudouin de Sebourc* is indebted to Marco Polo's account of the Assassins [Hashishin] for its story of a King of the *Rouge Montaingne* who has set up a *Paradis* in which he persuades gullible young men that if they do his bidding, they may have eternal life and eternal joy – and I have argued myself,[52] not quite so long but still many years ago, that the *Roman de Perceforest* owed its own picture of a rather similar tyrant that same tale of the Assassins. It is difficult, moreover, not to note the fact that Rusticien de Pise, who was also the deviser of a version of the *Tristan en prose*, seems to have composed Marco Polo's *Devisament* at Marco's dictation when they were both prisoners in Genoa in 1298–99:[53] surely, we feel, this suggests a sort of kinship,

46 Pliny, *Historia Naturalis*, VII, 1, trans. Antoine du Pinet, 1622.

47 Jennifer Goodman's recent *Chivalry and Exploration, 1298–1630* (Woodbridge, 1998) addresses some similar issues from the other direction: she argues that travel narratives such as Marco Polo's are shaped by late romance. My argument is complementary: that late romance is to a degree shaped by narratives of exploration – but what emerges, clearly, from both our approaches is the interplay between these two genres. I owe to Dennis Green a reference to a book which discusses something of this sort in relation to Classical Antiquity: J.S. Romm, *The Edges of the Earth in Ancient Thought: Geography, Exploration, and Fiction* (Princeton, 1992).

48 Or, of course, Ronsard: Ariosto's *Orlando Furioso* is, he says, a romance where 'les membres sont aucunement beaux mais le corps est . . . contrefait et monstrueux': Preface to the *Franciade*, in his *Œuvres complètes*, ed. P. Laumonier, 20 vols (Paris, 1983), XVI, p. 4.

49 *The Canterbury Tales* (London, 1985), p. 132.

50 Cf. Erich Auerbach: 'The world of knightly proving is a world of adventure. It not only contains a practically uninterrupted series of adventures; more specifically, it contains nothing but the requisites of adventure. Nothing is found in it which is not either accessory or preparatory to an adventure. It is a world specifically created and designed to give the knight an opportunity to prove himself': *Mimesis: The Representation of Reality in Western Literature*, trans. Willard Trask (Garden City, 1957), p. 119.

51 *The Book of Ser Marco Polo*, op. cit., I, pp. 121–29.

52 'Aroès the Enchanter: An Episode in the *Roman de Perceforest* and its Sources', *Medium Aevum*, 47 (1978), 30–39.

53 See Yule's introduction to his *The Book of Ser Marco Polo*, I, pp. 55–64.

especially when we realise that either he, or Marco Polo, seems to have insisted on a long final chapter, occupying something like a fifth of the travelogue, detailing the Great Khan's chivalric exploits. It is also the case that both Mandeville's *Book* and Marco Polo's *Devisament* are pretty consistently copied with, or at least bound with, romances of various sorts: Mandeville's and Marco Polo's, most particularly and most interestingly, with one or other of the Alexander romances.[54]

This last is an interesting point. The Alexander romances are, after all, not dissimilar to travel narratives themselves. Like Marco Polo's, like Mandeville's, Alexander's is an archetypal travel narrative, a disinterested journey in search of marvels, a journey governed only by an avid and insatiable curiosity:[55] 'Entrer veul es desers ou a tante *mervelle*' [I want to explore the desert where there are so many *marvels*].[56] And not necessarily to conquer or to put to the sword – but also for simple curiosity: as Emmanuèle Baumgartner points out, 'triompher de l'Orient ne signifie pas le soumettre et le faire sien'.[57] According to Alexander's (apocryphal) letter to Aristotle, the emperor continued eastwards only until he reached the point beyond which, the Indians told him, nothing worth seeing was to be found – at which point, again according to the letter, he commanded his army to retrace its steps. His story is replete with every marvel: so insatiable was his curiosity, according to legend, that it took him, it seems, into the heavens and deep into the oceans,[58] and, as he travelled onwards towards the bounds of the known world, he met dragons and flocks of man-eating bats, rhinoceros and nyctorax . . .[59] And if I suggested that this point is particularly significant, it is because one of the romances on which I have spent most time in this essay, the *Roman de Perceforest*, derives precisely from a fusion of Arthurian romance, with its quest structure, and the Alexander romance, with its journey structure: what it purports to tell us is how the Emperor Alexander, by some curious meteorological quirk, is driven out of his way somewhere in the Mediterranean and onto the coast of England where, distantly, he is the ancestor of King Arthur.

Now, my intention is not to suggest that our late-medieval authors, any more than their earlier counterparts, consciously modelled their new Arthuriana on what we may, I think, legitimately call the *genre* of the travel narrative. But they were, after all, practical men: in producing new Arthurian romances at all, so long after the great prose romances had found their canonical form, they were pandering no doubt to a public taste for *merveilles* and not just for sober story-telling. It is, I think, legitimate to imagine that late-medieval story-tellers

54 For instance, in BL Bib.Reg. XIX, D. I (which also contains *Le Livre d'Alexandre* and Jehan le Venelais's *Vengeance d'Alexandre*), in Oxford, Bodleian Library, 264.

55 Alexander, according to legend, wrote to his mentor Aristotle to explain that he continued into the furthest East only so that 'rien ne m'echappât dans les lieux inconnus'; see Céard, op. cit., p. 57, and cf. Campbell, *The Witness and the Other World*, pp. 68–69.

56 Alexandre de Paris, *Le Roman d'Alexandre*, ed. E.C. Armstrong et al., presented by Laurence Harf-Lancner (Paris, 1994), branch III, vs. 2297.

57 In an interesting article, 'L'Orient d'Alexandre', *Bien Dire et Bien Aprandre: Revue de Médiévistique: sp. issue: Le Roman d'Alexandre*, 6 (1999), 8–15 (14).

58 Alexandre de Paris, *Le Roman d'Alexandre*, branch III, vss 389–499, 4967–5061.

59 Alexandre de Paris, *Le Roman d'Alexandre*, branch III, vss 1179 ff.

might have noticed a trend – and set out, to a greater or lesser degree, to meet it, recognising, and exploiting, the fact that after all the quest and the journey are, as structuring devices, isomorphic. What is produced, I suggest, are textual hybrids[60] which disrupt romance decorum and self-consciously stage their own escapism. Like Marco Polo and like John de Mandeville, whose ostensible goals become little more than an excuse reached, if at all, with a sort of lacklustre dutifulness, travel, discovery, 'tourism', ethnography almost,[61] become the point, rather than the achievement of a real, emotional end-point: these are, one might say, stories of *errance* [wanderings, journeys] and not of knights errant.[62]

60 Of the sort which François Suard, for instance, discusses for other late-medieval narrative genres: see 'Chanson de geste et roman devant le matériau folklorique', in *Mittelalterbilder aus neuer Perspektive. Diskussionsanstösse zu amour courtois, Subjektivität, in der Dichtung und Strategien der Erzählens. Würzburg Kolloquium, 1984*, ed. E. Ruhe and R. Behrens (Munich, 1985), pp. 364–77.

61 *Yale French Studies* (59 [1980]) devoted a volume to the origins of anthropological writing, which it finds in the sixteenth century; I would be much inclined to set it earlier, in the later Middle Ages, precisely with the early travellers like Marco Polo. Mary Baine Campbell, *Wonder and Science: Imagining Worlds in Early Modern Europe* (Ithaca, NY, 1999), suggests in the same vein that what readers derive from travel writings is 'ethnographic pleasure'.

62 Although what I am describing here is not specific to romance: I have argued elsewhere for something rather similar in late epics like *Tristan de Nanteuil* (see 'The Lure of the Hybrid: *Tristan de Nanteuil*: *chanson de geste* arthurienne?', *Arthurian Literature* XVIII [2001], 77–87).

Reconsidering Malory

CAROLINE D. ECKHARDT

> Historye is a perpetuel conseruatryce of thoos thynges that haue be doone before this presente tyme. . . . (Caxton, Proem to Higden's *Polychronicon*[1])

Writing in England in the second half of the fifteenth century (he completed the *Morte Darthur* between 4 March 1469 and 3 March 1470),[2] Sir Thomas Malory has long been recognized as one of the most important synthesizers and interpreters of the Arthurian legend. Like his twelfth-century literary ancestor Geoffrey of Monmouth and some of his more recent French predecessors, Malory used a wide range of antecedent materials and his own imagination to create an extensive textual fabric, encompassing a great many episodes, characters and themes, in which he presented the rise and fall of the Arthurian kingdom. As Derek Brewer, for example, has described it,

> The whole book may be said to follow a roughly threefold movement. Movement I . . . shows Arthur's upward rise; Movement II . . . shows the varied greatness of the knights of the Round Table and the peak of Arthur's glory; in Movement III the wheel of Fortune, starting at its height, goes on to its downward movement, showing the downfall of the Round Table and of Arthur, Lancelot and Guenevere.[3]

Among Arthurian scholars and many generations of readers the greatness of Malory's achievement is not at question, but the nature of that achievement continues to be debated. This essay will begin with a brief overview of some of the main preoccupations of Malory criticism, though instead of providing a chronological survey,[4] I will use the commentary offered by William Caxton,

1 William Caxton, 'Prohemye' to Ralph Higden's *Polychronicon*, in W.J.B. Crotch, *The Prologues and Epilogues of William Caxton* (London, 1928), p. 65.

2 Documentary evidence of the life of Sir Thomas Malory of Newbold Revel in Warwickshire, who is generally (if not unanimously) regarded as the author of the *Morte Darthur*, is summarized by P.J.C. Field, 'The Malory Life-Records', in *A Companion to Malory*, ed. Elizabeth Archibald and A.S.G. Edwards (Cambridge, 1996), pp. 115–30; see p. 126 for the *Morte Darthur*'s date of completion, which is based on a statement at the end of the text.

3 *The Morte Darthur, Parts Seven and Eight*, by Sir Thomas Malory, ed. and intro. D.S. Brewer (Evanston, IL, 1974), p. 40.

4 Overviews of Malory scholarship include Page West Life, *Sir Thomas Malory and the Morte Darthur: A Survey of Scholarship and Annotated Bibliography* (Charlottesville, VA, 1980), pp. 1–42; James W. Spisak, 'Introduction: Recent Trends in Malory Studies', in *Studies in Malory*, ed. James W. Spisak (Kalamazoo, 1985), pp. 1–12; Marylyn Jackson Parins, 'Introduction' in

Malory's first printer, as a point of access. I will then focus on the question of what Malory chose to preserve in his construction of the Arthurian past, before considering a sampling of ways in which aspects of Malory's work have, in turn, been preserved in later renderings of the *Morte Darthur*. 'Reconsidering Malory', as implied by the title of this essay, thus involves seeing Malory as both object and agent.

I

The earliest known readings of Malory are represented in the first extant textual witnesses, Caxton's printed edition of 1485 and the single known manuscript copy, called the Winchester Manuscript (now British Library MS Additional 59678).[5] Because this manuscript came to light only in 1934 and was not available in print until 1947, the first 450 years of Malory criticism, more or less, were based on the text of Caxton, whose work is doubly important because, in a prescient way, the preface he provided in his edition broaches the main issues that were to engage readers and scholars for centuries to come.[6]

Caxton begins his preface by explaining that 'many noble and dyuers gentylmen of thys royame of Englond' visited him to request that he print 'th'ystorye of the sayd noble kyng and conquerour Kyng Arthur and of his knyghtes' – rather than printing the exploits of worthies from other countries – 'consyderyng that he [Arthur] was a man borne wythin this royame and kyng and emperour of the same'.[7] This passage initiates the placement of the Arthurian narrative into the discourse around the growth of English national identity and nationalism. However, Caxton also situates the narrative within the context of transnational literary production, reporting that Arthur is 'more spoken of beyonde the see' with 'moo bookes made of his noble actes than there be in Englond' – for overseas, he says, there are Arthurian books in Dutch, Italian,

Malory: The Critical Heritage (London, 1988), pp. 1–39; and James P. Carley, 'England', in *Medieval Arthurian Literature: A Guide to Recent Research*, ed. Norris J. Lacy (New York, 1996), pp. 1–82, esp. pp. 33–42. After Carley's work, for annual annotated listings see the *Bibliographical Bulletin of the International Arthurian Society*; some issues of *The Year's Work in English Studies* carry annual overviews.

5 The standard editions of Caxton and the Winchester Manuscript are *Caxton's Malory, A New Edition of Sir Thomas Malory's Le Morte Darthur*, ed. James W. Spisak, et al., 2 vols (Berkeley, 1983); and *The Works of Sir Thomas Malory*, ed. Eugene Vinaver, rev. P.J.C. Field, 3rd ed., 3 vols (Oxford, 1990), both of which will be cited here. Facsimile editions of both these early texts are available: *Sir Thomas Malory, Le Morte D'Arthur, Printed by William Caxton, 1485, Reproduced in facsimile from the copy in the Pierpont Morgan Library*, intro. Paul Needham (London, 1976); and *The Winchester Malory: A Facsimile*, intro. N.R. Ker (London, 1976). Two other copies made prior to 1500 are sometimes included in discussions of the early textual history: a partial second copy of Caxton's 1485 edition and Wynkyn de Worde's printed edition of 1498. For lists of editions, see, to 1983, Parins, *Malory: The Critical Heritage*, pp. 40–46; to 1985, Barry Gaines, *Sir Thomas Malory: An Anecdotal Bibliography of Editions, 1485–1985* (New York, 1990); and since 1985, the annual listings in the *Bibliographical Bulletin of the International Arthurian Society*.

6 Cf. Elizabeth Kirk, ' "Clerkes, Poetes and Historiographs": The *Morte Darthur* and Caxton's "Poetics" of Fiction', in *Studies in Malory*, pp. 275–95; Kirk remarks that Caxton 'identified the questions to be asked about Malory' (p. 276).

7 *Caxton's Malory*, I.1.

Spanish and Greek as well as in French.[8] He recognizes the French context in particular by describing the Arthurian volume from which he is printing as 'a copye vnto me delyuerd, whyche copye Syr Thomas Malorye dyd take oute of certeyn bookes of Frensshe and reduced it into Englysshe';[9] he does not explain who delivered this volume to him, or whether he had more than one such book at hand.

Further, Caxton suggests the generic instability of the Arthurian narrative, relating it implicitly to both historiographical and fictional genres. In his (perhaps partly invented) account of the discussion with those 'noble and dyuers gentylmen' who asked him to print the history of King Arthur, he represents himself as having initially expressed doubt as to whether he should fulfill their request, because 'dyuers men holde oppynyon that there was no suche Arthur, and that alle suche bookes as been maad of hym ben but fayned and fables'.[10] An unidentified speaker – 'one in specyal' among the 'noble and dyuers gentylmen' – is said to respond to this demurral by advocating evidence for Arthur's existence and pronouncing that 'al these thynges consydered there can no man resonably gaynsaye but there was a kyng of thys lande named Arthur'.[11] Acquiescing if not wholly agreeing, Caxton asserts the aesthetic appeal of the book he has decided to print, but still hedges the question of its historicity: 'for to passe the tyme thys book shal be plesaunte to rede in, but for to gyue fayth and byleue that al is trewe that is conteyned herin, ye be at your lyberte'.[12] This reluctance to place the *Morte Darthur* firmly in the category of historiographical texts, whose truth-claims Caxton elsewhere vigorously defends, leaves its generic status open.[13]

Most significant, Caxton initiates the placement of this Arthurian narrative into the discourses of literary use-value when he exhorts readers, several times over, to use the text as an inducement to good conduct. One such exhortation, resonant with Biblical and Chaucerian echoes, frames Malory's work within the contexts of moral literature, both religious and secular, as well as juxtaposing types of conduct by positioning 'vertue' between 'hate' and 'synne':

> For herein may be seen noble chyualrye, curtosye, humanyte, frendlynesse, hardynesse, loue, frendshyp, cowardyse, murdre, hate, vertue, and synne. Doo after the good and leue the euyl, and it shal brynge you to good fame and renommee. . . . al is wryton for our doctryne and for to beware that we falle not to vyce ne synne, but t'excersyse and folowe vertu . . . and after thys shorte and transytorye lyf to come vnto euerlastyng blysse in heuen . . . Amen.[14]

8 *Caxton's Malory*, I. 2.

9 *Caxton's Malory*, I. 2. At the end of the book (I. 600) Caxton reiterates the French context by the title that he gives to the work, *Le Morte Darthur* (rather than using the English equivalent).

10 *Caxton's Malory*, I. 1.

11 *Caxton's Malory*, I. 2.

12 *Caxton's Malory*, I. 3.

13 In the Proem to the *Polycronicon*, for example, Caxton argues that 'by the redyng of historyes' one can become wise, for a person 'syttynge in his chambre or studye maye rede knowe and vnderstande the polytyke and noble actes of alle the worlde . . . And the conflyctes errours. Troubles & vexacions done in the sayd vnyuersal worlde Jn suche wyse as he had ben and seen them. in the propre places where as they were done.' Caxton, *The Prologues and Epilogues*, p. 64.

14 *Caxton's Malory*, I. 3. The word 'vertu(e)' maintained its earlier meaning of 'power', but its

And so, in 1485, many of the later critical controversies were anticipated if not actually joined. To the nationalist justification for disseminating the story of Arthur that is urged by the visiting 'gentylmen' can be linked subsequent discussions of Malory's political context in the Wars of the Roses, including not only his own role and affiliation, which was almost certainly Lancastrian, but also such larger topics as England's imperial ambitions at the time and the effect of their failure (by 1453 England had lost its former French territories).[15] To the translingual distribution of the Arthurian legend, Caxton's reticence about the origins of the copy that was 'delyuerd' to him, and his description of Malory's having 'reduced' French books into English, can be linked subsequent considerations of the *Morte Darthur*'s textual history, the work's sources and what Malory did with them, and the remarkable prose style that resulted.[16] To the question of the narrative's ficticity or historicity can be linked later studies of the *Morte Darthur*'s relationship to medieval genres such as romance, chronicle, 'tale', epic, tragedy and other forms.[17] And to Caxton's insistence on themes of good and evil, vertu and synne, pleasure and faith can be linked the hundreds of analyses of those and further themes (adultery, fortune, destiny, alienation, betrayal, etc.) as displayed through the actions and choices made by Malory's characters.

Finally, Caxton's recurrent characterization of his Arthurian book and its subject as 'noble' – for example, toward the end of his preface he describes the work as 'the noble and ioyous hystorye of the grete conquerour and excellent kyng, Kyng Arthur, somtyme kyng of thys noble royalme'[18] – anticipates many other assessments that involve strong value-judgments, from Roger Ascham's angry accusation, in 1545, that the 'whole pleasure' of the *Morte Darthur*

semantic range had predominantly positive usages that sort oddly with 'hate' and 'synne'. The Pauline precept that 'all that is written, is written for our doctrine (instruction)', Romans 15.4, was often cited, e.g. by Chaucer in the 'Nun's Priest's Tale' and the 'Retraction' (Caxton had printed the Canterbury Tales in 1476[?] and 1483[?]), and by Caxton in other prologues as well as this one. See Kirk, pp. 277–80, and William A. Kretzschmar, Jr., 'Caxton's Sense of History', *Journal of English and Germanic Philology*, 91 (1992), 510–28, esp. 519–26.

15 Felicity Riddy, 'Contextualizing *Le Morte Darthur*: Empire and Civil War', in *A Companion to Malory*, pp. 55–73. Cf. Patricia Clare Ingham, *Sovereign Fantasies: Arthurian Romance and the Making of Britain* (Philadelphia, 2001), pp. 192–226; Ingham delineates connections between the Grail and contemporary coronation ritual, the behavior of Arthur's knights and the rhetoric of crusading, etc.

16 Scholarship on the topics of textual history, sources and style is voluminous. For recent work on the relationship between the Winchester Manuscript and Caxton's edition see *The Malory Debate: Essays on the Texts of Le Morte Darthur*, ed. Bonnie Wheeler, Robert L. Kindrick and Michael N. Salda (Cambridge, 2000). The differences between the Winchester and Caxton versions led Eugene Vinaver to believe that Malory wrote not one long narrative but multiple shorter tales, and thus his edition of the Winchester manuscript (see n. 5) is entitled *The Works of Sir Thomas Malory*, but many scholars have returned to the traditional title of *Morte Darthur*, as used here. For overviews about Malory's use of his sources and his style, see Terence McCarthy, 'Malory and His Sources', in *A Companion to Malory*, pp. 75–96; Jeremy Smith, 'Language and Style in Malory', in *A Companion to Malory*, pp. 97–113; and Mark Lambert, *Malory: Style and Vision in Le Morte Darthur* (New Haven, 1975).

17 Malory's work has been described, e.g., '(in alphabetical order) as an "Arthuriad", an "Arthurian compendium", a compilation of tales, an epic, a history, a long prose fiction, a novel, a redaction (of its French sources), a romance, a tragedy, a translation.' See Ruth Morse, 'Back to the Future: Malory's Genres', *Arthuriana*, 7.3 (1997), 100–23, here citing 100.

18 *Caxton's Malory*, I. 3.

'standeth . . . in open mans slaughter, and bold bawdrye',[19] to encomia such as Jill Mann's assessment that 'the emotional power of Malory's writing . . . has made it the most influential and enduring of the many medieval versions of the Arthurian story . . .'.[20] It would not be accurate to say that Malory's critical heritage consists of footnotes to Caxton, but in many respects Caxton has surely led the way.

II

Caxton's preface shows him and the unidentified visiting gentlemen engaged in the act of 'considering' the Arthurian legend. Malory left no such preface, but we can envisage him too considering the nature of his writing project as he translated, combined, reduced, untangled and performed the other types of transformations that scholars have identified. Other studies have examined what is different in Malory, i.e., what he changed as he synthesized and reconstructed the Arthurian legend, but the emphasis here will instead be on what he retained and transmitted. This perspective entails reconsidering his work through the concept of cultural preservation, or, as Caxton put it in his preface to Higden's *Polychronicon*:

> Historye is a perpetuel conseruatryce of thoos thynges that haue be doone before this presente tyme and also a cotydyan wytnesse of bienfayttes of malefaytes grete Actes and tryumphal vyctoryes of all maner peple. And also yf the terryble feyned Fables of Poetes haue moche styred and moeued men to pyte and conseruynge of Justyce How moche more is to be supposed that Historye assertryce of veryte and as moder of alle philosophye moeuynge our maners to vertue reformeth and reconcyleth ner hande alle thoos men whiche thurgh the Infyrmyte of oure mortal nature hath ledde the mooste parte of theyr lyf in Ocyosyte and myspended theyr tyme passed ryght soone oute of Remembraunce Of whiche lyf and deth is egal oblyuyon The fruytes of vertue ben Immortall Specyally whanne they ben wrapped in the benefyce of hystoryes.[21]

It is of course not 'history' that is the perpetual conservator, the daily witness, the advocate of verity and the mother of all philosophy – it is the writer, who, from the vantage point of a later time, makes decisions about what is worthy of preservation from the residue that can be discovered, surmised, or invented to represent the past. Despite the differences that Caxton posits, both historian and poet are understood to be practitioners of the process of 'conserving' (evidently the historian conserves truth, the poet justice), and their own subjectivities help determine which elements of the past will live or die. At the end of the day, historians and poets, and one might say scholars too, keep or reify what they think matters.

19 *The English Works of Roger Ascham*, ed. William Aldis Wright (Cambridge, 1904), cited in Parins, *Malory: The Critical Heritage*, pp. 56–57.

20 Jill Mann, *The Narrative of Distance, the Distance of Narrative in Malory's Morte Darthur, The William Matthews Lectures 1991* (London, 1991), p. 2.

21 Caxton, 'Prohemye' to *Polychronicon*, in *Prologues and Epilogues*, pp. 65–66.

Malory of course 'conserved' a wide range of the constituent elements of his sources, retaining plots, characterizations, settings, points of view and so forth as he made his complex synthesis. I will discuss here only a small cluster of such characteristics, each relating in different ways to a recurrent concept in his Arthurian world: the high value put on individual agency expressed in both solitary and communal pursuits. Despite the interventions of fortune, prophecy, magic, or miracle, it is human choices and actions that drive the narrative onwards and constitute its interest.

The tale of Balin, for example, includes several mysterious elements, such as a knight who can make himself invisible and a horn, blown by an unseen hunter, that somehow signals or anticipates Balin's death. However, these potential gestures towards the occult are not pursued as such. Instead, they are recounted in an utterly matter-of-fact way that insists that attention remain directed to 'realistic' human actions, such as proposing to ride the better of two available horses, or entering a castle where dancing and feasting are underway. Here is the moment of deadly intervention by the invisible knight:

> And as they [Balin and another knight] were evyn before Arthurs pavilion, ther com one invisible and smote the knyght that wente with Balyn thorowoute the body with a spere.
>
> 'Alas!' seyde the knyght, 'I am slayne. . . . Therefore take my horse that is bettir than youres, and ryde to the damesell and folow the queste that I was in as she woll lede you, and revenge my deth whan ye may'.[22]

Eventually the knight who 'destroyeth many good knyghtes, for he goth invisible'[23] is killed by Balin, who then learns that, in this as other situations, his actions have unexpected consequences. But the invisibility itself, which in the hands of a different writer could be used to exploit special effects of eeriness or even terror, is here not allowed any interest at all. Similarly, the weird horn signal is neither commented upon nor explained:

> And soo he [Balin] herd an horne blowe as it had ben the dethe of a best. 'That blast,' said Balyn, 'is blowen for me, for I am the pryse, and yet am I not dede.' Anone withal he sawe an honderd ladyes and many knyghtes that welcommed hym with fayr semblaunt and made him passyng good chere unto his syght, and ledde hym into the castel, and ther was daunsynge and mynstralsye and alle maner of joye.[24]

It is the actions of Balin himself, and his brother Balan and the many ladies and knights who participate in this section of the *Morte Darthur*, that matter, despite the influence of fate, destiny and unknown powers that constitute the context within which they act.

Curiously enough, the scribes of the Winchester Manuscript seem to have visually reproduced this characteristic. As if to call attention to the presence of the king and the many other characters, the scribes regularly wrote all the text's

22 Malory, *Works*, I. 80. Cf. a second such episode on I. 81.
23 Malory, *Works*, I. 83.
24 Malory, *Works*, I. 88.

hym self in a launde stoode. Anone as Sir Lucyus sawe
Sir Gawayne he sayde all on hyght thou art welcom I wys
for thou sekyst aftir sorow here thou shalt be sone ovirmacched
Sir Launcelot was wroth at hys grymme wordys and
gurde to hym with his swerde aboven uppon hys bryght
helme that the raylyng bloode felle downe to his feete And
Sir Gawayne wyth his longe swerde leyde on faste that
iij. amerallys deyde thorow the dynte of his hondis And
so Lovel fayled nat in the prees he slew a kynge and a deuke that
knyghtes were noble Than the Romaynes releved whan
they sye her lorde so hampred they chaced and choppedde
doune many of oure knyghtes good and in that rebukyng
they bare the bolde Bedwere to the colde erthe and wyth a
rauke swerde he was merveylously wounded yet sir
Launcelot and sir Lovel rescowed hym blythe. With that come
in kynge Arthure with the knyghtes of the Table Rounde and
rescowed the ryche men that nere were lyke to ascape
at that tyme for ofte tymes thorow envy grete hardynesse
is shewed that hath bene the deth of many kyd knyghtes for
thoughe they speke fayre many one unto other yet whan
they be in batayle eyther wolde beste be praysed
Now as kynge Arthure had a syght of the Emperour
Lucyus for kynge nother for Captayne he taryed
no lenger and eyther with her swerdys swapped at other so
Sir Lucyus with his swerde hit Arthure overthwarte the nose
and gaff hym a wounde nyghe unto the tunge Sir Arthure
was wroth and gaff hym another with all the myght that in his
arme was leved that frome the creste of his helme unto
the bare pappys hit wente adowne and so ended the Emperour
Than the kyng mette with Sir Cador his kene Cousyn
and prayde hym kylle downe clene for love of sir Kay

How Sir Gawayne slew iij. admyrallys in batayle

How kyng Arthure slew the Emperoure of Rome sir Lucyus

33. Sir Thomas Malory, *Morte Darthur*, British Libary Manuscript Add. 59678, f. 86v, by permission of the British Library

proper names in red ink and in a slightly more formal script than the rest of the text.[25] On folio 86v of the Winchester manuscript (Fig. 33), for example, which recounts part of Arthur's struggle against the Romans, the names constitute a lively reiteration of color on the page. To rubricate names throughout a text in this way must have represented a significant additional investment of time, as N.R. Ker, editor of the facsimile edition, explains: 'Personal names are very numerous, sometimes as many as two dozen on a page, and the scribes must have found the task of distinguishing them very laborious, particularly as they changed pen each time a name came up. . . . The distinguishing of personal names was evidently a matter of great consequence to the scribes.'[26] Whether the makers of the Winchester Manuscript understood Malory's interest in a multiplicity of characters, or coincidentally displayed all these names for another reason, any user of this manuscript would see Malory's constructed Arthurian world, at least in a literal sense, as dominated by the presentation of names.[27]

In accordance with the concept that events are crucially (though not exclusively) driven by human actions, Malory preserves and transmits a social ideology in which a great deal of freedom is allocated to men of the knightly class. For them, the opportunity for singular adventure, initiative and private choice is an everyday phenomenon, surprises and challenges are a normal component of experience, and time seems elastic – knights can wander for months or years at a time, but return, as it were, to the same page on the calendar, and in the meantime they do not worry about mundane responsibilities at home. As has long been noted, however, Malory's Arthurian society attempts to sustain an array of conflicting values, and this strong endorsement of individualism exists in tension with the alternative desire for companionship and community. The communal drive is expressed most strongly through the Round Table, whose function as a resident company of knights risks being undercut by the demands of adventuring, as Arthur recognizes at the start of the Grail quest, when he sadly predicts that after his knights 'departe frome hense I am sure they all shall never mete more togydir in thys worlde. . . . Wherefore hit shall greve me ryght sore, the departicion of thys felyship.'[28] The communal drive also extends beyond the Round Table membership, being evident as well in the glimpses of fathers and sons, or leaders and their companions, or lords and ladies in their castles along with the members of their households. Even a hermit may have the companionship of a 'fair child', like the one who answers Sir Lavaine's banging on the gate in search of assistance for the wounded Lancelot:

25 In giving this special treatment to the names, the two scribes who wrote this manuscript were presumably executing decisions made by someone responsible for the overall design of the volume; N.R. Ker notes that 'Scribe A was probably the leading scribe' (*The Winchester Malory: A Facsimile*, p. xiv). Andrew Lynch also remarks upon the importance of naming in Malory and notes the special attention given to names in the Winchester MS ('Good Name and Narrative in Malory', *Nottingham Medieval Studies*, 34 [1990], 141–51, esp. p. 143).

26 *The Winchester Malory: A Facsimile*, p. xiv. See further images at <http://www.imagesonline.bl.uk>.

27 By 'user' I intend not only actual readers, but also anyone who, lacking full literacy, might look at the book and discern, or be told, that the red words were all names.

28 Malory, *Works*, II. 866–67.

> And than sir Lavayne bete on the gate with the but of hys speare and cryed faste, 'Lat in, for Jesus sake!'
>
> And anone ther cam a fayre chylde to hem and asked them what they wolde.
>
> 'Fayre sone,' seyde sir Lavayne, 'go and pray thy lorde the ermyte for Goddys sake to late in here a knyght that ys full sore wounded. . . .'
>
> So the chylde wente in lyghtly, and than he brought the ermyte whych was a passynge lycly man.[29]

The hermit, it turns out, had attended the tournament at which Lancelot was wounded. Furthermore, having formerly been 'one of the felyship' of the Round Table,[30] he recognizes Lancelot by an old scar on his cheek. Even those who have ostensibly chosen an isolated or unworldly way of life are often revealed to have societal affiliations that they value.

Through situations such as this one, which briefly brings into view a fair child and a former knight of the court, the focus of attention is constantly diffused onto multiple personalities. To be sure, the very name *Morte Darthur* identifies the king as the central figure, and, as Edward Donald Kennedy has shown, Malory takes an extensive interest in the characterization of Arthur, making him 'a better king than he was in the sources' and establishing a detailed contrast between Arthur as a basically good ruler and the tyrant King Mark.[31]

Nevertheless, as has often been noted, Arthur's main knights often have more activity, agency and discretionary mobility than he does, and for considerable stretches of the narrative Tristan, Lancelot, Galahad or other members of the Round Table are foregrounded while the king recedes into the background. Arthurian society is only intermittently king-centered, being at other times demographically dense, populated with hundreds of characters, many of whom we cannot easily remember, for they are anonymous or appear only briefly. The extreme example is the profusion of more than a hundred knights whose names are listed when Arthur's fellowship gathers in an attempt to cure Sir Urry of his wound.[32] In this type of society – with attention deflected away from the king for sustained intervals and distributed among many other individuals – perhaps Sir Thomas Malory, Knight, saw an ancestral place of importance for figures such as himself.

Despite this displacement of the king's centrality, however, there is no shift towards a Chaucerian empathetic recognition of many levels and constituent elements of society. Instead, Malory preserves and transmits admiration for 'noble' ways of life and standards of decorum. There is a proper way to do things, a sense of custom, ritual, formality and ceremony, and in many situations an explicit hierarchy. For example, hospitality is regularly extended to strangers, if they are traveling knights; in contrast, lowly travelers are nearly invisible. Early in his reign, when Arthur has drawn the sword from the stone, the commons support his claim to the crown,[33] but in much of the *Morte Darthur*

29 Malory, *Works*, II. 1074–75.
30 Malory, *Works*, II. 1075.
31 Edward Donald Kennedy, 'Malory's King Mark and King Arthur', *King Arthur: A Casebook*, ed. and intro. Edward Donald Kennedy (New York, 1996), pp. 139–71, esp. p. 161.
32 Malory, *Works*, III. 1146–50.
33 Malory, *Works*, I. 15–19.

if there is an occasional glimpse of ordinary people, it is usually not to their favor. Near the end, for example, Sir Lucan sees looters pillaging and killing the wounded on the battlefield when the last fight has been won and lost:

> So sir Lucan departed, for he was grevously wounded in many placis; and so as he yode he saw and harkened by the moonelyght how that pyllours and robbers were com into the fylde to pylle and to robbe many a full noble knyght . . . . And who that were nat dede all oute, there they slewe them for their harneys and their ryches.[34]

Though he would have belonged to the gentry, not the aristocracy, 'noble' is one of Malory's favorite words,[35] and his perspective is firmly that of the knightly class. It is also primarily male, as is shown, for example, in the interest in battles and in tournaments, and in Sir Ector's final tribute to the dead Lancelot, with its summation of chivalric virtues:

> . . . 'thou sir Launcelot . . . thou were never matched of erthely knyghtes hande. And thou were the curtest knyght that ever bare shelde! And thou were the truest frende to thy lovar that ever bestrade hors, and thou were the trewest lover, of a synful man, that ever loved woman, and thou were the kyndest man that ever strake wyth swerde. And thou were the godelyest persone that ever cam emonge prees of knyghtes, and thou was the mekest man and the jentyllest that ever ete in halle emonge ladyes, and thou were the sternest knyght to thy mortal foo that ever put spere in the reeste.'[36]

The civilization constituted by these norms and codes is not coextensive with either national or regional identity, for behavioral and ethical codes as defined by the fellowship of the Round Table are transnationally acknowledged, even if not always observed. Wherever the Grail seekers go, for instance, they meet strangers who understand their ways, though sometimes from oppositional stances of hostility. Virtually everyone speaks the same language, even if they use it to challenge each other. This is perhaps not a mere narrative convention, but more profoundly an assumption that European aristocratic and Christian expectations and ideas will be intelligible anywhere that Arthur or his companions might find themselves. Arthur's empire is not only a vast, unpacified realm of innumerable territories and personalities; it is also an empire of the mind, with the presumption of mutually comprehended ideologies and aristocratic values.

34 Malory, *Works*, III. 1237–38.

35 On Malory's gentry status and interests, see Field, 'The Malory Life-Records', in *A Companion to Malory*, p. 115; Karen Cherewatuk, ' "Gentyl" Audiences and "Grete Bookes": Chivalric Manuals and the *Morte Darthur*', *Arthurian Literature* XV (1997), 205–16; Raluca Radulescu, '*John Vale's Book* and Sir Thomas Malory's *Le Morte Darthur*: A Political Agenda', *Arthuriana*, 9.4 (1999), 69–80; and Hyonjin Kim, *The Knight Without the Sword: A Social Landscape of Malorian Chivalry* (Cambridge, 2000). In the Winchester text the word 'noble' occurs 440 times, or, including forms such as 'nobelest', 'noblesse', etc., 505 times. It is one of the most frequent terms after function-words such as 'of', 'an', 'aftir', common verbs, pronouns, etc., and names such as 'Arthure' and 'Launcelot'. See *A Concordance to the Works of Sir Thomas Malory*, ed. Tomomi Kato (Tokyo, 1974).

36 Malory, *Works*, III. 1259.

In an important passage in which Malory mourns England's turning away from Arthur to follow Mordred, a betrayal which meant the passing of the noble world he had constructed, he acknowledges that instability, its crucial weakness, characterizes his own time as well:

> Lo, ye all Englysshemen, se ye nat what a myschyff here was? For he that was the moste kynge and nobelyst knyght of the worlde, and moste loved the felyshyp of noble knyghtes, and by hym they all were upholdyn, and yet myght nat thes Englyshemen holde them contente with hym. Lo thus was the olde custom and usayges of thys londe, and men say that we of thys londe have nat yet loste that custom. Alas! Thys ys a greate defaughte of us Englysshemen, for there may no thynge us please no terme.[37]

Given what the life-records suggest about his own role as a man and a soldier, Malory may not have been a distinguished exemplar of the values represented in Ector's praise of Lancelot or in this characterization of Arthur, 'the moste kynge and nobelyst knyght of the worlde', but in his role as writer he was surely a noble 'conservator', as Caxton might have put it.

III

Following Caxton's edition of 1485, the *Morte Darthur* was printed again, more or less complete, in 1498, 1529, 1557, ca. 1578 and 1634, after which there was a hiatus for nearly two hundred years until two editions appeared in 1816, to be followed by seven more editions or printings and a dozen adaptations and abridgements prior to 1900.[38] And of course the twentieth century saw Malories of many descriptions, including children's books, modernizations or selections intended for the reading public, textbooks for students and critical editions for scholars, along with a great many versions of the Arthurian legend in print and electronic media in which more distant relationships to Malory can be discerned. Though space does not permit discussion of the diverse ways in which the profusion of editors, adaptors and illustrators responsible for these many renderings has reconsidered Malory, I will briefly discuss a small set of examples, including illustrations, to suggest ways in which some of these 'conservators' have tended to preserve Malory, while others have veered away from concepts (such as those sketched above) that his narrative conveys.

The tendency toward emotional tension, even madness, which in the *Morte Darthur* is associated with the adulterous love and the conflict of loyalties it entails, has also been a focus of interest and an opportunity for visual depiction by some of his later redactors. In an illustration by Andrew Wyeth for a modernized Malory, for example (see Fig. 34), a tormented Lancelot turns his back on an

37 Malory, *Works*, III. 1229.

38 Editions and adaptations are listed in Parins, *Malory: The Critical Heritage*, pp. 40–46; see also A.S.G. Edwards, 'The Reception of Malory's Morte Darthur', in *A Companion to Malory*, pp. 241–52. Several items pertinent to Malory are included in 'Arthurian Literature, Art, and Film, 1995–1999', ed. Norris J. Lacy and Raymond H. Thompson, *Arthurian Literature* XVIII (2001), 193–255.

34. Lancelot and Guenever

anxious Guenevere; he chews his knuckles and knits his brow, yet retains something of his heroic stature because of the way his body dominates the scene. This book was published in 1943, in wartime, when conflicts between desire and duty may have had a special urgency.[39] Allowing for the complete difference of medium and idiom, Wyeth's Lancelot may be regarded as a lineal extension of Malory's, preserving assumptions and values that are not inconsistent with his.

In contrast, sometimes a redactor's glance backwards, reconsidering Malory, sees something other than what Malory seems to have seen. For example, in Aubrey Beardsley's illustrations to the *Morte Darthur*, published at the end of the nineteenth century,[40] characters who in Malory were 'noble' despite their faults are interpreted with strange or exaggerated traits that nudge them almost in the direction of ugliness. Beardsley's figures are often awkward, joyless, grotesque, or in other respects more sharply negative than in the text of Malory that they accompany. Particularly disturbing is his picture of Guenevere (Fig. 35) when she has become a nun at Amesbury after Arthur's death: she appears as a hunched and massive figure that occludes the shape of the female body as such and dominates the frame with scarcely relieved blackness. In the absence of grace or beauty, Guenevere's power has almost become menace. As Aymer Vallance remarked,

39 *Arthur Pendragon of Britain: A Romantic Narrative by Sir Thomas Malory as edited from Le Morte Darthur*, by John W. Donaldson, illus. Andrew Wyeth (New York, 1943), illus. facing page 276. Fig. 34 by permission of Andrew Wyeth.

40 Beardsley's illustrations were first published in *Le Morte Darthvr By Sir Thomas Malory, Knt, The Introduction By Professor Rhys, The Designs by Aubrey Beardsley* (London, pub. in parts, 1893–94). They are available in facsimile: *Beardsley's Illustrations for Le Morte Darthur, Reproduced in Facsimile. . .*, Arranged by Edmund V. Gillon, Jr. (New York, 1972).

35. Guenevere at Amesbury

> . . . Beardsley did not really find the subject of the 'Morte Darthur' congenial . . . . Not only was Beardsley out of sympathy with the 'Morte', but he was actually heard to boast that he had never taken the trouble to read it. He could not, it is true, avoid dipping into its pages . . . for such bare suggestions as were indispensable for affording themes for the more important pictures; but his reading was desultory. . . .[41]

Beardsley's distaste for Malory has produced distortion, one might argue, rather than preservation, though seeing ugliness in Guenevere or in the love affair is not unique to him.

Sometimes a contrast to Malory's work as 'conservator' is achieved not through distortion, but through omission. In Sidney Lanier's 1950 rendering, for example, the scene in which Lancelot is discovered in Guenevere's bedroom is omitted; the bland statement 'So it befell that the queen was again accused of treason and was condemned to the fire, while Sir Launcelot was away' suffices to

41 Aymer Vallance, 'Foreword', in *The Birth Life and Acts of King Arthur . . . as Written by Sir Thomas Malory . . . with many original designs by Aubrey Beardsley. . .*, intro. John Rhys (New York, 1927), p. vij. Fig. 35 by permission from the facsimile ed. (n. 40).

36. Guenevere at the stake

explain why she must be rescued from the stake.[42] Similarly, Malory's pervasive interest in battle is frequently elided or minimized in nineteenth- and twentieth-century representations. As Andrew Lynch has pointed out, in the nineteenth century there developed a 'radical re-emphasis of *Le Morte Darthur* . . . when . . . versions of Malory consistently disparaged, downplayed, or falsely moralised his major narrative preoccupation – the description of knightly combat'.[43] Battle descriptions, once presumably of great interest to readers but later found to be tedious and repetitious, are often bypassed or suppressed both in selections made for abridged versions and in the choice of scenes to illustrate, though Lynch finds battle to have been 'Malory's most passionate interest and predominant thematic matter'.[44]

Such renderings of Malory involve extension (Wyeth), distortion (Beardsley) and omission (Lanier and the versions that minimize combat). In a further distancing from the 'noble' legacy of Malory, certain redactions have endorsed qualities antithetical to his, reflecting alternative ideologies of preservation. Perhaps as a concomitant of democratization, for example, sometimes the Arthurian characters are reduced towards the everyday. One such interpretation is conveyed by the picture of Guenevere at the stake in a modernized abridgment and adaptation of Malory published in 1929 by Henry Gilbert and illustrated by Frances Brundage (see Fig. 36).[45] Though the text in this version says that

42 *King Arthur and His Knights of the Round Table, from Sir Thomas Malory's Le Morte d'Arthur*, ed. Sidney Lanier, illus. Florian (New York, 1950), p. 245.

43 Andrew Lynch, 'Malory Moralisé: The Disarming of *Le Morte Darthur*, 1800–1918', *Arthuriana*, 9.4 (1999), 81–93, esp. pp. 81–82.

44 Lynch, 'Malory Moralisé', p. 82.

45 Henry Gilbert, *King Arthur*, illustrations by Frances Brundage (Chicago, 1929), illus. p. 164.

Guenevere, about to be led to the stake, 'would bear herself proudly like a queen', and that at the stake 'she stood, pale and still',[46] in the illustration she is sitting down on the faggots of wood, clutching her hands in anxiety, gazing a little upwards, not particularly beautiful, somewhat bedraggled – almost a generic picture of woman as victim, with only the indistinct headgear suggesting that this is the queen. What is preserved here is the surface of the narrative, not its qualities of hierarchy, nobility, or chivalry, nor the expectation that the queen should stand tall, because she *is* a queen. Here, as with Beardsley, a different value-system is operating, but this one may deviate even further from Malory, for Beardsley's Guenevere, visually dominating and powerful, remains compelling in her own way, while Brundage's is merely ordinary.

Just as Malory reconsidered the Arthurian past, so more recent editions, printings and adaptations of the *Morte Darthur* have reconsidered what he wrote. It has been suggested here that part of the cohesion of his long and varied work[47] comes from its representation of an Arthurian past characterized by human agency and the correlative values of individualism, fellowship and an aristocratic hierarchy of virtues. The synthesis he achieved is nevertheless a shaky one, vulnerable to tensions and disruptions, and some of the qualities visible in later reconsiderations, especially the tendency to reduce his 'noble' personages – appreciated as such since Caxton's time – towards ordinariness would further destabilize that synthesis. However, as Malory's own work shows, the Arthurian past is always open to further layers of both change and preservation according to the positions, temporal and ideological, from which it is seen by each new 'conservator'.

46 Gilbert, *King Arthur*, pp. 163, 165.

47 For the term 'cohesion' ('coherent') see D.S. Brewer, ed., *The Morte Darthur*, pp. 2, 9.

The Old Order Changeth: King Arthur in the Modern World

ALAN LUPACK

In Alfred, Lord Tennyson's 'The Passing of Arthur', Bedivere, the last survivor of the fellowship of the Round Table, asks Arthur, who is about to leave in the barge for Avalon, where he should go now that he must make his way ' ". . . companionless, / And the days darken round me, and the years, / Among new men, strange faces, other minds." And slowly answered Arthur from the barge', Tennyson writes, ' "The old order changeth, yielding place to new, / And God fulfils himself in many ways, / Lest one good custom should corrupt the world" '.[1]

The paradox that Arthur uses to console Bedivere – how, after all, can a *good* custom corrupt the world? – seems to apply to Arthurian literature and art as much as it does to the passing of Arthur in the poem, where it suggests the need for change, growth, evolution. Stagnation is the enemy of the human spirit: without change there is no growth from the level of the beasts towards the level of the angels, a metaphor as important in Tennyson's poem (and to which I will return below) as it was to the Elizabethan world picture. Stagnation is the enemy of art and legend as well. Stories remain vital by changing, and no story is more adaptable than that of Arthur with its large cast of characters and its complex of fascinating narratives. Like Bedivere, the Arthurian legends have gone forth and been adapted anew 'Among new men [and women], strange faces, other minds' than those of the medieval authors who popularized the Matter of Britain. Though the fortunes of Arthur have risen and fallen throughout the ages, he has remained a presence, sometimes more, sometimes less dominant in literary and cultural history.

In discussing the fortunes of Arthur, one must keep in mind that the Arthurian legend is many stories at the same time that it is one story – something that great writers like Malory and Tennyson know intuitively but that modern critics have sometimes forgotten. The legend is comprised of a complex of stories – the stories of Lancelot and Guinevere; Tristan and Isolt; Sir Gawain, who has been portrayed as both model of courtly behavior and near-brute; the Holy Grail and its heroes, from Perceval and Galahad to Launfal and Dagonet to Indiana Jones;

1 Alfred Tennyson, *Idylls of the King and a Selection of Poems*, ed. George Barker (New York, 1961), p. 251.

Elaine of Astolat, who dies of unrequited love for Lancelot; Morgan le Fay, who throughout her history is transformed from healer to wicked magician, to ally and mother of Mordred, to feminist heroine; Merlin, who, in various works, is a magician, prophet, warrior, shapeshifter, superstitious humbug, descendant of the devil or of an alien race from outer space; and others too numerous to name. Indeed, it is the range of characters and stories that make up the Arthurian legend that gives it its vitality.

But in keeping with the theme of this volume, this essay will focus on the figure of Arthur. Although many of the works called 'Arthurian' say little or nothing about the king himself, he is always the symbolic source and the center of the legend, and, in almost every age in which stories about him have been written, he appears as the literal center of major, and sometimes minor, works. A representative sampling of these works demonstrates the fortunes of Arthur in English and American cultural history.

A little more than a century after Caxton published Malory's *Morte d'Arthur*, an Elizabethan playwright named Thomas Hughes wrote a tragedy called *The Misfortunes of Arthur* (1587). Drawing on the chronicle tradition descending ultimately from Geoffrey of Monmouth to dramatize Arthur's downfall, Hughes recounts Gueneuora's betrayal of Arthur with Mordred, Mordred's usurpation, Arthur's return from his wars on the continent, and the final battle with Mordred. On the one hand, the *Misfortunes* is in the tradition of the medieval tragedy of fortune. Arthur complains about Fortune's fickleness, and the chorus proclaims that Fortune overturns the lofty. Arthur's ally Cador sums up the inevitable turning of the wheel of Fortune: 'thus *Fortune* gibes: / She hoyseth vp to hurle the deeper downe';[2] and the messenger who reports events of the battle observes that: 'There *Fortune* laid the prime of *Brytaines pride,* / There laide her pompe, all topsie turvie turnde'.[3]

However, despite the play's medieval roots, it has been thoroughly adapted to the conventions of its time. Besides using numerous classical allusions, it adopts many of the conventions of the revenge tragedy popularized by Renaissance interest in Senecan drama. The action of the *Misfortunes* begins, as does *Hamlet*, with a ghost calling for revenge – in this case, the ghost of Gorlois, first husband of Igerna, seeking revenge on the house of Uther Pendragon. The play makes abundant use of stichomythia, the line-for-line exchanges typical of Senecan style. The major gory action of the *Misfortunes*, including the events of the final battle up to the killing of Mordred and the fatal wounding of Arthur, is reported by a messenger and not depicted on the stage.

Though not one of the great works of Renaissance drama, *The Misfortunes of Arthur* is a good example of how Arthurian material has been adapted for a new audience. In the seventeenth century, there are other such examples. John Dryden's 'dramatic opera' *King Arthur*, the music for which was composed by Henry Purcell, was originally written in 1684 during the reign of Charles II (who ruled 1660–1685) and, according to Dryden's preface, revised radically to reflect

2 Thomas Hughes, *The Misfortunes of Arthur*, in *Early English Classical Tragedies* (Oxford, 1912), p. 284.

3 Hughes, p. 279.

a new political situation, the reign of William and Mary (1689–1702), for its publication in 1691 and first performance in January of 1692. Dryden's original intention in writing the play was apparently to honor King Charles as a modern incarnation of Arthur, a position that would have been less politic when it was actually published and performed.

The action of the play seems strange to a modern audience. The well known characters of romance are generally absent; only Arthur and Merlin appear. Guinevere is replaced as the object of Arthur's love by Emmeline, the blind daughter of Arthur's ally Conon, Duke of Cornwall. She is loved, in turn, both by the Saxon leader Oswald and by his magician Osmond. The play builds on the chronicle tradition of Arthur's battles with the Saxons; but unlike *The Misfortunes of Arthur* and other Renaissance plays dealing with the chronicle material, Dryden's account is a heroic Restoration play that is as interested in amorous as dynastic conflict. Dryden does dramatize 'several problems related to the empiricist philosophy that arose in the latter half of the seventeenth century in England, including reliability of the senses as a basis for knowledge . . .',[4] and this supports 'the controlling motif in the opera, the motif of perception'.[5] But in the end the play is not a study of philosophical concepts but rather a melodrama drawing on the idiom of contemporary ideas as well as contemporary drama.

The military struggle between Arthur and Oswald, who, as James Merriman has observed, are 'nothing but a pair of Restoration beaux',[6] is subordinated to their struggle for Emmeline; Arthur even offers to share his kingdom with Oswald if he will surrender Emmeline. Both conflicts culminate in a single combat in which Arthur is the victor. But before this resolution is possible, Merlin must overcome the magic of the heathen sorcerer Osmond who enchants a forest and binds Emmeline with a charm that can be overcome only when the spell on the forest is broken.

In contrast to the wicked, deceptive heathen Osmond, who even betrays Oswald because of his own lust for Emmeline, Merlin uses his magic to enlighten Arthur and others, a function that is depicted symbolically by his literally curing Emmeline of her blindness. In the end, Merlin restores order in such a way that even the enemy is accommodated. He predicts not only Arthur's fame as the first of the three Christian Worthies but also the eventual union of Britons and Saxons who will be bound together 'in perpetual Peace' by 'One Common tongue, one Common Faith'.[7] Yet, despite the harmonious resolution, Dryden's play remains 'a commercial product whose direct modern heir is the Broadway musical'[8] and not one of the highpoints of Arthurian literature. Nevertheless, it demonstrates the way in which Arthur can be adapted to the tastes of an age, just as modern dramas like *Camelot* and modern films do.

4 Eric Jager, 'Educating the Senses: Empiricism in Dryden's *King Arthur*', *Restoration: Studies in English Literary Culture, 1660–1700* (1987), 107.

5 J.M. Armistead, 'Dryden's *King Arthur* and the Literary Tradition: A Way of Seeing', *Studies in Philology*, 85.1 (1988), 57.

6 James Merriman, *The Flower of Kings: A Study of the Arthurian Legend in England Between 1485 and 1835* (Lawrence, KS, 1973), p. 63.

7 John Dryden, *King Arthur or The British Worthy*, in *The Works of John Dryden*, vol. 16, ed. Vinton A. Dearing (Berkeley, 1996), p. 60.

8 Merriman, *The Flower of Kings*, p. 64.

Other adaptations of the story of King Arthur followed Dryden's play. The physician Richard Blackmore, for example, wrote two epics, *Prince Arthur* in 1695 and *King Arthur* in 1697, in which Arthur's life and wars represent those of William III. The poems combine an allegory of the Glorious Revolution and the reign of William and Mary with Miltonic trappings, without Miltonic art, I fear, to produce a roman à clef in which demonic forces oppose Arthur and heavenly forces assist him. It is difficult to say whether these long poems have moved Arthurian literature up or down on the wheel of fortune; but in any case the poems surely adapt the Matter of Britain to the political concerns and the poetic style of the age.

In the eighteenth century, an age known for rationality and satire, the wheel of Arthur's fortunes is generally considered to be at a low point, but there are some fascinating developments in Arthur's story, including a version of the tale of Tom Thumb dramatized by Henry Fielding in a play called *Tom Thumb* (1730), which was revised as *The Tragedy of Tragedies* (1731). Drawing on a tradition found in chapbooks of the seventeenth and eighteenth centuries, Fielding makes Tom Thumb a knight of Arthur's court, whose very conception was engineered by Merlin; and he uses the somewhat absurd story as a means of satirizing everything from the politics and drama of his day to doctors and lawyers.

Arthur himself has a relatively minor role, but he is unmistakably not the hero of medieval romance. He is married not to Guinevere of fabled beauty but to Queen Dollallolla, a big-bosomed, bawdy, boozing broad who is herself in love with Tom Thumb. In one of the jokes of the play, she weighs her virtue against the diminutive knight and finds that he is the heavier. In *The Tragedy of Tragedies*, Arthur himself feels a pain within his breast when he sees Glumdalca, the queen of the Giants, who has been captured by Tom Thumb – though Arthur is at first not sure whether it arises 'from Love, / Or only the Wind-cholick'.[9] Whether Arthur's pangs are caused by Glumdalca or by gas, the old order of courtly love has yielded place to something new. Glumdalca in turn is in love with Tom and wants him to fill the bed formerly occupied by her twenty giant husbands. But Tom is promised to Arthur's daughter Huncamunca; and the Parson who is to marry them wishes, in one of a number of mock-heroic similes in the play, that they will propagate and fill the land with Tom Thumbs just as maggots breed in a Cheshire cheese until 'by thousands, and ten thousands they increase, / Till one continued Maggot fills the rotten Cheese'.[10]

Arthur himself does nothing heroic in the play. When Lord Grizzle, who loves Huncamunca, leads a rebellion against the king, it is Tom who beheads him, only to be eaten by a cow before he can enjoy his triumph. When the queen kills the messenger who brings news of Tom's death, she sets off a train of murders, six in all, that parodies the bloody endings of heroic tragedy. In a final satiric flourish, Fielding has Arthur, the last left alive, kill himself. In a Preface to *The Tragedy of Tragedies*, Fielding notes that the tragedy teaches two lessons: the first, exemplified by Tom's death, is that 'Human Happiness is exceeding

9 Henry Fielding, *Tom Thumb and the Tragedy of Tragedies*, ed. L.J. Morrissey (1730 and 1731; repr. Berkeley, 1970), p. 57.
10 Fielding, *Tom Thumb and the Tragedy of Tragedies*, p. 79.

transient'; and the second, exemplified by the death of all the other characters, is that 'Death is the certain End of all Men'.[11] The banality of the morals is of course part of the satire, especially as it contrasts with the tragic complexity usually involved in the death of Arthur.

But Arthur's fortunes were to rise again. Even in the eighteenth century there was the beginning of a resurgence. Bishop Percy, in his *Reliques of Ancient English Poetry* (1765), included Arthurian ballads and considered Arthurian material to be as instructive as the Classics. And Arthur makes a more dignified, though not more entertaining, appearance in Richard Hole's *Arthur or the Northern Enchantment* (1789) than he did in Fielding's burlesque.

It is not, however, until the Victorians take up Arthur that he becomes the amazingly popular figure that he is today. Arthur's popularity is due partly to the publication of three new editions of Malory's *Morte d'Arthur* early in the nineteenth century (two in 1816 and one in 1817) and the rediscovery and transformation of this great work by artists and poets. Chief among them was Alfred Tennyson, whose interest in Arthur spanned most of his creative life.

A central event in Tennyson's life was the death of his beloved friend Arthur Hallam at the age of twenty-two in 1833. This tragedy informed much of Tennyson's poetry for the rest of his life and led directly to the writing of one of the greatest English elegiac poems, *In Memoriam*. As John D. Rosenberg has so perceptively observed, it is no coincidence that a draft of Tennyson's 'Morte d'Arthur', which later became part of the idyll 'The Passing of Arthur', 'appears in the same notebook that contains the earliest sections of *In Memoriam*'.[12]

Added to this personal association of King Arthur with Arthur Hallam are larger patterns that make the *Idylls* much more than an idealization of a lost friend. As the *Idylls of the King* grew from the 'Morte d'Arthur' to the completed collection, Tennyson maintained a thematic and structural consistency that not only is compelling in its own right but also seems to be a perfect reflection of the Victorian age. In addition to – and probably more essential than – his stated theme of soul at war with sense, Tennyson consistently balances 'the true and the false', appearance and reality; and he presents characters who, like all of us, must cope with the fact that things are sometimes better and often worse than they seem. The resulting tensions thus have a universal significance at the same time that they are a metaphor for an age that was itself torn between faith and doubt, hope and despair.

Arthur is most prominent in the two idylls that frame the body of the work, 'The Coming of Arthur' and 'The Passing of Arthur', but he plays an important symbolic role in others. He is the 'stainless King' and the 'blameless King'.[13] So perfect is he that Tennyson first defies tradition by making Uther and Igraine conceive Arthur after the death of Gorloïs and then creates an alternate story of a mystical coming of Arthur. Bellicent (the name Tennyson gives to the mother of Gawain and his brothers) reports that Bleys, Merlin's 'master', told her that

11 Fielding, *Tom Thumb and the Tragedy of Tragedies*, pp. 43–44.

12 John D. Rosenberg, 'Tennyson and the Passing of Arthur', in *The Passing of Arthur: New Essays in Arthurian Tradition*, ed. Christopher Baswell and William Sharpe (New York, 1988), p. 229.

13 Tennyson, *Idylls of the King and a Selection of Poems*, pp. 118, 120.

on the night that Uther died, he and Merlin saw a ship 'Bright with a shining people on the decks',[14] and then waves washing the shore. The ninth wave carried a baby to Merlin's feet, a baby whom the mage recognized as an heir for Uther.

Arthur's dedication to his duty; the recognition that there is an order to the world and that each person has a role to play; that departing from that role, even for what some may see as a higher cause (like seeking the Grail), is a flaw – all of these things make Arthur the superior being he is. In fact, in the evolutionary scheme of the poem, Arthur has evolved beyond most men and thus can be an example to them. In the wonderful description of Camelot, we hear of the scenes carved around the castle:

> And four great zones of sculpture, set betwixt
> With many a mystic symbol, gird the hall:
> And in the lowest beasts are slaying men,
> And in the second men are slaying beasts,
> And on the third are warriors, perfect men,
> And on the fourth are men with growing wings,
> And over all one statue in the mould
> Of Arthur, made by Merlin, with a crown,
> And peaked wings pointed to the Northern Star.
> And eastward fronts the statue, and the crown
> And both the wings are made of gold, and flame
> At sunrise till the people in far fields,
> Wasted so often by the heathen hordes,
> Behold it, crying, 'We have still a King.'[15]

This image of Arthur, the Arthur who has slain the beasts in his kingdom and the beast in himself and who has progressed – should we say evolved? – beyond most men so that he approaches the level of the angels (an image that combines medieval and Renaissance ideas of the chain of being with nineteenth-century notions of evolution), this Arthur hovers over the *Idylls* as his statue does over Camelot. And even in those idylls in which he is not the central figure, he is the symbolic point of light, the moral exemplar to which his knights and indeed all in his kingdom look for order and direction.

Guinevere herself calls Arthur 'the faultless King, / That passionate perfection', a compliment qualified when she adds, 'But who can gaze upon the Sun in heaven?'[16] It is this formidable Arthur before whom Guinevere 'grovell'd with her face against the floor'[17] when Arthur visits her in the nunnery – a scene that appalled some nineteenth-century writers as much as it does modern feminist critics. But who can blame her for groveling when Arthur appears so intimidating, almost other-worldly? Arthur's helmet is crested with a golden dragon, his visor is lowered, and Guinevere does not even see his face,

14 Tennyson, *Idylls of the King and a Selection of Poems*, p. 23.
15 Tennyson, *Idylls of the King and a Selection of Poems*, p. 176.
16 Tennyson, *Idylls of the King and a Selection of Poems*, p. 141.
17 Tennyson, *Idylls of the King and a Selection of Poems*, p. 234.

Which then was as an angel's, but she saw,
Wet with the mists and smitten by the lights,
The Dragon of the great Pendragonship
Blaze, making all the night a steam of fire.[18]

We empathize with Guinevere, not wanting to gaze upon the Sun of perfection, not wanting to meet the eyes of the blameless king when she feels she has committed an act so blameworthy that it has brought down a kingdom. It is hard not to feel that Arthur is too perfect, too stern. Even in this final meeting, one of a number of great dramatic scenes in the poem, wherein Arthur forgives and says he still loves Guinevere, he reminds her that she has 'spoilt the purpose of my life'.[19]

If we may forgive and even love the Arthur of the idylls, even as we remind ourselves of his flaw of flawlessness, it is because he stands for something. He lives by a code and demands that his knights live by a code. Gareth, departing for Camelot, says he must 'Live pure, speak true, right wrong, follow the King – / Else, wherefore born?'[20] But as Gareth approaches Camelot, he meets Merlin – another of those great dramatic scenes in the *Idylls* – and the mage tells the young, idealistic knight that the King ' "Will bind thee by such vows, as is a shame / A man should not be bound by, yet the which / No man can keep . . ." ' The specifics of the code in the *Idylls* are spelled out in the final meeting between Arthur and Guinevere[21] but may be summarized as keeping down the base in man, that is, overcoming the beastly part of human nature.

Tennyson's epic is a highpoint in the fortunes of Arthur because Tennyson, as did Malory and most of the best writers of Arthurian literature throughout the ages, realized that Camelot is about codes. And Tennyson's importance in the development of Arthurian literature is in part the result of his turning knighthood into a moral matter, as he does in the *Idylls* and in his extremely popular and influential poem 'Sir Galahad', in which Galahad's strength is as the strength of ten because his heart is pure.

Just as Tennyson is the central nineteenth-century figure in the development of the story of Arthur, so T.H. White is central to the twentieth century. And like Tennyson, White looked to Malory and, also like Tennyson, radically altered the form and content to make his own comment on the fortunes of Arthur. Yet, like other authors, medieval and modern, he saw the story of Arthur as a tragedy. White published the first three parts as separate books and then gathered them together with the fourth part and published the whole as *The Once and Future King* in 1958. In a 1939 journal entry, White refers to the parts of his Arthuriad as his 'quadruplets'.[22] White originally planned a tetralogy that was to treat what he called 'the Doom of Arthur' and even intended that the fourth volume would 'be in the form of a straightforward play or tragedy'.[23] But at some stage he

18 Tennyson, *Idylls of the King and a Selection of Poems*, pp. 238–39.
19 Tennyson, *Idylls of the King and a Selection of Poems*, p. 235.
20 Tennyson, *Idylls of the King and a Selection of Poems*, p. 30.
21 Tennyson, *Idylls of the King and a Selection of Poems*, p. 236.
22 Cited in Elisabeth Brewer, *T.H. White's The Once and Future King* (Cambridge, 1993), p. 17.
23 T.H. White, *Letters to a Friend: The Correspondence Between T.H. White and L.J. Potts*, ed. François Gallix (New York, 1982), pp. 109, 111.

decided to abandon that plan and to shift from a four-part to a five-part book, intending to conclude with *The Book of Merlyn*.

At the same time that White was developing this five-part structure, his conception of the book was shifting from a classical tragedy to something more in line with what he says he 'suddenly discovered', that is, that 'the central theme of *Morte d'Arthur* is to find an antidote to war'.[24] Nevertheless, his sense of the work as a tragedy is still evident. In the 1958 *Once and Future King*, at the end of the second part, 'The Queen of Air and Darkness', White writes that though most of Malory's book – and by implication his own – deals with knights and quests, 'the narrative is a whole, and it deals with the reasons why the young man came to grief at the end. It is the tragedy, the Aristotelian and comprehensive tragedy, of sin coming home to roost'[25] (which might serve as a description of *The Misfortunes of Arthur* as well). *The Book of Merlyn* is important in understanding White's artistry in *The Once and Future King*, not so much because it is the most blatant exploration of the theme of war, which remains part of the point of the book in its ultimate revision, but mainly because it is the key to a brilliant experiment in artistic construction, in which the book grows up with the characters as it progresses from a children's story to a *bildungsroman*, to a romance, to a tragedy, to a philosophical treatise.

But the omission of *The Book of Merlyn* was the right decision. It forced White to conclude his book with the tragic ending that it has. Since true tragedy involves triumph, ending with the tragedy requires ending with the triumph of Arthur, a triumph that involves a code. Arthur's great achievement in *The Once and Future King* is to apply what he has learned from Merlin and to arrive at the notion that Might does not make Right but that Might must be used for Right. It is Arthur's dedication to law and justice, the basis of his simple but profound code, that Mordred uses against him. Like all true villains, from Iago to Osama, Mordred knows that using people's strengths against them can do more harm than using their weaknesses. But it is also this code – the idea of 'fighting for truth, and to help weak people, and to redress wrongs'[26] – that is the candle in the wind that Arthur passes on to young Tom Malory.

In the end, time, so essential to the book, is part of its ultimate theme. There is not enough time in a person's life to solve the great problems like war and human iniquity and the tragic consequences that result from them, and not enough time to teach the things that make it possible to solve these problems, not even enough time for someone like Merlin who lives many lifetimes. Thus art and culture, embodied in the young Tom Malory, become crucial so that each generation is not always starting anew, so that the code can be preserved and absorbed even when Merlin or some Merlin figure like T.H. White is not around to teach. Malory's presence in the novel, accepted because of the pattern of anachronism and the muddled medieval time in which the story takes place, allows White to announce that the conclusion of his tale is not 'The End' but 'THE BEGINNING'. White's Merlin said that 'the best thing for being sad . . . is

24 White, *Letters to a Friend*, p. 120.
25 T.H. White, *The Once and Future King* (1958; repr. New York, 1967), p. 312.
26 White, *Once and Future King*, p. 636.

to learn something'.[27] The ending of *The Once and Future King* implies that the best answer to macrocosmic sorrows like war and human evil is indeed to learn something – from the examples of books like Malory's *Morte D'Arthur* and White's own Arthuriad.

In America, where Arthur's story is probably more popular than it is in Britain, there is a long tradition of seeing Arthur and his realm in moral terms. Indeed the concept of moral knighthood is one of the main ways that Americans democratize the legends and adapt them to American values and ideals. It is a tradition that extends beyond works in which Arthur is the central figure but is clearly present in some of those as well. The moral code that Arthur represents and that defines knighthood and at times kingship is a key element in the popularizing of chivalric tales in the nineteenth and early twentieth centuries and in the notion that tales about Arthur and his knights – those very tales that Roger Ascham rightly described as dealing with open manslaughter and bold bawdry – were suitable models of moral conduct for children.

In 1893, a minister named William Byron Forbush founded an organization called The Knights of King Arthur, originally for boys between the ages of thirteen and sixteen, a time when they 'are said by psychologists to be in the knightly period, and it is just then that they respond to the ritual, regalia and the glamor of exclusiveness'.[28] The general plan outlined by Forbush was fairly simple and flexible. Each castle (as the local clubs were called) is 'a fraternity, private but not secret, self-governing and under the control of the local church. It is based upon the oldest English Christian legend, that of the Round Table. It is a revival of the nobler side of medieval chivalry. The thought is to fulfill the prophecy of King Arthur that he would return to re-establish a kingdom of righteousness, honor and service.'[29]

Forbush's concept of the legends as suitable to American youth was based on his understanding of the Arthurian material, an understanding that came largely from Tennyson. In fact, the boys in the club were advised to read the *Idylls of the King*; and to advance to the degree of Knight, a boy had to memorize the lines from Tennyson's 'Guinevere' which begin 'In that fair Order of my Table Round',[30] the lines that contain the impossible vows to which Arthur makes his knights swear.

In *The Boys' Round Table*, the manual for the Knights of King Arthur, Forbush and his co-author Frank Masseck noted that 'Although the framework of the order is a monarchy, there is nothing dictatorial about its management',[31] as can be seen in the fact that in each castle all the boys adopted the name of an Arthurian knight or of some other hero of their choice, but being King Arthur was an elected position; and it was the King Arthur who was to lead the club, guided by

27 White, *Once and Future King*, p. 183.

28 William Byron Forbush, *The Coming Generation* (New York, 1912), p. 352.

29 William Byron Forbush and Dascomb Forbush, *The Knights of King Arthur: How to Begin and What to Do* (Oberlin, OH, 1915), p. 4.

30 William Byron Forbush and Dascomb Forbush, *The Knights of King Arthur: The Merlin's Book of Advanced Work* (Oberlin, OH, 1916), p. 27.

31 William Byron Forbush and Frank Lincoln Masseck, *The Boys' Round Table: A Manual of the International Order of the Knights of King Arthur* (6th ed., rewritten, Potsdam, NY, 1908), p. 18.

an adult called the 'Merlin' but not ruled by him. Forbush wrote that 'the most cogent reason yet given for the roundness of the [Arthur's] table is that at a round table there is no head, and so there can be no jealousy. Thus we have, in a democracy under leadership, the ideal form of organization for boys.'[32] In his book on the *Queens of Avalon*, the sister group for girls, Forbush observed that those who are attracted by the poetry of legends such as those surrounding Avalon and dreams of places like Utopia and the New Atlantas (Forbush's spelling) 'may even think it fair to place the real Avalon on the shores of the New World, toward which all such dreams have tended'.[33]

Forbush's notion of Arthur's returning through his organization and of Avalon's being located on the shores of the New World may have been romantic enthusiasms, but in a very real sense Arthur, or at least the stories surrounding him, did indeed have a rebirth through the Knights of King Arthur and related groups. After all, because of Forbush's clubs and the organizations they influenced, a quarter of a million youngsters – not to mention the Merlins and Ladies of the Lake guiding them – were taught to read and to dream about and to imitate in their daily lives the legends and the code of Camelot.

Among the many Arthurian books written for children in the wake of Forbush's Knights of King Arthur and other Arthurian youth groups were four volumes by Howard Pyle that retold the tales of Camelot. Especially in the first of these, *The Story of King Arthur and His Knights* (1903), Pyle is fond of moralizing and thus democratizing knighthood and kingship by suggesting that what makes an individual knightly or kingly is the way he acts, the code by which he lives. Early in the book, just after Arthur has drawn the sword from the anvil, Pyle writes:

> Thus Arthur achieved the adventure of the sword that day and entered into his birthright of royalty. Wherefore, may God grant His Grace unto you all that ye too may likewise succeed in your undertakings. For any man may be a king in that life in which he is placed if so he may draw forth the sword of success from out of the iron of circumstance. Wherefore when your time of assay cometh, I do hope it may be with you as it was with Arthur that day, and that ye too may achieve success with entire satisfaction unto yourself and to your great glory and perfect happiness.[34]

Pyle adapts his version of the Arthurian story in other ways as well. One of the most interesting is seen in the prediction of Arthur's return in the final book in his series, *The Story of the Grail and the Passing of Arthur* (1910). According to tradition Arthur will come back at a time of great need for the people of Britain, but for Pyle his return is a sign of the return of a golden age. In Pyle, there is none of Malory's ambiguity. The King lies in Avalon until 'all shall be peace and concord amongst men'. Everyone can play a part in Arthur's return by living 'at peace with other men' and wishing them well and doing them well: 'then will King Arthur awake from his sleep'. Ironically, Pyle, writing in 1910, sees this

32 Forbush and Masseck, *The Boys' Round Table*, p. 29.
33 William Byron Forbush, *The Queens of Avalon* (4th ed.; Boston, 1925), p. 11.
34 Howard Pyle, *The Story of King Arthur and His Knights* (New York, 1903), p. 35.

time as 'nigh at hand' because 'less and less is there war within the world, and more and more is there peace and concord and good will amongst men'.[35]

By instilling his story with an early-twentieth-century optimism expressed through recurring images of an Edenic world, which seem to speak to American dreamers in every generation, and especially by providing direct and indirect examples of how young people of the time could be like the knights of Arthur's court and even like Arthur himself, Pyle transformed the legends of Camelot into a story that reflects and speaks to his own age.

How important versions of the Arthurian legend written for children and the moral codes underlying them can be is demonstrated in the novels of John Steinbeck. The influence of Malory is evident in many of his works, from his earliest novel, *Cup of Gold* (1936), to the posthumously published *Acts of King Arthur and His Noble Knights* (1976). As he noted in the Introduction to the *Acts*, it was a version of Malory designed for youngsters from which he developed 'my sense of right and wrong, my feeling of noblesse oblige, and any thought I may have against the oppressor and for the oppressed'.[36] Thus Malory's *Morte* helped to shape all of Steinbeck's novels. Even in books like *The Grapes of Wrath*, which are more dependent on Biblical than Arthurian themes, the overriding sympathy for the downtrodden results from the author's early reading of that version of Malory and his understanding of the code embodied in those tales.

In *Tortilla Flat* (1935), for example, Steinbeck translates the Arthurian realm into the modern world. Though he 'avoided the dangers of too close a parallel' to Malory's account of the Arthurian legend,[37] Steinbeck nevertheless created an overlay of Arthurian allusion to ennoble the lower-class characters of the novel. Steinbeck himself said that *Tortilla Flat*

> has a very definite theme. I thought it was clear enough. I have expected that the plan of the Arthurian cycle would be recognized, that my Gawaine and my Launcelot, my Arthur and Galahad would be recognized. Even the incident of the Sangreal in the search in the forest is not clear enough I guess. The form is that of the Malory version, the coming of Arthur and the mystic quality of owning a house, the forming of the round table, the adventure of the knights and finally, the mystic translation of Danny[38]

the Arthur-figure in the book. These comments, written in a letter in 1934, prior to the book's publication, reflect Steinbeck's concern that those reading the manuscript were missing the Arthurian theme in the book. To make the link more obvious, therefore, Steinbeck added chapter headings that imitated those in the Caxton edition of Malory.[39] Steinbeck also added a sentence to the preface

35 Howard Pyle, *The Story of the Grail and the Passing of Arthur* (New York, 1910), p. 246.

36 John Steinbeck, *The Acts of King Arthur and His Noble Knights*, ed. Chase Horton (1976; New York, 1977), p. 4.

37 Arthur F. Kinney, 'The Arthurian Cycle in *Tortilla Flat*', *Modern Fiction Studies*, 11.1 (1965), 11–20, repr. in *Steinbeck: A Collection of Critical Essays*, ed. Robert Murray Davis (Englewood Cliffs, NJ, 1972), p. 46.

38 John Steinbeck, *Steinbeck: A Life in Letters*, ed. Elaine Steinbeck and Robert Wallsten (New York, 1975), pp. 96–97.

39 See Joseph Fontenrose, '*Tortilla Flat* and the Creation of a Legend', in *The Short Novels of John Steinbeck*, ed. Jackson J. Benson (Durham, NC, 1990), pp. 24–25.

to make the Arthurian connection more explicit. He wrote: 'For Danny's house was not unlike the Round Table, and Danny's friends were not unlike the knights of it.'[40] Perhaps such blatant devices were necessary because the characters of *Tortilla Flat* are in many ways just the opposite of our idealized view of Arthur and the knights of the Round Table. The main concern of Steinbeck's 'knights' seems to be obtaining a bottle of wine; and if one of them obtains such a treasure, he is not eager to share it, even with his friends, the symbolic companions of the Round Table.

Despite their shortcomings, Danny and his friends have their own code of ethics, a code to which they adhere as rigidly as if it were a sworn vow of knighthood. That code is evident in the incident involving the character called the Pirate. They know that for a long time the Pirate has been earning but never spending a quarter a day and that he must have amassed what to them is a fortune. As a means of getting the money, which is buried in the woods, they devise a plan. They invite the Pirate and his five dogs to live in Danny's house, scare him with stories of buried treasure discovered and stolen by others, and wait for him to bring the money into the house for safekeeping. When the Pirate confides that he has been saving his 'two bitses' to fulfill a vow to buy a gold candlestick for St. Francis of Assisi if a sick dog would recover – 'And . . . that dog got well' – they realize they cannot violate the sanctity of his promise: 'it was over, all hope of diverting the money. . . . There was nothing in the world they could do about it.'[41] The knights of *Tortilla Flat* are, in fact, common men, in some ways the most common of men. Yet they follow an uncommonly noble code. When Big Joe Portagee, a newcomer to their circle, steals the Pirate's savings, the companions, led by Danny, administer a rough justice. They beat him, cut him, and pour salt in his wounds. But when he returns the money, they welcome him back into their company.

While Steinbeck translates Arthurian characters into the modern world in *Tortilla Flat* and other novels, like *Sweet Thursday*, another American novelist, Thomas Berger, actually sets his Arthurian story, *Arthur Rex* (1978), in medieval Camelot. Berger has noted that, as a boy, he 'preferred the pleasure of the imagination to those of experience' and read incessantly;[42] he mentions with great fondness his 'own boyhood King Arthur . . . the work of one Elizabeth Lodor Merchant', a gift from his father at Christmas in 1931.[43] That childhood reading no doubt inspired Berger to write *Arthur Rex*, one of his most popular novels, in which he questions the Arthurian code, almost as if he were responding from a twentieth-century perspective to the notion of impossible vows in Tennyson's *Idylls* as he develops the novel's theme of the dangerous ideal.

Like the legend itself, Berger's novel is full of paradoxes and ironies. For instance, after Arthur pulls the sword from the stone and assumes the throne, he quickly discovers the burden of kingship. One of the first of those discoveries is that a monarch has fewer liberties than his subjects do. 'Captive of many laws,

40 John Steinbeck, *Tortilla Flat* (New York, 1935), p. 9.
41 Steinbeck, *Tortilla Flat*, p. 119.
42 Douglas Hughes, 'Thomas Berger's Elan: An Interview', *Confrontation*, 12 (Summer 1976), 24.
43 Brooks Landon, *Thomas Berger* (New York, 1989), pp. 6–7.

ordinances, traditions, customs, and moreover, prophecies', all of which conspire to guarantee that he 'is never free to do his will',[44] Arthur feels that he is 'fundamentally a slave'.[45] Kingship reveals to Arthur some other unpleasant realities, such as the fact that doing good may lead to evil. His marriage shatters in large part because of his own selfless actions. Arthur extols Launcelot's virtues to Guinevere and assigns Launcelot not to the quest, for which he longs, but to the queen's side as her protector and defender. As Berger writes, out of his admiration for his friend and his desire that his wife 'be at one with him in his enthusiasms . . . King Arthur took every opportunity to bring Guinevere and Sir Launcelot together'.[46] What makes the love triangle of king, queen, and knight so curious is that they all have only the deepest affection for each other; 'and all throughout their lives Arthur and Guinevere and Launcelot did love one another, though each pair in a different way'.[47] Moreover, the dissolution of Arthur's household mirrors the dissolution of his fabled Order, a noble concept that leads ultimately to war and to the deaths of every knight of the Round Table.

This idea that evil consequences can result from good intentions suggests what is perhaps *the* theme of *Arthur Rex*: that extreme adherence to moral rules can be more damaging than lapses in morality. This is not to suggest that Berger finds it wrong to want to be better and to make things better, that is, to have a code. In fact, such a principle is the essence of Arthur's character and the Arthurian story, even for Berger. But in Berger's novel, the desire to make things *perfect* without admitting human failings usually causes more trouble than outright imperfection does. Thus he seems to favor a realistic rather than an impossibly idealistic code.

Interestingly, Berger's female characters seem best able to articulate this notion of the pursuit of the dangerous ideal. Late in the novel, for instance, when Launcelot says that his war with Arthur is not the result of any hatred between the two, Guinevere thinks to herself, 'Nay, it hath happened because of men and their laws and their principles!'[48] In effect, she implies that idealism itself is responsible for many of the world's problems. This notion is echoed by Morgan la Fey, Arthur's half-sister and his greatest nemesis. Throughout the novel, Morgan repeatedly seeks to undermine Arthur's kingdom, especially by counseling Mordred on the 'remarkable satisfaction' of bringing pain to others and on the significance of evil as a way of 'serv[ing] Life',[49] advice that registers all too easily and too well on Arthur's bastard son. Finally, however, Morgan enters the Convent of the Little Sisters of Poverty and Pain, for after a long career in the service of evil she comes to believe that corruption 'were sooner brought amongst humankind by the forces of virtue, and from this moment on she was notable for her piety'.[50] She even becomes mother superior of the convent that Guinevere eventually joins.

Similarly, the Lady of the Lake, who serves as the antithesis to Morgan's

44 Thomas Berger, *Arthur Rex: A Legendary Novel* (New York, 1978), p. 65.
45 Berger, *Arthur Rex*, p. 78.
46 Berger, *Arthur Rex*, p. 217.
47 Berger, *Arthur Rex*, p. 153.
48 Berger, *Arthur Rex*, p. 442.
49 Berger, *Arthur Rex*, p. 224.
50 Berger, *Arthur Rex*, p. 453.

villainy, tells Arthur and his knights that no quest should be conducted blindly. The principles of chivalry, she suggests, must admit some alteration; otherwise, those principles become mere abstractions. One good custom could then, we might say, corrupt the world. And the knights – even the kings – who grow obsessed with 'adherence to the letter'[51] stop being men and become instead 'abstract example[s] for-argument's-sake'.[52] To have a noble purpose is good, she says; 'but to be so intent upon it as to see only its end is folly. Never to be distracted is to serve nothing but Vanity.'[53]

At one point in the novel, Arthur tells Kay not to seek perfection at arms, either in himself or in others. But immediately afterward Arthur hears of Launcelot's prowess and 'must have him'. When Guinevere reminds Arthur of his warning about perfection-seeking to Kay, he says, 'As we know, absolute perfection is found only in Heaven. But if 'tis gallant to seek it as a vassal, it is obligatory to seek it as a king. We know at the outset, if even the Christ Himself did die as man, that we shall necessarily and ultimately fail. But we can fail gloriously, and glory doth come only from a quest which is impossible of attainment.'[54] Thus Arthur points to another paradox of the legends. The quest for perfection is doomed to failure, but it makes Arthur the glorious symbol that he has become.

Later, on the battlefield at Salisbury Plain, the Lady of the Lake appears in order to instruct the wounded king. When Arthur wonders if he could have ruled more wisely, she reassures him,

> Thou couldst not have done better than thou didst. . . . Thine obligation was to maintain power in as decent a way as would be yet the most effective, and a Camelot without Guinevere, a Round Table without Launcelot, were inconceivable, as would be an Arthur who put to death his best friend and his queen. All human beings must perform according to their nature.[55]

The implication here is that no one can be perfect, and so for Arthur to feel guilt for not being something that he could not be – indeed that no one could be – because of his nature, which is human nature, is unnatural.

Berger recognizes that nature and human nature are such that even those with high moral standards may have their downfall. He says of Arthur's reign:

> this was the only time that a king had set out to rule on principles of absolute virtue, and to fight evil and to champion the good, and though it was not the first time that a king fell out with his followers, it was unique in happening not by wicked design but rather by the helpless accidents of fine men who meant well and who loved one another dearly.[56]

Let us return to where we began, to Bedivere on the shore – one of the haunting images of the legends. In Berger's account, Bedivere says to Arthur as he lies in the barge that the king might gather new knights to establish a Round Table once more. But Arthur knows that the old order changes. He says, 'now

51 Berger, *Arthur Rex*, p. 312.
52 Berger, *Arthur Rex*, p. 431.
53 Berger, *Arthur Rex*, p. 105.
54 Berger, *Arthur Rex*, pp. 95–97.
55 Berger, *Arthur Rex*, p. 484.
56 Berger, *Arthur Rex*, p. 447.

hath come an end to Britain as we knew it', and he predicts a 'darkening epoch to come'. Arthur knows that a Launcelot or a Tristram or a Gawain or even a Kay or a Bedivere will not soon be seen again. But he tells Bedivere to 'thank God in joy that for a little while we were able to make an interregnum in the human cycle of barbarism and decadence'. When Arthur's barge disappears into the fog, Bedivere lies down and dies 'a happy death, for he did not feel that he had lived in futility'.[57] He had been a part of something great, something that, paradoxically, is joyous as it is sad, that lasts as it passes. The old order changeth, but we know that Arthur will come again as he has so many times before in the modern world and that even as the wheel of his fortunes turns and brings him low, it will rise again because the brilliant complex of stories surrounding the king, the fascinating cast of characters in the legend, and the values and ideals they represent will keep it turning.

57 Berger, *Arthur Rex*, p. 495.

Index

[The index identifies substantial discussions of major characters, themes and authors but does not include less prominent references, particularly to ubiquitous names such as Arthur, Merlin or Gawain. It lists titles of works discussed in the volume, but provides simply a cross-reference to the author's name, if known. Finally, there is a deliberate though minor stylistic inconsistency for the sake of clarity: in the extensive entry for 'manuscripts' a colon rather than a comma separates the manuscript number from the corresponding page numbers.]

ARTHURIAN STUDIES

I	ASPECTS OF MALORY, *edited by Toshiyuki Takamiya and Derek Brewer*
II	THE ALLITERATIVE *MORTE ARTHURE*: A Reassessment of the Poem, *edited by Karl Heinz Göller*
III	THE ARTHURIAN BIBLIOGRAPHY, I: Author Listing, *edited by C. E. Pickford and R. W. Last*
IV	THE CHARACTER OF KING ARTHUR IN MEDIEVAL LITERATURE, *Rosemary Morris*
V	PERCEVAL: The Story of the Grail, by Chrétien de Troyes, *translated by Nigel Bryant*
VI	THE ARTHURIAN BIBLIOGRAPHY, II: Subject Index, *edited by C. E. Pickford and R. W. Last*
VII	THE LEGEND OF ARTHUR IN THE MIDDLE AGES, *edited by P. B. Grout, R. A. Lodge, C. E. Pickford and E. K. C. Varty*
VIII	THE ROMANCE OF YDER, *edited and translated by Alison Adams*
IX	THE RETURN OF KING ARTHUR, *Beverly Taylor and Elisabeth Brewer*
X	ARTHUR'S KINGDOM OF ADVENTURE: The World of Malory's *Morte Darthur, Muriel Whitaker*
XI	KNIGHTHOOD IN THE *MORTE DARTHUR*, *Beverly Kennedy*
XII	LE ROMAN DE TRISTAN EN PROSE, tome I, *edited by Renée L. Curtis*
XIII	LE ROMAN DE TRISTAN EN PROSE, tome II, *edited by Renée L. Curtis*
XIV	LE ROMAN DE TRISTAN EN PROSE, tome III, *edited by Renée L. Curtis*
XV	LOVE'S MASKS: Identity, Intertextuality, and Meaning in the Old French Tristan Poems, *Merritt R. Blakeslee*
XVI	THE CHANGING FACE OF ARTHURIAN ROMANCE: Essays on Arthurian Prose Romances in memory of Cedric E. Pickford, *edited by Alison Adams, Armel H. Diverres, Karen Stern and Kenneth Varty*
XVII	REWARDS AND PUNISHMENTS IN THE ARTHURIAN ROMANCES AND LYRIC POETRY OF MEDIEVAL FRANCE: Essays presented to Kenneth Varty on the occasion of his sixtieth birthday, *edited by Peter V. Davies and Angus J. Kennedy*
XVIII	CEI AND THE ARTHURIAN LEGEND, *Linda Gowans*
XIX	LAȜAMON'S *BRUT*: The Poem and its Sources, *Françoise H. M. Le Saux*
XX	READING THE *MORTE DARTHUR*, *Terence McCarthy*, reprinted as AN INTRODUCTION TO MALORY
XXI	CAMELOT REGAINED: The Arthurian Revival and Tennyson, 1800–1849, *Roger Simpson*
XXII	THE LEGENDS OF KING ARTHUR IN ART, *Muriel Whitaker*
XXIII	GOTTFRIED VON STRASSBURG AND THE MEDIEVAL TRISTAN LEGEND: Papers from an Anglo-North American symposium, *edited with an introduction by Adrian Stevens and Roy Wisbey*
XXIV	ARTHURIAN POETS: CHARLES WILLIAMS, *edited and introduced by David Llewellyn Dodds*
XXV	AN INDEX OF THEMES AND MOTIFS IN TWELFTH-CENTURY FRENCH ARTHURIAN POETRY, *E. H. Ruck*
XXVI	CHRÉTIEN DE TROYES AND THE GERMAN MIDDLE AGES: Papers from an international symposium, *edited with an introduction by Martin H. Jones and Roy Wisbey*

XXVII SIR GAWAIN AND THE GREEN KNIGHT: Sources and Analogues, *compiled by Elisabeth Brewer*

XXVIII CLIGÉS by Chrétien de Troyes, *edited by Stewart Gregory and Claude Luttrell*

XXIX THE LIFE AND TIMES OF SIR THOMAS MALORY, *P. J. C. Field*

XXX T. H. WHITE'S *THE ONCE AND FUTURE KING*, *Elisabeth Brewer*

XXXI ARTHURIAN BIBLIOGRAPHY, III: 1978–1992, Author Listing and Subject Index, *compiled by Caroline Palmer*

XXXII ARTHURIAN POETS: JOHN MASEFIELD, *edited and introduced by David Llewellyn Dodds*

XXXIII THE TEXT AND TRADITION OF LAȜAMON'S *BRUT*, *edited by Françoise Le Saux*

XXXIV CHIVALRY IN TWELFTH-CENTURY GERMANY: The Works of Hartmann von Aue, *W. H. Jackson*

XXXV THE TWO VERSIONS OF MALORY'S *MORTE DARTHUR*: Multiple Negation and the Editing of the Text, *Ingrid Tieken-Boon van Ostade*

XXXVI RECONSTRUCTING CAMELOT: French Romantic Medievalism and the Arthurian Tradition, *Michael Glencross*

XXXVII A COMPANION TO MALORY, *edited by Elizabeth Archibald and A. S. G. Edwards*

XXXVIII A COMPANION TO THE *GAWAIN*-POET, *edited by Derek Brewer and Jonathan Gibson*

XXXIX MALORY'S BOOK OF ARMS: The Narrative of Combat in *Le Morte Darthur*, *Andrew Lynch*

XL MALORY: TEXTS AND SOURCES, *P. J. C. Field*

XLI KING ARTHUR IN AMERICA, *Alan Lupack and Barbara Tepa Lupack*

XLII THE SOCIAL AND LITERARY CONTEXTS OF MALORY'S *MORTE DARTHUR*, *edited by D. Thomas Hanks Jr*

XLIII THE GENESIS OF NARRATIVE IN MALORY'S *MORTE DARTHUR*, *Elizabeth Edwards*

XLIV GLASTONBURY ABBEY AND THE ARTHURIAN TRADITION, *edited by James P. Carley*

XLV THE KNIGHT WITHOUT THE SWORD: A Social Landscape of Malorian Chivalry, *Hyonjin Kim*

XLVI ULRICH VON ZATZIKHOVEN'S *LANZELET*: Narrative Style and Entertainment, *Nicola McLelland*

XLVII THE MALORY DEBATE: Essays on the Texts of *Le Morte Darthur*, *edited by Bonnie Wheeler, Robert L. Kindrick and Michael N. Salda*

XLVIII MERLIN AND THE GRAIL: *Joseph of Arimathea, Merlin, Perceval*: The Trilogy of Arthurian romances attributed to Robert de Boron, *translated by Nigel Bryant*

XLIX ARTHURIAN BIBLIOGRAPHY IV: 1993–1998, Author Listing and Subject Index, *compiled by Elaine Barber*

L *DIU CRÔNE* AND THE MEDIEVAL ARTHURIAN CYCLE, *Neil Thomas*

LI NEW DIRECTIONS IN ARTHURIAN STUDIES, *edited by Alan Lupack*

LII KING ARTHUR IN MUSIC, *edited by Richard Barber*

LIII THE BOOK OF LANCELOT: The Middle Dutch *Lancelot* Compilation and the Medieval Tradition of Narrative Cycles, *Bart Besamusca*

LIV A COMPANION TO THE *LANCELOT-GRAIL* CYCLE, *edited by Carol Dover*

LV THE GENTRY CONTEXT FOR MALORY'S *MORTE DARTHUR*, *Raluca L. Radulescu*

LVI *PARZIVAL*: WITH *TITUREL* AND THE *LOVE LYRICS*, *translated by Cyril Edwards*

LVII ARTHURIAN STUDIES IN HONOUR OF P. J. C. FIELD, *edited by Bonnie Wheeler*

LVIII THE LEGEND OF THE GRAIL, *Nigel Bryant*

LIX THE GRAIL LEGEND IN MODERN LITERATURE, *John B. Marino*

LX RE-VIEWING *LE MORTE DARTHUR*: Texts and Contexts, Characters and Themes, *edited by K. S. Whetter and Raluca L. Radulescu*

LXI THE SCOTS AND MEDIEVAL ARTHURIAN LEGEND, *edited by Rhiannon Purdie and Nicola Royan*

LXII WIRNT VON GRAVENBERG'S *WIGALOIS*: Intertextuality and Interpretation, *Neil Thomas*

LXIII A COMPANION TO CHRÉTIEN DE TROYES, *edited by Norris J. Lacy and Joan Tasker Grimbert*